# THE
# Downtown
# Jews

# THE
# Downtown
# JEWS

## Portraits of an Immigrant Generation

**RONALD SANDERS**

**Foreword by HASIA R. DINER**

**BARNES & NOBLE**

NEW YORK

*For Beverly*

*A socially prominent Jewish lady . . . had written to the editor asking why so much space was given to the ridiculous performances of the ignorant, foreign East Side Jews and none to the uptown Hebrews. I told her. I had the satisfaction of telling her about the comparative beauty, significance and character of the uptown and downtown Jews. I must have talked well, for she threatened and tried to have me fired, as she put it.*

THE AUTOBIOGRAPHY OF LINCOLN STEFFENS

# CONTENTS

*Acknowledgments*                                                    IX

*Foreword*                                                           XI


Prologue                                                              1

1.  Russia, 1881                                                      7

2.  New York, 1882                                                   40

3.  The Radicals of Rivington Street                                56

4.  Anarchists, Socialists, and Labor Unions                        80

5.  The Yiddish Labor Press Begins                                  97

6.  Sweatshop Poets                                                125

7.  The Founding of *The Jewish Daily Forward*                     147

8.  How a Publicist Became a Man of Letters                        179

9.  Interlude: With Yankees                                         203

10. A "Russian" Bemoans His Exile in America                       224

11. Cahan Returns to the *Forward*; or,
    The Fable of the Birds                                          244

12. Yiddish Theater, I: The Beginnings                             275

13. Yiddish Theater, II:
    The Feud Between Cahan and Jacob Gordin                        298

14. 1905     324

15. A Bundle of Letters     347

16. Lords of the Press     370

17. Jewish Labor Comes of Age     391

18. The Exile Is an American at Last     413

19. The Long Twilight     435

*Appendix:* Some Notes on Transliteration, and a Glossary     453

*Bibliography and Notes*     459

*Index*     465

# Acknowledgments

⁓

THROUGH THE YEARS IN WHICH I HAVE PURSUED THE INTERESTS reflected in this book, I have received help and suggestions from more people than I can remember; but in taking this occasion to thank them all, I would like to single out a special few for mention:

First, Shlomo Katz, the editor of *Midstream,* my foremost teacher in Jewish cultural matters, who answered innumerable questions and provided more solutions for this book than he imagines.

Then, the various veterans of the world of Lower East Side arts, journalism, and politics with whom I have spoken through the years, especially Leon Forem, Henry Greenfield, Alexander Kahn, Mendel Osherowitch, Bernard G. Richards, Hillel Rogoff, Zvee Scooler, Isaac Bashevis Singer, and various other members of the staff of *The Jewish Daily Forward.*

Also, two men in the publishing world who have been most helpful in the conception and execution of this book, the late Roger Klein, and David Segal.

And above all my wife, Beverly Gingold Sanders, who brings me life and the strength to go on writing.

# FOREWORD

⟨~⟩

RONALD SANDERS OFFERED THE READING PUBLIC *THE DOWNTOWN Jews* amidst a flurry of writing about New York and its immigrant Jewish enclave. He did so at a time when Americans of all sorts, but in particular the children and grandchildren of the immigrants of the "great wave" who had flooded the United States in the last decades of the nineteenth century and the early ones of the twentieth, began to search for their roots. In the political and cultural realm they fomented what historians have labeled an "ethnic revival," and as part of that project, they began to tell the story of their forbears' arrival in America and to describe the kinds of communities that their immigrant ancestors had built in their new home.

For America's Jews that story had to be told from the vantage point of a very particular place in New York, the area usually defined as having extended south from Houston Street and east from the Bowery—namely, the Lower East Side. The story also encompassed a particular time—the 1880s through the 1920s—when, on those New York streets, the world's largest Jewish neighborhood formed and immigrant men and women created a dense concentration of not just lived life, but of newspapers and strikes, of theaters and cafes, of politics, passions, street culture, argumentation, and social protest.

*The Downtown Jews* originally appeared in 1969, just about halfway through a sixteen-year period in American letters when a spate of works introduced, or better reintroduced, the American public to that place and time. This reintroduction began in 1960, when two Lower East Side novels that had been published to great acclaim long before, and then faded from view, came back as reissues. Abraham Cahan's *The Rise of David Levinsky* (1917) and Henry Roth's *Call It Sleep* (1934) both returned to print that year. Cahan's novel played a pivotal role in setting the stage for *The Downtown Jews* since Sanders's book would twin the narratives of Cahan and his fictional alter ego, Levinsky. These two novels were followed in 1962 by Moses Rischin's *The Promised City*, a revised Harvard doctoral dissertation which Sanders would employ as the scholarly spine for his longer and later work. In 1967 the Jewish Museum mounted a major exhibition on the history of the Jewish Lower East Side, "Portal to America." The beautifully illustrated catalog of the same title made it possible for those who had not had the chance to come to New York and see the artifacts of the immigrant era, including enormous blow-ups of pages of the *Jewish Daily Forward*, to experience the exhibition from afar. Several other books appeared later in the 1960s, including the 1966 reissue of Hutchins Hapgood's 1902 reportorial foray into the "Hebrew Quarter," *The Spirit of the Ghetto* and Milton Hindus's *The Jewish East Side* (1969). They helped set the stage for the publication of *The Downtown Jews*.

Flanking the Sanders book from the other end of the notable era, and no doubt inspired by his, 1970 saw the reprint of more fiction from Cahan—*Yekl and the Imported Bridegroom*, a group of short stories written by the hero of *The Downtown Jews*. One of those stories, "Yekl," would reach a much wider audience in 1975 when it came out in the form of the movie, "Hester Street," directed by Joan Micklin Silver. In 1971 Isaac Metzker also dipped into the Cahan legend, so shaped by Sanders, in his *A Bintel Brief*, a compilation and translation of some of the juiciest advice letters sent to and answered by the enigmatic editor and publisher of the *Forward*, letters which

revealed much about the texture of life in the immigrant neighborhood, its stresses, opportunities, and disruptions. Anzia Yezierska's
1925 novel *The Bread Givers* came out in 1975, packaged as a rediscovered text to give voice to the women of the Lower East Side. Its
reissue offered a generation forged in the era of feminism a work of
their own.

The high point of this publishing epoch was reached in 1976,
with the release of the biggest of them all and the one which may
have played a role in eclipsing *The Downtown Jews*. Irving Howe's
masterwork *World of Our Fathers*, a big book in every sense of the
word, took a panoramic view of the Lower East Side. Though Cahan
functioned as an important character (but only one among many),
within its pages the world of the Lower East Side expanded in mul-
tiple directions well beyond the orbit, however large, of the *Forward*
and its editor.

The scope of *World of Our Fathers* pushed *The Downtown Jews*
to the margins. Howe's book rendered Sanders's too small. Sanders
decision to tell the Lower East Side story through Cahan may indeed
have been its main liability as a book. The subject of the Lower East
Side could not be encompassed by means of one individual, however important, and by virtue of having done so Sanders necessarily
offered less than a complex history of a complicated community. On
the other hand, it fell short of being a comprehensive biography, given
that Sanders spent much time on the history of the Yiddish theater,
Yiddish literature, socialism, and the Jewish labor movement, often
taking his eye off Cahan, and then returning to him.

These shortcomings and Howe's subsequent bestselling work
splashed on its larger canvas should not, however, dim the importance of *The Downtown Jews*. It still reads as a rich text, which allows
readers to see the world of the Lower East Side through the eyes of
one key individual, to hear its sounds through his voice, and to measure the changes in the neighborhood and in the political, cultural,

and economic lives of its Jewish denizen by his activism. Well-written, devoid of cloying sentimentality which the subject could, and often did, inspire in other writers, *The Downtown Jews* deserves a fresh look by a new generation.

HASIA R. DINER
JUNE 2008

# UNEARTHING TWO STATUES

In Arabians Märchenbuche
Sehen wir verwünschte Prinzen . . .
> —HEINRICH HEINE, *Prinzessin Sabbath*

In die alte bobba mayses
Kummen for gilgulim printzen . . .
> —CHAIM NACHMAN BIALIK'S
> Yiddish adaptation of *Prinzessin Sabbath*

NEW YORK CITY IS A KIND OF ARCHAEOLOGICAL MOUND, ITS layers all on the surface, requiring an effort of the imagination to uncover their meaning as an excavator does with his tools. In some places the histories of the various layers are dramatic enough to be widely known: on Lafayette Street, for example, stands an Italian Renaissance palace which once housed the foremost public library of New York and then the Hebrew Immigrant Aid Society, and is now the home of the New York Shakespeare Festival company. Other histories are more obscure, and must be painstakingly unearthed.

My interest is in that branch of the study which one might call ethnic archaeology. New York is of course extremely rich for students of this subject, many of its neighborhoods containing layer on layer of ethnic deposits, one group succeeding to the buildings and institutions of another. It is often particularly fruitful to observe the interplay that persists between certain groups, such as between Negro and Puerto Rican, or East European Jew and German. For example, in a small park on the Grand Concourse in the Bronx, immediately surrounded by a neighborhood that is still largely made up of East European Jews and their offspring, there is a monument depicting the legendary Lorelei. This bit of paganism might seem merely amusing in a park that is faced by a church at one end and by a synagogue at the other; but, upon closer examination, one perceives that it is a monument to the German—and Jewish—poet Heinrich Heine, whose profile stands in bas-relief upon the pedestal, surrounded by figures of the mythic Rhine maidens about whom he wrote his most famous poem. This monument has a history something like that of the beleaguered and ultimately exiled poet to whom it is dedicated. Originally commissioned by the Empress Elisabeth of Austria as a gift to Heine's native Düsseldorf, it was turned down by that city under the influence of an anti-Semitic movement there. Other German cities rejected it on similar grounds, but finally, a group of German-Americans heard of the statue and raised money to have it brought to this spot and unveiled in 1899, more than ten years after work upon it had been begun. This group of exiles from Germany, consisting of many more Gentiles than Jews, recognized full well what were the affinities between themselves and both the monument and its subject when they inscribed at its side: *Ihrem grossen Dichter die Deutschen in Amerika* ("To their great poet the Germans in America."). It was only subsequently that the surrounding neighborhood, then still semirural, came to be settled by large numbers of Jews.

This symbol of the relationship that existed for a time between Germans and Jews in New York stands far north of the terrain in which that relationship was really enacted, the Lower East Side of Manhattan—the main threshold, in its day, of the mass immigration of East European Jews to America. When one burrows southward through the city, pushing closer and closer to New York's origins, one comes upon the vestiges of the furthest, northern- and westernmost extension of the Lower East Side Jewish culture in the vicinity of Union Square. The most politically radical wing of that culture reached this traditional scene of labor demonstrations in the nineteen-twenties, when the Yiddish communist newspaper, the *Freiheit* ("Freedom"), stationed itself here along with Communist Party headquarters. It was here, during the Depression, that unemployed Jewish radicals used to gather and sing:

> *The old capitalist system,*
> *It's good enough for Norman Thomas,*
> *It's good enough for the Jewish* shammes *(beadle),*
> *But it's not good enough for me.*

But one of the last visible signs of the extension of the Jewish Lower East Side culture to this area is, once again, inscribed by the German culture that preceded it. A block from the Square stands a building which now serves as the central receiving depot for the large department store to which it is attached, but which was once the Irving Place Theater. Built by German-Americans to house productions in their native language—it also was the scene of the last major fund-raising rally for the Heine monument, in 1899—it bears the trademark of its makers in its elaborate, vaguely baroque, bas-relief work over entranceways and windows that are now either wholly or partially obscured with brick. Luchow's Restaurant, visible down at the end of the street, is the last living representative of the era of German-American glory once reflected at this spot. But later on, an era of Yiddish glory was reflected here, too; for it was in this same theater that Maurice Schwartz, in August, 1918, launched the company that was to become, in another location and under the name "The Yiddish Art Theater," the center of a Jewish cultural renaissance on Second Avenue.

The stretch of Second Avenue which begins at Fourteenth Street two blocks east of Irving Place and extends southward the fourteen blocks to Houston Street, and which was the main boulevard of the

Yiddish artistic culture of New York during the nineteen-twenties and thirties, was a latecomer to the expanding Jewish-immigrant population center and had previously been largely German. The signs of that earlier epoch are still visible, in building inscriptions—the neighborhood's "Freie Bibliothek u. Lesehalle" is, as it happens, *still* a public library—and in the sculptured heads that adorn many façades, especially on the side streets. The later period of Jewish culture, though waning, is still represented by living vestiges: a Yiddish publishing house continues to reside above a theater in which Yiddish productions once took place, but which now houses a girlie show; at one theater a Yiddish musical-comedy company continues to appear in an annual production; some of the old Jewish restaurants are there to this day; a music store remains, its shelves filled with song sheets in Yiddish, and with records which can bring back the sounds of an era partly characterized by music halls in which a performer like Aaron Lebedeff sang:

> *Rumania, Rumania, Rumania, Rumania . . .*
> *Geven amol a land a zisse, a sheyne.*

"Once there was a country, sweet and beautiful."

But in other places the signs have vanished without a trace: the site of a great old Rumanian-Jewish restaurant where gypsy violins once played is, at this moment, a hole in the ground, about to be replaced by a church, and that of one of the greatest of all the Yiddish theaters is now, and has been for many years, a parking lot. The best traditions of Second Avenue are manifested in the places where other cultures have taken over—the former Yiddish theater that is now one of the city's main showplaces of Negro musical talent, or the stretch of St. Mark's Place that is a center of the hippie "scene."

One must probe deeper, farther southward, to find the more imposing vestiges of the old Jewish culture—south of Houston Street and slightly to the east of Second Avenue, where that culture had its main centers prior to the First World War. At Orchard Street, for example, stretching southward for blocks, is the teeming market of sidewalk stalls—containing mostly articles of clothing at bargains frequently arrived at by heated, on-the-spot discussions—that constitutes the remaining echo of the old Lower East Side of pushcarts and street peddlers. Nowadays, there are no pushcarts, and the sellers usually own the stores in front of which their stalls are set up; furthermore, the discussions sometimes slip into Spanish as readily as they do into Yiddish. But the air crackles with the agitation of old; and all around, crisscrossed with the fire-escape façades that have become their trademark, are the tenements, dreary in the day when they were primarily filled with Jewish immigrants, drearier still today.

Going eastward for two blocks on Delancey Street—from where one can gaze across the Williamsburg Bridge, leading to that Brooklyn promised land which attracted many Jews in their first wave of emigration from the Lower East Side—and then turning southward again at Essex, one can now begin to glimpse the very sources of the Jewish quarter; for it is at the foot of this street that the East European Jewish settlement began, in the eighteen-seventies, when this, too, was still largely a German neighborhood. Though many of the original buildings are still visible, there have been some major alterations in the overall scene since that time, not only because of the blocks of relatively recent housing developments which rise massively to the left, but also because of substantial changes made a longer time ago, when the Yiddish culture here was at its pinnacle. For one part of the intersection of Essex Street with Canal Street and with East Broadway is the site of Seward Park, which was built in place of a block of tenements demolished at the turn of the century, and another part of the intersection is dominated by the ten-story office building of *The Jewish Daily Forward,* built in 1911–1912. This latter structure, housing what is still the largest-circulating Yiddish newspaper in the world, was once the main "skyscraper" of the Lower East Side, and the principal nerve center of the entire

Jewish quarter. It dominated the lives of those who hated it as much as of those who loved it.

In the lobby of the *Forward* Building, dim and quiet, there is a bronze bust. It is of Abraham Cahan, one of the founders of the *Forward* and its first editor, who ruled over the paper's destiny for half a century until his death in 1951 at the age of ninety-one. As editor of the *Forward* and a talented writer in English as well, Cahan was one of the most powerful men on the Jewish Lower East Side— perhaps the most powerful for a time—as well as one of the most articulate witnesses of its inner and outer experience.

This statue was the goal of my expedition, the key to my research. From it unfolds the history I want to tell, a history which only ends here, and begins in nineteenth-century Russia.

CHAPTER 1

# RUSSIA, 1881

Then Verochka found herself in the city; she saw a cellar where young girls were shut up. She touched the lock, the lock fell; she said to the young girls: "Go out!" and they went out. She saw then a room where young girls lay paralyzed. She said to them: "Arise!" They arose, and all ran into the country, light-hearted and laughing. Verochka followed them, and in her happiness cried out:

"How pleasant it is to be with them! How sad it was to be alone! How pleasant it is to be with the free young girls who run in the fields, so lithe and joyous!"

—N. G. CHERNYSHEVSKY, *What Is to Be Done?*

O my sweet Marianna! believe me, I am not laughing at you; and my words are the simple truth. You now, all of you, Russian women, are more capable, and loftier too, than we men.

—IVAN TURGENEV, *Virgin Soil*

THE RUSSIAN REVOLUTIONARY MOVEMENT OF THE NINETEENTH century was distinguished by the presence within its ranks of a large number of courageous young women. One of the most outstanding of these was Sophia Perovskaya, a daughter of a prominent aristocratic family, who had run away from home at the age of seventeen and joined a group which sent young men and women into factories to preach socialism to the workers. That had been in the time of the *Narodnikii,* a peaceful era of "going to the people," which ended in 1873 and 1874 with a vast wave of arrests by the Tsarist police.

Perovskaya was among those arrested, and she spent four years in prison, until she was finally acquitted in a mass trial which was meant to break the back of the radical movement, but which inspired it with renewed moral strength instead.

The growing police persecution finally caused the revolutionaries to retaliate with a policy of violence. This new turn was signaled by the act of another young woman, Vera Zasulich, a typesetter for the underground newspaper *Land and Liberty,* who, on January 24, 1878, shot General Trepov, the St. Petersburg chief of police, in protest against his severe maltreatment of a political prisoner. Although Trepov was gravely wounded, he did not die, and the trial of his would-be assassin in March was turned by her defense lawyer into a vigorous indictment of police brutality. To the surprise of everyone, Zasulich was acquitted. The Tsar immediately issued an order that she be arrested again, but an enthusiastic crowd which had formed around her in the street after her release spirited her away from the oncoming police. She left the country and settled in Geneva, amidst worldwide acclaim for her heroism.

Her act soon became a source of inspiration for others. Only a few weeks after her acquittal, the Kiev chief of police was assassinated by a revolutionary, and in August General Mezentzev, another high officer of the St. Petersburg police, was stabbed to death in broad daylight by Sergey Kravchinsky, the editor of *Land and Liberty,* who managed to get away and escape into exile. Inevitably, the growing mood of violence began to be focused upon the person of Tsar Alexander II himself. That summer, a Jewish engineering student named Solomon Wittenberg was caught trying to lay a mine where the Tsar's excursion yacht was due to land in Odessa harbor; he was quickly sentenced and executed. The following April, Alexander Solovyov, a revolutionary already wanted by the police, fired upon the Tsar in a public square in St. Petersburg. He missed, but he was dealt with summarily nonetheless and was executed in a few weeks' time. The pace of executions and assassinations continued to grow, and by the summer of 1879 the government and the extremist wing of the revolutionary movement were in a state of violent warfare with one another.

The movement itself soon split over the issue of terrorism, and two new parties came into being. One of them, known as *Chornyi Peredel* ("Black Repartition," i.e., repartition of the soil), continued the old policy of peaceful preachment of socialism among the masses; the other, called *Narodnaya Volya* ("People's Will"), adopted a policy of terrorism. Ironically, Vera Zasulich repudiated terrorism from her exile in Geneva and gave her support to *Chornyi Peredel*. Sophia Perovskaya, on the other hand, joined *Narodnaya Volya* and became a member of its Executive Committee.

At a meeting held in August, 1879, the Executive Committee of *Narodnaya Volya* "sentenced" Alexander II to death. The members decided to blow up the Imperial train that November when it carried the Tsar back to Petersburg from his summer residence in the Crimea. To make sure they would not miss, they divided themselves into two forces. One was led by Andrey Zhelyabov, a powerfully built young man who had been born a serf and had studied law at the University of Odessa on a scholarship. One day at the beginning of October he made an appearance in the small town of Alexandrovsk, which was on the Imperial train route, and gave out that he was a merchant setting himself up in business there. With his "wife" and two assistants, he established a tannery by day and mined the railroad track at night. Meanwhile, farther along the Imperial route, in a suburb of Moscow, a similar dual enterprise was under way. A merchant named Sukhorukov and his wife had bought a house near the railroad tracks, and had engaged some laborers to dig an ice cellar in their kitchen floor. In reality, this couple were Leo Hartmann, a young revolutionary of German extraction, and Sophia Perovskaya; the "ice cellar" was the entrance to a tunnel being dug all the way to the tracks, where an explosive charge was to be laid. Throughout the two months that it took to dig the tunnel, some bottles of nitroglycerine were kept in the house; should the police ever come to arrest the conspirators, Perovskaya was to fire on the bottles, killing them all.

The Tsar's train passed through Alexandrovsk on the morning of November 18, but when Zhelyabov tried to explode the mine that he and his associates had so carefully laid, it did not go off. The reason for this failure was never discovered. The task of carrying out the planned assassination now devolved upon Hartmann, Perovskaya, and their associates. At about nine o'clock on the evening of the nineteenth, Perovskaya, the group's lookout, watched a train approach; this, according to information she and Hartmann possessed, was the Imperial retinue train, sent in advance of the Tsar's own train to test the safety of the route. She let it go by. When the second train arrived nearly an hour and a half later, she gave a signal; there was a loud explosion. The cars were smashed and derailed, but the damage was not so severe as had been expected. No one aboard was seriously injured, but this made no difference anyway as it turned out, for the Tsar was not even there. He had taken the first train after all.

This failure only increased the determination of the Executive Committee to carry out its aim, and a rapid succession of attempts upon the life of the Tsar was staged during the course of the following year. In February an enormous charge of dynamite was set off under the dining room of the Winter Palace; it had been placed there by a young revolutionary who had obtained a job the preceding autumn as a palace carpenter. But though the casualties this time were quite severe—eleven persons were killed and over fifty wounded, most of them members of the palace guard—the result was essentially the same as before: the dining room was only slightly damaged, and besides, the Tsar had not yet even come in for dinner when the explosion occurred. Subsequent attempts to kill the Emperor by setting up charges in the street, along routes frequented by him, also came to nought.

By this time the lives of the conspirators were completely absorbed in their one overriding purpose, and though they managed to welcome the arrival of 1881 with a New Year's Eve party that was notable for its merriment, they were in an apocalyptic mood, and seemed fully prepared to face the prospect that they might not survive the year. Zhelyabov and Perovskaya now were lovers, and were the acknowledged leaders of the movement. To their colleagues, they seemed to find no time for thoughts of personal happiness.

Even before the end of the year, the work was under way for the most ambitious assassination plot of all, the one that would not fail. At the beginning of December, a basement storefront had been purchased in St. Petersburg on Malaya Sadovaya Street, a thoroughfare frequently traveled by the Tsar in his stately processions to and from the Winter Palace. Here two conspirators disguised as a married couple established a cheese store, which served as a cover for a tunnel that was dug under the street. A charge was to be placed in this tunnel and set off at some moment to be determined. But the conspirators had decided not to rely on this plan alone; in addition, four men were selected and trained as bomb-throwers, who would be prepared to deal with the Tsar face to face if necessary. Furthermore, if the Tsar should somehow escape even them, Zhelyabov was prepared to attack him with dagger and pistol.

The conspiracy received a great blow on February 27, when Zhelyabov was discovered and arrested; but Perovskaya took over the command alone and proceeded with the plan to assassinate the Tsar on March 1, the day of a military parade. The tunnel under Malaya Sadovaya Street was mined and, on the appointed morning, the four bomb-throwers went to various locations along the Emperor's route, each carrying his bomb wrapped in a newspaper or handkerchief. Perovskaya was stationed at the parade site. The Tsar arrived at the parade that afternoon by a route other than the one along Malaya Sadovaya Street, and when Perovskaya saw that he was going back to the palace the same way, she signaled to two of the bomb-throwers, stationed at the parade with her, to proceed to another predetermined site, along the Yekaterininsky Canal. They arrived there on foot ahead of the Imperial carriage, which had stopped en route to enable the Tsar to pay a brief visit to his cousin, the Grand Duchess Catherine. When the carriage finally appeared, one of the bomb-throwers—a nineteen-year-old student named Rysakov—ran up to it and threw his parcel among the horses' legs. The bomb went off. One of the Tsar's Cossack guards and a butcher's delivery boy who had been passing by were mortally wounded by the explosion. The Imperial carriage was partly damaged, but the Emperor himself received only mild cuts and bruises, and was otherwise unharmed. Rysakov was caught and held by some bystanders. The Emperor was helped down from the carriage and, against the protests of his guardsmen, insisted upon surveying the scene. As he did so, a man in the gathering crowd made a sudden movement toward him, and there was a second explosion.

This time, when the smoke cleared, the Tsar lay mortally wounded in a pool of blood, his clothing in tatters. Next to him lay his assassin, Ignaty Grinevitsky, unconscious and also dying. Other wounded bystanders lay about. After a few moments some of the Tsar's men gained control of themselves sufficiently to lift the semiconscious Alexander onto a sleigh and start back to the palace. The sleigh left a trail of blood in the street. A few hours later both the Tsar and his assassin were dead.

The police moved swiftly against the conspirators. By the next evening young Rysakov had broken down and begun to inform; the following night the police raided the apartment that had served as headquarters for the plot. The apartment had been rented by another fake married couple, a man named Sablin and a Jewish girl named Hessia Helfman. When the police arrived Sablin fired several shots at them and then killed himself. Helfman was taken prisoner. The next morning Timofey Mikhailov, one of the two remaining bomb-throwers, was found and arrested. The cheese store on Malaya Sadovaya Street was raided but found unoccupied. Sophia Perovskaya remained at large several days more, concerned all the while with schemes for helping Zhelyabov to escape; for this reason she imprudently remained in Petersburg. On March 10 she was spotted on the Nevsky Prospekt and was arrested. Rysakov, deluded by promises of clemency, identified her and described the role she had played in the conspiracy. A few days later, Nikolay Kibalchich, who had constructed the bombs and served as the scientific technician of the conspiracy, was arrested and also identified by Rysakov.

On March 26 the trial began of the six conspirators who were in custody: Zhelyabov, the two bomb-throwers Mikhailov and Rysakov, Kibalchich, Hessia Helfman, and Sophia Perovskaya. Zhelyabov conducted his own defense; the others had legal counsel. Rysakov faced the death penalty despite the promises of clemency he had been given for his informing. All but Mikhailov and Helfman pleaded guilty of participation in the slaying of the Emperor. Three days after the trial began, all the defendants were found guilty and sentenced to be hanged. The following day Hessia Helfman informed the authorities that she was pregnant—she had been the mistress of Nikolay Kolotkevich, another member of the Executive Committee, who had been arrested in February—and her sentence was thereupon postponed until after the birth of her child. Later her sentence was commuted, but she and her infant daughter both died in prison. The five others were hanged in a public square on April 3. "Kibalchich and Zhelyabov were very calm," wrote a correspondent of the *Kölnische Zeitung,* "Timofey Mikhailov was pale but firm, Rysakov was liver-colored. Sophia Perovskaya displayed extraordinary moral strength. Her cheeks even preserved their rosy color, while her face, always serious, without the slightest trace of parade, was full of true courage and endless abnegation. Her look was calm and peaceful; not the slightest sign of ostentation could be observed in it." Her last known utterance had been a letter written from prison consoling her mother.

Their minds and hearts filled with these scenes of martyrdom, the surviving members of *Narodnaya Volya* throughout the Empire now awaited the mass uprising of the peasantry that they believed would follow the assassination. But except for a few scattered and minor disturbances, nothing happened until the early part of May, when a wave of anti-Jewish pogroms broke out in southern Russia. In Kiev, Elizabethgrad, and Balta, and subsequently in scores of other communities, angry mobs ransacked Jewish homes and stores, injuring and killing many. It was a new chapter in the old history of constant and sometimes volatile hatred of the Jews by the Ukrainian peasantry. After a while, it began to dawn upon observers that there also might be some connection between these outbursts and the atmosphere of revolutionary crisis in the land. The revolutionaries were the first to formulate a theory linking the two phenomena: the pogroms, some of them said, were the first rumblings of a genuine revolution. The Jews of the Ukraine, they observed, had long functioned as middlemen between the Ukrainian peasantry and their oppressors—Jews, for example, had usually served as rent collectors for absentee landlords. The peasants, then, were taking the first step in a general revolt against their oppressors. A succession of issues of the underground journal of *Narodnaya Volya* carried discussions and proclamations on this question. Some members of the Executive Committee were even enthusiastic about the pogroms; others were more cautious in their attitude, but still were inclined to accept the theory of the pogroms as a prelude to revolution. Even many Jewish members of the organization accepted this view, although there were heavy hearts among them. No peasant uprising followed, however. In time there came the realization that the pogroms, far from opening a path toward revolution, had really worked as a diversion of potentially revolutionary energies. None but the forces of reaction had profited from them. Indeed, it had become evident after a while that not only were the police doing little to put down the riots, but were at times actually making efforts to turn the rioters upon the Jews. Although it was not likely that the authorities had instigated the pogroms to begin with, they clearly had made use of them, recognizing anti-Jewish sentiments as a trait common to the government and the peasantry, and the pogroms as an exercise harmless to everyone but Jews.

The assassination produced other results as well: In the ensuing months, both *Narodnaya Volya* and the moderate *Chornyi Peredel* headed rapidly toward extinction, and the Russian revolutionary movement faltered for almost a decade. But the foremost outcome of the event was one that could never have been anticipated—a major turning point in the history of the Jews of Russia. For the pogroms of 1881 had a galvanizing effect upon them. Many Jewish intellectuals hitherto associated with the Russian radical movement now began seeking new formulations for their revolutionary outlook that would accommodate the fact, hitherto ignored by them as much as possible, that they were Jews. A "Lovers of Zion" movement—the precursor of political Zionism—came into being and sent its first group of young settlers to Palestine the year after the pogroms. Most of the Jewish revolutionaries, however, resisted Zionism as a Utopian and hence bourgeois ideal, preferring to seek some kind of distillation of social-ism and Jewish identity on Russian soil. The formula for such a distil-lation was slower to evolve than the Zionist one was; but a socialist and diasporic Jewish nationalism did eventually emerge in Russia in the following decade.

But these stirrings were the responses of merely a small revolu-tionary elite; it was above all the Jewish masses who were affected by the pogroms of 1881, and their response was the most momentous of all. By the middle of the following year, it became evident that a mass Jewish exodus had begun, mainly from the areas in southern Russia where the pogroms had taken place, and mainly in the direction of America. Charitable organizations of middle-class western European Jews, most notably the formidable *Alliance Israélite Universelle*, fearing a large and embarrassing influx of impoverished Russian Jews into their own countries, quickly established a series of way sta-tions throughout Austria and Germany that facilitated the migrants' journeys to Hamburg and other North Sea ports, and provided them with steamship tickets to America. In 1882, more than 13,000 Jewish immigrants reached the ports of New York, Philadelphia, and

Baltimore, as compared with less than 6,000 in the previous year. This was only the beginning; the number was to go on multiplying in the years to come.

A Russian crisis had thus proven itself to be a matter of Jewish destiny. This was an ironic outcome, for though the great majority of Russian Jewry had been physically a part of the Empire since the Polish partitions at the end of the eighteenth century, they scarcely felt any cultural or spiritual identification with it. By 1881, only a small intelligentsia had achieved any such identification; but the masses had by then, if anything, come to feel more alienated from their surroundings than ever, reinforced in their sense of Jewish separateness by a special history of persecution that the Tsars had imposed upon them. There is a national element in all of Jewish history, but this is generally rather abstract; the Jews of Russia, on the other hand, living in a contiguous territory called the Pale of Settlement that Tsarist law had imposed, and speaking a common Judeo-German, or Yiddish, language, were suddenly discovering their own concrete national identity in the midst of a crisis that began the breaking up of their community.

By origin, the civilization of the Jews of Russia was a disengaged fragment of Central Europe. Spurred on by the pogroms that accompanied the Crusades and later by the mania that fixed upon them the blame for the Black Plague of 1348, groups of Jews from the Rhineland and other parts of Germany had migrated eastward and obtained asylum under the Polish kings, who were eager to have a talented mercantile class established within their domains. The Jewish settlers were grateful for this reception, but not so much so that they were willing to renounce their Germanic culture for the less developed one of their new Slavic environment. In general, an eastward movement of German settlers into the underdeveloped Slavic regions was going on at this time, and the Rhineland Jews who had migrated to Poland undoubtedly saw themselves as a part of it in spite of everything. Even in their new home, they continued to identify themselves as *Ashkenazim* ("Germans," in Medieval Hebrew), and to speak the same Judeo-German dialect—which is to say, a pure Medieval German dialect with Hebrew accretions—as that spoken by their cousins to the west.

Indeed, it is most likely that the Ashkenazic Jews of Germany and of Poland (both of these are only vague geographical designations when one is speaking of the Middle Ages) went on thinking of themselves as a single community, and ceased to do so only with the outbreak of the German religious wars of the sixteenth century. This was a moment of tremendous upheaval in Central and Eastern Europe, and for its Jews in particular. More than a century of turmoil which benighted Germany until 1648 left the region in such spiritual disarray that it did not recover and reenter the mainstream of Western culture for another hundred years. This was also the case with its Jews. During that same period of turmoil until 1648, the Polish branch of Ashkenazic Jewry rose to become the spiritual center of world Judaism. But its very brilliance at this time eventually became a source of cultural retardation; for while Jewish life in Germany had been so shaken up that a path into modern Western culture was opened, Polish Jewry had come under the grip of a rabbinical establishment which outside cultural influences would not easily penetrate.

This barrier to Western cultural influence that surrounded Polish Jewry was further shored up by a disaster which struck in 1648, the year in which Germany and its Jews reached the end of their travail. A Cossack revolt broke out in the Ukraine—which was then still ruled by the Poles—under the leadership of the Hetman Bogdan Chmelnitzky. This uprising eventually transformed the political structure and subsequent history of Eastern Europe, by removing the Ukraine from Polish hands and bringing it into the Russian Empire. It also brought devastation to the Jews of the region, for Chmelnitzky's Cossacks, like their peasant successors in the Ukraine in 1881, vented their wrath at absentee Polish landlords upon the

Jews who collected the rent—and upon all other Jewish men, women, and children in their path. The scenes of rape, torture, and slaughter that took place remained a horrifying memory to East European Jews for generations to come. In an instant, the greater part of Polish Jewry was reduced to poverty and spiritual darkness.

The divergence that had now taken place in the cultural paths of the two main branches of Ashkenazic Jewry became dramatically evident during the course of the eighteenth century. In Germany, the humanism and passion for German culture represented by the Jewish philosopher Moses Mendelssohn helped illumine the way for reconciliation between Jewish traditions and the civilization of Enlightenment Europe. Mendelssohn conceived Judaism to be as rational a faith as a philosopher of his day could desire. Gratefully accepting this view, an emerging German-Jewish bourgeoisie stepped forth from its ghettoes and embraced, once again, the old dream of a Judeo-German culture; revived in *Hochdeutsch* after an eclipse of several centuries, that dream would now seem brighter than ever.

The Jews of Eastern Europe, on the other hand, were at this very moment moving further away from that dream, into a deepening oriental obscurity and religious fundamentalism. Almost immediately after the Chmelnitzky pogroms, the moral vacuum left by that disaster had been filled by an onrush of Jewish chiliasm from the Middle East. In the sixteen-sixties, the appearance of the false messiah Sabbatai Zevi of Izmir had a shaking impact upon Jewish communities throughout the world, but nowhere so much as in Eastern Europe. It was in the resulting atmosphere of spiritual anxiety that the Hasidic movement was founded in the eighteenth century by a Galician Jew of extraordinary charismatic powers named Israel ben Eliezer, known to his followers as the Baal Shem Tov ("Master of the Good Name"—that is, of the sacred name of the Lord). Although there was considerable resistance to this movement within the rabbinical establishment, there was scarcely a corner of East European Jewry that did not feel the influence of its mystical and lyrical religiosity, which blessed the condition of the abject and the poor. Hasidism was ultimately to inspire numerous revolutionary currents among East European Jews, including the thrust toward socialism on the part of many of them, but one of its first effects after an initial wave of spiritual inspiration had passed was a reinforcement, albeit in fresher terms, of the prevailing atmosphere of religious obscurantism.

Hasidism was the contemporary of the Mendelssohnian Enlightenment in Germany, and was also the final gesture of Polish Jewry as a single historical entity. In 1772 the partitioning of Poland was begun, and by the end of the century, while a large portion of Polish-Galician Jewry found itself under Austrian domination, most of the Jews of Eastern Europe were now subjects of the Russian Empire. This completed the three-centuries-old history of divergence between East European and German Jewry. At the same time, the first glimmers of an effort at a reconciliation between the cultures of the two communities made their appearance. For by the end of the eighteenth century, in the next wave after the first onrush of Hasidism, the mood of the German-Jewish Enlightenment had started to gain entry into Eastern Europe. One strain of Enlightenment arose in Galicia, the old heartland of the Hasidic movement and now, under Austrian rule, a conduit of High German culture into Eastern Europe. Another strain appeared in Lithuania, traditionally an outpost of rabbinical rationalism against the more fundamentalist spiritual currents from the south, and readily susceptible to the winds of Enlightenment from nearby Koenigsberg—Kant's home—and other Hanseatic cities. Among the Jews of Russia, this latter strain was the more important one, since Lithuania was also now part of the Empire. These two areas became the centers, then, of a new movement, an East European Jewish version of the German-Jewish Enlightenment, to which its adherents gave the Hebrew name *Haskalah*.

The broader aims of the Haskalah were the same as those of the movement which had inspired it: to reconcile Jewish traditions to Western culture and educate the Jewish masses in that culture.

But there was one major difference. Whereas Moses Mendelssohn considered the German language to be the proper vehicle—indeed, virtually the *chosen* vehicle—for such a reconciliation, the *maskilim* ("men of the Haskalah") accorded this status to Hebrew. In both cases, the decisive factor involved was a somewhat contemptuous attitude toward the Judeo-German dialect, which no one yet considered to be a *language*. The Enlightenment culture of eighteenth- and early nineteenth-century Europe was essentially Brahmin in outlook, and dominated by the notion of a single standard of high culture to which all men should aspire. There was in this none of the fondness for folk utterance that was later to characterize the Romantic movement. Moses Mendelssohn could see in the Judeo-German dialect of his coreligionists nothing but the wretched gropings of an oppressed and ill-educated people toward the language of Lessing and Goethe; he would guide them along the path to full articulateness. As for Mendelssohn's East European counterparts, the maskilim, they were witnesses to an even more alienated condition. The dialect spoken by the Jews around them had almost nothing whatsoever to do with the languages of the other peoples amidst whom they lived. Many of the more European-minded among the Jews of Russia and Galicia were already reaching the conclusion Mendelssohn had reached, that what their tongues naturally yearned to articulate was good *Hochdeutsch,* and they were at first more likely to have their children learn this than either Russian or Polish, for these two languages had not yet, at the beginning of the nineteenth century, quite proclaimed their legitimacy to the civilized world. But the maskilim were, for all their secularist tendencies, enough the products of Polish rabbinical traditions and Hasidic influence to look upon the Jews of Eastern Europe less as exiles from Germany than as exiles from the Land of Israel, and to note that the Hebrew component of the dialect they spoke was perhaps as important as the German. As the Haskalah saw it then, Hebrew was what the Judeo-German dialect—written, after all, in Hebrew letters—was really aspiring to become. The East

European Jewish version of the Mendelssohnian Enlightenment thus also became, quite uniquely, a Hebrew literary renaissance.

Of course, there was an innate contradiction in the effort to write for a people in a language other than the one they spoke. Haskalah won adherents from one generation to the next, but these remained a small elite whose ability to read the Hebrew writings of the maskilim—something that only the most highly educated could do—was, ironically, the outcome of their training in the rabbinical academies against which they were rebelling. The typical maskil was merely a genteel protester against an elite background that continued to shape his life and to shield him from overexposure to the world around him. Reluctant to speak the crude tongue of his own masses— he usually preferred to converse in German—he must indeed have often wished that his home environment were that Mendelssohnian Central Europe in which the universe of Germanism provided a continuum of cultural advancement from the meanest ghetto dialect to the phrases and thoughts of a Goethe. This state of cultural alienation from the folk whom they wished to uplift remained an insoluble problem for the Hebraists until the late nineteenth century, when the energies of Zionism—not thought of by the early maskilim—helped to create a Hebrew-speaking Jewish people in Palestine. But even then, the Hebrew-speaking folk had come out of the linguistic revival and not the other way around; for the Hebrew revival—which was, in a sense, one of many such national cultural awakenings going on in Central and Eastern Europe at the time—was the only one among its contemporaries which never had a village to which to go and discover its own ancient and spontaneous rhythms.

Meanwhile, the fact remained that there *was* a folk language being spoken by the Jews of Eastern Europe; its only failing seemed to be its incapacity, until the latter half of the nineteenth century, to persuade many members of the educated classes that it deserved any attention at all. It did not even have a name of its own—the term "Yiddish" (which is, after all, simply the word in that language for

"Jewish") did not come into wide use until the eighteen-nineties—and it was quite frequently called, simply and contemptuously, *zhargon*. Seduced by Germanism in spite of themselves, the maskilim thought of this dialect only as a debased German, and those among them who first began writing in it so as to reach a larger audience often loaded their prose with *Hochdeutsch*. This was done in part, perhaps, out of nostalgia for a "higher" medium of expression, but it was mainly for the purpose of trying to wean the Russian-Jewish masses to good German. The foremost exponent of this technique was also the man who was the first to write prose more or less regularly in *zhargon* (continuing also to write in Hebrew all the while), Isaac Meir Dick of Vilna. A teacher and a maskil, Dick discovered in the eighteen-thirties the uses of the Russian-Jewish dialect for a kind of moral fable (even when writing fiction, the maskilim were relentlessly didactic) built around scenes from the common folk life. These tales became immensely popular, and Dick undoubtedly grew aware of the literary legitimacy of the language he used in them. *Zhargon* had, after all, become something quite different even from the Medieval Judeo-German in which it had originated; full of Slavic accretions and of a flavor all its own, it could not but awaken responses in a sensitive literary ear. But Dick was not able to rid himself entirely of the loftiness of Haskalah attitudes, and his language remained full of inappropriate Germanisms, giving off the air of Tevya the Dairyman trapped uncomfortably in a starched collar.

Despite the touch of condescension in Dick's efforts, there even existed a literary tradition for Judeo-German, but it had lapsed long before he began writing. The didactic uses of the language had been discovered with brilliant results around 1600 by a Polish rabbi named Jacob ben Isaac Ashkenazi, who published at that time a long, explanatory paraphrase of the Pentateuch in Judeo-German. The reason for such a literary work was indicated by its title, *Tzeyna u'Reyna,* which simply means "Go Forth and See" in Hebrew, but which is grammatically in—Hebraic exoticism!—the *feminine* plural imperative. This book, in other words, was written expressly for ladies, who received no education in Hebrew but were nonetheless entitled, as Rabbi Jacob ben Isaac well understood, to some acquaintance with the sacred literature. Yet it is clear that the author did not proceed on the strength of condescension alone, for the book he wrote is fresh and vivid, and though its diction is somewhat more German than was the dialect that had evolved among Russian Jews by the early part of the nineteenth century, it was still capable at that time of serving as a model for good writing. Its homely literary virtues had in fact enabled it to survive those two hundred years as a major classic, for no pious Jewish woman to that day would be without her *Teitsh-Khumesh,* as it was popularly called (*Teitsh,* showing clearly its kinship with *Deutsch,* remained a widely used term for the Judeo-German dialect; *Khumesh* is the Yiddish—and Hebrew—word for Pentateuch). And though they would scarcely have admitted it, many men not blessed with a good Hebrew education read the book as well.

This, then, was the traditional status of *written* Judeo-German: a mere women's language that men also read, but on the sly. This deprecation of the language was a reflection of the general attitude of the traditional East European Jewish culture toward women and the less educated. In the two centuries following the work of Rabbi Jacob ben Isaac, only Hasidism had made an organized attempt to challenge this state of mind—although it must be said that Hasidism treated women better in fancy than in fact. Otherwise, nothing broke that centuries-long rule of lofty and austere cultural masculinity, the equivalent of which in Western Christian Europe had been dislodged by the Renaissance. Yet the relics of the history of Judeo-German culture show signs that it, too, but for the special circumstances of its history, might have yielded to the general Renaissance trend of vernacular languages toward serving as vehicles for a lighter literature—ostensibly directed at ladies, but increasingly capable of capturing even scholars with its charms—than any for which the ancient tongues were reserved.

This is suggested by the career of the earliest known Judeo-German writer, Elijah Bochur—known in Christian Europe as Elia Levita—whose approach to the relative uses of his own classical and vernacular linguistic heritage was quite similar to that of many of the humanists of that Renaissance Italy in which he spent most of his adult life (he was born in Bavaria in 1469, and he died in Venice in 1549). Like Petrarch writing austere works in Latin and then turning to Italian in his lyrical moods, Elijah Bochur produced several large and important works of Hebrew grammar and also wrote poems in Judeo-German. Among these latter works, there has come down to us a tale of chivalry written in *terza rima* about a knight named Bova, and hence known as the *Bova-Book*. It was based on an Italian romance published in 1497 called *Buovo d'Antona*, which was itself an adaptation of the fourteenth-century English tale *Bevys of Hamptoun*. In his preface the author makes it quite clear that the work is aimed at women. This was implicitly recognized by subsequent East European Jewish tradition, for the term *Bova-Mayse* ("Bova story"), which came to be used for any similarly fantastic tale, eventually mingled with the word for "grandmother"—*bobba*—to become *bobba-mayse,* a somewhat condescending term meaning "old wives' tale."

By the middle of the nineteenth century, the climate for writing again in *zhargon* had greatly improved even over the time when Isaac Meir Dick had first begun to write in it. Liberalism, and the ardent concern over women's rights that came with it into educated Russian circles, helped improve the attitude toward Judeo-German, as did Romanticism, with its passion for the folk tongues of Europe. But the old opprobrium attaching to the language was nevertheless not easily overcome. The first true master of Yiddish prose—indeed, the term "*Yiddish* prose" can first be properly used only for his works— Sholom Abramovich, who wrote under the pen name of Mendele Moicher S'forim ("Mendele the Book-Seller"), never fully overcame an attitude of profound ambivalence toward the language in which he made his fame and toward the culture that produced it. Born in Lithuania in 1835, Abramovich was a maskil by early training and inclination who wrote a number of didactic works in Hebrew while still in his twenties. But the mood of "going to the people" which arose among educated Russians after the emancipation of the serfs in 1861 provoked a new interest among maskilim in the possibilities of writing in Judeo-German, as Isaac Meir Dick had done. "I observed the life of my people and I wished to impart to them Jewish tales in the holy tongue [Hebrew]," Abramovich later wrote of his inner conflict at the time. "The bulk of them, however, did not understand this language, but rather spoke Yiddish. What profit accrues to the writer for all his thoughts and all his labors if he does not serve his people by them?" But this realization placed him upon the horns of a dilemma. "In my time," he went on, "the Yiddish language was a hollow vessel, containing only gibes and nonsense, the work of fools who could not talk like human beings. . . . If one in ten [of our writers] ever reminded himself of the 'accursed tongue' and dared to write something in it, he would hide it beneath his holy prayer shawl, so that his shame might not be discovered to damage his good name." In 1864 Abramovich decided to give it a try anyway, hiding his good name under a *nom-de-plume* which was to become celebrated.

Mendele Moicher S'forim developed a Yiddish literary style of genuine authenticity and quality, but the warmth of his prose style has no counterpart in the attitude expressed in his writings of contempt toward the lives of abjection and ignorance that he considered most of the Jews of Russia to be leading. Twentieth-century readers at all familiar with the Yiddish literary tradition tend to see it through the glow of Sholem Aleichem's affection for the Russian-Jewish village folk and tolerance of their foibles. But this was by no means the mood of Mendele Moicher S'forim, even though he was later recognized to be the "grandfather of Yiddish literature" by its practitioners and was claimed by Sholem Aleichem as his master. It was only in a spirit of ironic scorn that Mendele had been able to take up Yiddish and give it a place in history for almost the first time in over two hundred years. Uncertain even of its ability to assure his literary immortality, he eventually translated all his major Yiddish works into Hebrew—and thereby also became the main founder of a modern Hebrew narrative prose.

Yiddish had thus begun by the eighteen-sixties to break down the obstacle of Hebraism that had stood in the way of its development; but another obstacle was now arising, in the form of Russian language and culture. A brilliant Russian literary awakening was taking place, and it was inevitable that educated Jews should begin being drawn to it.

This, too, was an outcome of the Haskalah, as well as of increasing efforts on the part of the Russian government to assimilate its Jews. In both respects, the model for a reconciliation between the Jews and Russian culture had been provided, as with so many elements in East European Jewish life, by Germany. Tsars Nicholas I and Alexander II had been greatly impressed at the ways in which the Mendelssohnian Enlightenment and the subsequent Reform movement in German Judaism had transformed the Jews of Germany into good subjects of their various princes, and they sought to effectuate the same transformation in Russia by creating a government-sponsored educational system for their Jewish population. This program met with great resistance, but nevertheless, by the eighteen-sixties, a small assimilationist rabbinate had come into being in Russia; these rabbis urged their flocks to be—in the fashion of German Reform Judaism—"Russians of the Mosaic Faith." During the halcyon days immediately following the emancipation of the serfs, when even the exiled revolutionary Alexander Herzen began looking upon Tsar Alexander II as a vehicle for liberal aspirations, many Russian Jews regarded the Emperor as a savior of their people. These passions soon cooled toward Alexander II, and they later found no object whatsoever in Alexander III; but the fact remained that a class of Russified Jews was coming into being. Some were even winning the rare privilege—later circumscribed by a *numerus clausus*—of a gymnasium and university education for their sons, and for their daughters.

But this process did not produce merely the Russified Jewish bourgeoisie that the Tsars had hoped for. Russian spiritual life in the eighteen-sixties and seventies was a teeming cauldron of ideas, and the young Jews who received gymnasium and university educations could not be uninfluenced by the new currents. It was in particular the radical movement, an overwhelming force in the universities at this time, which drew young Jews in large numbers and became, ironically, a more powerful agent for their Russification than any that the government had created. A movement which seemed to recognize no distinction between Gentile and Jew, or between noble and peasant, and which sought to create a whole society in which its attitudes would prevail was naturally most attractive to a group entering it from the outer margins of society.

However, there were problems implicit in the participation of Jews in a peasant-oriented movement, as the pogroms of 1881 finally demonstrated. It was, in fact, not until the later infusion of Marxism into the Russian revolutionary movement, providing a myth of class struggle which could encompass the Jewish masses, who were rapidly becoming proletarianized, that Jews could participate in the movement without apparent contradiction. Marxism was scornful of the peasantry. But it was fully a decade after 1881 before Marxism became a significant factor in the Russian revolutionary movement, and until that time, a whole generation of Jewish radicals were left with the task of recovering from the shock of an apparent betrayal by a faith which had seemed to be their salvation. The history of this trauma, which reduced many from total belief to total disillusionment, is the central story in the lives of the young Jewish radicals of 1881. In many cases, their story is somewhat like that of the person whose marriage has ended in divorce in spite of himself, but whose heart has never ceased to yearn for the estranged, unloving spouse.

Such, for example, was the story of Abraham Cahan.

Born in 1860 in a village just outside of Vilna, Abraham Cahan grew up in that city whose Jewish community was so large and culturally brilliant that Napoleon, passing through there on his doomed path toward Moscow, had called it "the Jerusalem of Lithuania." Vilna had long been eminent for its outstanding rabbinical traditions, but in the eighteenth century it became particularly celebrated in the Jewish world for being the seat of Rabbi Elijah the *Gaon* (roughly, "genius"), the foremost spokesman of those forces which remained opposed to the Hasidic movement. Long after his death Vilna remained the principal rallying ground of the *misnagdim* (literally, "opponents," of the Hasidic movement), and in the more southerly and more Hasidically inclined regions of East European Jewry, the word *Litvak* ("Lithuanian Jew") came to be a synonym for a skeptic and a cold-hearted rationalist. This estimate may not have been entirely just, since Vilna and nearby Kovno were also the centers of a great tradition of cantorial singing—ever a major expression of the sentimental elements in the Jewish soul—and were the first places in which secular artistic and intellectual currents arose with any strength among East European Jews. Nevertheless, a rational and practical streak was always clearly in evidence among Litvaks, who were, for example, the first in Eastern Europe to discover to any wide extent that it was possible for them to trim their beards and dress like "Germans" (i.e., like Western Europeans), and still be pious Jews. They were a main spearhead for Russification among the Jews of the Empire.

Abraham Cahan was thoroughly a Litvak from his earliest days, combining a capacity for romantic outbursts of spiritual passion as fervent as the cantorial singing which he loved with a remarkable talent for the practical. The grandson of a rabbi, he was at first expected by his family to become a rabbi too; since time immemorial, this station in life had been the highest toward which pious East European Jews aspired for their sons. Abraham was even a good Talmudic student for a while; but his family had reached the point of the break-down of tradition. His father, the rabbi's son, had already fallen short of what the family had regarded as its birthright for several gen-erations, for he was not a rabbi but merely a *melammed*, a teacher on the elementary levels of the Jewish educational system. Traditionally, the *melammed* was a man who lived on the margins of sustenance and was regarded as something of a failure by society. Shakhne Cahan was no exception to this, but his plight was somewhat aggra-vated by the scorn of his eminent father and of his wife, the daughter of a prosperous jeweler whose delight at giving her away to the prom-ising son of a great rabbi had long since faded with his promise. In time, the family had concluded that the life of the spirit had best remain purely a private matter for Shakhne, and a great-uncle who ran a prosperous distillery in Vilna summoned him to preside over the company tavern in 1865.

From Abraham's earliest childhood, his mother made it clear to him which of the family's trodden paths represented glory and which disaster: "You have a mirror before your eyes," she would say to him, referring ominously to his father. The boy got the idea, and was for a time a zealous student and an extreme religious enthu-siast. But Shakhne, whose failures had apparently persuaded him that the Talmud was not the sole source of principles by which a life might be governed, wanted something of a secular education for his son as well, and Abraham was sent for a time to one of the schools for Jewish boys that had been established by the government's Russification program. This worked even better than Shakhne had hoped; for Abraham, whose character was marked by a tendency toward obsessive spurts, first in favor of one interest or ideal and then in favor of another, gave up his passion for religion, became an athe-ist, and embraced Russian culture.

For most pious Jewish homes, Russian culture still meant baptism and forced service in the Tsar's armies; Abraham's new passion was therefore not popular with his family. But the boy's interests were no longer in their world anyway; rather, from the age of about fourteen, he began to look longingly in the direction in which the sons—and the daughters—of some of the wealthier Vilna Jewish families were beginning to go, speeded on by the government's new policies for Russifying Jews and by the virtues of *protektsiya* ("pull"—above all, bribes), toward the gymnasiums and the universities. Abraham's parents were too poor to obtain this kind of education for him even had they thought it desirable, but he was determined to find some way of getting it. For a time he studied Latin and Greek on his own in hopes of entering a gymnasium, but he did this at an age beyond that of most entrants, when he was already eligible for the draft. He soon found out that he could gain exemption from military service only by staying on where he was by then enrolled, in the Jewish Teachers' Institute of Vilna, one of the schools of "higher" education established by the Russification program. And so, reluctantly, he settled down to the inferior education he was receiving there—which at least was in Russian—and to the prospect of a career as a teacher in government Jewish schools.

But life at the Institute proved to be not as barren of the new currents in Russian-Jewish life as young Cahan had at first expected. Even there, one could experience some of the charms of Russian student life that he had once thought reserved only for those who followed the elite route of the gymnasium and the university. "At the Institute," he later wrote of those days in his memoirs, "were several students about whom it used to be said that they had *barishnyas*." (The word *barishnya* is Russian, and it means "lady" in the old sense of the word, implying refinement or high social status.) "This meant that they were friendly with girl gymnasium students, or with other intellectual girls. [There were no girls at the Institute.] No improper relations were implied by this—absolutely none. Someone who 'had *barishnyas*' simply played the role of a cavalier with them. He used to go for walks with them, visit them in their parents' homes, honor their 'women's rights,' lend them books to read and bestow attention upon them in other chivalrous ways." These were of course Jewish rather than Gentile girls, but in the context of Jewish life at the time they were very Russian indeed. They spoke Russian, adored Russian literature, and expected their cavaliers to behave toward them in the current Russian fashion of idealizing and exalting women. In the case of their relations with boys from the Institute, they could usually get away with demanding extra displays of admiration; for, standing as he did merely at the margin of the truly Russian way of life he so longed for, the Institute boy was always zealous to gain acceptance by a gymnasium girl. Acceptance was sufficient, and "having a *barishnya*" did not necessarily mean being loved by her. "It only meant," Cahan explained, "that [a boy] knew how to get to know people; that he was no *yeshiva-bokher* and knew how to play the role of a cavalier." A *yeshiva-bokher* is a Talmud student; in this context it implies someone utterly unworldly, shy and un-Russian, who is afflicted with the fear endemic to pious Jews of even having so much as mere comradely relations with women outside of marriage. When a *barishnya* sensed that her cavalier was really a Talmud student deep within his pounding heart, she knew that favors were available beyond the call of mere chivalry.

She could often, for example, even get her admirer to write school compositions for her. Cahan discovered this one day when he was out walking with a friend of his from the Institute. In the street they met two girls who were wearing the brown-skirted uniform of gymnasium students; "apparently they were acquaintances of my friend—especially the taller of the two girls. We stopped, he greeted them and introduced me. The words 'I have the honor to introduce Mr. So-and-so and Miss So-and-so,' and the whole ceremony, were no longer anything new to me. And yet the whole thing would upset me every time and bring color to my pale cheeks. All the more so when I was being introduced to a 'brown-skirt.'" Cahan's yeshiva-bred shyness, still strong, was compounded by the fact that he was somewhat cross-eyed and was overly persuaded that girls therefore found him ugly. "The taller of the two gymnasium girls was not especially pretty. But her eyes—they were black—sparkled with vivacity. She had a request to make of my companion. Her Russian teacher, who was also our dean, had assigned a composition, and she wanted him to write it for her.

"'When does it have to be in?' he asked.

"'The f'rteenth,' she replied."

Her way of slurring the word was highly Russian and colloquial, a way of demonstrating to Cahan's friend that her Russian accent was really more authentic—and less Jewish—than his, despite her difficulties writing compositions in the language; also, Cahan observed, it was a way of flirting. "Several times she found a pretext for repeating the word, for flirting again by means of her good Russian pronunciation. Then her black, vivacious eyes sparkled coquettishly at my friend, and her not especially pretty mouth smiled coquettishly too. I perceived all this as clearly as I saw that the composition was not the point. . . . The girl didn't make a good impression on me, neither with her face nor with her flirtatious manner. But, nevertheless, she was a *barishnya!* A gymnasium girl, after all! I envied her cavalier for the sparkling glances she gave him."

Cahan happened to meet this girl again at a party not long afterward. During the course of the evening, he did not get to talk to her much, but when the time came to go home and escorts were assigned to each of the girls, Cahan found that he was to take her home because she lived near him. He discovered to his surprise that she did not seem at all displeased about this. On the way home they soon found themselves wandering a bit. They went into a park. "It was late, and quiet all around; no sign of anyone. It was a moonlit night. The air was filled with a silver glow. We sat and talked, and she began turning the conversation in a playful direction. She was making light-hearted remarks and flirting unabashedly.

"'Give me a hundred kisses!' she said to me, not in Russian but in Yiddish.

"She said this in a joking tone. But she gazed into my face with her coquettish, vivacious smile.

" 'No!' I replied, ashamed, my heart pounding.

" 'Give me a thousand kisses,' she said again, jokingly.

" 'No!'

" 'Ten thousand, twenty thousand.'

" 'No!'

" 'A million kisses!'

" 'No!'

"I thought she was making fun of me. I didn't come near her. And so I took her home."

He did not easily forget the incident, however. "Afterwards I began taking myself to task for being such a fool. At first I both had understood and not understood her. It was incredible to me. Did she really mean for me to kiss her, then?—me, with my cross-eyes? No, she was surely making fun of me. . . . But why, then, had she been glad that I was to be her escort home? And why did she wander out of our way with me . . . so late at night? . . . When I became a bit more acquainted with the ways of the world I no longer had any doubt as to the meaning of that scene."

Cahan eventually did enjoy the acquaintance of a fair number of gymnasium girls, but he still found it hard to overcome his shyness. "Every time a group of boys and girls that I wasn't a part of would walk by, I would think to myself that their world was forbidden fruit for me, that they were more important than I was." He would often wander by himself into a cafe frequented by the young intellectuals and students of Vilna, to sit there and try to feel himself a part of its atmosphere. But "I didn't feel comfortable there; it was as though I was trying to insinuate myself into a world too high for me." What he now was beginning to aspire to was a world beyond that of the flirtatious *barishnyas* who went around with the Institute boys, one in which the girls were preoccupied with nobler thoughts and acts than coquetry and did not jokingly refer to women's "emancipation" as *a-man-tze-patzye* ("to slap a man," in Yiddish).

Specifically, Cahan was now beginning to have inklings of the activities of students who were involved in the revolutionary movement. "Near the railroad tracks . . . I used to see several young men and a few *barishnyas* whom I suspected to be members of an underground group. . . . They were dressed like anyone else, they talked like anyone else . . . but a certain manner, a certain expression on their faces, and the special intimacy with which they behaved toward one another—all this was testimony that they belonged to another world. Among them were a few gymnasium graduates, two or three boys still in gymnasium, a few from the trade school, and some gymnasium girls. These were all Jews. But together with them was always a young Christian, a very handsome, blond young man who wore the uniform of the Vilna Railroad School." Cahan's own contact with Christians was still rare, and normally a Jew's ability to have Christian friends was a sign of his having truly "arrived" socially; but here was a society in which Jew and Christian mingled without any ceremony and pretension, in which any distinction between the two did not even seem to exist. "I used to picture to myself the hidden world in which [these people] moved; and they themselves seemed to me to be mysterious, extraordinary creatures. My imagination cloaked them in a life of secrecy, danger and courage. . . . I have said how I used to feel jealous of every group of young intellectuals with whom I was not personally acquainted. I would feel excluded. . . . But my feeling toward this group was quite different. I looked with completely different eyes upon the *barishnyas* with whom these mysterious young men went about. I thought of them as girls of a higher sort. Their distance aroused no jealousy in me. They simply belonged to another world."

But Cahan was soon to become a part of this world. "At the beginning of the summer of 1880, when I was between my third and my fourth year at school, I made my first acquaintance with the secret literature [of the revolutionary movement]. It turned out that two of my friends belonged to the Vilna underground *kruzhok* ("circle," in Russian), and they gave me socialist writings, the first I had ever read. Afterwards, they introduced me to other members, and I was admitted into the revolutionary family. This brought about a transformation in me that influenced my entire life." Cahan was soon regularly attending the meetings of the Vilna revolutionary *kruzhok*, which was affiliated with *Narodnaya Volya.*

These meetings took place in the apartment of a young Gentile named Vladimir Sokolov, a bachelor who earned enough money to provide for his simple personal needs by giving private lessons in various subjects. Though only in his early thirties, Sokolov was a good ten years older than most of the members of the *kruzhok* over which he presided, and he represented to them a figure of maturity and wisdom, from whom they received their first lessons in the principles of socialism. The blond young man in the uniform of the railroad school, a Pole named Anton Gnatowski, was a boarder in Sokolov's apartment; he looked upon his host as an elder brother and teacher. In general, Sokolov showed a comradely warmth to all the members of the circle which Cahan, whom he was soon addressing in the familiar form, found overwhelming. Eventually Sokolov was even calling him "Cahanchik" (or "Caganchik"), a form of address as affectionate as it was Russian. To be addressed in this way by an older man, a revolutionary, a Gentile, filled the former *yeshiva-bokher* with a thrill of excitement. "I could scarcely believe this was really happening." He had been won over to the revolutionary movement heart and soul: "a religious enthusiasm was burning within me." Eagerly, he pored over the literature of the movement, and reread Chernyshevsky's *What Is to Be Done?,* a book which bored him when he had tried it a few years before, but which now inspired him with its vision of how men and women were to live in complete equality in the new society to come.

Cahan received word of the assassination of Tsar Alexander II on the evening of March 1, when he was sitting in the study hall of the Teachers' Institute. A student entered saying that the director had ordered all to close their books and go out into the corridor. They did so, and in the corridor the director soon appeared, a tall, dignified Russian Gentile in a black frock coat and a starched shirt. "Gentlemen," he said sadly, "close your books. There will be no lessons tomorrow. Our Emperor has suddenly passed away." Nothing was said of how the Tsar had died, and Cahan and others wondered if the news meant that he had been assassinated. Later that evening, with the help of some friends, Cahan left the school building through a window—the students, who slept in, were not free to go out on a Sunday night, as this was. Cahan was being sent as an unofficial emissary to find out what had happened; he headed straight for Sokolov's apartment. The members of the *kruzhok* who had gathered there were able to tell him that the Tsar had been killed by an explosion, but no one had any further information as yet.

In the next few days the details of the assassination became known to everyone; these were received along with the news of the arrest of each of the conspirators. There was sadness about the arrests among the radicals, but for the most part Sokolov and many other members of the *kruzhok* were in a state of excited anticipation as they awaited the revolutionary upheavals that were to come. Cahan, suddenly discovering the practical streak in himself, was unable to become convinced that such upheavals were really in the offing. He noticed that everyday life in Vilna seemed to be going on exactly as before. The police were no stricter than they had ever been, business and transportation went on as usual—Cahan had the eerie impression that the world simply regarded an Imperial assassination as an everyday occurrence. Perplexed, he went to Sokolov and asked him why nothing was happening.

"Be patient, Cahanchik!" Sokolov replied. "You have to be patient. Did you ever think that Alexander would fall so soon? What do you know about what they're getting ready to do in the 'center'?"

The "center" referred to was the Executive Committee, which was at that very time being reduced to a shambles, as Cahan and presumably Sokolov well knew. Cahan felt an unhappy pang of suspicion: could it be that his mentor Sokolov was politically naive? To have such a realization was like growing years older in an instant.

The news of the executions made an indelible imprint upon Cahan's youthful imagination. "The description of the scene [in the newspapers]," Cahan wrote four decades after the event, "caused me to break down and cry. Zhelyabov, Kibalchich, Perovskaya, Mikhailov and Rysakov—their last minutes before the gallows, how each of them met the end—all this has never left my mind."

These images made a far deeper impression upon him at the time than did the subsequent news of the pogroms in the distant Ukraine. "I must admit, this matter [of the pogroms] was of little interest to me and to the other Jewish members of our *kruzhok*. We considered ourselves to be 'human beings, not Jews.' Jewish matters had no special appeal for us. There was one solution to all the problems of the world, and only one: socialism. That was our supreme principle." And yet it was troubling even to Cahan and his Jewish comrades in revolution when some members of the underground positively endorsed the pogroms—all the more so, when it eventually became clear that the pogroms were a betrayal of the revolution and not a step in its fulfillment. In spite of Cahan's protestations of universalism, there seemed to be a delicate line, impossible to avoid, between being a good revolutionary and being more aware of one's own Jewishness than revolutionary principles could easily allow.

The irony is that Cahan's own revolutionary destiny, like the destiny of the revolution itself, came to a Jewish outcome anyway, despite his intentions to the contrary. After graduating from the Institute that spring, Cahan went to work in the fall as a teacher in a Jewish school in the town of Velizh, White Russia, some distance from Vilna. But despite the distance from his home, his underground associations began catching up with him there, and one day the police called upon him to search his room. By chance, they found nothing incriminating—they spotted a copy of Marx's *Capital,* then still little known in Russia, but Cahan coolly informed them that it was a treatise on business enterprise—but he knew that he was now being watched. When the news arrived of the arrests of some of his old comrades back home, he decided that he had better leave the country, at least for the time being. He left Velizh and went into hiding.

His plan, at first, was to go to Switzerland, which was then a Mecca for socialist exiles from Russia. But while traveling southward to a point at which he could cross the border more easily, he ran into a Jew named Belkin, who was soliciting potential settlers for Palestine. Belkin tried to win Cahan over to the Love of Zion program. In doing so, he described a controversy that was arising among young Jewish radicals in the wake of the pogroms. Some of them, having turned to a purely "national" solution to the Jewish question, were advocating emigration to Palestine, while others who were still opposed to an unmitigated Jewish nationalism but were now persuaded that there was little future for Jews in Russia planned to establish communistic colonies in the United States. The communal ideal still had some strength among Russian radicals in these pre-Marxist days, especially in Kiev, where a communal movement had flourished a few years before. It was now especially the Jewish radicals of Kiev who were afire with the ideals of this new communal movement which they called, in Hebrew, *Am Olam* ("Eternal People"), and which focused its aspirations upon America, whose history of communistic settlements was still fresh in the minds of Europeans.

Belkin did not succeed in turning Cahan into a "Palestinian," but his account of the *Am Olam* movement was something else again. "There took shape before me," Cahan later wrote, "a fantastic picture of a communistic way of life in distant America, a life in which there would not be any notion of 'mine' and 'thine,' in which all men would be brothers and everyone would be happy." The imagination of Cahan, the romantic dreamer, soared for at least a moment in cantorial song—but is it possible that the practical side of his spirit did not then come to the rescue? Surely, Cahan knew that communistic colonies were not for him, not even for a moment; he had been a dedicated "loner" all of his young life. But what other excuse could he provide himself for this sudden desire that rose up in him to go to America? As he headed farther south, toward the regions that had been immediately affected by the pogroms, he began to encounter the masses of Jewish emigrants who were streaming toward the New World. Was there, quite simply, an impulse deep within him to join his destiny to theirs? He could scarcely admit it to himself; but, once he made his decision to go to America, this was, in effect, precisely what he had done.

CHAPTER 2

# NEW YORK, 1882

⌒

When she heard what I wanted to do she shook her head and
frowned. She said, in substance, that America was a land of dollars,
not of education, and that she wanted me to be an educated man.
—ABRAHAM CAHAN, *The Rise of David Levinsky*

"I CONJURE UP THE GORGEOUSNESS OF THE SPECTACLE AS IT
appeared to me on that clear June morning," Cahan wrote years later,
using the voice of his fictional protagonist, David Levinsky. "The
magnificent verdure of Staten Island, the tender blue of sea and sky,
the dignified bustle of passing craft—above all, those floating, squat-
ting, multitudinously windowed palaces which I subsequently learned
to call ferries." The vast spread of New York harbor, with its many
islands, channels, and bays, still had a somewhat rustic look in June
of 1882, when Cahan arrived there by train and ferry after docking at
Philadelphia. The Statue of Liberty was not yet standing, Ellis Island
was bare, and there was nothing to be seen of that huge fortress of
stone, brick, and glass skyscrapers that the observer coming up the
harbor sees at the southern end of Manhattan Island today. At that
time, the tallest edifice in New York was a ten-story slab that stood
at the foot of Broadway just beyond Battery Park; a cluster of large
commercial buildings surrounded it, but north of them the highest
structures to be seen were the numerous church spires, which them-

selves yielded to the hegemony of treetops farther north as the city quickly faded off into semi-rural and rural suburbs. Only one clear sign of the titanic growth to come was in view, just to the right: the lofty towers and cables of the Brooklyn Bridge, which was nearing completion and was already casting a shadow over its environs which seemed to command the subsequent urban growth that would match its immensity if not its grace.

The immigrant reception center of New York was still located in the squat, hexagonal structure called Castle Garden that stood in Battery Park at the southernmost tip of Manhattan Island. Built originally as a fort, the last in a long line of artillery positions dating back to Dutch times that had given the Battery its name, it had been converted into New York's main opera house and civic center a few years after the War of 1812. Standing as it did at the gateway to the city—and, in effect, to America—it also served for a time as the site of receptions for distinguished European visitors. Lafayette was received here in 1824, and Louis Kossuth, the Hungarian revolutionary leader, in 1851. Kossuth in particular was a symbol to many Europeans who had despaired of the struggle for liberty at home, and Castle Garden had come to stand for a spiritual as well as a physical arrival. It was therefore a kind of historic fulfillment when, in 1855, after the newly built Academy of Music on Fourteenth Street became the main seat of opera in New York, Castle Garden was converted into the United States government's main immigrant clearinghouse.

This had happened in a time when immigration was still thought of in terms of the yeoman ideal that the early colonial settlement in America was considered to represent. New arrivals were not yet perceived as "the wretched refuse of your teeming shores," but as adventurous and enterprising wanderers who had broken loose from the trammels of an overripe civilization to seek freedom of opportunity in a country that was still largely frontier. It was only in the decades following the Civil War that the character of the immigration began to change. This was, in part, a reflection of the changes that were taking place in American society. After its victory over the Southern agrarian society, the old Yankee civilization of small entrepreneurs and modest commercial aristocracies had begun yielding place to an emerging class of industrial barons dedicated to the creation of immense consolidations of power and wealth. In turn, the economic system that these men were creating was bringing new classes into being at the bottom of the social and economic scale, to serve their engines of production. The fundament of these new classes was a new type of immigrant that began arriving in the same period, the restless overgrowth of obsolescent peasantries, seeking not necessarily entre-preneurial opportunities, but mere employment.

The first waves of these industrial-age immigrants, dwellers at the margins of sustenance in their home countries and often again in America, were primarily from Ireland, Germany, and other parts of Northern Europe. But in the latter part of the nineteenth century these gradually gave way to Italians, East Europeans, Jews, and Chinese, in a movement further and further along the spectrum of exoticism that began provoking "nativist" reactions from white Americans of more traditional stock. Castle Garden underwent a dramatic change of character, filling up with unprecedentedly large masses of impecu-nious arrivals, many of whom remained there to be fed and housed until claimed by a relative or a potential employer, speaking a babel of foreign tongues, taxing the hygienic capacities of the old building. "The stench was terrible," Cahan recalled of the one night he spent in Castle Garden, "as if a thousand cats were living there." More adequate facilities were needed for this inundation; it was not long after this that work was begun on a new, much larger immigration center on Ellis Island.

The city outside the gate of Castle Garden was already begin-ning to show signs, despite its still-peaceful look from the harbor, of the social and economic transformation that was taking place in the country at large; indeed, New York was the nerve center of that transformation, and had been its harbinger for many years. If Boston had been the Athens of the old Yankee civilization, New York was the Rome of the new empire represented by the words "Wall Street." New York had begun to boom shortly after the War of 1812, with the commencement of work on the Erie Canal upstate. The sweet reasonableness and genteel prosperity of the Knickerbocker era was soon replaced by the brute rationality of expansive power. Buildings were razed to make way for bigger ones, and the lines of streets were redrawn. A city commission laid out a street plan for the entire northern part of Manhattan Island, which was then still largely farmland and forest; and New York, which had grown up alongside the paths of loping cows and of creaking wagon-loads to the sea, suddenly began to become, to the north of Houston Street, an exercise in urban geometry, a stark rectangular grid of numbered streets and avenues. But this highly rationalized pattern was the only constant, for within the rectangles the city became a seething realm of change that was virtually unrecognizable from one generation to the next. "It is never the same city for a dozen years altogether," a resident wrote in *Harper's Magazine* in 1856. "A man born in New York forty years ago finds nothing, absolutely nothing, of the New York he knew. If he chances to stumble upon a few old houses not yet leveled, he is fortunate. But the landmarks, the objects which marked the city to him, as a city, are gone."

Yet these were mere preliminaries to the immense outburst of wealth and power that was to hit the city after the Civil War. In the fifties, the gentility of the old mercantile aristocracy still reigned supreme, despite the intrusions of such brash parvenus as John Jacob Astor, who foreshadowed personalities and powers to come, and the seat of New York's best society resided in the quietly elegant brownstone town houses that were going up in and around Washington Square, Lower Fifth Avenue, and Gramercy Park. But by the seventies and eighties this world was watching the growing indications of its own obsolescence. "When I was a girl," Newland Archer's mother observes in Edith Wharton's *The Age of Innocence,* "we knew everybody between the Battery and Canal Street; and only the people one knew had carriages. It was perfectly easy to place anyone then; now one can't tell, and I prefer not to try." Appropriately, this novel depicting the twilight of Mrs. Archer's way of life opens on an evening in the early seventies in a box at the Academy of Music, during a performance of Gounod's *Faust* with Christine Nilsson in the role of Marguerite. There is an ironic foreshadowing here, for it was with a performance by Nilsson in *Faust* that the Metropolitan Opera House was to make its debut in October, 1883. The idea for building the Metropolitan had come to William Henry Vanderbilt, one of the new industrial plutocracy, after he had been consistently refused the social distinction of owning a box in the Academy of Music. Recognizing a power at his disposal greater than mere entrenched snobbery, he gathered together his peers to build an opera house of their own. It was erected farther north than the old Academy of Music, closer to the frontier where the new barons were also building their residential palaces on upper Fifth Avenue. The opera company at the Academy of Music was forced to close down soon thereafter, leaving Fourteenth Street to the German immigrants, to the new mass retailing centers, to the prostitutes, and to Tammany Hall.

For if a new class of roughneck millionaires was blazing a trail uptown, an equivalent class of roughneck political barons, dealing in votes as the magnates dealt in dollars, was emerging out of the slums left in the wake of the city's northward growth. New York's first major political boss, William Marcy Tweed, born in the shanties of Cherry Street on the Lower East Side, had transformed Tammany Hall—the Democratic Party organization of Manhattan—into the instrument of a new type of political power. This power was founded mainly upon the organization's abilities to win and control the loyalties of the city's poor by doing favors for them. It was a method especially likely to be effective with immigrants, for whom the organization could serve as a protector, provider, and guide into the rough-and-tumble processes of making one's way in America. In Tweed's day, the two main immigrant groups of New York were the Germans and the Irish; but whereas the Germans were too foreign, too attached to social and political institutions they had brought to America with them, and too rapid in their ascent into middle-class occupations to be amenable to the Tammany approach to politics, the more plebeian Irish took to it with relish. Tammany became virtually an Irish institution, and Tweed, himself of Scottish descent, was followed after his demise in the seventies by a succession of Irish bosses that was to last until the nineteen-twenties, when the Italians achieved supremacy in the organization. New York's special pattern of ethnic politics was now beginning to emerge.

So also was the rich ethnic variety in its population, for which New York was to become celebrated, beginning to articulate itself at this time. The first major non-Anglo-Saxon immigrant group to arrive had been the Irish, first in the eighteen-twenties and thirties with the growth of job opportunities caused by the Erie Canal boom, and then again in the late forties and the fifties as a result of the potato famine in Ireland. The large Irish laboring class that thereby grew up in the city easily fell victim to the vagaries of the business cycle, and masses of Irish poor became a fact of New York life by the time of the Civil War. The first neighborhood into which Irish immigrants had gathered in large numbers was at the foot of Mulberry Street and around Chatham Square, just a few blocks northeast of City Hall. Like many slum neighborhoods, this one had been built with high social aspirations; but it stood upon the site of a pond, and when the streets and houses there had begun to sag, the original well-to-do residents fled and left them to the poor. In each succeeding generation, the natives of this district, known as the "Five Points" because of the five intersecting streets that formed it, either climbed the social scale and moved on to better neighborhoods or stayed on in deepening squalor. By 1882, when it housed the most poverty-stricken members of several ethnic groups, it had become the major preoccupation not only of Police Headquarters, which stood a few blocks north on Mulberry

Street, but of the celebrated reform journalist Jacob Riis, himself an immigrant, who stalked its streets at night searching for material for his articles and dreaming dreams of urban improvement.

The Germans were the next major immigrant group to arrive, beginning in the forties, when the liberal mood in Germany was growing restless at the outmoded and seemingly intractable social and political structure of that country. High-minded and industrious, the German immigrants eschewed the worst slum districts and established themselves in the areas, east of Chatham Square, into which the socially rising elements of the Irish population had settled. These areas constitute the Lower East Side of Manhattan, which was to go on being the principal immigrant neighborhood of the city. Largely a lower-middle-class neighborhood during the first wave of Irish and German settlement in it, its German sectors in particular so came to bear the stamp of its inhabitants as to be known to New Yorkers at large as "Dutchtown" ("Dutch" being here a corruption of *Deutsch*). The community life of "Dutchtown" was characterized not only by an air of well-scrubbed and industrious sobriety, but also, after 1878, when the Bismarckian anti-Socialist law brought an influx of refugee intellectuals, by cultural institutions of a high caliber. There was a proliferation of German-language newspapers, socialist and otherwise, and of German theaters and concert halls from the foot of the Bowery all the way up to Irving Place. The entire area came to be filled with crowded beer halls, cafes, and restaurants. To a certain extent, this German community life provided a paradigm for the Jewish one that was to follow it.

Before the seventies there had never been more than fleetingly a distinct Jewish neighborhood in New York. The old Sephardic Jewish settlers of the seventeenth and eighteenth centuries had clustered from time to time around the succession of synagogue buildings that their congregation had occupied, but with their ascent into the upper middle classes they had become dispersed throughout the better neighborhoods of the city. The next great wave of Jewish immigrants, the German Jews and German-speaking Jews from Central Europe, arrived as an integral part of the general German immigration and tended, even with their synagogues and other Jewish communal institutions, to remain culturally a part of the German community at large. If German *Jews* were to be found in clusters anywhere in the city, it was not so much in their dwellings as in their places of business. As was the case with Jews in Germany itself, the German-Jewish immigrants in New York (and in other American cities) entered the burgeoning consumer industries of the day with a rather high degree of concentration. Within the system of mercantile arteries that had grown through Lower Manhattan by the middle of the nineteenth century, certain sectors became thick with wholesale and retail establishments run by German Jews.

This was especially the case in the garment trades, which, as clothing increasingly became an item of mass production and consumption, emerged as preeminent among the specialties of German Jews; and the concentration was especially heavy along arteries which connected the main areas of German settlement on the Lower East Side with the principal downtown shopping districts on and around Broadway, to the west. Grand Street, one of the major shopping streets in New York in the seventies, was one such artery, and it grew thick with German-Jewish retail shops. Canal Street, roughly parallel to Grand and two blocks to the south of it, was another, and it became the main center for German-Jewish wholesalers. This arrangement formed the basis of a socioeconomic system which, with the later mass influx of Jews from Eastern Europe, and with the concomitant rapid growth of garment production at home, was to run its innumerable veins through the surrounding tangle of residential streets right into the tenements themselves. The clear line of distinction between residence and business establishment would begin to disappear.

It was after 1870 that the appetite to seek one's fortune in America spread *en masse* from Germany to communities of Yiddish-speaking Jews in parts of Poland that were adjacent to it. In their first wave, some of these new arrivals from the districts of Suwalki and Great Poland began to cluster at the corner of Bayard and Mott Streets, just a block north of the Five Points (later to become the heart of Chinatown). But many of these Polish Jews were tailors attracted by New York's growing garment industry, and since they often brought their work home from the shops of the German-Jewish merchants who farmed it out to them, it was natural for them to seek to live closer to where these shops were concentrated. In time a settlement of Polish Jews came into being at the very foot of Canal Street, where it met Essex Street and East Broadway. This is the neighborhood into which the Russian Jews surged when they began arriving in 1882.

The Jewish neighborhood that was thus coming into being was characterized by a high degree of integration of domestic life and commercial activity. The street at one's doorstep was the beginning point of some avenue of entry into the world of American economic opportunity. There were various routes that could be followed. One was the way of the pushcart: this mobile establishment could be rented at very low rates and filled with the overflowings of Canal Street's wholesale stores, from full-fledged articles of clothing down to the merest scraps of ribbon and cloth. In a sense, the pushcart was the urban-era version of the wagon that the German-Jewish peddler of the previous generation had taken into the towns of the frontier, out of which he had built his retail empires. From the pushcart the next step, for those who made it, was "customer-peddling," going from door to door taking orders for second-hand clothing or buying clothing with which to fill such orders. Success at customer-peddling could in turn produce enough capital for the next step, that of actually setting up a store of one's own. Until that point, the essence of success was an ability to maintain a virtually nonexistent margin of overhead; indeed, nothing was over the head of the beginning peddler but the dusty sky of Manhattan, framed between the tenement ledges.

Other economic routes followed the direction of manufacturing rather than of retailing. At first, the clothing industry was run by men whose main activity was selling, and for whom the process of manufacturing the goods they sold essentially was something that could be carried on in the back of the shop. As trade expanded— men's clothing became an item of standardized mass production and consumption earlier than women's wear did—it became necessary to transform the nature of the old shop industry in one of two ways: either to expand one's business into a large-scale manufacturing and merchandising enterprise all housed under one roof, or to farm out a segment of the manufacturing process. A few chose the former course exclusively, but most resorted to the latter either partially or completely. The merchant-manufacturer would buy the raw material and have it cut in his shop; he would then hire out the cut material to contractors, who took it to their own shops and supervised the sewing and other work required to transform it into finished goods. The contractors then resold the merchandise to the manufacturer, who in turn sold it wholesale or retail on the open market.

This process brought into being a unique phenomenon: the Lower East Side clothing contractor. The equivalent in the realm of manufacturing to the pushcart peddler, he too tried to work with virtually no overhead. Very few contractors in this stage of the New York garment industry rented lofts to serve as their shops; rather, they used their own homes for this purpose. Some rented equipment themselves, but in most cases the contractor's hired help brought their own sewing machines. The hiring of workers by the contractor was done in a daily shape-up—the amount of work available naturally varied greatly from one day to the next—on the street. The main center for this activity was at the intersection of Hester Street—which ran midway between and parallel to Canal and Grand Streets—with Ludlow Street. Hester Street was the main pushcart artery as well. Consequently, at about eight o'clock in the morning this intersection was perhaps the noisiest and most densely crowded spot in New York. The din of furious negotiating and hiring and firing eventually brought to it a name that became celebrated in Lower East Side folklore—the *Khazzer-Mark* ("Pig Market").

As housing conditions grew worse on the Lower East Side, the unique form of domestic industry evolved by the clothing contractors inevitably gave rise to conditions of unimaginable squalor. "The homes of the Hebrew quarter are its workshops also," wrote Jacob Riis in his study of New York slum conditions in the eighteen-eighties, *How the Other Half Lives*. "You are made fully aware of it before you have travelled the length of a single block in any of these East Side streets, by the whir of a thousand sewing-machines, worked at high pressure from earliest dawn till mind and muscle give out together. Every member of the family, from the youngest to the oldest, bears a hand, shut in the qualmy rooms, where meals are cooked and clothing washed and dried besides, the live-long day. It is not unusual to find a dozen persons—men, women and children—at work in a single small room." Later, Riis describes how he once followed a typical contractor, bent under the bundle of goods he had just hired from the manufacturer, through the streets, into a Ludlow Street tenement and "up two flights of dark stairs, three, four, with new smells of cabbage, of onions, of frying fish, on every landing, whirring sewing-machines behind closed doors betraying what goes on within, to the door that opens to admit the bundle and the man. . . . Five men and a woman, two young girls, not fifteen, and a boy who says unasked that he is fifteen, and lies in saying it, are at the machines sewing knickerbockers, 'knee-pants' in the Ludlow Street dialect. The floor is littered ankle-deep with half-sewn garments. In the alcove, on a couch of many dozens of 'pants' ready for the finisher, a bare-legged baby with pinched face is asleep. A fence of piled-up clothing keeps him from rolling off on the floor. The faces, hands, and arms to the elbows of everyone in the room are black with the color of the cloth on which they are working." This was a typical "sweatshop."

The "sweating-system," as it was called, reached these depths only with the great influx of Jews from southern Russia that began in 1882. The earlier Jewish immigrants from western Poland were largely skilled tailors, practitioners of a trade that had been quite low on the social and economic scale in the old country, but that formed a basis for relative economic well-being in America. On the other hand, few of the Jews arriving from southern Russia were skilled in the garment trades; theirs was not so much a selective emigration, founded upon the anticipation of specific economic opportunities in America, as a mass flight which cut across a wide variety of occupations and social positions. As a matter of fact, their emigration to America wrought a kind of social revolution among them. Men who had been relatively well-to-do in the old country, their fortunes now left behind them, were reduced to penury and to the necessity of flinging themselves as unskilled labor upon the mercies of the "Pig Market" in order to gain a livelihood. Others who perhaps might have been their hired hands in Russia, now flourishing on the basis of a head start or a temperamental capacity to survive in New York's entrepreneurial jungle, were often the men who hired them. But it was the men of learning, the pinnacle of the social scale at home, who fell most severely of all in the passage to America. When David Levinsky, a Talmudic scholar, leaves Castle Garden with a tailor whose acquaintance he has made aboard ship, they are confronted in the street by a contractor. The latter has come to the Battery, as many contractors did, to find the cheapest labor of all, among the "greenhorns" fresh off the boat. Discovering that Levinsky's companion, Gitelson, is a tailor, he hires him on the spot; then, turning to Levinsky, he asks:

"And what was your occupation? You have no trade, have you?"

"I read Talmud," Levinsky replies.

"I see," the contractor says, "but that's no business in America." He gives Levinsky a quarter and sends him forth into the world to fare for himself.

But despite this initial rebuff, Levinsky, too, finds work in the garment trades; for it was this industry, with its superabundance of jobs requiring little or no previous training and not much physical strength, and with its already well-established network of Jewish connections, that became the major source of employment for the Russian-Jewish immigrant masses pouring into New York. At first, most of the new arrivals regarded a job as a finisher or a baster—sewing or cutting required more skill—as merely a first step, a chance to take a breath, until one got started in America. Some planned to go on from there and start businesses of their own from their savings; others hoped to save enough money to pay for schooling in a profession. Few or none, at first, thought they had settled into the occupation of ordinary garment worker for the rest of their lives. The intolerable working conditions were therefore ignored; they were simply hurdles to leap over in one's journey toward the American rewards that seemed to await all who were patient and strong.

The sweatshop was a natural sojourning place for the more cultivated and intellectual of the Russian-Jewish immigrants. Neither the hurly-burly of pushcart peddling nor the brutalities of contracting appealed to their sensibilities as a rule, and they preferred doing straightforward toil—especially if, like Cahan, they were Russian-bred radicals, imbued with the tradition of "going to the people"—until such time as they obtained training in some skilled trade or profession. Certain garment-trade occupations, such as shirtmaking, in which the work was light and routine enough to enable those engaged in it to let their minds wander or converse with their fellow workers or even read a book lying open on the table, became established as preserves for intellectuals. The result was a situation perhaps unique in history: an industry that contained a large class of proletarian intellectuals, who brought an articulate class consciousness right into the shops at a time when such an attitude still normally, elsewhere in the world, had to be imparted to workers by intellectuals from the outside. It was a class which had from the outset an opportunity to view, with educated eyes, the underside of the American entrepreneurial adventure.

Although, like Cahan, the first of these intellectuals to arrive in America thought of themselves as exiled Russian radicals rather than as Jewish immigrants—they conscientiously spoke Russian rather than Yiddish among themselves—they were driven by a natural dialectic of circumstance into identifying their lot with that of the Russian-Jewish immigrant masses, and thereby into taking up positions of moral leadership among them. Indeed, there was a vacuum of moral leadership among the Jewish immigrants in America that had to be filled. The role that had normally been played by the rabbinate in Eastern Europe was now, for a moment, going to be taken up by the immigrant anticlerical intelligentsia, since East European rabbis still disdained to go to America in any significant numbers. But, ironically, the radical immigrant intellectuals shared some of the traditional attitudes of the rabbinate, in the depths of their souls. They harbored, for example, a similar disdain for those who were less spiritually and intellectually exalted than themselves. In the sweat-shop situation, this deep-lying attitude gave reinforcement to the working-class pride that their ideology committed them to develop; for, as Russian intellectuals, they were readily able to muster special resources of contempt toward the former tailors and cart-drivers who had become the shop bosses of the Lower East Side. This double-edged class attitude was further reinforced by an ethnic one: for even if the intellectuals as a group were far and away the most "Russian" of the Jewish immigrants, the new arrivals of 1882 and after were in general more Russian (and, on the whole, better educated) than their immediate predecessors, the tailors from Suwalki and Great Poland. It is a tradition of long standing for Russian Jews to regard themselves as more refined than Polish Jews. Thus, the new arrivals of 1882, both intellectual and ordinary worker alike, all of them "greenhorns" from Russia seeking employment at the hands of their Polish-Jewish and German-Jewish predecessors, found their lives converging into a common destiny.

When Cahan saw this scene unfolding before him in his first days in New York, he viewed it with mingled excitement and dismay. "While human nature was thus growing smaller," David Levinsky observed of it, "the human world as a whole was growing larger, more complex, more heartless, and more interesting." Cahan concluded years later that "it was unpleasant to me. But it also was invigorating to me, like the strong, healthy smell of a freshly plowed field." A strange mingling of despair and restless anticipation filled his being. He walked the streets constantly, his senses pulsating with the new detail and experience that crowded around him, searching for something without knowing what. "The streets swarmed with Yiddish-speaking immigrants," David Levinsky wrote. "The signboards were in English and Yiddish, some of them in Russian. The scurry and hustle of the people were not merely overwhelmingly greater, both in volume and intensity, than in my native town. It was of another sort. The swing and step of the pedestrians, the voices and manner of the street peddlers, and a hundred and one other things seemed to testify to far more self-confidence and energy, to larger ambitions and wider scopes, than did the appearance of the crowds in my birthplace." There was considerable poverty, to be sure, far more than the immigrant had been led to anticipate before his arrival, but even this seemed to be "of another sort," less hopeless, than in the old country. In the course of his wanderings through the streets, David Levinsky sees a family being evicted:

> A mother and her two little boys were watching their pile of furniture and other household goods on the sidewalk while the passers-by were dropping coins into a saucer placed on one of the chairs to enable the family to move into new quarters.
>
> What puzzled me was the nature of the furniture. For in my birthplace chairs and a couch like those I now saw on the sidewalk would be a sign of prosperity. But then anything was to be expected of a country where the poorest devil wore a hat and a starched collar.

The essence of the experience that America promised to yield seemed to be revealing itself in scenes like these.

In his walks, Cahan often stopped at the very center of the Jewish quarter, in Rutgers Square, the meeting point of Essex, Canal, and East Broadway, to absorb the bustling pageant all around. He knew that whatever the destiny of the Jewish immigrants in America was to be, its gestation was taking place right here. Did he also have any inkling that he was gazing upon the locus of an imperial seat—the consummation of his own American destiny—over which he was to preside one day?

CHAPTER 3

# THE RADICALS OF RIVINGTON STREET

*How can you be happy when in the country where you were born people are dying of hunger, where the government takes from the people their last penny and compels them to go forth and beg for a crust of bread? Perhaps you do not know this; and if you know it, what have you done for your brethren?*
——"STEPNIAK" (SERGEY KRAVCHINSKY), *Underground Russia*

ON A SUNNY AFTERNOON IN JUNE OF 1882, THE MONTH OF Cahan's arrival in America, a group of Jewish immigrants sitting on the grass outside of Castle Garden saw a white barge appear in the harbor and approach the dock just in front of them. When it landed, a young, well-dressed man stepped off, walked up to the immigrants and, to their surprise, began addressing them in German. He told them that he had jobs for about five hundred men, at two dollars a day plus meals. The effect of this announcement was electrifying. Some of the men had been here for days and even weeks, they and their families eating meals provided by charitable organizations of German-American Jews, waiting for some economic opening into the American world beyond the gate of the immigrant center. Now such a channel was presenting itself, and at a rate of pay considerably higher than what many established residents of the Lower East Side were receiving at the time. Few of the immigrants asked the well-dressed young man about the nature of the work being offered. He had said simply that it involved loading and unloading ships, but he assured them that they would be provided with wheelbarrows and that the work would not be too heavy. He easily obtained the five hundred workers he desired.

At about a quarter to six the following morning, the immigrants at Castle Garden were awakened by the sound of a ship's whistle. They hurriedly got dressed, took leave of their families, and walked out onto the waiting barge. As the boat pulled away, they were given their breakfast: a piece of white bread and a tin cup filled with milk. Lunch and supper were to be pretty much the same, with coffee instead of the milk. The immigrants barely had time to finish eating before the barge arrived at its destination. They descended onto a dock where a foreman stood, shouting at them in English and endeavoring to make himself understood by emphasis and vigorous gesticulation. In this way, he and his assistants showed the new workers to their various assignments. The work proved to be not so light as the young man had promised. An observer might well have asked, as he watched these underfed immigrants staggering under their heavy loads: what had made them so desirable as longshoremen in the first place?

It was not until the afternoon of the third day of work that an incident occurred which shed light upon this question. One of the immigrants, taking a short break from his chores, happened to stroll from the dock area out onto the street. There he was suddenly accosted by two brawny men in work clothes, who proceeded to pummel him. His cries for help brought the police, who broke up the fight and sent the immigrant back onto the dock. When his fellow workers saw his state of disarray, they gathered around him in excitement. What had brought on this assault? He was unable to say. After a brief discussion, it was decided that two of the immigrants who knew a little English would go out onto the street and try to find out what was going on. When they reached the street, they were immediately surrounded by a crowd of angry workingmen; their English came to the rescue, as they asked in bewilderment why they were being attacked.

Fists were lowered, the two immigrants were taken to a saloon, and there they received an explanation.

They learned that five thousand longshoremen, many of them immigrants themselves, from Ireland, were on strike in New York that week, seeking a five-cent raise in their twenty-cent hourly wage. The strike was the result of years of effort on the part of the union to inculcate a spirit of solidarity among the dock workers; and now its success was being threatened by the Jewish immigrants who had been hired at Castle Garden. The two emissaries listened sympathetically and then, pointing out that few of the Jewish immigrants knew what a union or a scab was, suggested that the longshoremen send a committee to Castle Garden that evening to state their case. The longshoremen agreed to do so.

A large crowd gathered for the meeting that was held that evening on the grass of Battery Park. Several of the union leaders were exiled Social Democrats from Germany, and they addressed the assembled immigrants in German. There was also one speaker from among the immigrants themselves, a radical Jewish intellectual from St. Petersburg named Miravich, who addressed the crowd in Russian. He called upon his fellow immigrants to demonstrate solidarity with the working class of their adopted land. After a discussion a vote was taken, and an overwhelming majority decided not to work at the dock any longer. A plan of action was formulated for the following day, which was payday.

The next morning the immigrants got onto the barge as usual, ate their meager breakfasts, and descended onto the dock where they had worked the past three days. This time, however, they refused to work, and demanded to be paid immediately. The foremen, quickly recovering from their surprise, suddenly charged into the immigrants and drove them back onto the barge. The boat headed for another dock and moored near it, far enough away so that the occupants could not get off. They sat there for the rest of the morning and part of the afternoon, without getting lunch, until the barge began to move again at about three o'clock. It returned to the dock where they had been working; the foremen were there, ready to distribute the week's pay. The paying began, but suddenly there was a commotion as the first workers on line discovered that their pay envelopes contained only $1.70, instead of the six dollars they had expected. There was a scuffle, but police were present and broke it up. A discussion was held. The foremen argued that the pay was less because the cost of the "meals" had been deducted. After a long debate on this point, the workers finally agreed to a deduction of meal costs at the rate of a dollar a day. This meant that $1.30 was still due each worker, and they were paid accordingly. Leaving the dock on foot for the first time, the immigrant workers were greeted by a crowd of jubilant longshoremen, who accompanied them back to Castle Garden.

That evening, in another meeting in Battery Park, the Jewish immigrants were invited by the longshoremen to take part in a mass labor demonstration scheduled for the following Monday. On the appointed day, about a thousand Jewish immigrants joined five thousand dock workers in a march from Battery Park more than two miles up Broadway to Union Square, where a rally was held.

So far as is known, this episode was the first instance of Jewish labor organization in America.

For the time being, nothing permanent was to come of it. This same group of immigrant Jewish workers was soon scattered far and wide through the fragmented economy of the Lower East Side and elsewhere, carrying peddler's baskets, pushing pushcarts, crowding into sweatshops, assisting in a multitude of small shops and factories. Even if the spirit of enterprise were not predominant among the immigrants, the conditions under which they worked were still too diffuse and unstable for any notion of labor solidarity to arise readily and take hold. The Knights of Labor, still the chief organization of unions in America at this time, was to make some attempts at unionizing Jewish immigrant workers in the months to come, but without success. The unions of Jewish workers created by the Knights tended to be *ad hoc* organizations which came into being for a strike and fell apart immediately afterward, whether the strike was successful or not. The ambitions of most of the Jewish immigrant workers still lay elsewhere than in the shop. Besides, they were unable to breathe easily in the quasi-Christian atmosphere of the Knights' organization. It soon became clear that if they could be unionized at all, it would have to be under the leadership of fellow Jewish immigrants, who understood their view of things and spoke their language.

But the Jewish immigrant intelligentsia that would eventually perform this function were, for the time being, still too caught up in the romantic mood of the Russian revolutionary movement to be able to immerse themselves in the prosaic tasks of labor organization in America. Typical of their attitude was that of the young St. Petersburg radical, Miravich, who had addressed the immigrants in Russian at the meeting in Battery Park. The New York German Social Democratic leaders present that night were impressed enough with his speech to want to set him up as the leader of a socialist discussion group which would, hopefully, attract some of the "Russian" immigrants to the cause. The organization was created in the following weeks. Though its principal language of discourse was ostensibly to be Russian— which few enough immigrants would understand to begin with—it was resolutely, like all the discussion groups it was modeled after, given a German name: the *Propaganda Verein*. Miravich was to preside over the meetings of this group, which was to be a forum for socialist ideas among, in effect, that small immigrant elite which knew Russian well enough to participate, most of whom were committed socialists already. There was no thought of finding ways of reaching out to the uninitiated masses, or of creating any kind of labor organization for practical ends. Such tasks were not for the likes of Miravich, who, though physically installed on the Lower East Side of New York, still lived spiritually in the world of Zhelyabov, Perovskaya, and the other martyrs of *Narodnaya Volya*. Shortly after arriving in the United States, his wife gave birth to a son, whom they named Andrey Zhelyabov Miravich.

Among the more intellectual Jewish immigrants, the *Propaganda Verein* soon attracted considerable attention. Its second meeting, on the evening of Friday, July 27, drew a large crowd. Cahan, who had a job in a cigar factory—another favorite occupation among the intellectuals—was among those present. The meeting place was a hall at 125 Rivington Street, one of the numerous tenements on the Lower East Side that had been converted into a building of assembly rooms to serve a community which had a passion for after-hours lectures. Although it was a hot night, the hall had filled beyond its capacity; more than five hundred persons squeezed into the chairs and lined themselves up against the walls.

The first speaker was Sergey Schewitsch, a Russian aristocrat by origin who had lived in Germany for a time and was now one of the editors of the New York *Volks Zeitung*, a German-language daily that had become the foremost socialist organ in America. He was well chosen as an opening speaker, for he had a special luster in the eyes of the Russian-Jewish intellectuals. This was not only because of his origins, but because he was married to Helene von Racowitz, the woman, partly Jewish in origin, for whom Ferdinand Lassalle had given his life in a duel. These associations breathed the very essence of the romantic radicalism of mid-nineteenth century Europe, typified by the figure of Ferdinand Lassalle and his restless gropings beyond his middle-class Jewish origins in search of a gesture that would transform him, now into an aristocrat, now into a proletarian. Every Russian-Jewish radical had a touch of Lassalle in his heart, which was at this moment turned toward the figure of Sergey Schewitsch as he began addressing the audience in Russian.

"The pogroms," he said, "that have forced you, Russian Jews, to seek a new home were the work of ignorant peasants who did not understand what they were doing. When the day of understanding comes to them they will attack, not Jewish homes, not the Jewish inhabitants of Elizabethgrad, Balta or Kiev, but the Tsar's palace in St. Petersburg. There they will indeed make a pogrom. They will do away with the rule of despotism and organize a government founded upon freedom, equality and brotherhood." He went on in this vein; there was not a word in his speech about the situation of the work-ingman in America. After he had finished, he was followed by two anarchist speakers, who addressed the audience in German.

After they had spoken, Miravich stood up and announced that the floor was open to anyone who wished to say something. To his surprise, the aisle suddenly filled with a mass of people who surged toward the platform, each person striving to get there before the oth-ers and be the first to speak. He hastily retreated from his original open invitation, and asked for a show of hands. No one in the crowd forming at the foot of the platform heard him say this; but Cahan, sitting in a seat near the front of the hall, found himself thrusting his hand into the air. He was recognized by the chair. With a pounding heart, he stood up and made his way to the platform. As he started to speak, he noticed some people at the door in the rear who had been about to leave; his first words made them stop and listen.

"We are now in a country that is relatively free," he said, in Russian. "We are seeking a new home here. But we must not forget the great struggle for freedom that we left behind in our old home. While we are here worrying only about ourselves, our comrades over there are struggling and are being tortured in Russian prisons—our heroes, our martyrs."

These words were spoken quickly, in a tone that was quite modest compared with that of the other speakers, but they had an appeal-ing forthrightness, and were delivered in a lilt that had some of the musicality of the speaker's home city of Vilna. He spoke with evident sincerity, and in a high state of emotion. These were the qualities that had arrested his audience. He went on:

"No, we must not forget the fight for freedom in our old home. There is not much we can do from so far away—but we can collect money, for example. We must support that sacred movement. The Russian revolutionary struggle should lie deep in our hearts. We must not forget the martyrs who are being tortured in their Siberian exiles." When he finished, there was an outburst of thunderous applause. The young speaker, his initial shyness gone, listened in astonishment and delight.

Miravich stood up to make a few final remarks and close the meeting. A group then gathered around young Cahan, still on the platform, to find out who he was, and to talk some more about the things he had said. Miravich joined the conversation. He and Cahan introduced themselves to each other, and Cahan asked him about the nature of the *Propaganda Verein*. Miravich explained that the purpose of the organization was to propagate socialism among the Jewish immigrants.

"If this is for Jewish immigrants," Cahan said, "then why were the speeches in Russian and German?"

"What other language should they be in?" Miravich replied. "What Jew doesn't know Russian?" Being from St. Petersburg, Miravich had grown up among a community of Jews so highly assimilated to Russian culture that they were hardly any longer aware of how untypical they were.

"My father, for example," Cahan said to him, "knows very little Russian."

Cahan then went on to suggest that some of the meetings be conducted in Yiddish. But at this time, though Yiddish had begun to show its possibilities as a vehicle for fiction and poetry, it was still scarcely thought of as a language in which serious philosophical or political discussions could be held. Miravich clearly thought that the idea was ridiculous.

"All right, then," he said sarcastically, "will you give a talk in Yiddish?"

"Why not?" Cahan retorted.

The next thing Cahan knew, he had accepted an assignment: at the forthcoming meeting of the *Propaganda Verein* the following Friday evening, he would give a lecture on socialist theory, in Yiddish.

The whole thing had come about more in jest than in earnest, but once he was launched on the project, Cahan went about it with a characteristic outburst of obsessive zeal. So far as he knew, this was to be the first Yiddish-language socialist speech ever delivered on American soil. He decided therefore to make much of the occasion. With a natural instinct for publicity, he designed a handbill announcing the lecture, which he had printed at his own expense. These he distributed in the street after working hours each day, helped in this task by Bernard Weinstein, a sixteen-year-old immigrant from Odessa who worked on the bench next to him in the cigar factory. Weinstein had, in fact, been listening to Cahan's workbench lectures on socialist theory for weeks, and was already his passionate disciple. Cahan's experience as a teacher had stood him in good stead; he knew how to win a pupil's ear. Now he would try his techniques on a larger and generally more mature audience.

The meeting took place that Friday evening in the meeting hall of the New York anarchists, which was located behind a German saloon on East 6th Street. A crowd of about four hundred men and women gathered to hear Cahan speak. He had prepared a discussion of Marx's theory of surplus value, the class struggle, and the transition from capitalism to socialism. This would be rather heavy going for the uneducated Yiddish-speaking workingmen who formed the bulk of his audience. Few of them had ever even heard of Karl Marx, much less of the difficult concepts that formed the stuff of his theories. But Cahan himself had only recently begun reading Marx, and this was an advantage, for he had the born teacher's capacity to be at his best with material he was only just absorbing himself, to recapitulate for students the stages of his own understanding. Furthermore, he had a remarkable talent for providing vivid illustrative examples. During his speech, for example, he depicted the capitalist system as a human pyramid in which the rich stood upon the shoulders of the poor, its enormously broad base formed by the proletariat and its tiny apex by the wealthiest capitalists. Even the dullest head in the audience could thereby summon up an image of the toppling of the system. He spoke for two hours, but he never lost the attention of his listeners. When he finished he was greeted by tumultuous applause, and he felt again the thrill he had felt at this sound the week before. He had managed to convey Marxian ideas in Yiddish, which meant that he had been able to popularize them, to present them in terms that were simple, homely, and vivid. This was truly a demonstration of the Russian radical ideal of "going to the people." What did it matter if some of the subtleties were lost? The point was to convey a revolutionary passion.

Miravich was now persuaded that his skepticism had been ill-founded, and he invited Cahan to lecture in Yiddish again the following week. Cahan accepted. His second Yiddish lecture the next Friday evening took place in a much larger hall, on Suffolk Street; but, despite its size, the place was filled to overflowing, and many people stood or sat in the aisles. As he spoke, Cahan even spotted one small group standing on a table; among them was a girl wearing a pince-nez—very much the *barishnya* type, Cahan noted. His eyes kept falling upon her during his lecture. In places, his talk grew a little more furious than it had been the week before. At one point, he even called upon the audience to charge up Fifth Avenue with axes and swords. Of course, neither he nor his listeners were quite sure yet where Fifth Avenue was; the remark was meant as an intoxicant for the soul rather than as a real call to action. Such was the mood of those days.

Cahan soon developed a considerable reputation as a socialist speaker, and his life became filled with an unflagging succession of engagements. His mind and spirit had found a life in America; but his hands were still occupied with a dreary daytime round. He had quit the job at the cigar factory after a few weeks, but had then gone to work in a tin factory, which he found equally oppressive.

The lectures, delivered purely for the cause, did not bring him any income. He therefore decided to set out on a course of self-education that would make him more eligible for some intellectual occupation. Working with *Appleton's English Grammar* and a pile of newspapers every night, he soon improved his English to such a degree that he was able to begin giving English lessons to other immigrants. Only three months after his arrival in America, he had developed a thriving trade teaching English to rising young peddlers. The situation brought out all his innate feelings of superiority to the uneducated parvenus whom he taught; but it also liberated him. He was soon able to earn enough from these lessons to quit his factory job.

But English had now become his latest obsession, and he could not settle for a merely relative competence in it. That fall, he asked permission of the principal of a Lower East Side grammar school to sit in on classes there. This was granted, and for the next three months Cahan attended lessons in reading, arithmetic, and geography among a class of thirteen-year-old boys, for the purpose of perfecting his English. He was eventually able to speak the language with little trace of a foreign accent. By the summer of 1883, a year after his arrival in America, he was already contributing free-lance articles about the Lower East Side to American newspapers, and in the fall he obtained a position in the evening school of the local branch of the Young Men's Hebrew Association as an English teacher for immigrants. He was now able to earn a satisfactory living and keep his days free for socialist activities and for participation in the rich cultural life of the Lower East Side.

Because of its character as a European and working-class neighborhood, the Lower East Side was a magnet for foreign-born intellectuals of various persuasions, nationalities, and ethnic origins. Its lively cultural life and innumerable cafes made it also an attraction to growing numbers of native Americans who sought richer intellectual fare than their own Yankee civilization seemed to offer. The area thus became a kind of Left Bank, whose *ad hoc* university was scattered through the various tenement assembly rooms in which lectures and meetings were forever taking place. These lectures were not the province of socialists exclusively. Cahan, for example, also went to Felix Adler's lectures on Ethical Culture, which fascinated him with its rationalist religious philosophy, even though he found it unacceptably bourgeois in the last analysis. More appealing among the nonsocialist doctrines then popular on the Lower East Side, for Cahan and for other Russian-Jewish intellectuals, was Comtean positivism. One of the popular lecturers of this school was a Scottish-born workman named Edward King, whose gentleness and simplicity of manner won him many admirers among the Jewish immigrants. But the chief exponent of positivism and perhaps the major spiritual force in the neighborhood in the early eighties was a Russian nobleman of German extraction whose name had been Vladimir Heins, and who now called himself William Frey. Frey had emigrated to the United States in 1875 in order to found a Christian communist colony in Kansas. This venture failed, but in the meantime Frey had discovered Comtean positivism, out of which he had worked a distillation all his own that included his communist theories. This did not seem at all inconsistent to him, even though Comte had ardently opposed communism. Frey's communist theory was so Utopian, however, that in practise it was no more revolutionary than Comte's own doctrine anyway. It was based primarily upon the hope that mankind would become good through a spontaneous and willful act of self-regeneration on the part of every individual; this was to be achieved through such demonstrations of self-discipline as the refusal to eat meat. The doctrine thus became in practise a kind of bourgeois individualism that bordered on mere eccentricity. Cahan and other orthodox socialists viewed it with amused interest; but it had quite a vogue among many Jewish immigrants. One follower of Frey used to prepare a vegetarian soup whose terrible taste he invested with moral significance. "He assured me," Cahan said, "that it was something wonderful, and that he could feel himself getting healthier with every spoonful."

Less public, but far more intense spiritually, were the regular informal gatherings of the young "Russian" socialist intellectuals. At this time, their lives still revolved around the communal movement that had brought so many of them to the United States in the first place. The movement was not exclusively concentrated in agricultural colonies, even though these had been its principal goal. The Kiev *Am Olam* group had tried founding such a colony in New Jersey, but this quickly failed, and the only rural commune of the movement still in existence by the fall of 1883 was the one maintained by the Odessa *Am Olam* group in Oregon, which was called "New Odessa." But even this commune had representatives in New York; its New York secretary, Paul Kaplan, lived in an attic room adjoining that of Cahan on Clinton Street. The *Am Olam* groups from Kiev and Vilna maintained urban communes in New York. The boys and girls living together in one of these communal apartments would work on the outside in various jobs, but would share all income and chores at home. Cahan was a frequent visitor at the Vilna commune, on Essex Street near Grand, and an occasional boarder there, but he was never able to bring himself to consider settling down in it. Another place he frequented, along with many of the other young immigrant intellectuals, was the apartment of Nikolay Aleinikoff, the leading light of the Kiev *Am Olam* group. Slightly older than the others, Aleinikoff was a forceful personality who had quickly made himself one of the chief spokesmen for the Jewish immigrant community in New York. It was, in particular, the wealthy representatives of the German-Jewish community in the city who looked upon him as such, and they had appointed him the superintendent of the Lower East Side branch of the YMHA, where Cahan taught evening school, and where Aleinikoff's apartment was located.

It was above all nostalgia for Russia and for its revolutionary movement that held these young people together and dominated their lives. Starting with New Year's Eve of 1882, the "Russian" colony began holding an annual New Year's party that was to become a major Lower East Side institution. On March 13, 1883, the first anniversary—on the Western calendar—of the assassination of Alexander II, a solemn public ceremony commemorating the martyrs of *Narodnaya Volya* was staged by them; this, too, was to become an annual event. The young Russians of New York also continued to circulate among themselves the issues which reached New York of the waning party organ of *Narodnaya Volya,* and other specimens of underground literature. In the summer of 1883, two books of exceptional interest to them appeared. One was an account of the Russian revolutionary movement written from his London exile by Sergey Kravchinsky, the assassin of General Mezentzev, under the pseudonym of "Stepniak"; it was published in an English translation (an edition in the original Russian was not to appear for several years) entitled *Underground Russia.* This book was very important to Cahan, who, having participated in only a provincial *kruzhok,* knew scarcely more than the general public did about what had happened in March, 1881. It also gave vivid biographical sketches of the martyred leaders of *Narodnaya Volya.* More important in this latter respect, however, was the book published in Geneva that same summer, in Russian, called *Calendar of Narodnaya Volya.* The biographies in this book were given in terms of the major dates in the history of the underground movement. For Cahan the book remained, ever afterward, "one of the priceless souvenirs of my youth."

Shortly afterward, Cahan even had an opportunity to see a fragment of the *Narodnaya Volya* legend in the flesh. Cahan's attic apartment had an extra bed in it which often served as a hotel facility for young Russians who were passing through; early one morning, when a young man from Odessa named Moscowitz was sleeping there, he and Cahan were awakened by a loud knocking at the door. When they opened it, they saw standing there a blond-bearded Russian Gentile in his early thirties who had come looking for Moscowitz. To Cahan's astonishment, the visitor turned out to be none other than Leo Hartmann, Sophia Perovskaya's false husband in the attempt to bomb the Tsar's train in November, 1879. Hartmann had been sent abroad in the fall of 1880 by the *Narodnaya Volya* Executive Committee, to act as its emissary and try to collect funds for the movement. In Paris he had almost been extradited, but was spared, thanks to the intervention of Georges Clemenceau, Victor Hugo, and other luminaries, on condition that he leave France immediately. He went to London, where he stayed long enough for a brief romantic involvement with the niece of Frederick Engels' wife, and then sailed for New York, where he arrived in July, 1881. Finding himself threatened with extradition again, he had gone to Canada briefly and then back to London; but public opinion in the United States had intervened in his favor, as in France, and he had now returned to New York. Cahan could scarcely contain all the questions he wanted to ask Hartmann, and, a few weeks after this first encounter, when the latter came to spend a few nights in his apartment, the torrent broke forth. Hartmann, who had already displayed to the American press a talent for romanticizing his own history, was glad to answer questions for his admirer. Cahan listened with special interest to his descriptions of Sophia Perovskaya. One evening Hartmann pulled out a black silk kerchief which he said had belonged to her. "When he showed it to me," Cahan later wrote, "I took it into my hands and gazed upon it like a holy object."

But Hartmann, unlike his young host, had already had his fill of living for the revolution. He had made application for American citizenship by now, and, in anticipation of a business career, was learning the electrician's trade, which had fascinated him since his days of working in the technology of assassination. He had recently invented a tie clasp that could be illuminated electrically, and during his stay with Cahan he and his host went around to storekeepers in the evenings trying to sell this product. Clothing dealers all over the Lower East Side would look up in surprise to see one or the other of these two men coming in through the door, his face glowing in the light of his illuminated necktie. One storekeeper was going to give them an order, when he observed the wire leading from Cahan's tie to his pocket, bulging with the stuffed bottle that served as a battery; he promptly sent him out of the store. They never came that close again to making a sale.

Although Cahan was beginning to have second thoughts about the exalted notion he had once held of Hartmann's character, these days were a great pleasure to him. They had a carefree Russian quality, like Hartmann himself, with his childlike passion for telling jokes until all hours of the night, and his light-hearted aristocrat's way of getting into debt. One evening, in the midst of their roamings as tie-clasp salesmen, Cahan stopped in the street to listen to a sentimental Italian melody being played by an organ grinder. Cahan's old passion for cantorial music had long since found its natural extension in a love for Italian opera; shortly after his arrival in the United States he had fulfilled a lifelong ambition by going to hear Adelina Patti sing at the Academy of Music. Now, something about the organ grinder's music filled him with an ineffable joy.

"What kind of a salesman are you," Hartmann chided him merrily, "stopping to listen to music during business?"

"Like inventor, like salesman," Cahan replied, laughing.

By this time the *Propaganda Verein* had dissolved, and Cahan took part in the creation, toward the end of 1884, of a successor which sought to proclaim its independence from German tutelage with a stridently Russian title: *Ruskii Rabochii Soyuz* ("Russian Workers' Union"). There were two other founders of the organization along with Cahan: Nikolay Aleinikoff, Cahan's supervisor at the YMHA, and Bernard Weinstein, Cahan's old co-worker at the cigar factory, now eighteen years old and an active participant in Lower East Side socialist affairs. This was an odd combination in some ways. Aleinikoff was more than ten years older than Weinstein, and there was something of a generation gap between them. The holder of a Russian university degree, Aleinikoff was an immigrant of the most soulful and aristocratic type and not temperamentally suited to mingle with ordinary Jewish workingmen. Like Miravich, he preferred dwelling upon general questions of principle to becoming involved in the practical problems of the immigrant masses. Young Weinstein, on the other hand, though intellectually inclined, was himself a workingman, and had more Jewish than Russian culture in his background. The Russian revolutionary nostalgia imparted to him by men like Aleinikoff was the yeast that raised up his spirit to a life of activism, but it was his experience as a worker in the factories that gave him a sense of the practical direction in which he was to go as a socialist.

The difference between his own and Cahan's experience at Stachelberg's cigar factory is significant in this respect. As it happened, in 1882 Stachelberg's was the place of work of a cigar maker in his early thirties who not only was the head of the union there, but was on his way to becoming the leading figure in the American labor movement: Samuel Gompers. In his several weeks working there, Cahan never met Gompers, nor did he even know of the union leader's existence. The impressionable Weinstein, on the other hand, had often noticed how—on another floor from that upon which he and Cahan worked—groups of workers used to congregate around an impressive-looking young man whom they kept calling "president." Weinstein talked to him one day—he spoke Yiddish and Gompers replied in German—telling him about the socialist and labor activities of the Jewish immigrants. Gompers listened patiently, offered advice, and gave the boy his card; he was about to leave the shop for good and devote all his time to union affairs. Weinstein never called on Gompers, but this brief meeting had made a profound impression on him. He did not come to share any of Gompers' contempt for high-minded socialist intellectuals—rather, he continued to have a somewhat exalted opinion of them—but he was beginning to recognize how limited their preoccupations were.

Cahan stood in an ambiguous position between his two collaborators. Aleinikoff, of course, represented the world with which he most wanted to identify—but this world was, in fact, not wholeheartedly inclined to embrace a mere graduate of the Vilna Teachers' Institute. Unlike Aleinikoff, he had been poor, and had been a work- man for a time himself. Indeed, partly as a result of this, he had a popular touch with the masses, as was shown in his lectures, and this gave him a certain distinction among the masses greater than that of such Lower East Side aristocrats as Aleinikoff and Miravich. He was thus inclined in both directions, that of the aristocrats and that of the masses, and had a unique position among both that he was beginning to appreciate. There was a natural, populist's *mystique* that he sensed passing between himself and any group of workers before whom he stood up to speak, based upon a background of autodidacticism that he shared with them in common and that Aleinikoff did not have, and upon something of the paternalist instinct of the rabbi standing before his flock that he once had been destined to be. It was a tribute to this natural communion that took place between himself and the Jewish workers when, in the fall of 1884, a group of tailors asked him to help them form a union. He did so, though he disdained any fur- ther involvement in the union's affairs. Yet he had come to perceive once again that he had a certain advantage over men like Aleinikoff and Miravich in making claims to a life of socialist fulfillment.

The *Ruskii Rabochii Soyuz,* with its uneasy alliance between Weinstein and Aleinikoff, fell apart in a few months. Aleinikoff removed himself from further activities of this nature, and turned to the study of law. Meanwhile, Cahan had found a collaborator for another such enterprise who was somewhat more like himself. Louis Miller—whose family name had been Bandes, but who had adopted this pseudonym while escaping the Tsarist police and had kept it— was the younger brother of one of Cahan's old comrades in the Vilna *kruzhok.* Like Cahan, Miller had received a rabbinical education in his youth and had then repudiated it to make his own way into Russian culture and the revolutionary movement. Together they cre- ated a new socialist discussion society which they called, in English this time, the Jewish Labor Lyceum. Although its first lecture was delivered in German by Alexander Jonas, the editor-in-chief of the New York *Volks Zeitung,* it was, like its immediate predecessor, freer of German tutelage than the *Propaganda Verein* had been. Most of its lectures were delivered in Russian, but Yiddish lectures were also given, by Cahan, Miller and another immigrant intellectual named Michael Zametkin.

The Yiddish-speaking colony of the Lower East Side was now growing with extreme rapidity, and so it was natural for Cahan and his friends to begin thinking of a discussion group that conducted its sessions exclusively in Yiddish. Edward King, the Scottish-born positivist, who was a frequent visitor to Cahan's attic apartment, was fascinated by the genuine working-class culture that Yiddish seemed to represent, and he urged Cahan to organize such a group. With his help, Cahan and Weinstein got together with another immigrant from Vilna named Chaim Rayevsky in February, 1885, and founded an organization which they called the *Russisher-Yiddisher Arbeiter Verein* ("Russian-Jewish Workers' Union"). This was the first such group to be purely Yiddish-speaking. It took something of the burden of Yiddish from Cahan's and Miller's Labor Lyceum, allowing that to remain more purely Russian.

It was in the same month as that in which the "Russian-Jewish Workers' Union" was founded that Cahan's bachelorhood came to an end. His bride was a plain but pleasant-looking and highly intellectual girl from Kiev named Anna Bronstein; she was the girl with the pince-nez who had stood on the table to hear him deliver his second Yiddish lecture that night on Suffolk Street almost three years before. Since then, their paths had often crossed at the gatherings of the Kiev *Am Olam* group, of which she was a member. Anna was a gymnasium graduate, who was as passionately attached to French literature as she was to Russian. In general, she had something more of the aesthete about her than her husband had, his interest in the arts tending to range from melodies of a type which she found unduly sentimental to books which she considered to be endowed with far more moral solemnity than artistic value. Even in her involvement in socialism there was perhaps a touch of dilettantism which was ultimately bound to be irksome to her young husband's puritanical spirit. But these potential sources of tension between them were obscured for the time being beneath the euphoria of love's first days and of still undiminishing common visions of revolution and youthful gallantry in Russia.

Nostalgia was still the chief energy for the political views of the Cahans and their friends. Unlike the Social Democrats of the New York *Volks Zeitung,* the Russian immigrant intellectuals eschewed systematic theorizing about revolution. As ever, the Germans were inclined to be professorial, the Russians to be dashing and sentimental. Whereas the Germans had been steeped in Marxist thought for a generation and were already passing into the more tranquil mood that anticipated the coming of Bernsteinian Revisionism, the Russians were still Bakuninists, who tended to translate the glimmers of Marxism that were now beginning to reach them into cavalier notions of their own. Hair-splitting ideological distinctions had no appeal for them. The difference between anarchism and Marxism—between Social Revolutionaries and Social Democrats, to use the terms that the Germans applied—seemed merely academic to the Russian immigrants. Why couldn't one be both? Any belaboring of the point seemed to be a sullying of the purity—indeed, the innocence—of the vision for which Zhelyabov, Perovskaya, and their associates had given their lives. Cahan described himself as both an anarchist and a socialist; intellectually, he felt uneasy about the contradiction he sensed in this, but for the time being he wanted to follow only his heart.

In the meantime, the large and scattered community of German radicals in America was becoming rent by this distinction. In the course of the preceding half-century, American political radicalism—and whatever there had come to be of a socialist movement in America—had fallen virtually entirely under the domination of

German immigrants. The failure of the 1848 revolution had brought a number of German radicals of real distinction to America, including Wilhelm Weitling, the self-educated tailor whose communist ideals had formed the effective beginning point of the German socialist tradition. By the time of his death in New York in 1871, Weitling had succeeded in organizing a group of German-American labor societies into an *Allgemeine Arbeiterbund* ("General Workingmen's League"), which was to be the kernel of a socialist party. The prospects for socialism on American soil seemed so good at that time that, in the following year, the International Workingmen's Association (later known as the "First International") decided, on Karl Marx's authority, to transfer its headquarters from the European hotbeds of dissent in the organization to distant and peaceful New York. In the next four years the International completed its march toward extinction, but not through any fault of the American branch of the movement. By 1877, twenty-four socialist daily and weekly newspapers were being published in the United States, four of them in the German language. In this same year thirty-eight labor delegates, most of them German immigrants, gathered in convention at Newark, New Jersey, and created the Socialist Labor Party of America, after the model of the Social Democratic Party of Germany, which had been founded two years before.

But the split in the International that had been brought about by the anarchists under the leadership of Michael Bakunin had reached the United States, and an anarchist faction soon arose in the Socialist Labor Party. While the SLP leadership leaned further and further in the direction of an American-style gradualism, the anarchist faction argued with increasing vehemence the continuing validity of violent tactics. Finally the anarchists broke away from the SLP altogether in 1881, and formed their own Revolutionary Socialist Labor Party. Despite their dissenting view about tactics, they still considered their program to be essentially a Marxist one—at least until the end of the following year, when the nature of their endeavor was completely transformed by the arrival in New York of Germany's preeminent exponent of anarchist terrorism, Johann Most.

Born in Augsburg, Bavaria, in 1846, of parents who were not yet legally married, Johann Most seemed destined from the outset to live his life outside the conventions of the petit-bourgeois society into which he had been born. From his earliest childhood, the world seemed to him a vast conspiracy of cruelty. His father, who had had an adventurous youth, had become reduced to earning his living as a copyist in a lawyer's office; his mother, whom he adored, died while he was still a small child. His father soon remarried, but the relationship between the boy and his stepmother became one of constant and bitter conflict. When he was twelve years old, an illness of five years' standing culminated in a facial infection which required surgery; when the operation was over, his face was left permanently deformed by a large swelling on the left side. He had dreamed of becoming an actor, and for the rest of his life Most believed that he would have done so but for this misfortune.

His career as an agitator began shortly after this, when he organized a strike against a despotic teacher in the trade school he was attending; he was promptly expelled. He was then apprenticed to a bookbinder, and at the age of seventeen became a journeyman in his trade, wandering through Germany, Austria, Hungary, and Switzerland. In Switzerland he became a member of the Zurich section of the First International, and went to work as a professional socialist agitator. Spending the next few years in and out of prison, he developed into a professional journalist and became editor of a Bavarian socialist newspaper in 1873; the following year he was elected to the Reichstag as a socialist deputy, but he then went on to serve two more prison terms. It was while he was serving the second sentence that the Anti-Socialist Law of 1878 was passed, requiring that all socialists, whether free or in prison, be expelled from the country.

Most settled in London, and there his anarchist temperament began to assert itself. He became closely associated with the colony of

Russian terrorist exiles there, and this led to a conflict with the exiled leadership of the German Social Democratic Party, from which he was expelled in 1880. Shortly thereafter he established an anarchist newspaper of his own, *Die Freiheit* ("Freedom"). When news reached Most of the assassination of Alexander II, he published an issue of his paper bearing a red border and the headline: "Hail to the Slayers of the Tyrant." An accompanying article advocated the further use of political assassinations in countries throughout the world. For this he was arrested and sentenced to eighteen months in prison.

Upon his release in October, 1882, Most received an invitation from the New York Social Revolutionary Club to do a lecture tour of the United States. He not only accepted the invitation, but decided to settle permanently in the United States, and he arranged to have the *Freiheit* transferred to New York. Among Lower East Side radicals, there was some consternation about Most's forthcoming arrival into their midst; nevertheless, his cause was championed not only by anarchists but by some moderates, who argued that America should stand as a refuge for all political exiles, no matter what their persuasion. Preeminent among these latter was the good-hearted Edward King, whom the anarchists gratefully—and shrewdly—asked to be the chairman of Most's reception committee. King accepted, and presided over the ceremony held in the Great Hall of Cooper Union in honor of Most when he arrived on December 18. Cahan attended the event, standing in back of the packed hall next to William Frey's wife, who turned to him at one point and exclaimed, "King should be ashamed of himself!"

After a socialist lecture tour to Chicago, St. Louis, and other cities, Most returned to New York and resumed publication of the *Freiheit* in an office in anarchist headquarters on East 6th Street. He was soon a storm center of radical politics in America. He published articles on the use of dynamite and portions of the *Revolutionary Catechism* of Bakunin and Nechayev. He also wrote a pamphlet called *Science of Revolutionary Warfare,* "a manual of instruction in the use and preparation of nitroglycerine, dynamite, gun-cotton, fulminating mercury, bombs, fuses, poisons, etc." As labor tension in America increased, Most seemed to many observers—above all, to the police—to be the spark that could ignite the fuse of revolutionary upheaval at any moment.

CHAPTER 4

# ANARCHISTS, SOCIALISTS,
# AND LABOR UNIONS

⌒

Wer schafft das Gold zu Tage?
Wer hämmert Erz und Stein?
Wer webet Tuch und Seide?
Wer bauet Korn und Wein?
Wer gibt den Reichen all' ihr Brot—
Und lebt dabei in bitt'rer Not?
Das sind die Arbeitsmänner, das Proletariat.
—SONG COMPOSED IN PRISON BY JOHANN MOST

I saw how professions of radicalism and sensationalism concentrated all the forces of organized society against a labor movement
and nullified in advance normal, necessary activity. . . . I saw the
danger of entangling alliances with intellectuals who did not understand that to experiment with the labor movement was to experiment with human life.
—SAMUEL GOMPERS, *Seventy Years of Life and Labor*

IN THE DECADE PRIOR TO 1886, THE GROWING LABOR UNREST IN
America had come to focus increasingly upon the movement to
achieve an eight-hour working day. This remained a distant dream,
however, and May 1, 1886, which had been chosen as the target
date for its realization, became a day for angry mass demonstrations
instead. One took place in New York, and ended with the arrest of
Johann Most and many others; another took place in Chicago and

culminated similarly in mass arrests. In Chicago, a public meeting to protest police tactics was called three days later by the editors of a German-language anarchist newspaper published there, called the *Arbeiter Zeitung.* The meeting was held in Haymarket Square, an open place at the center of a warehouse district, which had become established as a site for radical assemblages. Only some twelve or thirteen hundred people showed up, and the Mayor of Chicago, who stopped by to check on the proceedings, concluded that this gathering was a relatively mild affair. A sudden rainfall arrived as the last speaker stood on the platform, and he hurried to make his closing remarks. At that moment a column of one hundred and eighty policemen entered the square.

The captain in charge walked up to the platform and demanded that the meeting disperse. Eager to avoid violence on this occasion, the speakers began to descend. Suddenly a fuse bomb flew through the air from somewhere and exploded on the ground near the column of policemen. One of them fell dead. Recovering themselves, the police opened fire on the crowd. Many of the workers were armed, and they fired back. When the riot had ended, six more policemen and four other persons were dead; about fifty persons were wounded. The shock of this event was soon felt throughout America.

In the next few days, the Chicago police arrested not only the leaders of the May 4 meeting, but virtually all the remaining staff of the *Arbeiter Zeitung.* Of the ten men thus rounded up, one of them, Rudolph Schnaubel, escaped and fled the country, and another gained immunity by turning state's evidence; the remaining eight were placed on trial for complicity in the murder of the patrolman who had been killed by the bomb. The trial was grossly unfair. Most of the jurors had admitted when being examined that they hated all anarchists; many of them had professed from the outset a desire to see the accused men hanged. The popular press in Chicago and elsewhere shrilly doled out the death sentence in advance. Nothing more than guilt by association was established. Indeed, the one man whom the prosecution claimed was the actual bomb-thrower was Rudolph Schnaubel, who had fled the country. The trial was more a public vendetta against anarchism than a legal proceeding. All eight defendants were found guilty, and seven of them were sentenced to be hanged.

The months that followed, during which the case was appealed to higher courts, was a time of growing rage among radicals throughout America. Anarchists and Social Democrats forgot their quarrels with one another for the time being in a common show of solidarity with the eight victims of injustice in Chicago. Angry public meetings were held throughout the country, sometimes ending in violent scuffles with the police. In New York, even the usually peaceable Sergey Schewitsch shouted to a crowd as it was being dispersed by the police: "Next time come armed, comrades!"

But, despite these moments of emotional heat, Schewitsch, Jonas, and the rest of the New York *Volks Zeitung* circle had not abandoned their overall reformist approach to socialism in America. Indeed, that very fall, they led the way in the most decisive bid socialism had ever made to achieve power within the constitutional structure of the United States. In the New York mayoralty election of that year, Henry George ran as a candidate on a ticket sponsored both by his own Single Taxers and by a largely German socialist and labor coalition, led by the Central Labor Union of New York and the *Volks Zeitung*. George, who sought the abolition of landed property, was no critic of capitalism in general and hence not really a socialist. Rather, he was one of a line of Jeffersonian radicals whose moral vigor, utter Americanness, and opposition to the rich made them recurringly, throughout the history of America, the focus of a wide range of radical aspirations. The moral force of his presence had the effect of cleansing the atmosphere of New York politics in general that year. Both major parties responded to it by nominating men of far better character than was customary at the time. The Republicans offered as their candidate Theodore Roosevelt, then only twenty-seven years old and a fledgling New York state assemblyman who was already well respected for his independence of judgment and lofty moral approach to political questions. The Tammany-dominated Democrats also did somewhat better than usual, nominating Abram S. Hewitt, an honorable man even if a mediocre one.

Hewitt won the election, but Henry George ran second, winning 68,000 votes to Hewitt's 90,000; Roosevelt came in third, with just a little over 60,000 votes. George's supporters claimed, with some justification, that the Tammany machine had fixed the election results. The air was filled with a feeling that a moral victory had been won by democratic socialism.

Unfortunately, the Henry George coalition between socialists and Single Taxers broke up soon after the election. Later that year a debate was held in Miner's Theater, on Eighth Avenue near Twenty-third Street, between Schewitsch and Henry George, in which the sophisticated Russo-German Social Democrat succeeded in making the Single Taxer's naive social philosophy look ridiculous. Socialism was again without an immediate prospect of entry into the American political establishment, and for a moment the violent mood of the previous spring was revived. This was fanned by the winds that now blew from the wretched denouement of the Haymarket Affair. The judgment of the Chicago court had been reaffirmed, on appeal, by the Illinois Supreme Court; an appeal then made to the United States Supreme Court had been dismissed on grounds that the court had no jurisdiction in the matter. Two of the seven condemned men appealed to the governor of Illinois for clemency, and their sentences were reduced to life imprisonment. A third killed himself in his cell. The remaining four went to the gallows on November 11, 1887. Their conduct in their last moments was heroic. August Spies, the thirty-two-year-old editor of the *Arbeiter Zeitung,* cried out from beneath the hangman's hood: "There will come a time when our silence will be more powerful than the voices you strangle today!" The last to go to the gallows was Albert Parsons, the one American-born member of the group, who shouted, as the trap was sprung, "Let the voice of the people be heard!"

For the Russian radicals in particular, the parallels between the fate of the Chicago anarchists and that of the leaders of *Narodnaya Volya* were dramatically clear. "For us," Cahan said, "the thirteenth of March was the sacred anniversary of the martyrs of the Russian revolution, and the eleventh of November was that of the martyrs of the American labor movement." For some, the fact that the Chicago verdict was more unjust than the St. Petersburg one was a confirmation of their unflagging revolutionary convictions. Twenty-two-year-old Emma Goldman, a Jewish immigrant from Russia, was persuaded by it that the American social and political order was no better than that of Tsarist Russia. For her, this meant that the constitutionalist approach of the New York Social Democrats was a sham. She went on to become Johann Most's most ardent disciple.

Others, however, while moved by the heroism and tragic fate of the Chicago martyrs, were also struck by the example they offered of the futility of the anarchist position. Even in Russia, where liberal democracy did not exist, terrorism had failed; the American political system at least seemed to provide an alternative way toward the realization of a more just social order. The Henry George campaign in particular had given grounds for reflections of this sort on the part of New York radicals. For Cahan, that campaign had made the American political system seem relevant to his ideals for the first time. Until then, he had witnessed only what seemed to be a corrupt and bombastic political circus, the tone of which had been set by Tammany Hall. In 1884, during the Cleveland campaign for the presidency, he had been appalled to see voters being bribed outside the polls. "For Russian socialists, the ballot was a sacred ideal," he wrote, yet here in America, "the naive immigrant was being taught to sell it for a few dollars." Yet even at that time, he had been struck by the fact that a candidate of more or less socialistic tendencies, Benjamin F. Butler, had been able to run for the presidency on the Greenback and

Labor Party ticket. Now, in 1887, Cahan was beginning to believe that the editors of the New York *Volks Zeitung* were right in expecting a socialist party to find its way soon into the American system. This was beginning to happen in the liberal democracies of Western Europe; why not, then, in America too?

Cahan thus found himself, immediately after the execution of the Chicago anarchists, torn between his heart and his mind. His heart still yearned after the vision of manhood represented by the bold convictions and the heroism of a Zhelyabov or an August Spies. For a while, he had been caught up in the general atmosphere of rage that accompanied the executions of the Chicago anarchists, but now that they were over, the political atmosphere was suddenly calm again and Cahan found his spirit plunged into a turmoil. For the first time, he felt driven to seek a conclusion to the moral conflict within him. He carefully reread Marx's *Capital,* and also studied Engels' *Socialism: Utopian and Scientific* and Plekhanov's *Our Differences.* A former *Narodnik,* Georgy Plekhanov was now struggling to make Marxism the ruling ideology of the Russian revolutionary movement. His arguments, as well as those of Engels, stressed the founding of socialism upon the real social and economic forces operating in the world, and not upon the mere Utopian convictions of a small elite. Cahan was convinced now that the anarchists were just such a Utopian elite. One day he went to see M. Bachmann, one of the prominent German anarchists of New York, and plied him with questions. The anarchists opposed all systems of elections as manifestations of the tyranny of the majority over the minority; but how, then, Cahan asked him, were any decisions to be made, how was any order to be established? Cahan gave an example of the problem: a group of men are sitting in a room; some of them, finding the room unbearably stuffy, demand that the windows be opened, while others, fearing the cold, demand with equal vehemence that the windows remain shut. How, Cahan asked, is a decision to be arrived at? Bachmann replied that this, or any other such problem, could be solved by "the intrinsic goodness of human nature." The shortcomings of anarchism were thus demonstrated to Cahan's satisfaction; a few days later, he went to see Alexander Jonas at the editorial offices of the *Volks Zeitung* and, after a long conversation, reached his decision. By the end of December, he had become a member of the Socialist Labor Party. "When I got my membership card," he wrote, "I felt as if a stone had been lifted from my heart."

Cahan's conversion to social democracy took place during a general turning point in the ideological development of the Lower East Side Jewish radicals. For many of them, the old euphoria of revolutionary nostalgia was coming to an end under the impact of present realities. The unceasing flow of Jewish immigrants was at last bringing a clearly definable Jewish proletariat into being. The social and economic lines were less fluid than they had been a few years before. There was virtually not a square inch of space left on Hester Street for fledgling peddlers, and the typical Jewish immigrant now was more likely than he once had been to remain a worker for some time, condemned to long hours in crowded and filthy sweatshops. The task of organizing the Jewish workers was both more necessary and more possible than ever.

This task was now about to be assumed mainly by a group of younger immigrants—among them Cahan's old colleague, Bernard Weinstein—who were more prone than such members of the elder Lower East Side elite as Aleinikoff and Miravich to pursue the pragmatic meanings of radicalism in America all the way into the prosaic chores of labor-union organization. Although Cahan was soon to discover that he had many affinities with these younger men, they came by their moderate social democratic convictions with far greater ease than he had done. This was an advantage of their greater youth, for the nostalgias of 1881 were less vivid and restraining for them than for Cahan or for the still older Aleinikoff, and they had furthermore come of age politically at a moment when the differences between anarchism and social democracy had become more clearly defined than ever before. For example, by the middle of the decade of the eighties, the anarchists had at last openly declared their opposition to labor unions as "palliatives," mere concessions to the capitalist system. They were not to maintain this rigid stance for very long, but they did so long enough to drive all the proponents of unionism among the Lower East Side intelligentsia into the social-democratic camp. The all-out battle between anarchists and social democrats, focused mainly upon the issue of unionism, that was now being joined was to dominate the political life of the Lower East Side Jewish immigrants for the remainder of the decade.

The course of this new history can be traced back to an evening in April, 1885, two months after Cahan, Weinstein, and Rayevsky had founded the *Russisher-Yiddisher Arbeiter Verein.* Two young brothers, Mitya and Nyuma Gretch, had recently arrived in New York from their native Odessa, and had become ardent disciples of the *Volks Zeitung.* Nyuma in particular, who was soon to be a worker in the Socialist Labor Party organization, was persuaded that the Jewish worker had to be taken in hand ideologically and led away from the perils of anarchism. He had decided that what was needed was a Yiddish-language equivalent to the *Volks Zeitung.* There was still no Yiddish labor press in New York, and the only Yiddish paper that did exist, *Die Yiddishe Gazetten,* was conservative in its politics and orthodox in its religious views—in other words, it had no relevance to political matters that were now becoming crucial on the Lower East Side. The *Volks Zeitung* gave Gretch the use of its pages to advertise the April night meeting of Jewish workers at which he hoped a Yiddish social democratic newspaper could be brought into being.

The meeting brought together an unprecedented assortment of groups. Members of the *Russisher-Yiddisher Arbeiter Verein* were present, although Cahan himself was not, since he still thought of himself at this time as more an anarchist than a social democrat. Also present was a substantial number of Hungarian-Jewish and Galician-Jewish tailors from further uptown, ardent readers of the *Volks*

*Zeitung,* their German being far better than that of most Jewish immigrants from Russia, Poland, or Lithuania. They had also been in America a longer time and were, on the whole, better educated. The very fact that they were now, for the first time, coming together with the newer Jewish immigrants was a prospect for more stable labor organization than ever before.

As it turned out, the Gretch brothers could not raise enough support to create a Yiddish newspaper, but the meeting did produce an organization, the first of its kind to include a representation from *all* the East European Jewish groups of New York. It was called the *Yiddisher Arbeiter Verein,* and the freedom from Russianness suggested by its very title was indicative of the new turn it was to take. Repudiating elite revolutionary attitudes from the outset, it immediately went to work at a task unprecedented for this type of group: organizing Jewish labor unions. This it did with notable success. Even Cahan, though still claiming to be an anarchist, became caught up enough in the momentum of its success to help in the founding of a union under its auspices. Cahan also contributed his services as a lecturer; Nyuma Gretch was delighted to have him, although, wary of his anarchism, he insisted upon going over the text of every one of Cahan's talks in advance.

Yet, despite Gretch's watchful eye, anarchism gradually infiltrated his organization. The *Yiddisher Arbeiter Verein* campaigned for Henry George in the fall of 1886, but immediately after the election an anarchist faction in its midst came to the surface. The dissension grew worse in the months preceding the execution of the Chicago anarchists, and ensued in an open split in July, 1887. The leadership of the *Yiddisher Arbeiter Verein* was still social democratic, but the anarchists were by now the larger faction, and they withdrew and formed an organization of their own, which they called the Pioneers of Liberty. Johann Most was the chief moral inspiration for this new group. "I was not an anarchist, but a Mostoist," one participant later wrote, to describe his feelings of the time. The Friday night meetings of the Pioneers of Liberty on Orchard Street soon came to be filled regularly with capacity crowds.

The remaining social-democratic faction of the *Yiddisher Arbeiter Verein* decided to reconstitute themselves as an official component of the Socialist Labor Party. At this time the policy of the SLP was to organize itself in distinct ethnic units. This was considered desirable because of the still overwhelmingly foreign, and primarily German, composition of the party. By this method of segregation, groups of "Americans" in the party could organize into separate branches of their own, and thereby help foster the Americanization that was eagerly sought after for the SLP. Consequently, such non-German and non-American groups as the Bohemian cigar makers and the "Russian" (in fact, mostly Jewish) garment workers of New York already had their own party branches. But until the fall of 1887, no separate status as Jews had been accorded to the large Jewish element in the party; in this respect, the SLP was still following the pattern that had been established by the older Jewish immigrant elite when they defined themselves as Russians. The *Yiddisher Arbeiter Verein* had changed all that, however; a touch of Jewish nationalism was now in the air. The surviving, social-democratic rump of Gretch's organization became the first expressly Jewish branch of the SLP. "Branch 8" thus came into being on the Lower East Side as a rival to the anarchist Jewish organization, the Pioneers of Liberty. It, too, held regular Friday night meetings; both groups conducted their affairs in Yiddish as much as possible, although good speakers in that language were still hard to find.

It was out of Branch 8 that there came the initiative which finally brought into being a strong and permanent Jewish trade-union movement. The model, as was so often the case, came from the Germans. In 1885, the *Volks Zeitung* and a group of representatives of German labor had created an organization intended to spread the influence of socialism among the German-speaking workers of New York, which they called the *Vereinigte Deutsche Gewerkschaften* ("United

German Trades"). After campaigning for Henry George in the fall of 1886, the United German Trades took on larger ambitions, seeking to become the nucleus of a national confederation of labor unions, a German-speaking version of the American Federation of Labor, which had been founded earlier in the same year. Inspired by the example of the United German Trades, a nineteen-year-old shirt-maker and aspiring journalist named Jacob Magidoff proposed at a meeting of Branch 8 in the fall of 1888 that a similar organization of Yiddish-speaking workers be formed. This idea was heartily endorsed by the German social democrats, who offered the facilities of the United German Trades for such a project. A three-man committee, made up of Magidoff, Bernard Weinstein, and a young man named Lederer, was assigned by the members of Branch 8 to examine the prospects for forming such an organization. Then Branch 17, the "Russian" branch of the SLP in New York, offered to the project a three-man committee of its own; the time had come to recognize that Russian simply was not the language or the form of identification of the Jewish immigrant masses. One of the three men sent by Branch 17 was Leo Bandes, Cahan's old comrade from the Vilna *kruzhok* and the older brother of Louis Miller, Cahan's partner in the Labor Lyceum. Twenty-eight years old, he was the oldest member of the joint six-man committee that was formed. The two others from Branch 17 were a young man named Stuchkoff, and a nineteen-year-old immigrant from Riga named Morris Hillkowitz.

Hillkowitz—who was to become well known years later under the Americanized name of Hillquit—was a representative example of those younger Jewish radical intellectuals who had come to America, "cast about for a promising field of practical work," as he later wrote, "and discovered it among their own countrymen." Like many of the older immigrant elite, he knew virtually no Yiddish when he came to New York. But, having been born and raised in the old Hanseatic city of Riga, he had spoken German from childhood. This was to prove to be a great advantage in the career he was now entering upon, as an organizer of Jewish labor in New York. "We all began perfecting our Yiddish," he wrote of this period. "Those of us who knew German had a somewhat easier task than those who spoke only Russian and had to labor at it word by word and idiom by idiom."

At its first meeting, the six-man committee appointed Hillkowitz and Bernard Weinstein to investigate the state of organized Jewish labor in New York. They carried out their assignment on foot, going from typesetters' basements, to bakeries, to garment lofts. "There had been, we knew," Hillquit wrote, "unions of shirtmakers, cloak operators and bakery workers at one time or another. We thought them dormant. We found them dead." They were able to discover only two unions still in existence—the typesetters, members of a trade in which craft consciousness always was strong, and the choristers, employees of the two Yiddish theater companies that then existed on the Bowery, among whom resentment at the cavalier treatment doled out to them by the "stars" was ever an incentive to solidarity. It was clear that any Jewish equivalent to the United German Trades would have to begin by *creating* the very unions that were to make up the federation it comprised.

The six-man committee decided to go ahead despite the difficulties it was faced with, and on the evening of October 9, it drew up the charter of an organization called the *Vereinigte Yiddishe Gewerkschaften;* the name was translated into English, in accordance with a euphemistic usage then fashionable, as the "United Hebrew Trades." Weinstein was designated the recording secretary of the new organization, and Hillkowitz its corresponding secretary—both posts being considerably more precise in name than in function. The first contribution to its treasury—the sum of ten dollars—was made by the United German Trades, which had contributed the meeting room for this occasion. Thus chartered and capitalized, the United Hebrew Trades went to work.

Like its predecessor, the *Yiddisher Arbeiter Verein,* the new organization sent its representatives right out onto the streets and into the shops to create unions. In some cases, these "walking dele-gates" were able to carry out their assignment fairly easily. Hillkowitz, for example, who had worked for a time as a shirtmaker, was quickly able to persuade his former colleagues to organize a shirtmakers' union. In other cases, it was not so easy to break through established habits and prejudices. In the case of the Jewish bakery workers of the Lower East Side, for example, the United Hebrew Trades found itself running into hostility from an unexpected quarter—that of saloon keepers. The Jewish bakers' union, now defunct, that had existed a few years earlier had followed the fashion of the German unions of the time by establishing its headquarters in a saloon. Indeed, the saloon was a very important element in German politi-cal life in New York, but this was one respect in which the Jews, notoriously diffident toward alcoholic beverages, did not, for the most part, follow the German lead. The bakers, however, were an exception to this, and even after their union collapsed they continued to be devoted beer-drinkers. By the end of 1888, when the United Hebrew Trades approached them, their after-hours loyalties were about evenly divided between two German saloons, one on Orchard Street and the other on Ludlow, which competed for their patronage. The appearance of the United Hebrew Trades was therefore considered by the two saloon keepers to be a threat to one or the other of them, or both; if a Jewish bakers' union was orga-nized again, it would either confine itself to one saloon, or would depart from the saloons altogether. Consequently, the UHT dele-gates were met with considerable hostility by the management in both places. In the end, the saloon keepers' worst fears were real-ized, for the bakers' union headquarters was set up in a tenement meeting hall.

The United Hebrew Trades grew rapidly, and developed a highly efficient technique of organization. This was made dramatically evi-dent in a strike that broke out in January, 1890, among the knee-pants makers. The knee-pants trade was at this time, as Hillkowitz put it, the "sweatshop industry *par excellence*," employing about a thousand workers scattered through tiny tenement rooms all over the Lower East Side. The wages were fairly decent for the time—about six or seven dollars a week, on the average—but working conditions were quite bad, and abuses at the hands of the contractors were rife. The workers had to bring their own sewing machines, and, since they could not be certain that work would be available from one day to the next, they usually had to carry their machines on their backs to and from the shop each day. They could be dismissed at the slightest whim of the contractor, and there were frequent cases of contractors absconding with the week's wages. Since most of the workers were "green," illiterate, and eager to get their start in America, they usually accepted these conditions as part of the necessities of life. Few of them knew anything about labor unions. A few of the more intellectually alert knee-pants workers were in contact with the United Hebrew Trades, but the strike that broke out in January was spontaneous, and took everyone by surprise.

When news of the strike reached UHT headquarters, representatives were promptly dispatched to seek out its leadership. Under their guidance a strike committee was quickly formed, a meeting hall was hired and established as strike headquarters, and a vigorous schedule of mass meetings was set up. In effect, the UHT gave the striking workers an on-the-spot, practical course in union organization and tactics; the meetings also served the purpose of establishing an unwonted physical contiguity among the workers, which would provide them with the rudiments of a sense of solidarity. In this way, enthusiasm for the strike was sustained over a length of time unprecedented in a sweatshop industry. After a week of unbroken work stoppage, a mob of contractors stormed the meeting hall one day and demanded a settlement. The strikers had won. An agreement was made to the effect that, henceforth, the employers would provide sewing machines and other equipment, and would see to various specified improvements in working conditions. But the most important result of all, in the eyes of the UHT, was the creation of a permanent Knee-Pants Makers' Union.

In general, the year 1890 was to prove to be a major turning-point in the history of the fledgling Jewish labor movement of New York. Even before the knee-pants makers' strike was over, a similar spontaneous work stoppage, which was to develop into a lengthy and crucial showdown between workers and employers, occurred in the cloakmakers' shops. The manufacture of ladies' cloaks, which had been exclusively a European and a luxury industry a few decades before, had been brought to America by German-Jewish immigrants, who turned the cloak into the first mass-produced women's garment; it was the opening wedge of what was to become, in a few years, a huge mass industry in women's garments which would revolutionize feminine dressing habits and be a central element in the economic life of the Lower East Side. At the beginning of 1890, the cloak-making industry was already the largest single employer of Jewish immigrant labor in America, but it was not yet unionized. When the strike broke out, the United Hebrew Trades, eager to gain this prize, sent a three-man committee headed by Bernard Weinstein to the *ad hoc* headquarters that the strike leaders had established at 92 Hester Street. The cloakmakers asked that the committee appoint a man to stay with them and lead their strike. Weinstein and one of the other committee members, M. Schach, were both occupied with other duties, and so they assigned to this task the third one among them, a twenty-four-year-old former knee-pants maker named Joseph Barondess.

This casual appointment was to have large repercussions, for Barondess, a magnetic and flamboyant personality, was to rise almost overnight to become the adored and powerful leader of the cloak-makers. In eight weeks of tireless effort, Barondess not only won the improvements in wages and working conditions that the strikers had sought in the first place, but brought into being a cloakmakers' union that had a membership of nearly three thousand—by far the largest organization of Jewish workers to date. Furthermore, a moral victory was achieved, in that the union won recognition and agreement to its terms not only from the contractors, as the knee-pants makers had done, but from the large manufacturers as well. Meyer Jonassen himself, the leading clothing manufacturer in New York, a wealthy "uptown" German Jew, had come to 92 Hester Street to put his signature onto the contract. From that moment on, Barondess was a kind of god in the eyes of the cloakmakers. A plush office was established for him with the union's meager funds, and Barondess soon gave abundant examples of the kingly behavior that was expected of him. A highly temperamental man, he would sometimes slap union members in the face; one of them was once heard to say: "It is an honor when such a man as Mister Barondess slaps me."

The leaders of the United Hebrew Trades began to suspect that they had created a Frankenstein monster. Many of them, in their personal contacts with Barondess, had thought him to be capricious and unreliable. Actually, he had more than a touch of the actor in him; shortly after his arrival in America in 1888, he had gone to work as a bit player in one of the Yiddish theatrical companies on the Bowery. Although his stage career had been brief and unsuccessful, he had never lost the air of the romantic, flamboyant artist that was the trademark of Yiddish actors: tall and handsome, he was capable of passing swiftly from laughter to tears, from lordly arrogance to childlike simplicity and humility. These qualities, combined with the rich Yiddish—more authentic than anything the lips of most of the UHT leaders could muster—of his native Kamenetsk-Podolsk enabled him to communicate to the hearts of the workers in a way that none of the established socialist leaders could. Indeed, he had no need of their socialist ideology to have his way in the world—this was one of the things that disturbed them. It is significant that Emma Goldman, who worked at Barondess' side during the cloakmakers' strike, thought it noteworthy about him that the mind of "this attractive lanky chap . . . was not of a scholarly type; it was of a practical turn." He had the visceral, spontaneous qualities that appealed to the anarchist spirit; he was himself something of an anarchist by nature.

This was the realization that began to dawn upon the alarmed socialists of the United Hebrew Trades in the weeks following the successful conclusion of the cloakmakers' strike. For, as the presence of Emma Goldman must have indicated to anyone who gave the matter some thought, the anarchists were losing their old contempt for labor unions, and had begun to woo the cloakmakers. There was considerable support for the anarchists among the rank-and-file union members already. The question was, which way would the unpredictable Barondess go?

CHAPTER 5

# THE YIDDISH LABOR PRESS BEGINS

Today our Biblical portion is about strikes: the cloak makers still have a little strike to finish up, the shirt makers are on strike, the pants makers are striking, even our teacher Moses called a mass meeting to talk about a strike. *Va'yak'hel Moishe,* Moses gathered the children of Israel together and said to them: *Sheyshes yommim te'asseh m'lokhoh,* more than six days a week you shouldn't work for the bosses, the seventh day you shall rest.

—*Der Proletarishker Maggid* ("THE PROLETARIAN PREACHER")

FROM ABOUT 1870 ON, VARIOUS ATTEMPTS HAD BEEN MADE TO establish Yiddish or Judeo-German newspapers in New York, but only one such paper was still in existence by the beginning of 1890. This was Kasriel Sarasohn's weekly, *Die Yiddishe Gazetten,* which had been founded in 1874, and which had become successful enough by 1885 to begin publishing a "daily" edition, called the *Tageblatt;* it appeared three or four times a week, on the average. Sarasohn aimed at an audience that was essentially pious in its Judaism and middle class in outlook if not necessarily yet in economic status. In the early days, Sarasohn used to obtain most of his copy directly from a Judeo-German newspaper in Mainz; later, as he began using his own material, the religious piety and political conservatism of his paper became more and more pronounced.

Troubled by Sarasohn's monopoly, the Jewish radicals of New York made increasing efforts from 1885 onward to found a Yiddish press of their own. It was Abraham Cahan who made the next major try after the failure of the attempt by the *Yiddisher Arbeiter Verein.* This was in the late spring of 1886, around the time of the trial of the Chicago anarchists. Spurred on by the success of his Yiddish lectures, Cahan and his partner in the *Russisher-Yiddisher Arbeiter Verein,* Chaim Rayevsky, decided to try applying a similar popular didactic style in journalism. Rayevsky, who was employed in a soap factory, offered all his savings—ten dollars—for the project. The two partners went to great lengths to cut costs to the minimum. They found a printer at the corner of Canal and Division Streets who was sufficiently sympathetic to let them have a large credit margin and a desk in the corner of his shop; this was their editorial office. The two editors worked at their enterprise in their spare time, Cahan between his lessons by day, Rayevsky after work at night. Since Cahan was the one who was free during normal business hours, it was he who went from store to store to solicit advertising. Often, instead of getting an ad, he ended up in a long argument about socialism with the storekeeper.

The first issue of their weekly, the *Neie Zeit* ("New Era"), appeared at the beginning of *Shavuos* (Pentecost). Cahan had persuaded a fellow immigrant from Lithuania, a budding linguistics scholar named Alexander Harkavy, to write an article for this issue linking the workers' lot with the theme of *Shavuos,* the giving of the Torah to Moses. Harkavy wrote a learned but popular-style article called "The Worker in Moses Our Teacher's Times." Cahan pursued this theme in his editorial, saying that socialism was the Torah of the workingmen of today. Cahan in fact believed this in a highly personal and somewhat mystical way, but the idea seemed a mere publicistic gimmick to many of his friends, who thought for the most part that his attempt to popularize socialism in print had turned into an exercise in vulgarity. "I've always known," one friend said to him only half in jest, "that Litvaks have a lot of nerve, but the nerve you've got, you and your *Neie Zeit,* is more than any Litvak has ever shown before.

Your paper will be a great success." But his prognostication, though based on sound principles, did not prove to be correct; the *Neie Zeit* had to give up after four issues.

At about the time that the third issue of the *Neie Zeit* appeared, a more ambitious rival got under way. Two immigrants who had worked in a factory in Massachusetts for several years, Moses Mintz and Abel Braslavsky, had come to New York determined to found a Yiddish workers' newspaper with the eight hundred dollars they had carefully saved. This was considerable capital, and they were able to establish their own editorial office and printing press. In emulation of their German model, they called their paper the New York *Yiddishe Volks-Zeitung*. Its ambitious format attracted advertisers far more easily than the *Neie Zeit* had been able to do. From the outset this project was looked upon with disapproval by the *Yiddisher Arbeiter Verein*, which still hoped to found a paper of its own, and which considered it a matter of principle that a socialist newspaper be published by a workers' association and not by private entrepreneurs. This attitude of disapproval was inherited in turn by the United Hebrew Trades, but despite such moral opposition the weekly *Yiddishe Volks-Zeitung* managed to last until 1889.

By that year, the Pioneers of Liberty had branches in several American cities, and was thriving so well that the anarchists decided it was time to try putting out a newspaper of their own. Enough money was collected to buy a printing press and set up an office, and an experienced editor, Joseph Jaffe, was brought from London, where a thriving Yiddish radical press had already existed for several years. *Die Wahrheit* ("The Truth"), as the new anarchist weekly was called, began publication on February 15, 1889. It was not an outstanding success, largely because Jaffe devoted a good deal of space to quarrels with his social-democratic rivals in London, to the neglect of American affairs. Considerable excitement was generated, however, by an event that the *Wahrheit* scheduled for the fall as a fund-raising enterprise: a "Yom Kippur Ball." This odd institution was to become an annual event on the Lower East Side for years to come. It was a sort of Jewish left-wing counterpart to the Black Mass, consisting of an enormous feast to be consumed while pious Jews everywhere were starting their twenty-four-hour fast for the solemn day of atonement, and of a pseudoreligious service, in which the traditional prayers for that day were revised in blasphemous ways and interspersed with revolutionary proclamations. But the *Wahrheit*'s Yom Kippur Ball ended in a riot, caused by angry observant Jews who had come to the meeting hall to break up the impious festivities. The anarchists managed to raise about five hundred dollars out of the sale of tickets all the same; but this was futile, since the *Wahrheit* had already ceased publication by then.

The Pioneers of Liberty were not through, however: they had money and they had a printing press. The *Wahrheit* experience had proven that they still did not have sufficient resources and following on their own to publish a newspaper successfully—but why do it on their own? The *Arbeiter Freind* in London, which Joseph Jaffe had edited, was published by anarchists in collaboration with social democrats; there the two groups had managed, at least until quite recently, to sink their differences and publish a "nonpartisan" labor newspaper. Looking to this model, and assuming that having the printing press would mean having the upper hand, the Pioneers of Liberty decided to invite representatives of the various Jewish social-democratic organizations in America to attend a convention at which the possibility of founding a coalition newspaper would be discussed.

The meeting took place on Christmas Day of 1889, in a small hall in one of the buildings of the Essex Street Market. The forty-seven delegates who came were from various parts of the country and represented some thirty Jewish radical and labor organizations. The foremost anarchist delegates present were the New York leader Roman Lewis, twenty-three-year-old Isadore Prenner, the Philadelphia leader, and a young Yiddish poet from Cincinnati named David Edelstadt. The social-democratic delegates also came from various parts of the country, but it was their New York leadership that predominated. Morris Hillkowitz and Bernard Weinstein were both there, as was Joseph Barondess, still a relatively unknown member of the knee-pants-makers' union. But the man who quickly came to the fore as the preeminent leader of this group was the twenty-three-year-old Louis Miller, Abraham Cahan's old partner in the Labor Lyceum of a few years before. Miller, who now made his living the way Cahan did, by teaching English in an evening school for immigrants, was known among Lower East Side radicals primarily for being the coeditor of a Russian-language socialist weekly, *Znamya* ("The Banner"). Somewhat more cosmopolitan than the United Hebrew Trades leaders in knowledge and experience, he was furthermore esteemed among them for his devastating polemical style. They had already drawn upon his services the previous summer, when they sent him to Paris as their delegate to the First Congress of the Second Socialist International.

It was Miller who was responsible for Cahan's presence at this meeting, for he had invited his good friend to attend as an observer. Since his conversion to social democracy two years before, Cahan had been giving less and less of his time to Yiddish publicistic work. He still gave occasional lectures in Yiddish, but he had not been interested in doing any Yiddish writing since the failure of the *Neie Zeit*. After his enrollment in the Socialist Labor Party, he had affiliated with New York's "American" branch, located on 8th Street near Broadway. He had become a regular contributor to the SLP's English-language weekly, the *Workmen's Advocate,* and was in general doing freelance journalism in English, contributing to such papers as the New York *Sun*. A book was now taking shape in his mind, a study of the relationship between Marxism and Darwinism, and he was deeply immersed in reading for this project. But the convening of this meeting had aroused his curiosity, and he had come, partly to see old friends, partly to find what would come of an idea he had once flirted with himself.

The room in which the meeting took place was small, and the participants and observers crowded into it, the delegates in front, the small audience in back behind a rope. The session was calm at the beginning, but it did not remain so; the young men present were fervent polemicists, and this was the first full-scale confrontation between their two factions since the dissolution of the *Yiddisher Arbeiter Verein* two years before. The social democrats were soon hotly denouncing the anarchist stress upon *gevalt-mittlen*—terrorist tactics—and the anarchists in turn decried the social democrats' enslavement to "palliatives." At one point, Isadore Prenner completely lost his temper and leaped onto a chair, shouting: "Down with all unions! Down with all palliatives that lead the workers astray!" Yet it was the anarchists, far more than the social democrats, who continued in their calmer moments to enunciate the vision of a nonpartisan Yiddish workers' newspaper—an idea which the social democrats, with growing vehemence, took to describing as *parveh lokshen:* "neutral noodles," neither milk nor meat, and hence *kosher* with anything.

The fact was that Miller and the UHT leaders had already formulated a somewhat different plan among themselves before coming to the meeting. With all that had happened in the last two years—in particular, with the growth of the UHT into a real power and no mere discussion group—the old Utopian ideal of a nonpartisan newspaper seemed out of the question to them. Even in London, where the social democrats were not nearly so powerful as they were in New York, the ideal was collapsing, the *Arbeiter Freind* breaking up in factional strife. At the socialist congress in Paris the previous summer, Miller had talked to Philip Krantz, the editor of the *Arbeiter Freind.* A social democrat, and one of the founders of the paper, Krantz now despaired of its future—it was he who had coined the term *parveh lokshen* to describe the "nonpartisan" idea. Miller and Krantz had discussed the possibility of a purely social-democratic newspaper in New York, and Krantz had expressed interest in being the editor of such a paper. Miller had still been thinking about this project when the anarchists gave out their call for the December 25 meeting. It had promptly occurred to him that this might be the occasion for sounding out the readiness of Jewish social democrats from all over the country to sponsor a paper entirely their own.

The meeting that day ended hotly but indecisively, with a decision to reconvene a few days later. In the meantime, the social democrats held a caucus. Cahan was invited to it, and he attended, his awakening interest now more than that of a mere observer. A vague notion of a nonpartisan newspaper had been one thing, but the real possibility of a social-democratic paper was something else entirely; the once-frustrated germ of a Yiddish journalist in Cahan was coming to life again at the prospect. A few of the social democrats, such as Cahan's and Miller's old associate in the Labor Lyceum, Michael Zametkin, refused to take part in the caucus, but most of them had little nostalgia left for the notion that anarchism and social democracy were merely two nuances of the same ideal. Not only was the idea of a social-democratic newspaper frankly discussed at the meeting, but a name for such a paper even was decided upon. It would be called the *Arbeiter Zeitung;* this invocation of the Chicago martyrs would be a clear social-democratic assertion of continuity in a heroic tradition that the anarchists claimed was exclusively their own.

By the time of the second meeting with the anarchists, there was little left to do but quarrel. The session ended in complete disarray, with the social democrats storming out of the meeting hall. They reconvened in a nearby apartment and confirmed their decision to start a weekly paper of their own. Miller and Hillkowitz assumed leadership in organizational planning and the collecting of funds for the new paper, which was to be run by a press association. Philip Krantz was sent for to come and be its editor.

These events had a remarkable effect upon Cahan. Until December 25 he was certain that he had become an "American" writer for once and for all—indeed, what else had there been for him to become? He occasionally submitted articles to Russian journals, but one could hardly make a career as a Russian writer living in America. As for Yiddish, its possibilities were represented mainly by such a journal as *Die Yiddishe Gazetten,* whose literary qualities were even more repellent to him than its politics. There hardly existed as yet, either in Russia or in America, any indication that Yiddish could be taken seriously as a vehicle for the kind of expository writing he wanted to do. Mendele Moicher S'forim had shown the language's virtues as a medium for evoking the folk life of East European Jews, and at that very moment, in Poland and Russia, a handful of younger Jewish writers were preparing to follow his lead in this respect. But it still seemed out of the question to write a serious essay in Yiddish comparing Darwinism and Marxism. And so, Cahan had been carefully polishing his English prose.

Yet it was hardly in his nature to be exclusively occupied with the lofty realms of social philosophy. A part of him always yearned for the satisfactions he obtained when lecturing in Yiddish to ordinary workingmen; a born *melammed,* he was quite addicted to that moment when, after a long and arduous groping for the right illuminative example, the light of understanding would suddenly come to some face in the audience that had hitherto been shadowed with perplexity. Cahan had a mind that naturally thought in concrete examples; in this respect he was the distinct product of an East European Jewish folk tradition, represented by the parable making of the Hasidic *rebbe* or by the homely style of the *maggid,* the traveling preacher whose Sabbath-afternoon sermons were usually an onrush of anecdote and apothegm. For him, finding and applying the example that was at once true, vivid, and popular yielded an intellectual satisfaction not unlike that which comes to most people when finding the solution to a mathematical problem. But the process had a touch of poetry about it for him as well, a poetry that echoed with the essence of the Yiddish language. English may have been for the side of him that was a social philosopher, but Yiddish was the natural expression of the folk teacher that was in him as well.

Cahan therefore knew, in a moment of awakening, that he wanted to have a hand in producing the *Arbeiter Zeitung;* but his feelings did not stop here. For, as he reflected upon the matter, he came to the conclusion that none of the other participants were as well qualified as he was to be the editor of the proposed paper. He alone had had several years of experience in American journalism—a popularizing field if there ever was one—and he knew he could apply some of its techniques in Yiddish. Indeed, he was, in general, the most American of the group that was forming around the paper, for neither Hillkowitz nor Miller had been in America so long as he nor become so involved in its institutions, and as for Krantz—it went without saying. Furthermore, he knew that none of the others, including Krantz, were so well grounded as he in Yiddish and its folkways, none of them had his instinct for the authentic Yiddish phrase. He was certain that neither Hillkowitz nor Miller understood the humble Jewish masses so well as he did; as for Krantz, he set out to confirm what he suspected already. Obtaining a bound volume of the *Arbeiter Freind,* he read it thoroughly and found, not at all to his surprise, that it was too dry and excessively formal to be a good Yiddish workingmen's paper. Not only was the style not popular enough, it was not even really Yiddish, Cahan felt; it was *Deitshmerish,* the sort of bastard German cultivated by those writers of Yiddish who sought to turn the language into a "higher" medium of expression. Cahan responded to this sort of diction with all his old contempt for the pretensions of those who had had a better formal education than he.

He noticed only one writer in the *Arbeiter Freind* who wrote Yiddish to his satisfaction. This was the poet Morris Winchevsky— also, incidentally, a Litvak—who was a frequent contributor of articles and feuilletons as well as verse. Winchevsky's style impressed Cahan as being genuinely Yiddish; but, on the other hand, he did not think it was a really popular style. Winchevsky wrote more as a poet than as a publicist, and Cahan felt that "his language was a little too high for the simplest Jewish worker."

Cahan met Krantz for the first time while walking through the streets with Joseph Barondess one day. He and Barondess were going from door to door soliciting funds for the newly formed *Arbeiter Zeitung* Publishing Association, Cahan busily discovering all the while that he could not bear the capricious and volatile temperament of his companion, who was then just on the brink of his meteoric rise to fame. Suddenly, there stood before them Bernard Weinstein and a big, barrel-chested man in his early thirties. Weinstein was escorting Krantz, who had just arrived from England, to the quarters that the United Hebrew Trades had found for him. Cahan was quite surprised when the introductions were made; he had expected Krantz to be more professorial in appearance. Furthermore, Krantz had an exuberant and thoroughly charming personal manner, and he spoke good Russian. Cahan was inclined to like him in spite of everything.

But personal charm could not stem the tide of Cahan's mounting ambitions, and tension soon arose between him and the newly arrived editor. At first, Krantz was somewhat bewildered at the constant stream of advice and criticism that came from Cahan at the *Arbeiter Zeitung* office day after day, even though the latter had no official position with the newspaper. After a while, Krantz got into the habit of changing the subject whenever Cahan brought up the matter of editorial policy. Cahan, who was twenty-nine years old and tended to look younger than his years, was certain that Krantz looked down upon him for his relative immaturity and seeming lack of experience. This only made him all the more vehement in his demands that he be heard. Relations between him and Krantz reached a point of crisis one day when he handed the latter a piece he had rewritten from an article in *Scribner's Magazine* by Henry M. Stanley, about cannibals in Africa. Cahan thought that popular science articles should be a regular element in the *Arbeiter Zeitung*. Krantz, who had already accepted two of Cahan's articles for publication in the first issue, read this one and handed it back without comment. Infuriated, Cahan promptly announced that he would have nothing more to do with the newspaper. But Miller and Hillkowitz, who had come to see the value of Cahan's continuing participation in the project, urged him to stay. He was persuaded to do so without much difficulty. In the end, the pressure of the approaching deadline forced Krantz to use Cahan's article about cannibals in the first issue anyway, along with his other two.

The first issue of the *Arbeiter Zeitung* came off the presses on the night of Thursday, March 6, 1890, datelined for the following morning. The paper was a four-page fold, journal size, with five columns to the page. Its headlines were all one column in width—in general, the format was quite conservative and dry, even by the standards of the time. The lead article, written by Krantz, was a solemn reiteration of "Our Program," intoned in the *Deitshmerish* style that Cahan so detested. "Our general goal *(Unser allgemeine Ziel)*," it began, "is the building of a social order on the principles of true freedom, equality and brotherhood, in place of the present capitalist order, which is founded upon oppression of the people, mass poverty, and internecine strife."

On the opposite side of the front page was an unsigned piece entitled "Two Worlds in the World," written in a Yiddish whose aggressively lowbrow tones seemed purposely to needle the style of Krantz's article. *Altz geyt vie geshmiert,* it begins—"Everything goes as if smeared (i.e., very smoothly) in the glittering parlors and salons of Fifth Avenue in New York." The first paragraph finishes describing this scene of wealth; the second paragraph sketches a scene of poverty. The article proceeds this way, juxtaposing scenes of wealth and poverty, with heavy-handed irony, in alternating paragraphs. A sketch depicting a musical soiré at the Vanderbilt home, for example, is followed by one of a Brooklyn stonecutter who dies of hunger and cold because he cannot find a job. The wedding of a millionaire's daughter, at which the dancing goes on all night, is contrasted with the all-night vigil of a group of newspaper peddlers, waiting in the cold for the early-morning edition. The final sketch shows the heirs of "the late Mr. Astor" gathering together eagerly to hear the reading of his will: "after *we* die," the last line reads, "we won't get such attention from our heirs, what do you think?"

The article was written, of course, by Cahan, who envisioned it as the first of a series which would always contrast the "two worlds in the world" in a way similar to this. The extreme crudeness of the idea did not trouble him, for the virtue of a newspaper, as he saw it, was its great richness of fabric, which allowed for accommodations to all tastes and levels of understanding. The writer did not have to invest his integrity and temperament in a single item in each issue. Rather, in any given issue, he could be several things at once: poet, feuilletonist, popular-science writer, socialist theoretician, storyteller, reporter, and so on—Cahan intended to try all these things. The informality of a Yiddish newspaper provided him with an opportunity to explore every aspect of his literary potential. In this first issue, he was already a sketch writer on page one, a popular-science writer (with his article on cannibals) on page three, and—also on page three—something considerably more ambitious as well; for his search for popular journalistic forms in Yiddish had brought him to a genuine literary idea.

Ever since his use of the theme of *Shavuos* to illustrate socialist principles, in the first issue of his *Neie Zeit* four years before, he had been interested in the idea of using Jewish folk-religious forms in this way. He was genuinely convinced that there was a moral and a deep-lying psychological link between religion and socialism—especially between Judaism and socialism; and he also knew from experience how thoroughly embedded religious conventions were in the Jewish folk imagination, even in that of a professed atheist like himself. Certain Jewish religious associations made the thoughts flow from him in vivid images despite the secularism of his conscious convictions; these same associations were rich and meaningful to the average working-man who would be reading the *Arbeiter Zeitung*—so why not use them? Why not recreate Jewish religious folklore in socialist terms?

For his first experiment with this idea, Cahan decided to take on the identity of the *maggid*, the traveling preacher of his Lithuanian-Jewish childhood. One of the important qualities of the maggid was his informality; his sermon was not an established part of the Sabbath services, but came rather in an interval between the regular morning and evening prayers. His talk would *begin* with a formal element in the liturgy—the *sidra,* or portion of the Pentateuch that was being read in the service that week—but it would soon take off amidst a cloud of homiletics in whatever direction his imagination would carry him. Cahan decided that he would write such a sermon each week, starting, as the traditional maggid did, with the Biblical portion of the week, but then taking off from it into a discussion of socialist matters. To emphasize the change in stress from religion to socialism, the column would be signed *Der Proletarishker Maggid* (the *k* in *proletarishker* conveys a conscientiously lowbrow air).

Cahan's *Sidra*—as the feature was regularly to be called—in the first issue of the *Arbeiter Zeitung* opens with a brief preface in which the Proletarian Maggid introduces himself to the reader. "Me," he says, "I'm from the town of Proletarishok. There I was born and there I've spent my whole life. Do you know, *raboysay* (folks), where Proletarishok is? Not far from Capitalishok. The two *shtetlakh* (towns) are as near to each other as, in New York for example, Fifth Avenue is to the Pig Market. . . ." There then follow contrasting descriptions of the ways of life in the two towns—leftover ideas, perhaps, from "Two Worlds in the World." After that the sermon itself begins.

The Biblical portion for the week in which Cahan is writing contains God's specifications to Moses for the building of a Sanctuary; for this purpose, a tax of half a shekel was imposed upon every Israelite, rich or poor: "The rich shall not give more, and the poor shall not give less than half a shekel, when they give an offering unto the Lord, to make an atonement for your souls." To the anticlerical Proletarian

Maggid, this arrangement is just like capitalism in its unfairness; he refers to capitalism as the "half-shekel" or "half-dollar" system. For every dollar the worker earns under this system, the Maggid says, he gets only half a dollar for himself (thus, the theory of surplus value!). But this is not the end of exploitation; when the worker gets home, he has to pay this half dollar to his landlord! Then, an element of topicality is introduced into the sermon to suggest the moral alternative to this arrangement: in Germany, the Maggid points out, the worker has just registered his protest against the capitalist system by voting overwhelmingly for the Social Democrats (now a legal party again for the first time after twelve years of antisocialist laws). From here the text makes another agile leap to the theme of the Purim holiday, which was to fall that week. Just as the Jews of Queen Esther's time had brought death to the tyrant Haman, so also, in the same week, did the workers of Russia bring death to Alexander II. The discourse goes on in this way, flitting rapidly from image to image and from example to example, interspersed with Biblical quotations, homilies, anecdotes, explanations, asides, all delivered in a manner as plebeian as a dish of potatoes. In its homely way, this column was one of Cahan's most ambitious literary efforts to date.

Krantz, Cahan, and the paper's other collaborators eagerly awaited the public's response to the first issue. It proved to be better than their most sanguine expectations: the entire edition of three thousand copies quickly sold out. In the ensuing days, the *Arbeiter Zeitung* became a prominent subject of conversation on the Lower East Side, the *Sidra* the feature most frequently discussed and praised. Relations between Krantz, who had little capacity for resentment in his nature, and Cahan improved virtually overnight. He extended to Cahan an open invitation to contribute whenever and whatever he liked, and to serve unofficially as one of the paper's editors. Cahan continued to do his *Sidra* every week, along with a great variety of other items under various pseudonyms. In a few weeks, the circulation of the paper had reached seven thousand, and the number of pages in an issue was increased to eight. An entirely new and important phenomenon had come into being on the Lower East Side.

The anarchists did not at all intend merely to sit back and watch this happen. In the first few months of that year, their point of view had been represented by a new weekly, *Der Morgenstern* ("The Morning Star"), which was privately published and edited by an anarchist printer named Ephraim London. But this modest enterprise had folded before the end of spring, and the Pioneers of Liberty decided once again to try to put out a newspaper collectively. The first issue of *Die Freie Arbeiter Stimme* ("The Free Voice of the Workingman") appeared on the Fourth of July. In format, it very closely resembled the *Arbeiter Zeitung* and sold, like the latter, for three cents a copy. Also like its rival, it began as a four-page fold, and expanded to eight pages a few weeks later—in both papers, this extra space was taken up largely with advertising, which more than paid for the added paper and printing costs. Indeed, *Die Freie Arbeiter Stimme* seemed a rather slavish imitation of its social-democratic counterpart; Roman Lewis, its editor, had never been noted for intellectual originality, despite his position as head of the New York Jewish anarchists. Numerous features were all but exact parallels of features in the *Arbeiter Zeitung*. But Cahan's *Sidra*, the success of which was most desirable of all to duplicate, was not imitated so easily. The first issue of the anarchist paper contained a feature called "Thoughts of a *Ba'al Makhshava* (man of reason)," which tried to recapture the spirit of Cahan's *Sidra*; but it lacked the element—the use of the weekly Biblical portion—that brought Cahan's feature to life. Subsequently, a closer equivalent was developed, called the *Haftarah* (the weekly segment from the prophets that is paired, in the Jewish liturgy, with the *sidra* and serves to elucidate it), but this was as weak in style as it was laden with intimations of dependency in concept.

There was one area, however, in which the anarchist paper had a distinct edge over its rival: poetry. Both papers had their share of *kitsch* poems written by regular contributors whose talents lay elsewhere. In the *Arbeiter Zeitung,* hortatory "poems" were occasionally contributed by Hillkowitz, intoning his verses in solemn *Deitshmerish,* and by Cahan, who thereby showed what was one of the areas in which he was totally lacking in any literary gifts; and at least one piece of bad verse was contributed to *Die Freie Arbeiter Stimme* in its early weeks by Joseph Barondess. But, whereas the social-democratic paper was embellished only from time to time with the verses of Morris Rosenfeld, who was a genuinely good poet, the anarchist paper carried a decent poem in almost every issue, either by Morris Winchevsky, who was still with the *Arbeiter Freind* in London, or by David Edelstadt of Cincinnati, who was to come to New York and take up the editorship of the paper by the end of the year.

*Die Freie Arbeiter Stimme* never attained more than half the circulation of the *Arbeiter Zeitung.* Still, this was better than any other predecessor had done, and the anarchist paper was able, for the time being, to maintain its precarious existence. Perhaps through the impact of the genuinely popular style of the *Arbeiter Zeitung,* perhaps because of other cultural changes that were in the air, there suddenly had come into being a Yiddish newspaper-reading audience large enough to support the two radical weeklies as well as the old orthodox paper put out by Sarasohn and some other more specialized journals besides. The cultural life of the Jewish community on the Lower East Side was at last throwing off German and "Russian" tutelage, and coming into its own.

Part of the success of the two radical papers was due to the excitement generated by the rivalry between them. Name-calling and jugular-vein polemicizing was part of the life's blood of the Russian-Jewish intellectuals—especially for Louis Miller, who did most of the *Arbeiter Zeitung*'s raging at the anarchists—and the newspaper audience loved it. The *Arbeiter Zeitung* would refer to anarchist doctrine as "warm ice cream," deeming it to be about as logical as that, and the *Freie Arbeiter Stimme* would ridicule the holier-than-thou attitude of the social democrats by calling them *die sich-bis'n-himmel-hoyber* ("the self-to-heaven-uplifters"), a piece of *Deitshmerish* which was too much even for the ear of Philip Krantz, who laughed until the tears came to his eyes when he first read it.

In general, Krantz liked to amuse himself by going to Sussman and Goldstein's Cafe, just down the block from the *Arbeiter Zeitung* office on Ludlow Street, there to sit over a glass of tea and read aloud, amidst peals of laughter, the passages in each issue of the anarchist paper that he found to be the most ridiculous. Sometimes one of the anarchists would be present to join in the merriment. On the other hand, some of the social democrats would occasionally walk over to the Sachs Brothers Cafe on Division Street near Pike, where the anarchists usually congregated. Here, too, the exchanges between them would usually remain on the level of good-natured banter, only occasionally slipping for an instant into the more venomous undercurrents that flowed between them. A more or less common success, defined by that large audience of passionately interested listeners and readers from all over the Lower East Side, had brought about something of a honeymoon in relations between the anarchist and social-democratic newspapers; but it did not last long. By that summer a renewed dispute had broken out in the cloakmaking industry, bringing to the fore once again the problematic figure of Joseph Barondess.

Despite the victory of the cloakmakers' union in March, many of the manufacturers had not yet become reconciled to the reality of union power, and were awaiting a new opportunity to challenge it. This came in the middle of May, when one manufacturer dismissed several of the sewing-machine operators in his shop—all of them union leaders—after an argument had broken out between them and him. All the other operators in the shop immediately walked out in protest. The manufacturer retaliated by locking out the operators in all his other shops. Seeing a definite showdown in the offing, other manufacturers followed suit and dismissed their unionized operators as well.

At this point the confrontation still had taken place only between the manufacturers and the sewing-machine operators—the people who assemble and finish the garments—at a moment when the slack summer season was approaching. It was the moment, in other words, when the operators' work was the most dispensable, and when the manufacturers could best afford a test of strength with them. But at the end of May, the dispute took a new turn. The cutters, who were much more in demand at that moment because they were already preparing goods for the fall season, and who had a union of their own separate from the cloakmakers', began walking out as a gesture of solidarity with the locked-out operators. Events thus produced a massive confrontation in the cloakmaking industry, a newly revived Manufacturers' Association on the one side, a fledgling cloakmakers' union of more than three thousand members, and its allies, on the other. Unlike the strike earlier in the year, this was a dispute between two entrenched power blocs, between union and manufacturers, rather than an organizing of hitherto unconsolidated workers against sweatshop conditions and the rule of small contractors. In fact, the contractors were now on the union's side, their representatives allied with the union leaders in an Amalgamated Board of Delegates.

At the head of this assemblage of workers and contractors stood Joseph Barondess, now at the height of his power. It was still an open question whether he was more an anarchist or a social democrat. Officially, he was still a member of the United Hebrew Trades and of the editorial board of the *Arbeiter Zeitung;* but he was also an occasional contributor to the *Freie Arbeiter Stimme,* and he seemed to be increasingly under the influence of an anarchist faction that was growing up among the union leadership. This latter group, which was organized into a fraternal workers' association that called itself the *Fortbildungs Verein* (roughly, "Self-Education Association"), was the surrogate of a new policy which had been articulated only that year by Saul Yanovsky, Philip Krantz's successor as editor of the now completely anarchist *Arbeiter Freind* of London. According to Yanovsky, the old sweeping condemnation of all unions as mere "palliatives" no longer applied; rather, there were good unions and bad ones, the good ones being those in which anarchist ideas had been made to predominate. Although the great majority of the cloakmakers were readers of the *Arbeiter Zeitung,* the anarchists were determined to make this union a "good" one, at least on its highest levels.

The success of this aspiration depended entirely, of course, on the ability of the anarchists to win and keep the heart of Barondess. For this purpose, they had a most effective instrument at their disposal. For if Barondess, an appealingly colorful figure in the eyes of any newspaperman in search of readable copy, had a passion for publicity in the wider world beyond the confines of the Lower East Side, the anarchists were able to gratify this passion through the services of a man whose talents for press agentry were decades ahead of the time in which he lived. This was the somewhat mysterious "Professor" Thomas Garside.

Nobody knew much about Garside's origins. He was a Gentile, apparently born in Scotland, and he had spent his early years in America in Baltimore, where his wife and children apparently still lived. Although he seemed in style and temperament to be naturally best suited to the task of selling patent medicines over the side of a wagon, he had somehow made his way into the ranks of the Socialist Labor Party by 1889, when he began to be known on the Lower East Side. The largely German SLP was then still endowed with very few speakers who could handle the English language as well as Garside could, and he became a valuable and well-paid asset to the party. Working out of New York, he toured the country giving socialist lectures. After a while, however, strange stories about his behavior on these tours began getting back to party headquarters. It was said, for example, that in the course of a single tour he had told an audience in Chicago that the eight-hour day was not a radical enough demand, and had then made an impassioned speech in favor of the eight-hour day in St. Louis. Other stories corroborated the impression that he was prone to change his line substantially, as if to suit his changing moods, from one moment to the next. Also, wherever he went, he would tell dramatic tales of how people were trying to assassinate him for his political beliefs.

This latter propensity reached its height of expression once in New Orleans, when he was spending the night in the home of a German SLP member named Bensch. In the middle of the night, the Bensch family were awakened by a cry for help from their guest's room. They rushed in and found him standing in great agitation in the midst of a room that was in disarray; he proceeded to tell them, in hair-raising detail, a story of how a man had come in through the window and tried to attack him with a razor. Garside had fought him off. The assailant got away, but he had, according to Garside, dropped the razor while making his escape, and it had fallen into the courtyard. Hosts and guest went down to the courtyard and, sure enough, found the razor lying on the ground. Garside said that the man had undoubtedly been hired by "the capitalists."

But Bensch's young son had picked up the razor and was examining it closely. Wasn't this Mr. Garside's razor?, he asked. The bearded Garside shook his head, protesting that he never used a razor. But, the boy insisted, he had seen it among Garside's possessions while helping him to unpack. No, Garside said, it was not his razor; it belonged to the assailant. The incident ended there, but Bensch found something suspect in Garside's story, which he relayed, along with the expression of his own suspicions, to party headquarters in New York. The party, too, decided that there was something wrong with the story. An investigation was held, and it ended in the dismissal of the flamboyant young speaker from the party. Pocketing his severance pay, Garside walked directly from SLP headquarters on East 4th Street to Johann Most's office at anarchist headquarters on East 6th Street, where he explained that he had been dismissed by the SLP because his revolutionary philosophy had been too extreme for them. The anarchists hired him as a speaker.

With the outbreak of the crisis in the cloakmaking industry in May, 1890, Garside was put to work by the anarchist faction of the union. The old-stock American bourgeoisie of New York, though not normally inclined to favor labor unions, were in this crisis sympathetic to the claims of an oppressed, slum, immigrant population against a group of bosses who also happened to be immigrants, but who were economic and social upstarts as well. Nothing could have been more useful to the union at this moment, then, than a good public-relations man who spoke English well and could provide the New York press with the human interest material it was suddenly so eager to obtain. Garside, who was in his early thirties, was a most attractive man, with a blond beard—Emma Goldman thought he "resembled somewhat the pictures of Christ"—and a resonant baritone voice; speaking in churches and on other platforms, he took the New York public by storm. This round of speaking engagements, the steady stream of press releases that flowed from his pen, and the fund-raising dinners over which he presided all tended to make him the union's unofficial policymaker as well as its chief representative to the general public. But he was careful always to seem to yield first place to Barondess, for whom he created the title, "King of the Cloak Makers." This name was eagerly taken up by the press, who was making its first full-fledged discovery of the Jewish Lower East Side, and for whom Barondess became its hero of the moment, the ideal figure of a noble and suffering Jew.

On its pages, the *Arbeiter Zeitung* was solidly in support of the union, and no expression of second thoughts was to be found there. But behind the scenes, although Barondess was not, for the moment, fair game for open expressions of discontent on the part of the social democrats, much was said in criticism of Garside. Cahan remembered Garside's history with the SLP, and tried to persuade union leaders that he was a charlatan. Among some union people there were beginning to be rumbles of dissatisfaction at the large sums of money Garside was spending for luncheon conferences with newspapermen and dinners with prospective donors. Scattered rumors were to be heard, seeming to attest to the duplicity of his nature. One story claimed that he was an ex-priest—clerical robes still evoked frightful images of pogroms for most Jewish immigrants— who had been thrown out of the Church for his anarchist views (Garside had, in fact, once studied for the *Protestant* ministry); another story depicted him as an *agent provocateur* in the hire of the manufacturers. It was already well established that the title of "professor" which he used for himself had no grounding in fact. But none of these things dimmed the popularity he had achieved in the eyes of most grateful rank-and-file union members—at least not for the time being.

It was not until July 15 that an opportunity arose for Garside to demonstrate his unreliability. On that day, a proposal for a settlement was presented by the Manufacturers' Association, providing for official recognition of the cloakmakers' union and for the arbitration of labor disputes—two of the principal union demands. Garside liked the proposal, as did the president of the cutters' union, which was still an autonomous entity within the strike coalition. But Barondess objected to the fact that it did not deal with two other major union demands: the fixing of piecework rates and the discharging of those who had worked as scabs during the strike. Fluctuating and inadequate piece rates were the chief reason that the workers ended up putting in long hours for very low pay; as for the issue of scabbing, it concerned the very essence of the union's power to strike effectively. Barondess, therefore, went home that evening convinced that the proposal was inadequate, and determined to try to persuade Garside and the president of the cutters' union to turn it down the next morning. But when Barondess awoke, he learned that they had gone ahead and signed an agreement with the manufacturers. The New York papers were already carrying the news that the strike was over; the *Arbeiter Zeitung* came out that afternoon with the words "Hurrah for the Cloak Makers" in large type on its front page.

But on the back page of the same edition of the *Arbeiter Zeitung* there was a retraction, inserted at the last minute, which announced that the strike had not yet been settled. That morning, Barondess had hurriedly organized a committee of his own union to oppose the settlement. They had gone to the *Arbeiter Zeitung* office and persuaded the staff of the paper that Garside and the cutters' union president had signed what was, Cahan acknowledged, "the worst agreement that could have been made." Cahan agreed to address a mass meeting of the union rank-and-file. He made two stipulations, however, both intended to create as unprejudiced an atmosphere as possible within which the workers could arrive at a decision about the agreement. In the first place, since the text of the agreement was in English, he requested that he function only in the role of Yiddish interpreter, offering no comments of his own. Second, he urged that the vote on the question of whether or not to accept the agreement be held by secret ballot, rather than by the show of hands which was the standard practice. Barondess and his committee accepted these terms.

The meeting was held the following evening at New Everett Hall on East 4th Street. More than fifteen hundred workers crowded into the hall. First they heard Barondess deliver his criticisms of the settlement, then they heard Cahan give a patient, point-by-point explanation of its terms. Two slips of paper were then handed out to each worker, one marked *arbeiten* ("work"), the other *streiken* ("strike"). Cahan explained that each person was to select the ballot he wanted, fold it, and hand it back to the ushers—and to carefully avoid looking at his neighbor in the process. This was done, the ballots were collected, and the tabulation began. It quickly became evident that the vote was overwhelmingly in favor of "strike"—in the final count, only twenty votes favored "work"—and a commotion broke out in the hall. "The enthusiasm was indescribable," Abraham Rosenberg, then a rising young union leader, wrote of this moment years later. "Men and women jumped onto the tables. Their voices could be heard ten blocks away. After the audience calmed down a little, the chairman of the meeting declared that money was the thing needed most, and that since it was lacking, he advised them to reconsider their decision. But he had hardly finished saying this when a man walked up to the table and, taking a ring from his finger, handed it to the chairman with the request that it be sold or pawned and the money be given to the strikers. . . . The chairman's table was covered with rings, watches, ear-rings, brooches, and other pieces of jewelry. Everyone was shouting that these offerings should be sold so the strike could go on. . . . Many cried. Others yelled and argued. The entire meeting gave the impression of an immense seething cauldron."

Garside's initiative had thus been repudiated, and the good will he had cultivated for Barondess among the newspapers suddenly began to dissolve. Joseph Pulitzer's *World,* hitherto a chief promoter of the cause of the King of the Cloak Makers, demoted him to "Baron de-Ess," and a campaign of vilification against him began in it and in other newspapers. Meanwhile, dissension broke out among the members of the Amalgamated Board of Delegates, and the cutters' union resigned from the coalition. While the contractors and the cloak operators continued striking, the cutters went back to work. But with the fall season approaching, it was now the services of the contractors and the operators that the manufacturers needed most of all. They could hold out no longer, and on July 25 they agreed to a settlement on Barondess' terms. It was the greatest victory the Jewish labor movement had ever won. Barondess was more of a hero than ever, and union membership rapidly multiplied, reaching seven thousand before the end of the year.

The flirtation between Barondess and the anarchists continued. Immediately after the strike, he appointed Roman Lewis assistant manager of the union. Even Garside continued to have Barondess' ear, in spite of everything that had happened. Barondess invited both Garside and Lewis to speak at a mass meeting of the cloakmakers held on the evening of September 12 in the Great Hall of Cooper Union. Garside, in his speech, urged the workers to continue to be ready to use dynamite when necessary to achieve their aims; Lewis spoke in a similar vein. These views were counterbalanced by Alexander Jonas, who gave a speech congratulating the union on its peaceable victory. But Cahan, when his turn came to speak, was still incensed at the anarchist fireworks that had preceded the speech of the *Volks Zeitung* editor. He accused the anarchists of using extravagant and violent-sounding rhetoric merely for the sake of effect, whereas "we social democrats," he said, "try to practise what we preach." He challenged both Garside and Lewis to debate with him publicly in the near future, the former in English, the latter in Yiddish. Both men accepted.

The English-language debate never took place, however, for Garside suddenly vanished from New York. None of the Lower East Side leaders were ever again to know of his whereabouts, although rumors would always be rife. The one most frequently to be heard was that he had become a detective.

The debate with Roman Lewis took place on the evening of September 30 in Clarendon Hall on East 13th Street. From the stage, Cahan could see Johann Most standing with Emma Goldman in the back of the hall throughout the debate. He later was told that, during his talk, Emma Goldman had kept muttering: "Laughable! Asinine!," but that Most had protested to her all the while that Cahan was, in fact, an excellent debater. The general consensus among those present, even among anarchists, was that Cahan had won a decisive victory. In the next day's *Arbeiter Zeitung,* Krantz wrote that it had been "like killing a fly with a cannon." The anarchists dismissed the outcome by arguing that it did not matter how Roman Lewis fared in a debate, since they recognized no man as their representative. Michael Zametkin replied to this point in the *Arbeiter Zeitung* by demanding to know if they would have said the same thing had Lewis won the debate. In the same issue, Louis Miller challenged the anarchists to choose someone to debate with him. No one came forth.

The battle royal now raging between the anarchists and the social democrats on the pages of their respective newspapers continued into the following year. Their bone of contention continued to be the person of Joseph Barondess, and the fury of the battle was in direct proportion to the force of his authority in the cloakmakers' union. But in the spring of 1891 his authority began to weaken. This was due to a series of blows, the first of which came during a brief strike in March. The union's picket committee discovered one day that a contractor named Greenbaum, himself a former union member, was running a shop with scab labor in Jamaica, Long Island. The committee was determined to bring Greenbaum's enterprise to a halt by physical force if necessary, and one evening they went to Jamaica and entered the shop. A fight broke out, and in the scuffle a stove was overturned, scattering burning coals all over the floor. Greenbaum's four-year-old son stepped on one of the coals and scorched his foot. Later, when he called the police, Greenbaum claimed that some of the union men had poured vitriol on the unfinished garments lying in the shop. That evening, Barondess and ten other members of the union executive were arrested.

The union leaders were held at a bail of $10,000 each. A union fund-raising campaign brought in enough money just to pay for Barondess' bail. At the trial—which further strained the union beyond its financial capacities—some union members sympathetic with their employers testified that they had seen Barondess giving out bottles of vitriol to the members of the picket committee. But there was no evidence available, and in the end charges were dismissed against all but one of the picket-committee members, Frank Reingold, who was found guilty of burglary and sentenced to five years in Sing Sing.

Barondess had no sooner been cleared of this charge than he was arrested again on another. A strike that had taken place in the clothing firm of Papkin and Marks had been settled in the union's favor. Among the terms of the settlement was an agreement by the employers to pay the union compensation for wages lost during the week of striking. Papkin accordingly made out a check for one hundred dollars; but, since the union had not yet established an account in its own name, the check was made out to Barondess. Papkin delivered it, then went to the police and charged Barondess with extortion. Barondess, he said, had threatened to continue the strike unless paid this amount. The union leader was arrested and held on bail again. The union raised more money to get him out.

Barondess was tried on May 2, and this time was found guilty; he was sentenced to twenty-one months in Sing Sing. His lawyer sought an appeal, and the hapless union leader waited in the Tombs, the city jail at Leonard and Centre Streets, for his next trial. Meanwhile the union organized a massive protest rally, which was held at Cooper Union on the evening of May 6; thousands were turned away. Anarchists, socialists, and even Samuel Gompers came together on the same platform to speak. "Who were the men that convicted Barondess?" Gompers asked rhetorically. "Every one of them belonged to the capitalistic class." Cahan spoke too, suppressing the rampant animosity which he felt toward Barondess on a personal level. Bail was raised for Barondess once again, and he was released a few days later. Thoroughly demoralized, Barondess heard a rumor one day shortly after his release that he might be taken into custody again, and he suddenly yielded to an uncontrollable impulse: jumping bail, he took a train to Montreal. There he was soon discovered, and was brought back to the Tombs.

The *Arbeiter Zeitung* could now no longer contain itself, and proceeded to launch a campaign of criticism of Barondess' character. The paper's staff sensed that some disillusionment with Barondess had begun to set in among union members, and had decided to try to seize the advantage. Cahan had already obtained a foothold of influence in the union after Barondess' arrest, when he was offered the position—which he accepted—of temporary administrator in Barondess' place. The *Arbeiter Zeitung* also took the initiative in organizing a fund-raising campaign to help the imprisoned Frank Reingold and his family. The *Freie Arbeiter Stimme* denounced this as mere publicity seeking. Perhaps because of anarchist opposition, the campaign had only very meager success.

Eventually both Barondess and Reingold were pardoned, in response to a petition that had been signed by fifteen thousand New York workers, both Jews and Gentiles. Barondess returned to his post as manager of the cloakmakers' union at the end of the summer of 1891; but his authority had been greatly shaken, and the social-democratic elements in the union were now more firmly in control. The decline of his power continued, and with it took place the decline of anarchist influence, both in the cloakmakers' union and in the Jewish labor movement in general. The fortunes of the *Freie Arbeiter Stimme* began to wane correspondingly. Toward the end of 1891, the typesetters employed by that paper—all members of a union loyal to the United Hebrew Trades—struck for higher wages. The anarchists thereupon accused the UHT and the *Arbeiter Zeitung* of a plot to strangle their newspaper, and tried to form a typesetters' union of their own. But by this time, the destiny of the beleaguered *Freie Arbeiter Stimme* had come to be bound up largely with that of its editor, the poet David Edelstadt, who was dying of tuberculosis. By the end of the year, Edelstadt had been forced to cease working, and he retired to Denver in search of a cure. The paper ceased publication shortly thereafter, putting out its last issue on January 22, 1892. Edelstadt died in the Denver Sanitarium on October 17, at the age of twenty-six. The ascendancy of the *Arbeiter Zeitung* among the Jewish unions was now completely unrivaled.

# CHAPTER 6

# SWEATSHOP POETS

O, gute freind! Ven ikh vell shtarbn
Trogt tzu mein kever unzer fohn—
Die freie fohn mit die royte farbn,
Bashpritzt mit blut fun arbetsman! . . .

Un ven ikh her die shverdn klingn
In letztn kampf fun blut un shmertz—
Tzum folk vell ikh fun kever zingn
Un vell bageistern zein hertz.

"O, good friend! When I die,
carry our flag to my grave—
the free flag with the red colors on it,
spattered with the blood of the workingman! . . .

And when I hear the clanging of swords
in the final battle of blood and woe—
I will sing to the people from my grave
and inspire their hearts."

DAVID EDELSTADT WROTE THESE LINES IN THE FIRST WEEKS OF
1889, when he was still more adept at German than at Yiddish. Though
their diction is plainer than that of most of the American Yiddish writings of the time, it still tends to be *Deitshmerish*. Furthermore, their
mood echoes more with Heine's "Two Grenadiers"—indeed, with
the whole revolutionary-romantic tradition of nineteenth-century

Europe—than with anything then to be found in Yiddish sources. But the attempt they represent at reconstructing a folk diction on the basis of a radical political inspiration reflects the meeting of elements that constitute the beginning point of modern Yiddish poetry.

Edelstadt's background, like that of many other Jewish immigrant radicals, was somewhat more Russian than Yiddish. He was born in 1866 in a village outside the Jewish Pale of Settlement, to a father who had served more than twenty years in the Russian army and was subsequently a policeman for a time—an occupation extremely rare among Russian Jews of his generation. Yet the elder Edelstadt does not seem to have been completely estranged from Jewish traditions, for during a brief time he hired a Lithuanian *melammed* to teach his son. This experience apparently made a deep impression upon the boy's imagination; like many Jews who begin life partially or wholly removed from the sources of their Jewish identity, young Edelstadt could, in the very rebelliousness and idealism of his nature, embrace experiences that, for others of a more conventional Jewish upbring-ing, would often represent the essence of a pious authoritarianism from which they seek to release themselves.

To be sure, in his first flush of adolescence, he was still very much a Russian: at the age of eleven he was already publishing Russian poems in a provincial newspaper, and in April, 1881, when he was thirteen years old, he wrote some poems in honor of the *Narodnaya Volya* leaders who had just been executed. But his response was more extreme a month later when the pogroms broke out in Kiev, where he was living with an elder half-brother: he fell ill as a result of them, and had to spend some time in a hospital. Later, his friends were to trace the tuberculosis which took his life at the age of twenty-six to this first illness of his, the nature of which is not clear. In any case, this was evidently the moment in which his radical conscience became confirmed as also a Jewish one; after leaving the hospital, he joined the Kiev *Am Olam* and went with its members to America.

The sixteen-year-old Edelstadt went to live with two elder half-brothers in Cincinnati. There he led a provincial version of the lives of the "Russian" radical immigrants of New York, eagerly reading the revolutionary literature that reached him from the country of his birth. Also like them, he obtained his "American" political education from German radicalism, reading papers like Most's *Die Freiheit* and Spies' *Arbeiter Zeitung.* The execution of the Chicago anarchists in November, 1887, evoking memories of the *Narodnaya Volya* executions, awakened an anarchist mood in his poetic spirit. It was this event which moved him to try writing poems again, some in Russian, and some in the language of his fellow Jewish immigrants from Russia. Like Hillkowitz—who also tried his hand at writing Yiddish verse, though with far less success—he painfully reconstructed his Yiddish from German, which he had learned at school in Russia and for which he had found frequent use in the largely German-Jewish community of Cincinnati. In February and March of 1889, he published his first Yiddish poems in the *Wahrheit,* and soon became the bard of the Yiddish-speaking anarchists of America. A bulwark of the *Freie Arbeiter Stimme,* he was naturally thought of as the successor to its editorship when Roman Lewis left to take a post with the cloakmakers' union.

Edelstadt's career was thus another manifestation of the way in which, at this time, a Russian-bred radicalism was combining with the specific circumstances of Jewish immigrant life in America to produce a Yiddish socialist culture. For him, as for other Jewish immigrant intellectuals, it was the energy of his radicalism that had recovered the spirit of the Jewish folk culture from which he had been at least partially alienated, and that had begun the process of transforming it into a literary culture. On Russian soil, radicalism might only have threatened to further alienation, but in America, it discovered Yiddish as a way of shoring itself up against the tendencies of American life to dull the edge of radical convictions. At this moment, in both Russia and America, a *general* Yiddish literary movement was coming into being for the first time—for Mendele Moicher S'forim, who was still active, had virtually been only an isolated cultural manifestation when he first began writing in Yiddish nearly three decades earlier. But it was only the American wing of this literary awakening that was in the first place a radical political movement. In Eastern Europe, the home soil of the Yiddish folk culture, the priority of elements was reversed: what began as primarily an aesthetic awakening only subsequently turned to the political radicalism that had been implicit in its populist mood from the outset. It was just around 1890 that two rather cosmopolitan Jews, Sholem Rabinowitz (Sholem Aleichem) in southern Russia and Isaac Loeb Peretz in Warsaw, were sitting down to recapture in writing the spirit of East European Jewish folk life that they had only recently rediscovered. Sholem Aleichem was never especially political, Peretz took to calling himself a socialist; but it was only later that their younger followers would seek to create a movement on East European soil that would explicitly identify Yiddishism and socialism as two aspects of a single ideal.

The East European Yiddish writers (those, that is, who reached personal and literary maturity on native soil, as distinguished from the "American" Yiddish writers, those who emigrated while still relatively immature) naturally wrote better prose fiction than their American counterparts did; the *shtetl* (the East European Jewish village) provided an entire, ready-made, Yiddish milieu, and the East European writers were dwelling right at the source. For the immigrant milieu of New York and other cities, it was never possible to create a prose diction that was both authentically Yiddish and authentically American at the same time. Americanization, which entered the immigrant Jewish culture like a torrent, only destroyed Yiddish, which in Eastern Europe had been—despite the appreciable Slavic element in it—founded upon a high degree of resistance to its linguistic environment. But poetry was another matter. The poet enjoys the luxury of being far more selective about his diction than the prose writer can be, and linguistic tendencies that might in general be culturally problematical are sometimes used by the poet to his own advantage. The American Yiddish poets were able to draw upon the elements of a cultural shock ultimately detrimental to the language in which they wrote, and turn them to advantage in a corpus of poems that were at least as good as any that were being written in Eastern Europe. Furthermore, the more distinctly ideological atmosphere of the American Yiddish culture as compared to the native East European one also had a more salutary effect upon the poets than upon prose writers. Yiddish prose writing in America was born in newspapers, and always—even in the case of fiction—maintained one foot in the feuilleton and the polemical editorial; poetry, once again, is more selective than prose fiction in relation to its environment, and the element of political radicalism in the American Yiddish culture provided the poets with a certain direction for the sensibility which worked well when it was not leading them into writing mere propaganda tracts in verse. Up to a point, noble political convictions have often served good poets well.

All these factors worked most interestingly in the case of Eliakum Zunser, a major Yiddish poet—perhaps the first major one—who managed, atypically, to bridge both the East European and the American Yiddish cultural worlds in his lifetime. Born in 1836 in Vilna, the capital of traditional Yiddish song, he had his poetical beginnings on the purest folk level, for he was by vocation a *badkhen*—a wedding bard. It was the function of the *badkhen* to enchant the ears of the wedding celebrants, moving them alternately to laughter and to tears, strengthening the hearts of the bride and the groom with lyrical wisdom, in an incessant flow of song that was often composed spontaneously at the moment of utterance. Zunser rose to the top of his profession early in life, and his songs were published in little booklets that were read by sobbing mothers and brides throughout Eastern Europe. But from the beginning there was an occasional touch of astringency and an incipient social consciousness in his work that

brought some of his lyrics to another plane than that of the master
*badkhen.* Even in this early poem, for example, written when he was
only fifteen years old and still an amateur performer at weddings, he
was already able to see the unhappier side of the traditional Jewish
way of arranging marriages:

> *Yiddishe shiddukhim, ver es veyss,*
> *Vie azoy a Yid a shiddukh tut—*
> *Dos trefft nor zeltn ven,*
> *Az die shiddukhim zoln zikh oyslozn gut . . .*
> *Es kummen die shadkhonim*
> *Mit dem falshn ponim*
> *Un shtelt far zey a groyzn glick;*
> *Zey tuen zikh nit badenkn,*
> *Az zey nemmen zikh oyfn halz a shtrick . . .*
> *Kukt nor, menshn, vie die eltern beyde*
> *Fuhrn dort a tokhter a kallah tzu der akeydah,*
> *Die oygn iz farbundn,*
> *Un dos hartz iz full mit vundn,*
> *Un der tatte geyt nokh bei der zeit;*
> *Nokh a por minut*
> *Tzi shlekht oder gut,*
> *Die khartah kummt nokh der tzeit . . .*

"Jewish marriages, who knows how a Jew makes a match—
but it seldom happens that the match works out well. . . . The
matchmakers arrive dissimulating, proffering images of great
happiness; you'd never know that they're putting a noose
around your neck. . . . Now look, ladies and gentlemen, at the
two parents leading their daughter, the bride, to the sacrificial
altar, eyes blindfolded, heart filled with wounds, the father
still by her side; just a few minutes more, for better or for
worse—then after a while the regrets begin. . . ."

Zunser's social impulse, evident in this poem, became somewhat more pronounced, and even took a brief political turn, in the

politically charged atmosphere of Russia in the sixties and seventies. Never more than a *naïf* in the world of politics, Zunser was inspired by the emancipation of the serfs and certain improvements in the Jewish lot in Russia to write two poems in the early sixties depicting Alexander II as a savior of the Jews. In the seventies his work manifested a more radical political tendency. But his poems did not take a distinctly socialist turn until he settled in the United States in the fall of 1889. New York acted as a catalyst for his political views in much the same way as it did for the average Jewish immigrant, who came to America to discover himself a full-fledged proletarian for the first time, and who thereupon discovered socialism as the religion of his salvation. For in this respect, as in many others, Zunser, who was no intellectual, tended to reflect spontaneously in his own spirit the collective experience of the Yiddish folk. Even while still en route to the American promised land, he had reflected the excited anticipation of the ordinary immigrant, writing on board ship a poem of praise for the New World called *Columbus un Vashington* (these were the two names associated with America that were likely to be known to even the simplest *shtetl* Jews, among whom the United States was sometimes known as *Columbusses medina*—"Columbus's state"). Later he also reflected the bitter disappointment of the hard, weary first months after arrival (a popular American-Yiddish epithet, expressive of this mood, went: *a klog tzu Columbussn!*—"a curse upon Columbus!"). In one of his earliest New York poems, Zunser contrasts the arriving immigrant's anticipation of happiness "in the good, free land" with the disillusionment of a friend whom he meets in the street six months after the latter had stepped off the boat. The friend describes his experiences since that moment:

> *Zeks monaten zikh gevalgert,*
> *Vu a tog un vu a nakht,*
> *Hunger hob ikh oykh gelitn,*
> *Mit mein bildung nisht gemakht;*

*Biz der noyt hot mikh getzvungn*
*Vern bigler in a shop,*
*Zekhtzn shtundn zikh tzu brennen,*
*Mit dem eizn klop un klop.*

*Den der boss nemt fun die greeneh*
*Arbeter far halb umsist,*
*Vill ikh billiger nit lozn—*
*Ruft er mir shoyn "sotzialist" . . .*

"Six months wandering around day and night, suffering hunger—my education was of no use to me; until sheer need forced me to become a presser in a [sweat] shop, there to burn myself up for sixteen hours [a day], clop-clopping with the iron. Then the boss gets some more workers from among the greenhorns for next to nothing [in wages], but I won't work for less—so now he calls me a 'socialist. . . .' "

Zunser's socialist mood reached its peak during his first year in America; in the summer of 1890, he contributed a poem to one of the first issues of the *Freie Arbeiter Stimme*, which was published on the front page under the jubilant heading: "Eliakum Zunser is ours—an anarchist!" But the poet was too mild a spirit for political controversy, and once he had settled down and opened a printer's shop to earn his livelihood (there was little demand for a *badkhen* in America), he drifted away from the clear ideological categories of either the anarchist or the social-democratic camp. Writing for an independent, mainly literary, weekly called the *Folks-Advokat*, he developed a Jewish socialist nationalism that anticipated both Bundism and Labor Zionism, ideologies which were to develop later in the decade, expressed in such lines as:

*Vie lang vestu, Yidl, arumgeyn un peddlen*
*Un falln tzu last bei die shkheynim in land,*
*Vos shreien in tzeitung un shtekhn vie nodlen:*
*"Der Yid iz a shnorrer un shtelt oys die hand"?*

"How long, my little Jew, are you going to go around peddling and being a burden to your neighbors in this country,
who are raising outcries in the newspapers that prick like
needles [to the effect that]: The Jew is a beggar with his hand
outstretched'?"

This sentiment was still similar to those of the orthodox socialists of
the Lower East Side, but not the one expressed a few lines later:

> *Zei besser a farmer un nem zikh tzu land!*

"Better that you become a farmer and betake yourself onto
the land!"

For most Lower East Side socialists, this ideal had not only passed
its moment of possible realization—New Odessa in Oregon, the last
of the *Am Olam* communes, had disintegrated in 1887—but it was
no longer even thought of as desirable: the onset of Marxism had
consigned such notions to the category of mere Utopianism. Zunser
had his laurels as the greatest Yiddish poet on the Lower East Side,
the elder statesman of its literary community, but the socialists had to
look elsewhere for the laureate of their own world view.

They found him in Morris Rosenfeld, the author of these lines
written at the beginning of 1893:

> *Es royshn in vork-shop zo shtark die mashinen*
> *Az oftmol in tummel ferlir ikh dem zinn,*
> *Ikh ver in zikh zelber ferzunken, ferloren,*
> *Mein "Ikh" vert dan bettel—ikh ver a mashine.*

"The machines in the workshop whir so loudly that I often
lose my senses in the din; I sink into myself and lose myself,
my 'I' is obliterated—I become a machine."

No other poet was to speak with such consistent authority as Rosenfeld
did of the sweatshop experience—an experience which came, largely

through his efforts, to be focused upon as the central symbol of Jewish immigrant sufferings in America. Himself the son of a tailor, Rosenfeld was born in the province of Suwalki, Poland, in 1862. His family moved to Warsaw when he was still a child, and he grew up there at the moment of the first flowering of a brilliant and cosmopolitan Jewish culture that was eventually to make Warsaw the Paris of the Yiddish-speaking world. The young Rosenfeld read Zunser and other Yiddish poets, and tried his own hand at writing verse in Yiddish. The pogroms of 1881, although they did not affect Warsaw Jewry directly, had a jolting impact upon Rosenfeld, and immediately after them he entered upon a period of restless casting about for a home, living at intervals in Amsterdam, New York, and London (in that order). In London, he settled down for a time in the East End among what was then a flourishing community of Yiddish-speaking radical intellectuals, and it was there that he first wrote Yiddish poems on socialist themes. But he did not publish anything until after his return to New York, to settle there permanently, in 1886.

Rosenfeld became the definitive poet of the Lower East Side, the one who most successfully arrived at a language and a set of metaphors for the Jewish immigrant experience. In the sweatshop, he found a vehicle for understanding and depicting Jewish folk life that was roughly the New World equivalent to what, at that same moment, was being discovered in the *shtetl* by Peretz and Sholem Aleichem. Like them, he was even able to find a folk vocabulary in his chosen literary milieu: in one poem, for example, he rhymes "singer" (of songs) with "Singer" (sewing machines). Of course, his milieu served more tenuously as a literary vehicle than did theirs, for his was the manifestation of a more alientated condition, and unlike them he regarded his milieu with scorn. In a sense, his attitude toward sweatshop and slum tenement was more like that of Mendele Moicher S'forim toward the *shtetl*—a perilous attitude, indeed, since both he and Mendele were ultimately seeking the downfall of the very institutions upon which their art was founded. Mendele survived artistically on a continuing dose of astringency in his personality, and on a return to Hebrew. Rosenfeld gradually tapered off into a kind of lingering wail, a generalized and sentimentalized sigh over the sufferings of the Jew and the workingman that lacked the toughness of his earlier sweatshop settings, but that also had its moments:

> *O, nit keyn gold'ner kammerton*
> *Shtimmt-on mein kell tzum zingn,*
> *Es kenn der vunk fun oybn on*
> *Mein shtimm nit makhn klingn;*
> *Dem shklafs a krekhtz, ven er iz mid,*
> *Nor vekt in mir die lieder—*
> *Un mit a flamm lebt-oyf mein lied,*
> *Far meine or'me brider.*

> *Derfar fargey ikh ohn a tzeit.*
> *Derfar vept-oys mein lebn:*
> *Vos kennen mir die or'me leit*
> *Far a baloynung gebn?*
> *Zey tzoln trern far a trer—*
> *Dos alles, vos zey konnen:—*
> *Ikh bin a trern-millionaire*
> *Un vein oyf die millionen . . .*

"O, it's not a golden tuning fork that sets my throat to singing, nor can a nod from on high make my voice resound; it's only the slave's groan, when he is tired, that awakens songs in me—and with a flame my song revives, for my poor brothers. For the sake of this I go on without respite. For this my life weeps away: what can the poor give me in payment? They pay teardrops for a tear—as much as they can: I am a teardrop millionaire, and I weep over my millions. . . ."

In a moment of equipoise between anger and self-pity, Rosenfeld had emerged as one of the best examples that can be found anywhere of the old socialist ideal of a self-contained proletarian literary culture. He had achieved this by an identification of his lot as a worker with his Jewishness (or Yiddishness), the latter serving as a richer and more historically reverberating poetic expression of the former. But, it must be said, that though this poetic formulation flowered in New York under Rosenfeld's pen, the seeds of it were first planted in London, during the brief season of Yiddish proletarian cultural activity that had begun in the East End in the early eighties and was moribund a decade later. In fact, Rosenfeld's vision is largely attributable to the influence of one man: the poet and feuilletonist Morris Winchevsky, who was the chief mentor of that East End Jewish culture when it was at its height. It was Winchevsky who first discovered the synthesis of ideology and urban milieu that provided Yiddish writers, especially poets, with a language adequate to describe the experience of Jews who had been transplanted from East European *shtetlakh* into large Western cities.

Winchevsky, who used several noms de plume during the course of his life, was born Lippe Ben-Zion Novakhovich on August 9, 1856, in a Lithuanian *shtetl*. His family already had a tradition of political activism and quasi-socialist leanings: his paternal grandfather had been killed fighting in the Polish uprising of 1831, and his widowed grandmother had thereupon devoted her life to community work for the poor. Her son—Winchevsky's father—was of a similar bent, and guests gleaned from among the poor were often to be seen sitting around his family's dinner table. Although superficially a true Lithuanian *misnagid,* the elder Novakhovich was from afar an admirer of the Hasidim, with their spirit of brotherhood and their devotion, in principle, to the notion of poverty as an outward form of spiritual purity. His unorthodox attitudes were imparted to his son Lippe, who received only fragmented elements of a Jewish education, combined with the rudiments of a modern one.

For a while, young Novakhovich prepared for entry into a gymnasium, with the intention of eventually studying at a university. But the family's money ran out, and so he went instead to the tuition-free

training college for state rabbis in Vilna (this was soon to be recon-
stituted as the Teachers' Institute, which Abraham Cahan went to
four years later). At this time, the school was even more a center of
student radicalism than it was to be by the time Cahan went there,
for young Jews of the progressive type were still not getting into the
gymnasiums in large numbers, and were studying at places like this
instead. When Novakhovich went there, radical agitation was being
led by a student named Aaron Sundelevich, who, despite the "rabbinical" education he was receiving at the Institute, was inclining
in the direction of complete revolutionary assimilationism; he was
always to scorn any separate Jewish identification within the radical
movement. On the other hand, Sundelevich's political mentor, a man
named Aaron Lieberman, who had been graduated from the Institute
several years before, was beginning, despite his early involvement with
the *Narodnikii* and their virtually exclusive passion for the peasantry,
to evolve a vision of Jewish autonomy within the revolutionary movement. This was still several years before the pogroms took place to
convince many others of the same idea; Lieberman later was to come
to be considered as the virtual father of the Jewish labor movement.
An active agitator among the Jewish students of Vilna, he won over
young Novakhovich as his disciple.

At this time, Hebrew was still primarily the literary vehicle of
Jewish nationalism or cultural autonomism in its various forms; only
Alexander Tzederbaum's Hebrew journal *Ha'Melitz* had granted
Yiddish a voice by putting out a supplement in that language, to which
Mendele Moicher S'forim was a regular contributor. Lieberman, seeking an outlet for his own ideas, naturally thought at first of writing
in Hebrew. But since none of the Hebrew periodicals existing at
that time were revolutionary or socialist in outlook—these Haskalah
journals had settled down to a stolid, bourgeois liberalism—he
founded one of his own, with the help of Novakhovich; they called
it *Ha'Emmes* ("The Truth"). Lieberman also began publishing
socialist proclamations in Hebrew and distributing them among

the Jewish students of Vilna; the young Abraham Cahan received one of these in 1876, several years before his moment of revolutionary awakening.

*Ha'Emmes* lasted only a few issues, and though another young socialist named Michael Radkinson had begun putting out a Hebrew journal, *Ha'Kol* ("The Voice"), to which Lieberman and Novakhovich became regular contributors, the latter two were growing aware of the futility of writing revolutionary tracts in Hebrew. One hoped to arouse the masses, but there were no Hebrew-speaking masses; this meant that one had to choose either to write for the Russian masses in their language—as Sundelevich had chosen to do—or for the Jewish masses in theirs. Lieberman and Novakhovich therefore decided to found a Yiddish supplement to *Ha'Kol*. The first issue appeared in October, 1877. So far as is known, this was the first regular vehicle for socialist ideas in Yiddish that ever existed.

In 1878, Lieberman discovered that he was being sought by the Tsarist police because of his political activities; he fled the country and eventually settled in London, then a major place of refuge for Russian revolutionary exiles. Novakhovich went to Koenigsberg and obtained a post as a bank clerk; but he was arrested in November, 1878, for carrying on a correspondence with Lieberman. He was about to be extradited to Russia, but the Jewish banker by whom he had been employed helped him escape to Denmark. From there he made his way to London, where his old collaboration with Lieberman was resumed.

By this time *Ha'Kol* had collapsed, but the two young radicals were more determined than ever to pursue their program of propagandizing in Yiddish. They made plans for a series of socialist pamphlets in *zhargon*. At the beginning of 1880, with the help of some exiled German Social Democrats, they organized a discussion group, the "Jewish Workers' Benefit and Education *Verein*." As in its New York counterparts a few years later, there were some initial strains in the effort to extricate the *Verein* from the German atmosphere that set the tone of radical immigrant activity all around it. Novakhovich discovered, in his first lectures, that he was having difficulty making the Yiddish-speaking workers understand the highly Germanized vocabulary that he had acquired in Koenigsberg and that had been reinforced in London radical immigrant circles. But he was, like Cahan, the offspring of a Lithuanian *shtetl,* and an authentic Yiddish speech soon returned to his lips.

At this point, personal tragedy intervened in these projects. One of the gathering places frequented by Lieberman and Novakhovich was an East End restaurant run by the latter's cousin, Rachel Sarasohn. Rachel was a young *agunah*—a woman whose husband had disappeared but had not yet been proven dead, and who was still not eligible to remarry. Lieberman was at this time thirty-six years old and unmarried. Gradually, a romance developed between him and Rachel. Then suddenly, in the fall of 1880, a letter arrived from Rachel's missing husband. He was in America, settled in Syracuse, New York, and he wanted her to join him; a steamship ticket was enclosed with the letter. She went, and Lieberman went with her, following her all the way to Syracuse. There one day he shot himself.

Stunned by his friend's suicide, Novakhovich withdrew from active political life. The Jewish Workers' Benefit and Education *Verein* fell apart. For the next four years, Novakhovich had virtually no other occupation than the clerkship in the Seligman Bank which provided him with his livelihood. Only in the latter part of 1881 did he devote himself for a time to a piece of writing: a paper on the pogroms in Russia, solicited by the august and conservative Anglo-Jewish Association.

But the vast Jewish exodus from Eastern Europe which ensued, and which for a time brought a heavy Jewish immigration into London and Manchester, eventually brought Novakhovich back to his calling as an agitator among Yiddish-speaking workers. Gathering together a group of supporters, he began publication of a weekly workers' newspaper in Yiddish in 1884. In the fullness of his long-brewing

Yiddishist-socialist pride, and of his determination to twit the upper-class Anglo-Jewish establishment (from whom he had to earn his living), he gave his newspaper the aggressively lowbrow name of *Dos Poylisher Yidl*. But this title could not long withstand the barrage of criticism to which it was subjected, from immigrant workers as well as from old Jewish banking families, and after fifteen issues the paper was given a more conventionally Judeo-German name: *Die Zukunft* ("The Future").

The paper, which was the first of its kind anywhere, had numerous obstacles to overcome. The chief difficulties were linguistic, for Novakhovich had as zealous a notion of the purity of Yiddish as did his younger fellow Litvak in New York, Abraham Cahan. He had made a concession to *Deitshmerish* in the paper's name, but he did his best not to do so in its content. But it was hard to get contributors to write the simple expository prose of a good newspaper article without veering into Germanic words and cadences. Novakhovich's St. Petersburg correspondent, Jacob Rombro—whose nom de plume was "BarMaro," an anagram of the Hebrew spelling of his last name—wrote in a diction that Novakhovich later described as being "like that of a goy speaking Yiddish." Rombro was later to improve somewhat, after coming to London and assuming the pen name of Philip Krantz, but never wholly to the satisfaction of all his Litvak critics, as time was to show. Linguistic matters on the paper were further complicated by the fact that its typesetter was a Galician Jew and its proofreader was from the Judeo-German-speaking part of Poland, with the result that, as Novakhovich put it, "both language and orthography were always a compromise." Nevertheless, this was the paper from which a younger generation of Yiddish writers were beginning to learn a conception of journalistic diction, from Morris Rosenfeld in London all the way to David Edelstadt in Cincinnati.

Encouraged by the modest success of his paper, Novakhovich returned to the idea he had developed with Lieberman of writing a series of propagandistic pamphlets in Yiddish. He wrote the first of these—called *Yehi Or* ("Let There Be Light," in Hebrew)—in the form of a dialogue between two ordinary workers; socialist ideas were thus developed in simple, everyday terms, in the conversational Yiddish of the immigrant masses. This was exactly the kind of writing in which Cahan later also excelled; indeed, Cahan was never likely to be able to read such works as this one by Novakhovich without a twinge of jealousy. Novakhovich named the two workers in his pamphlet "Morris" and "Hyman," and to complete his assumption of a working-class *persona* for literary purposes, he fictitiously designated the former as the author of the book, which was signed "Morris Winchevsky." This was his first use of the pseudonym by which he was to become almost exclusively identified in time, both in England and in America.

It was also around this time that he began writing poems seriously. Poetry was considered by the Yiddish-speaking intelligentsia to be an indispensable form of propagandizing. In general, verse can provide the uneducated worker with vivid phrases and images that engrave themselves upon the mind, but Yiddish in particular comes into its own in pithy sayings and homely metaphors. Unlike his younger disciples, Rosenfeld and Edelstadt, Novakhovich-Winchevsky does not seem to have come to the writing of poetry spontaneously; the other two were poets first and propagandists later, but Winchevsky developed in the reverse order. Unlike them, he was always at least as good in prose as he was in poetry, and he was perhaps better in the feuilleton—a central form of literary expression for Jewish intellectuals—than in any other literary form. Indeed, his best poems were usually feuilletons in verse, describing some scene of poverty or distress set against the background of Victorian London, such as this one, which incorporates an English refrain:

> *Lebn der Berze, dem Temple fun shvindl,*
> *Zeh ikh tog teglakh an orimess kind,*
> *Shteyendik ruhik un shtill vie a hindl,*
> *Nohent fun an altn man, velkher iz blind;*

*Shvebelakh trogendik,*
*Shtillerheit zogendik,*
*Betndik: "Koyft bei mir metches, mein Herr!*
*"Two boxes a penny, one penny the pair!"*

"Near the Stock Exchange, the Temple of swindle, I see every day a poor child standing still and silent as a puppy near an old man who is blind; carrying matches, quietly saying, imploring: 'Buy matches from me, sir! Two boxes, etc.' "

There is in this and other Winchevsky poems a conscientious awareness of milieu that was unprecedented in Yiddish poetry at the time. Winchevsky clearly has achieved this through an adaptation of British Victorian conventions: the atmosphere of this poem, highlighted by the English line, comes straight from Dickens and other, yet more banal, contemporary models. Even the sweatshop convention, which was brought into Yiddish by Winchevsky and then passed on to Rosenfeld, came directly from English Victorian literature: for it was around this time that Winchevsky captured the mood of Jewish workers in sweatshops everywhere with a Yiddish adaptation he did of Thomas Hood's "Song of the Shirt."

*Die Zukunft* came to an end a year after it began, in the summer of 1885. Despite its relative success, it was never more than a marginal operation financially, and it had depended for its existence mainly upon the good will of the printer, Rabinovich, who provided it with all its facilities, including "office space" in his shop. Rabinovich had always sought whatever means he could find to make the paper profitable, and this often meant taking in advertising of a sort of which Winchevsky and his socialist collaborators could only heartily disapprove. There was a constant state of crisis over this question. Finally, in August of 1885, Rabinovich brought matters to a head by printing an advertisement for a Parliamentary candidate who happened to be both rich and Jewish. Many socialists promptly denounced this as an extreme manifestation of the

Jewish "nationalist" turn of mind of which Rabinovich was always suspect among them. In response to these criticisms, Winchevsky ceased publication of the paper.

But by this time the Yiddish-speaking radical movement in London had found strength enough to begin putting out a collectively owned newspaper. Earlier that summer, in June, a group of Jewish workers and intellectuals had convened in an East End restaurant-hotel in which Winchevsky's correspondent Jacob Rombro, recently arrived from Russia, was boarding, and had created a monthly Yiddish newspaper which they called the *Arbeiter Freind*. Winchevsky was asked to be its editor, but he, fearing that taking the editorship of a paper openly sponsored by anarchists and socialists might threaten his position at the Seligman Bank, recommended that Rombro—now known as Philip Krantz—be given the job instead. Winchevsky unofficially collaborated with Krantz, and the first issue of the paper was put out on July 15. This was the beginning of a halcyon era of anarchist-socialist collaboration in London. Winchevsky, who was ever afterward to look back upon these years with infinite nostalgia, wrote huge quantities of poems and articles of all sorts for the *Arbeiter Freind*, which even brought him a wife: soon after the paper began publication, he married the daughter of the owners of the restaurant in which the paper had been founded. In December, 1886, the *Arbeiter Freind* became a weekly.

But, from this moment on, there took place a slow but steady decline into factional strife. As early as the fall of 1885, a running debate had been begun on the pages of the *Arbeiter Freind* between Philip Krantz, taking the social-democratic position, and Joseph Jaffe, speaking for the anarchist side. At first, this discussion was thought of by many of the paper's collaborators as merely academic. The debate did not become venomous, in fact, until 1889, when Jaffe became editor of the *Wahrheit* in New York and used his position there to deliver severe attacks upon the social-democratic faction in London. It was in the summer of that year that Krantz, a delegate to the First Congress of the Second International—in which anarchism was severely denounced—made contact with Louis Miller and discussed the possibility of going to New York. By the time he returned to London from the Congress, Krantz had become a bitter partisan in the battle against the anarchists. This was about the time when he coined the term *parveh lokshen* to describe the "nonpartisan" character of the *Arbeiter Freind*—a piece of polemical ingenuity which outraged Winchevsky.

The anarchist-socialist quarrel on the *Arbeiter Freind* seemed to Winchevsky to be nothing but a disaster. Refinements of ideology meant little to him; he cared only for the ideal of Jewish working-class brotherhood that the paper had represented at its inception. But even he and the other diehards of the "nonpartisanship" ideal found that there was no room left for them on the paper after Krantz had gone to New York and it had fallen completely under the control of the anarchist faction. Sadly, Winchevsky and the other "nonpartisans" withdrew in the spring of 1891 and founded a monthly of their own, *Die Freie Velt* ("The Free World"). Winchevsky never ceased to mourn the passing of the old coalition; his mood was expressed in such lines as these, published in the September, 1892, issue of *Die Freie Velt:*

> *O tzufall, O shikzal, O Gott—ver du bist,*
> *Nem altz fun mir, nem un gib es nit vieder,*
> *Nem altz, vos mein lebn derfreyt un farzist,*
> *Nem altz, oyb dikh ergert mein glick un fardrist,*
> *Nor loz mir die liebe tzu sey—meine brider!*

"O chance, O destiny, O God—whatever you are—take everything from me, take it all and give nothing back, take everything that gladdens and sweetens my life, take everything if my happiness troubles and aggrieves you—only leave me my love for them: my brothers!"

By this time, Winchevsky, now in his late thirties, was a kind of elder statesman among the Jewish radicals and workers of London. His poems and feuilletons were celebrated among them, his lectures were attended by large audiences. In the summer of 1893, he was sent to Zurich as a delegate to the Third Congress of the Second International. In the early part of 1894, he published a sequel to his pamphlet, *Yehi Or;* also a dialogue between "Morris" and "Hyman," this one showed its author's increasingly social-democratic leanings in spite of his "nonpartisanship," for it was a treatise on unions, called *Der Alef-Beys fun Trade-Unionism* ("The ABC of Trade-Unionism"). It was an even greater success than its predecessor, selling nearly three thousand copies in a few weeks. The grateful Jewish workers of London took to referring to Winchevsky, their teacher, as *Der Zeyde* ("The Grandfather")— a rare honor to be bestowed upon a young man in a culture that was still largely patriarchal in its public values. The title was to stay with him the rest of his life.

But this was a glow that reached him from a fading glory. The vast majority of Jewish workers emigrating from Eastern Europe had gone, and were continuing to go, to the United States. A Jewish workers' press and labor movement had come into being in New York and now was flourishing with a vitality far greater than that of its London counterpart. The Yiddish-speaking intellectuals of London had long since taken to publishing a large part of their writings in New York, and by the middle of 1894 a great many of them had gone to live there. Winchevsky had long been receiving invitations to come to New York, too—at the beginning of 1889, for example, the anarchist *Wahrheit,* in a first hopeful vision of "nonpartisan-ship," had asked him to come and be its editor—but he had thus far refused to leave London, with which so much of his youth had been bound up. By the fall of 1894, however, there was little left for him in London; his brother-in-law, Constantine Gallup, the editor of *Die Freie Velt,* had just died, and that paper was now clearly on its last legs, most of its staff fleeing to New York in search of a livelihood. He received another invitation from New York, to go there on a lecture tour, and this time he decided to go and settle there for good. He arrived in New York in October, just in time to become one of the central figures in a major controversy that had broken out at the *Arbeiter Zeitung.*

# CHAPTER 7

# THE FOUNDING OF
# *THE JEWISH DAILY FORWARD*

His heart is in France, his head in Russia and his belly in New York. New York has the most important part of him.

He is a social democrat—in other words, not an anarchist. But, on the other hand, he is a revolutionary and holds little store in the ballot. Why? Simply because this is more comfortable. Casting a ballot—this is done by hand, and it is work, something that has to be done here and now, whereas the social revolution is still far off and doesn't require much effort for the time being. Besides, voting is something you have to do every year, whereas a revolution, once you've got it over with, is a job put out of the way.

—"HE: A CHARACTER SKETCH," BY MORRIS WINCHEVSKY,
IN *Die Zukunft* (NEW YORK), MARCH, 1897.

The Socialist Labor Party must not get mixed up in union affairs. Absolute neutrality—this is the only tactic for the party to use. Any other is a disaster for it.

—LOUIS MILLER IN *Die Zukunft* (NEW YORK), MARCH, 1897.

IN AUGUST, 1891, IMMEDIATELY AFTER HIS BRIEF SPELL AS A stand-in for Joseph Barondess at the head of the cloakmakers' union, Abraham Cahan went to Europe as a delegate of the United Hebrew Trades to the Second Congress of the Second International. Louis Miller had had this assignment two years before, but Cahan, since his return to active work among the Jewish social democrats of New

York, had come to be widely recognized as the most articulate voice among them, and he now seemed the most natural choice for this job. He approached it with characteristic zeal. Nine years of activity among the Yiddish-speaking immigrants had awakened in him the germ of a Jewish nationalist that he once had not imagined to be there; on the first day of the Congress, which was held in Brussels, he took the assembled delegates by surprise with an announcement that he wished to submit for the agenda the question: "What shall be the stand of the organized workers of all countries concerning the Jewish Question?"

This caused considerable embarrassment. "The Jewish Question" had been a major issue in the classic struggles of European liberalism half a century before, and was thought to have been disposed of; but it was now emerging as an issue again with a wave of political anti-Semitism that was sweeping Austria, Germany, and France. This new anti-Semitism was of an unprecedented nature, for it formed the rhetoric of candidates for political office, who appealed not so much to mass prejudices against the Jewish religion in the manner of old as to popular resentments at the position of relative eminence and prosperity Jews had achieved in Western Europe since their emancipation. It was, in other words, a repudiation of the achievements of liberalism in the past half century. But the social democrats of the Second International, though some of them perhaps recognized that anti-Semitism would some day be a danger to socialism as well, were not for the time being concerned with a question that seemed mainly to be a family quarrel between the liberal and the conservative bourgeoisie. After all, if anti-Semitic politicians were arousing the anger of the masses against Jewish capitalists, few socialists at this moment were inclined to quibble with popular resentment against the Rothschilds, or to trouble themselves over the question of where the element of anticapitalism ended and that of anti-Semitism began.

Added to these grounds for annoyance with Cahan's proposal was the fact that so many of the prominent socialists of Europe were

Jews. By the last quarter of the nineteenth century, Marxian socialism had become as powerful in its appeal to young Jewish intellectuals in Western Europe as it was to their counterparts in Russia. As in
Russia, the typical Jewish socialist in Western Europe was the son of
a businessman who had risen on the wave of liberal capitalism that
passed through virtually all of Europe in mid-century; the father's
affluence had thus provided the son with the education that induced
him to repudiate paternal values. As a result, this younger generation
of Jewish socialists were often in a peculiarly ambivalent position.
If they were as vehement in their denunciations of the Rothschilds
as non-Jewish socialists were, there still remained, in spite of themselves, an element of family quarrel in their rhetoric; their dismay at
capitalists who were Jewish may have had a special poignancy to it,
and a special vehemence as a result, but it lacked the note of a more
sinister vindictiveness that often characterized the attitudes of their
non-Jewish comrades.

Because of all this, the Jews among the leaders of the Second
International preferred not having any discussions of the Jewish
Question arise to complicate the movement toward European socialist unity that had only just got under way. Furthermore, they were
worried about the attitudes of the nonsocialist world. Marx and
Lassalle, both Jews by origin, had been the founders of the socialist movement, and ever since their day Jewish names had been more
prominent among the socialist leadership than among the ruling
circles of financial capitalism. The Jews in the Second International
feared that if the movement were now to become openly involved in
the Jewish Question, bourgeois Europeans would become confirmed
in their suspicions that socialism was a Jewish plot to overthrow the
established, Christian order.

The upshot was, Cahan found to his astonishment, that the most
vehement opposition to his proposal began coming from the Jews
at the Congress. In the next two days after he had submitted it, he
was summoned to the quarters of both Paul Singer, the leader of

the German Social Democrats, and Viktor Adler, the leader of the Austrian Social Democrats—flattering attentions, indeed, from two of the greatest eminences in the worldwide socialist movement. Both of them Jews, each in turn strongly urged that Cahan withdraw his proposal. But the discovery of a moral weakness in someone who opposed him was all Cahan ever needed to inspire him to press his arguments even more vigorously than before. He would not be dissuaded. Next came an invitation from a different world altogether: the Chief Rabbi of Brussels wanted to see him. The rabbi also urged him to withdraw his proposal, for the sake of the well-being of the Jewish community in general. This plea from the heart of West European Jewish bourgeois well-being was bound to bring the reverse snobbery of Cahan's proletarian Yiddishness bristling to the surface; again he refused. If his proposal was a matter of Jewish principle before the socialists of Europe, it was also a matter of socialist principle before the European bourgeoisie, Jewish and Gentile alike.

It was not until the discussion of his proposal on the floor of the Congress began that Cahan's growing petulance toward his opposition was undercut by a wave of despair. Until that moment, he had not realized how deeply ingrained anti-Semitic sentiments were among some West European socialists. This was particularly the case with the French delegates, who had difficulty dissociating the word "Jew" from the word "Rothschild," and who were in no way prepared to assume what they thought would seem to their colleagues back home to be a "philo-Semitic" stance. Cahan had indeed caused an embarrassment, and he soon found that the most liberal-minded among the delegates were, at best, concerned with finding a face-saving way of disposing with the question as speedily as possible. In the end, a resolution was passed to the effect that the Socialist International condemned "both anti-Semitism and philo-Semitism." Cahan was overcome with disappointment and dismay.

This had proved to be a good object lesson for him on the differences between Europe and America. If, as he now well knew,

American soil did not permit a heroic and pure-hearted socialism of the *Narodnaya Volya* variety to flourish, it did not nourish the kind of powerful and relentless anti-Semitism that was traditional to continental Europe either. If it was easier to be a good socialist in Europe, it was easier for a radical like Cahan to be a good Jew in America. Indeed, it had been American soil which had begun to bring out the Jewish nationalist in him. This sentiment was now an additional element in his socialist pride, an affirmation of characteristics which defined him as something distinct from and opposed to the Anglo-Nordic middle-class establishment in America. But Jewish sentiments did not seem to work this way so readily in Europe, most notably in France.

In general, France had provided Cahan with some of his most shaking experiences on this, his first trip to Europe since his emigration to America. He had first stopped in London on his way to the Congress, and though he met there a number of his socialist idols— including Eleanor Marx-Aveling (who had said to him, to his astonishment, "We Jews have a special obligation to devote ourselves to the working class"), Sergey Kravchinsky, and Peter Lavrov—London had struck him as not significantly different from New York. There he met Morris Winchevsky, had a traditional anarchist-social democrat public debate with Saul Yanovsky, the editor of the *Arbeiter Freind,* and gave several lectures in Yiddish to workers. But when he crossed the Channel and landed in France, thus setting foot on the European continent for the first time since he had become an American, he found himself suddenly overcome with nostalgia. Now it was merely a stretch of *land,* however wide, that separated him from his native soil. In Paris, as it happened, the comrade at whose house he was to stay was a Jew from Vilna, a former gymnasium student and member of Cahan's revolutionary *kruzhok,* named David Gordon. Despite his education, Gordon was now making his living as a factory worker, and he lived in a working-class neighborhood. He and his wife were living the kind of simple proletarian existence that Cahan and his colleagues in New York, professional socialist intellectuals, had by now left behind them. Yet, as Cahan could not but notice enviously—for his own relations with his wife were anything but harmonious—the Gordons seemed to be completely happy; "he was always telling jokes and she was always laughing," he later wrote of them.

David Gordon had a sister named Eva—"Yeva" in the Russian pronunciation they used among themselves—who lived nearby and would come to visit him often. "She also was a lively and happy girl. She had a fine voice, and usually came in singing." On the wall in one corner of the apartment hung a picture of a young man, a Russian Gentile named Kashintzev, whom Yeva referred to as her fiancé. He was in jail at the moment, having been caught by the French government organizing a plot against the Russian regime. She told Cahan how she visited him regularly in prison, where they would always discuss plans for their marriage, which was to take place after he had served his sentence. Her brother and sister-in-law listened to all this with a noticeable lack of enthusiasm.

Yeva assumed the role of Cahan's guide during his stay in Paris. Together they walked the streets, visited the great open squares and boulevards—always dazzling, but especially so to a young man who had been weaned on the narrow streets of Vilna and of Lower Manhattan—ambled through parks and museums, sat in cafes. There they talked, either by themselves, or with Yeva's radical and Bohemian friends living on the Left Bank. One day, Yeva took Cahan to a cafe where they met an exiled young Polish revolutionary who turned out to be none other than Anton Gnatowski, the blond-haired railroad-school student from the Vilna *kruzhok*. Since that time, as Cahan learned in their conversation, Gnatowski had taken part in a plot to kill Alexander III in the same way his father had been killed before him, by a dynamite bomb. The assassination had been planned for the early part of 1887, but on March 1—six years to the day after the death of Alexander II—the plot was discovered and fifteen of the conspirators were arrested. Gnatowski had been among the few who escaped. Of those who were arrested, ten were sentenced to various terms and five were executed; among those who went to the scaffold was a twenty-one-year-old chemistry student named Alexander Ulyanov. Neither Gnatowski nor Cahan, at the moment they discussed this incident, could know that the death of Ulyanov would prove to have had major historical significance; for it was mainly this event that converted Ulyanov's younger brother, Vladimir, to the revolutionary cause, in which he would become known under the pseudonym of Lenin. This had happened in the same year that Cahan was converted to social democracy.

The conversation turned to old friends and associates, and Gnatowski informed Cahan that their old mentor from the Vilna *kruzhok,* Vladimir Sokolov, was now living in Paris too, and was married to Gnatowski's sister. Another comrade from the *kruzhok,* a Ukrainian Gentile named Kutcherevsky, had married a Jewish girl who used to attend their meetings in Vilna; Cahan remembered her well, having been struck at the time by her beauty. In general, the atmosphere of revolutionary comradeship that had meant so much to Cahan in Vilna seemed to be surviving here in Paris. Unlike his own circles in New York, where being Jewish had become a life's work, these Paris comrades continued to know no distinction between Jew and Gentile within the socialist brotherhood. It was as if they had somehow succeeded in transferring to Paris the comradely euphoria of a time of youth in Vilna that Cahan had thought was irrevocably gone. Certainly his own Vilna was no more: "What made the strongest impression upon me was what I heard [from Gnatowski] about Vilna. It seemed to me that everything had changed in the ten years I'd been away, that it was now a completely different city with different people in it. I have never had such a strong feeling of life passing me by as I did at that moment." Cahan took his leave of Gnatowski in a somber frame of mind.

The nostalgia of those few days in Paris continued to haunt him. The following summer he crossed the Atlantic again, but went only to London, to which he had been invited to give some lectures in Yiddish. While there, he not only paid another visit to Eleanor Marx and Edward Aveling, but also went to see Frederick Engels to discuss a Yiddish translation he proposed to do of the *Communist Manifesto*. But London did not trouble his spirit any more than it had done before. Rather, it was when he returned to the European continent in the summer of 1893, as a delegate to the Third Congress of the Second International, held that year in Zurich, that he felt the nostalgia of two years before reviving in him as strong as ever. The previous fall, his brother Isadore—fifteen years younger than he, and the only other child of Shakhne and Sarah Cahan—had come to the United States to settle there, and Cahan had only then realized how distant he had become from his parents, to whom he had not written since his earliest days in New York. He had resumed contact with them in the ensuing months, and had arranged to meet them in Europe this summer. Since it was still dangerous for Cahan to try returning to Russia, they held their get-together at a cousin's home in Vienna. It proved to be a week and a half of often almost unbearable tension. He and his parents—an elderly, frightened couple who looked upon him with mingled awe and suspicion—stood on opposite sides of a broad chasm of incomprehension which was bridged only now and then in instants of vivid recollection. For Cahan, the delight he felt each time in the first moment of recall turned quickly to pain at the ensuing realization of how irrecoverable the qualities of his past life had become. He fled Vienna quickly when the time was up, knowing that he would probably never see his parents again.

He went to Paris after the Congress and there wandered the streets restlessly, searching for some communion he could not define. "One of the small details that come to mind when I recall this visit of mine to Paris is bound up with a Russian-Jewish restaurant on a small street called Rue Flatters near Boulevard Port-Royal. I once went there to eat a Jewish meal. The crowd consisted of Jewish students, and the whole atmosphere of the place was Jewish-intellectual—not in the New York fashion, but more like back home. And anything that had the flavor of my old home had a magnetic effect upon me.

"A Jewish girl student sat in this restaurant talking to another girl, younger than she.

" 'You're being a bad girl,' she was saying to her, slowly shaking her head. Her eyes were half-closed, in an expression of half-joking, half-serious chiding.

"She didn't make a good impression on me, but her type was so saturated with the flavor of home that the picture has always remained in my mind."

Cahan visited his comrades from Vilna again on this trip, and found them to be much the same. Only one substantial change had taken place among them: Yeva Gordon was no longer there. She was now in America, married, not to her imprisoned Russian revolutionary, but to Philip Krantz.

Cahan's rivalry with Krantz had not really come to an end in those first successful weeks of the *Arbeiter Zeitung.* With the passage of time, Cahan had made his weight around the editorial office felt increasingly at Krantz's expense, and by the end of the first year of publication he had quietly pushed himself into an unofficial position of commanding leadership. In the latter part of 1891, the Jewish socialists found a way of accommodating this effective shift in power. A new social-democratic Yiddish monthly was in the offing; to be called *Die Zukunft* (not to be confused with Morris Winchevsky's short-lived London newspaper of the same name), it was envisioned as a journal that would devote more space than a weekly newspaper could to articles popularizing socialist theory and scientific knowledge. Since Krantz was something of a specialist in social and economic theory, it seemed quite natural that he should assume the direction of the new journal; this post could therefore be given to him in place of the editorship of the *Arbeiter Zeitung,* which Cahan would take. Krantz would not have to relinquish power at the newspaper entirely, either. Morris Hillkowitz had finished law school, and had decided to resign from his posts at the United Hebrew Trades and the *Arbeiter Zeitung* in order to go into full-time legal practice—this was when he changed his name officially to Hillquit; Krantz could therefore have the job as business manager of the *Arbeiter Zeitung* that Hillquit was vacating. By the end of the year, all these shifts had been accomplished, but not without a considerable increase in hostility between Krantz and Cahan.

In general, the *Arbeiter Zeitung* was well past the euphoria of its early days; success was exacting its toll in various ways. The newspaper now had a circulation of about ten thousand, and its principal sponsor, the United Hebrew Trades, had grown into a powerful federation comprising about a quarter of a million members; but, as in all cases of rapid institutional growth, the interlocking leadership of these two organizations had become bureaucratized to an unexpected degree. The visionary energies of their founders were now being replaced by the indispensable but unimaginative services of hard-working professionals. In the case of the newspaper, this process was bringing about a shift in real power from the *Arbeiter Zeitung* Publishing Association—the broad congress of union and socialist representatives which had been created at the paper's inception as the vehicle for the ideal of a collectively published socialist newspaper—to the Management Board, a permanent committee delegated by the Association to handle the newspaper's ordinary round of administrative detail. By the end of 1891, the Management Board had quietly taken on the power to make and not merely implement *Arbeiter Zeitung* policy, and had made itself into a self-enclosed, self-perpetuating establishment, which held the final word in the making or rejecting of appointments into its own midst. Most of the members of the Management Board also held high administrative positions in the United Hebrew Trades. The editorial staff of the *Arbeiter Zeitung* thus increasingly found themselves answerable to a bureaucratic will that was being imposed upon them from the outside.

At the time he assumed the official editorship of the *Arbeiter Zeitung,* Cahan still found the will of the Management Board to be nothing more than the kind of routine annoyance an editor must face when another organization holds his publication's purse strings. He felt he could deal with it. But Louis Miller saw the matter differently. This was a time of great emotional turmoil for Miller on a personal as well as on a professional level. In the past two years, both his brother—Cahan's old Vilna comrade, Leo Bandes—and his sister had died. He seems also to have been troubled around this time by some unhappy amorous experiences, for he was still a bachelor. All this exacerbated what was already, even in the best of times, an inordinate combative instinct on his part. As far as he was concerned, the regime of party hacks was not only squashing the poetry and moral vigor of the Jewish labor movement, but it was also showing the first signs of imposing policies that would prove to be destructive if they were not repudiated.

He made his views known in the March, 1892, issue of the newly inaugurated *Zukunft.* Although founded by the men who edited and wrote for the *Arbeiter Zeitung*—Cahan, Miller, Krantz, Hillquit, Zametkin, and others—*Die Zukunft* was not run by the *Arbeiter Zeitung* Publishing Association. Rather, it had been established as the organ of the Yiddish-speaking branches of the Socialist Labor Party throughout the country; on its publishing board, the representation of the UHT-dominated New York branch was therefore only a small minority. At this time, tensions were beginning to mount between what were, in effect, two major groupings among the Yiddish-speaking social democrats of America. One grouping was the growing New York bureaucratic establishment, centered in the leadership of the United Hebrew Trades and the Management Board of the *Arbeiter Zeitung;* the other was that of the relatively unruly and exuberant "provincial" Yiddish branches of the Socialist Labor Party in Boston, Philadelphia, Chicago, and other cities. *Die Zukunft* was the organ of the latter, in effect, and it was therefore from the outset a potential counterpoise to the mounting authoritarianism of the New York "clique," as Miller called them; more and more of the dissident intellectuals of New York—Miller, Cahan, and their friends—were therefore to be drawn to it as a place to make their dissenting views known on the side.

Miller's *Zukunft* article, published under a title ever poignant to offspring of the Russian revolutionary tradition, "What Is To Be Done?," hit Jewish socialist circles like a bombshell. It had been generally assumed that the pages of *Die Zukunft*—"a scientific-socialist monthly," as it was described on its cover—would not be used for intramural polemics. Miller was now already violating this canon of propriety in the magazine's second issue. But this was not the only thing that was surprising about Miller's article. For he did not stop short at denunciations of the party's present state of moral stagnation, division into factions, and submission to the rule of bureaucratic hacks at the expense of the influence of the intellectuals; he went on from there to caution against the perils of continuing the old crusade against the anarchists, a crusade that remained dear to the hearts of the ruling "clique" of the UHT. This must have given many readers pause. Less than a year before, Miller had still functioned as one of the chief bludgeons in the all-out war against the anarchists; what had happened since then to cause him to change his views so radically?

Chief among the things that had happened was that, though battles and skirmishes continued to take place, the anarchists had really already lost the war for domination over the Lower East Side. The *Freie Arbeiter Stimme* had just collapsed, and there were now signs of flagging convictions among some of the Jewish anarchist leadership (indeed, Roman Lewis, the head of the New York organization, was to announce his conversion to social democracy later that year). The Yiddish-speaking anarchists had been thoroughly routed in every area but one: the unions, where they were nevertheless now weakening. But the unions were precisely the area, Miller had come to realize, in which the old tactic of all-out war was not only not going to work but likely to produce adverse results. For the situation in the unions was complicated by the presence of a third combatant, a new rival to both the anarchists and the socialists which was clearly the most powerful of all: the American Federation of Labor.

Since its inception in 1886, the American Federation of Labor, under the leadership of Samuel Gompers, had risen to the brink of supremacy in the American labor movement. Gompers had achieved this success by aiming at the defeat of his organization's two major rivals for that supremacy—both of them predecessors to the AFL— the Knights of Labor and the Socialist Labor Party. By 1892 he had reduced the Knights of Labor to ineffectuality, and was now turning his guns full force upon the socialists. In this battle, Barondess' cloakmakers, the largest single labor union in New York City, was an important prize to be won. The AFL had already obtained the affiliation of many of the Jewish cloakmakers' unions in other cities, as well as that of most of the men's-clothing unions, those in New York included. The men's-clothing industry had come to be represented by a national organization created under the auspices of the AFL: the United Garment Workers. Gompers now hoped to create a similar national organization of women's-clothing workers that would be under his control, and that would win the allegiance of the New York cloakmakers away from the United Hebrew Trades.

These trends were already producing strange bedfellows. A master tactician, Gompers had quickly perceived that the anarchists in the cloakmakers' union—their own fortunes waning with the power of Barondess—were potential allies in his cause. They were ready to rally to his banner, not only because their hostility to the socialists made them willing to commit even this suicidal act in an effort to destroy the SLP, but because their own ideological commitments did not seem at this moment to be very far from those of Gompers. His "pure and simple unionism," with its stress on economic goals, had none of the overtones of violence that prevailed in the ideology of anarcho-syndicalism then gaining currency in Europe and America, but the two programs had a common aim of removing unionism from the political arena. Gompers did not scruple to cultivate the anarchists in the cloakmakers' union, despite his extreme distaste for revolutionaries. The social democrats in the union, partisans of the United Hebrew Trades, thus had begun finding themselves squeezed between the tactical pincers of the anarchists on the one hand and the Gompersists on the other.

Under these circumstances, one might have expected that Miller, as a social democrat, would have been inspired by this redoubled opposition to what was ostensibly his own cause to become more vehement than ever against the anarchists. But Miller not only knew that the AFL and not the anarchists was the force to be reckoned with, he also sensed that the mindless establishment which had emerged out of the United Hebrew Trades and the *Arbeiter Zeitung* Publishing Association was more of a threat to long-run social democratic aims than Gompers was. In a somewhat un-Russian fashion, he had concluded that a practical program for the improvement of the workers' lot, such as that presented by Gompers, took precedence over any effort to maintain socialist organizational and doctrinal purity merely for its own sake. America was, after all, ruled by a Constitution, not a Tsar, and one had to adapt one's political aims and tactics accordingly. Socialism remained a long-run ideal to be advocated through the press—the rightful arena of the intellectuals—and through political party organization. The unions, Miller had decided, were no longer its bailiwick. Miller's opposition to the rule of the bureaucrats had thus driven him into becoming the first Yankee-style "pragmatist" among the Jewish socialist intelligentsia of New York.

Miller's friend and fellow-Litvak Cahan was of a similarly practical turn of mind, but he was slower to come around to such a vehement formulation of his views. For him, in his position as editor of the *Arbeiter Zeitung*, practicality also meant being able to put up with the bureaucratic foibles of the UHT and the Management Board, where he had, incidentally, a number of ardent admirers. As for the unions, he had been deeply involved in their organizational affairs and internal squabbles, and was still not ready to renounce completely the ideal of socialist control over them. But his ability to adjust for the time being to trends in the socialist movement that he really liked no better than Miller did was above all due to a growing indifference that he felt at this time. The mood of nostalgia that had suddenly come upon him in the summer of 1891 was bearing down on him increasingly. The entire Lower East Side labor movement, his life's work for the better part of ten years, was beginning to seem unimportant to him. What was all this prosaic organizational work to a soul that had been bred on the gallantries of *Narodnaya Volya*? His writings in the *Arbeiter Zeitung* and *Die Zukunft* had been taking a more lyrical and reflective turn of late, and he was now thinking seriously of trying his hand at another sort of writing than that with which he had made his career thus far. Indeed, upon his return to New York from Europe in September, 1893, he was fairly certain that he would soon try to write a novel.

But it was precisely in the fall of 1893 that the brewing conflicts among Lower East Side socialists, and in the Socialist Labor Party in general, were coming to a head. An economic crisis had broken out that year, bringing widespread unemployment and labor unrest. The situation had given the anarchists a sudden new lease on life, and that spring, with some assistance from the American Federation of Labor, the *Freie Arbeiter Stimme* had resumed publication. The United Hebrew Trades had responded to this move by calling upon the Hebrew Typographical Union, one of its affiliates, to boycott the paper. But the strategy backfired: the anarchists succeeded in organizing a typographers' union of their own to print the newspaper, and the cloakmakers' union, still under Barondess' shaky leadership, retaliated against the attempted boycott by refusing to report its proceedings in the *Arbeiter Zeitung* any longer.

The socialists were not at all surprised at this new show of defiance by Barondess, but they were quite dismayed at the formation of a rival typographical union by the anarchists. The tactic of forming "dual unions" had been tried from time to time in the past on the Lower East Side—the socialists and the Knights of Labor had alternately used it against one another—but it had long since come to be regarded as forbidden behavior. This was a new outbreak of all-out war, however, and apparently anything was to be permitted. Deciding to retaliate in kind, the socialist faction in Barondess' Operators' and Cloak Makers' Union No. 1 broke away from that organization and formed a new union of their own, entirely loyal to the United Hebrew Trades. This new International Cloak Makers' Union immediately set out to organize other socialist "dual unions" like itself, in opposition to already existing anarchist and AFL unions. Entering into the men's-clothing industry, it created a rival organization to Gompers' United Garment Workers. By the beginning of 1894, the anarchists and Gompersists on the Lower East Side found themselves so besieged by the new socialist tactic of "dual unionism" that they formed a Yiddish coalition newspaper as a propaganda organ for their unions in opposition to the *Arbeiter Zeitung,* which they called the *Union Zeitung.*

But behind the scenes the *Arbeiter Zeitung* was itself becoming rent over the question of dual unionism. Cahan had become persuaded that the tactic was wrong, that it would only lead to the disruption and demoralization of the labor movement. He was beginning also to feel that the Socialist Labor Party in general was going in the wrong direction. He therefore was finally driven to ally himself openly with Miller in forming the core of an opposition within the ranks to the policies of the UHT and the Management Board. His position as editor of the *Arbeiter Zeitung* gave him important leverage in the emerging struggle, but it was by no means decisive, since he was now no longer free to do precisely what he wanted on its pages—he certainly could not express his disapproval of dual unionism there. Consequently, *Die Zukunft* increased in importance as a rallying point for the opposition represented by Cahan and Miller. The "provincial" branches that controlled this journal were growing more discontented than ever with the rule of the New York establishment. Many of them had never renounced the old ideal of "nonpartisanship" and continued to harbor anarchists in their midst; now many of them also had members who belonged to AFL unions. This growing resistance to the New York establishment expressed itself in the national convention of the Yiddish-speaking branches of the SLP that was held on January 1, 1894, in Newark, New Jersey, at which Cahan was elected to replace Philip Krantz as editor of *Die Zukunft*. Krantz, as antianarchist as ever, had been inclined to go along with the policies of the UHT leadership, and now he was paying for this. Cahan, who had pushed him out of an editorship for the second time in three years, must have seemed to him like some kind of pursuing demon.

Cahan's new-found zeal in the cause of opposition to the "clique" was not due to events in the Jewish labor movement alone. He had also been drawn to the struggle by something larger, for the crisis in the Lower East Side movement was proving to be simply a microcosm of a crisis that was taking place in the American labor movement in general. Even after his return to full-time Yiddish activity four years earlier, Cahan had not given up his affiliation with the "American" branch of the SLP in New York, and he continued to take pride in having what he considered to be a more intimate knowledge of American matters than any of his fellow Russian-Jewish intellectuals had. This pride was, in a sense, his practical, Litvak side taking revenge upon the world for the frustration of the romantic *Narodnik* within him; he would always exact this vengeance by seeking to demonstrate to everyone around him a superior grasp of the reality principle. In this case, he perceived a situation shaping up in American socialism in general about which he felt called upon to keep the Lower East Side enlightened, and so he rallied to the banner of Miller's vehemence.

In particular, what troubled Cahan was the personality of the man who had recently achieved the national leadership of the Socialist Labor Party, Daniel De Leon. Although he had been born in Curaçao (in 1852) to a family of Dutch Sephardic Jews and had obtained his education in Holland and Germany, De Leon was nevertheless a phenomenon of the trend toward Americanization and away from German domination that the SLP had been undergoing since about 1890. De Leon had settled in New York in 1874, taught school in Westchester, studied law at Columbia University, and then gone to Texas, where he set up a legal practice. This constituted a far more American kind of experience than most socialists were accustomed to at this time. Indeed, his first appearances as a radical were in purely American, somewhat pragmatic forms, outside the auspices of the SLP. He first made himself known in politics as a supporter of Henry George for mayor of New York in 1886—by then he had returned from Texas to take up a lectureship in international law at Columbia. In 1888, he joined the Knights of Labor. He did not become a socialist until after he had taken part in another utterly American phenomenon, the Bellamyite Nationalist Club of New York. These clubs had been formed under the inspiration of Edward Bellamy's Utopian novel, *Looking Backward,* for the purpose of discussing the prospects for the better world that it envisioned. The Bellamyite Nationalist movement became a focal point for the generating of socialist ideas, which were first beginning to gain currency at this time among Americans of radical leanings. Eventually, the New York Bellamyite Club converted itself into a branch of the Socialist Labor Party, but De Leon himself had become a socialist even before this happened. By 1891, he was already known throughout the country as a lecturer for the SLP, and he was the party's candidate for governor of New York that November.

Despite these mild beginnings, De Leon soon turned into a revolutionary Marxist of the most doctrinaire variety, and a hard-bitten combatant in socialist struggles. With the characteristic zeal of a convert, he came to stand for complete intolerance of all rivals to the SLP in the American labor movement. He favored all-out war against both the Knights of Labor and the AFL, and considered any effectively disruptive tactic to be legitimate, including that of dual unionism.

De Leon's personal qualities of stubbornness and intolerance of other points of view had aroused Cahan's dislike from the very first time they had met, back in the days of the Henry George campaign. De Leon and another man had shown up one day at a meeting of Yiddish-speaking radicals who had convened for the purpose of deciding whether the revolutionary cause would be served if they gave their support to Henry George. De Leon and his companion, also a Single Taxer, were insistent that the Jewish radicals should support not only Henry George, but his program as well. They "explained to us," wrote Cahan, who was present at the meeting, "that [they] had come from the Single Taxers, who wanted us to unite with them. I took the floor and said roughly the following: we are taking part in the Henry George campaign, not as Single Taxers, but as socialists, and we must remain apart. We cannot unite with any 'bourgeois' Henry Georgites."

When, in later years, De Leon turned up as a socialist, Cahan could not easily forget this early vehemence on his part for a bourgeois program. He felt that there were undertones of self-aggrandizement in De Leon's behavior. This feeling was borne out in 1890 on the occasion of De Leon's first official public lecture as a socialist, delivered at the Labor Lyceum of the "American" branch of the party, on East 4th Street. During the question period that followed the lecture, one of De Leon's points was contested by a man named Goldenstick; the audience was startled to hear the lecturer reply by addressing him as "Mr. Goldenstink." "One of the listeners," Cahan wrote, "an elderly American, thought he had simply made a mistake, and corrected him. De Leon laughed, and then proceeded to mispronounce the name again, this time in a different way." Cahan was shocked at this behavior, even though he had to admit that the lecture had been an excellent one. In the days that followed, he served as De Leon's escort through the headquarters of the various Jewish unions on the

Lower East Side. But there continued to be tension between Cahan and De Leon.

These feelings were aggravated during the winter of 1893–94, as Cahan emerged as a major opponent to the dual unionist policy that De Leon, now head of the SLP, strongly favored. Early in 1894, Mayor Gilroy of New York summoned to his office a group of labor leaders—including Gompers, De Leon, and Cahan—to discuss ways of dealing with the unemployment problem in the city. "In the conversation we had with the mayor," Cahan recorded, "De Leon endeavored to demonstrate to him that the working class was the creator of all the nation's wealth. To this Gilroy very politely replied that now was not the time to become involved in questions of political economy; rather, something practical had to be accomplished right here on the spot." Cahan thought that the mayor was right, despite the fact that Gilroy was a Tammany man and De Leon a socialist. Cahan said nothing about this in the mayor's office, but after the meeting he presented his views to De Leon. The latter responded angrily at first, but the two men became so absorbed in discussing the point that they decided to have lunch together. Over lunch, De Leon began demonstrating once again some of the flippancy that Cahan had first encountered in the "Goldenstink" episode. While talking about one of the Italian members of the SLP, a man named Merlino, De Leon took to referring to him as "Mambrino." This literary joke did not appeal to Cahan at all. At another point in the conversation, Cahan made reference to his old mentor, the Scottish-born workman-lecturer, Edward King.

"Oh, that faker!" De Leon exclaimed.

Cahan was astonished. "Comrade De Leon," he said, "I must ask you not to talk like that about a man for whom all of us in the Russian colony have the utmost respect. He is one of the finest men in New York."

"Ah, Cahan, Cahan!" he replied. "You're still very young."

This propensity on De Leon's part to aim barbs at decent men came to the fore again a short time later, in a way that was to shake the entire Socialist Labor Party. De Leon's target this time was a British-born writer and journalist named Charles Southern—a loyal and assiduous party worker, in the opinion of Cahan and many others. According to Cahan, the trouble had begun when Southern edited a small brochure about the party and inadvertently neglected to mention De Leon's name in it. Whether this was the source of De Leon's hostility or not, the fact remains that De Leon one day stood on a lecture platform and denounced a biography that Southern had written of Horace Greeley as being "antisocialist." He proceeded to attack Southern in a severe *ad hominem* fashion. In the question period, Cahan stood up to defend the book and its author, stressing in particular his view that attacks upon a man's person, whatever one might think of his writings, were unjustifiable. De Leon replied a few days later by publishing an article in the party newspaper, *The People*—of which he was the editor— roundly denouncing Southern, though never mentioning him by name. A party meeting was immediately called to discuss the question of ethics involved in De Leon's use of the pages of *The People* to denounce a high-ranking party worker. When Cahan's turn came to speak, he pointed out that De Leon himself, not long before his sudden onslaught against Southern, had once described the latter in conversation as being "true as steel."

"That's not true!" De Leon cried out from his seat, just a few rows behind Cahan's.

"If you say it isn't true," Cahan replied, wheeling around, "then you're a liar, and you know it!"

A commotion broke out in the hall. The chairman rapped his gavel for attention, and declared that Cahan's time was up. Then Meyer Gillis, one of the few members of the Management Board of the *Arbeiter Zeitung* who were not ardently pro–De Leon, proposed that Cahan's time be extended. This motion was passed, and Cahan went on to speak in glowing terms of Southern's character and service to the party.

His speech apparently had some effect, for, in a subsequent party meeting on the same question, De Leon backtracked a little and even tried at one point to persuade the members that the article in question, which had mentioned no names, was not about Southern at all. Nobody believed him. But De Leon remained a magnetic personality, and the victories he was winning at this time for the socialist movement brought him the continuing loyalty of the great majority of party members. The controversy over the article in *The People* fell into abeyance, and De Leon's badgering of Southern continued. Southern eventually quit the party.

Cahan was now utterly convinced that it was his mission to combat De Leon's influence in the SLP in general, and in the Jewish labor movement in particular. But this was the moment when De Leon's influence was at its height as much among the Jewish party workers as within the "American" branches of the SLP. De Leon's Jewish origins, combined with the utterly "American" qualities that he seemed to exemplify in their eyes, persuaded many Jewish socialists that he was the man destined to lead them to American victories. He had no group of followers anywhere in the movement more loyal than the "clique" that controlled the United Hebrew Trades and the Management Board of the *Arbeiter Zeitung*. The opposition to the "clique" that Louis Miller had initiated, largely on the basis of matters purely within the Jewish movement, was now reinforced by Cahan's feud with De Leon.

At this point in the struggle, some of the other intellectuals on the staff of the *Arbeiter Zeitung* were still undecided as to which side to take. Benjamin Feigenbaum, for example, a talented writer of articles popularizing history, was himself a recent convert from anarchism—he had been with the anarchist faction of the *Arbeiter Freind* in London—and was therefore still zealous about the struggle against the anarchists that De Leonism stood for on the Lower East Side. Michael Zametkin, Cahan's and Miller's old comrade of the lecture platform, also found it hard to relinquish the old ideal of socialist control of the unions. But these men were at least sympathetic to the claims of Cahan and Miller; Philip Krantz was something else again. Still smarting from his defeats at Cahan's hands, Krantz continued to uphold the banner of relentless opposition to all of socialism's rivals; this, after all, was the kind of socialist zeal, directed against the anarchists on the *Arbeiter Freind,* that had made him prominent in London and brought him to New York.

Krantz was soon able to find his tactical position in the intramural conflict that was shaping up. The appearance of the anarchist-AFL *Union Zeitung* at the beginning of 1894 persuaded the Management Board of the *Arbeiter Zeitung* that the time had come to move into a new area of journalistic activity. That undying Lower East Side institution, Kasriel Sarasohn's *Tageblatt,* was now a flourishing daily newspaper, with a circulation considerably larger than that of the *Arbeiter Zeitung.* The Yiddish labor press could no longer safely remain out of the daily field, and the Management Board accordingly began drawing up plans for a newspaper to be called the *Abend Blatt* ("Evening Paper").

Since Cahan's talents as an editor were universally acknowledged, the Management Board somewhat reluctantly offered the editorship of the proposed daily to the man who had once been their protégé and now was the foremost critic of their policies. It was clear that they meant to harness his talent for the new project without allowing any outlet for his ideas, and for this reason Cahan hesitated to accept the post. Besides, he was busy enough already: in addition to his editing chores at the *Arbeiter Zeitung* and *Die Zukunft,* his normal round of lecturing and organizing activities, and his continuing work as an English teacher for immigrants in evening school—still his most reliable source of income—he was beginning seriously to write belles-lettres. The *Arbeiter Zeitung* was at this time carrying the installments of a kind of didactic novel or extended moral fable he had written, called *How Raphael Na'aritzokh Became a Socialist.* Also, *Die Zukunft* was carrying long essays in literary criticism by him, and he was now getting to work trying to write fiction in English. These literary occupations were becoming far more important to him than the world of constant backbiting that was the Jewish labor movement. Cahan therefore hesitated at the *Abend Blatt* offer, although, recognizing its importance, he did not mean to reject it out of hand. But this moment of hesitation was all that was needed by those on the Management Board who had been most wary of offering him the job in the first place; they thereupon persuaded the Board to offer it to Krantz, who accepted it.

It was while Krantz was preparing to go to press with his first issue in the middle of October that word came of Morris Winchevsky's impending arrival in New York. By this time Winchevsky was a regular contributor to both the *Arbeiter Zeitung* and *Die Zukunft*, and his feuilleton series, "Scrambled Thoughts of a Mad Philosopher," had become perhaps the most popular feature in Yiddish journalism. Winchevsky—who gave the impression that he was still the old, somewhat naive apostle of socialist unity at all costs—was an important prize to be won, and Krantz wasted no time about making use of the talents of his erstwhile colleague. Landing in New York on October 13, Winchevsky was warmly greeted by a delegation of American Jewish socialists, and was handed a ticket for a performance of an important Yiddish play that was to take place in one of the Bowery theaters that very evening. The first issue of the *Abend Blatt*, which appeared on the afternoon of October 14, was thus able to feature a piece of drama criticism by Winchevsky.

But despite this initial show of graciousness on his part, Winchevsky was not to be won over so easily to the cause of Krantz and the Management Board. The "clique" was, after all, a force determined to ferret out and purge anarchists in the labor movement, and Winchevsky, though no anarchist himself, was still sentimentally attached to whatever remained of the old anarchist-socialist alliance. Furthermore, he could not forget Krantz's role in provoking a crisis between the anarchists and the social democrats at the old *Arbeiter Freind*, and was in particular still unable to forgive his old disciple's coinage of the term *parveh lokshen* to describe "nonpartisanship." As Winchevsky saw it, De Leon was now also a more extreme version of what he had long disliked about Krantz. In a matter of weeks, Winchevsky became an outspoken ally to the cause of Cahan and Miller.

Toward the end of the year, Winchevsky received an invitation from the Yiddish-speaking socialists of Boston to come and edit a proposed newspaper of their own. This was attractive; the Boston group had been foremost among the "provincial" branches in upholding the old ideal of "nonpartisanship"—anarchists and social democrats both belonged to the organization—and Winchevsky felt the pull of nostalgia toward this job. It would be gratifying to have his own newspaper far from the scene of factional strife that the Lower East Side had become. Furthermore, his wife and children were soon to arrive from London, and he had not yet worked out the matter of steady employment; the Boston offer would be a solution in this respect, too. But the Sixth Congress of the Yiddish-speaking sections of the SLP, which happened to be held in Boston that year, was at first opposed to the project. The majority at the Congress maintained that the Boston comrades would only add to the general atmosphere of disunity if they put out their own newspaper. The Boston delegates then offered a compromise: they proposed that their paper would not be an official journal of opinion in the manner of the *Arbeiter Zeitung,* but would be a purely "educational organ," stressing literature and other cultural matters, and presenting no opposition to established SLP policies. On this basis, the Congress gave its consent to the project.

Winchevsky moved to Boston, and the first issue of the new journal was put out on May 3, 1895. It was called *Der Emmes* ("The Truth"), a name rich with connotations for Winchevsky, since it was the Yiddish form of the name of the newspaper put out by his lamented friend Aaron Lieberman nearly two decades before. The name reflected the editor's personality in another way, too: it was utterly Yiddish, a repudiation of the *Deitshmerish* that was still normally placed over mastheads at this time. Indeed, Winchevsky seemed to feel that he had to reassure his readers of the German meaning of the title, for he placed the words *Die Wahrheit* (in Roman letters) in one corner of the masthead. Under the title stood the disclaimer that had enabled the paper to win the consent of the Yiddish-speaking branches at large: "A Weekly Family Paper for Literature and Enlightenment."

But Winchevsky soon showed that he was not prepared to live up to this innocent claim. In the August 19 issue he published an editorial that gave vent to the anger and despair he had felt at the condition of the socialist movement in America from the moment he arrived in the country. Entitled *Foyl oder Tzugefoylt?* ("Putrid or Putrefying?"), it was an excoriation of the De Leonists above all. Describing America as a country that had "many socialists but little socialism," Winchevsky laid the blame for this at the door of De Leon and his followers, whom he said were the creators of factional strife.

By this time, the quarrel between the De Leonists and anti-De Leonists in the SLP in general and the corresponding quarrel between the "clique" and the opposition in the Yiddish branches were fully two years old; but, until this moment, it had never been so openly alluded to in print. The revered "Grandfather" of the Yiddish-speaking intelligentsia, beloved all the more because of the widely held opinion that he was naive and unworldly to an extreme, had forced the issue at last; from now on, the old behind-the-scenes dispute was to be an open, all-out battle. Krantz promptly replied to Winchevsky in an editorial in the *Abend Blatt*, saying that such emotional reactions would only endanger the unity of socialism.

As the struggle thus entered a new phase, Cahan once again felt a strong urge to detach himself from it and from the Jewish labor movement in general. By now he had published two short stories in an American periodical, and he was starting on a novel in English; his work had already come to the attention of William Dean Howells, from whom he was receiving encouragement. He was seized by the compulsive zeal he had always felt for some exciting new enterprise, and he yearned to be able to spend all his time writing fiction. But, as if for spite, he had just become even more the principal rallying point for the opposition than he ever had been before; for Louis Miller, normally his partner in bearing the burden of dissidence, had just left on an extended trip to Europe as a way of dealing with his oppressive personal problems of the moment. Besides, the whole De Leon question, to which Cahan continued to feel a special calling, was at this moment becoming more acute than ever.

De Leon was bringing all the strife in the American labor movement to a head over the issue of "dual unionism." For a time, in the latter part of 1894, the crisis over this issue in the cloakmaking industry seemed to have found a peaceful resolution. Driven by the conditions of depression, the two opposing cloakmakers' unions— Barondess' original one, now under AFL control, and the De Leonist one that had been formed in opposition to it—had come together in a coalition. But later that fall Barondess had impulsively instigated a general strike in a last attempt to assert that he was still something more than a mere figurehead, and the result was a shattering of the coalition, and a division not into two, but into three rival cloakmakers' organizations; for now the old cloakmakers' union broke up into its Barondessist (anarchist) and AFL factions. The three fragments, the heirs to what had been the most splendid labor organization on the Lower East Side only four years before, did not last very long. The AFL splinter organization and the De Leonist union both collapsed before the end of 1895; the Barondessist group managed to last until the spring of 1896, even though Barondess himself had resigned a year earlier, never again to hold an official union position. Ultimately, the phoenix to rise from these ashes of unionism in the women's-garment industry would be an AFL organization.

De Leon had first tried to retrench diminishing SLP strength in the labor movement by resorting to a strategy of frontal attack.

Cultivating delegate strength at the AFL convention of 1894, he succeeded in having Gompers defeated for the presidency that year, for the first time since the Federation had been founded. But the following year Gompers regained the office—he would then hold it continuously for the rest of his life—and De Leon retreated and turned his attack upon the moribund Knights of Labor; here, too, he failed to gain control. His response to these defeats was to create, in December, 1895, the Socialist Trade and Labor Alliance, the SLP's bid to rival the AFL as a national labor federation. De Leon was determined to see the Socialist Trade and Labor Alliance reach into every AFL-dominated shop in the country and bring a rival union into being. The policy of dual unionism was now being put into operation more vigorously than ever before.

In the Jewish labor movement, the response to De Leon's renewed offensive was vivid. The Seventh Congress of the Yiddish-speaking branches of the SLP, which convened in New York that December 31, became the scene of the first live, public confrontation between the De Leonist "clique" and its opponents. The opposition was determined to gain reforms in the organizational structure of the Jewish labor movement that would give greater voice to the critics of De Leon's policies. They demanded that the *Arbeiter Zeitung* and the *Abend Blatt* be removed from the control, not only of the Management Board, but of the *Arbeiter Zeitung* Publishing Association in general, and be placed under the direct authority of the Yiddish-speaking branches of the SLP, like *Die Zukunft*. They also wanted the policy of the *Abend Blatt* to be less sectarian than it now was—to be more tolerant, in other words, of anarchism, Gompersism, and other labor-movement heresies. And above all, they wanted Philip Krantz to be removed from its editorship. Cahan's name was not explicitly stated in the context of these demands, but it was understood that he was the opposition's candidate to replace Krantz—to replace Krantz once again! The dissidents also made clear their wholehearted disapproval of the Socialist Trade and Labor Alliance.

The De Leonists did not have the strength to squash this rebellion against their authority, but they were able to divert it into a compromise: the Congress adjourned with an agreement to establish a Board of Arbitration, which would examine the issues in the dispute and make recommendations. The Board that was created was made up entirely of non-Yiddish-speaking leaders of the SLP, and while it included in its midst such an eminently fair-minded person as Alexander Jonas, still editor of the *Volks Zeitung;* its chairman turned out to be, unfortunately for the dissenters, De Leon himself! In the January 17 issue of *Der Emmes,* which appeared while the Board was deliberating, Winchevsky published an editorial calling into question the representativeness of such a group. He rightly sensed the danger to his own position, for his little enclave of power in Boston had become a major annoyance to the De Leonists. Indeed, this proved to be the final issue of *Der Emmes;* for one of the Board's recommendations was that, in the interest of party unity, Winchevsky's paper cease publication immediately. To Winchevsky's dismay, the Board proposed that he become instead a staff member of the *Abend Blatt,* which was to continue under Krantz's editorship, according to the Board's decision. As for the *Arbeiter Zeitung,* it was to be turned into a weekly supplement of the *Abend Blatt;* the Board conceded that Cahan should remain its editor, "even though he is nervous and extremely temperamental."

Upon hearing the Board's recommendations, Cahan promptly resigned from the editorship of the *Arbeiter Zeitung.* Talk was now under way among the opposition of forming a separate, independent socialist newspaper; after all, their ranks included, in Cahan and Winchevsky, two of the greatest talents in Yiddish journalism. Cahan was still uncertain whether to take all that had happened as a sign that he should quit the battlefield altogether. He was putting the finishing touches on his first novel, which was to be published that summer. Requests from English-language journals to contribute stories were coming in. As for Yiddish writing, his recent inclination to do work of a more literary sort made his association with *Die Zukunft*—which, under his editorship, had gradually shifted its emphasis from popular science and history to serious literary criticism—more satisfying than any further involvements he might take on in the field of Yiddish newspaper work. Shying away from any further direct and personal participation in the battle over the New York Yiddish press for the moment, he settled for composing a reflective essay on the character of the Management Board of the *Arbeiter Zeitung* Publishing Association, which he published in the July issue of *Die Zukunft*. In it, he characterized the Management Board as a "House of Lords" and called for a truly democratic "House of Commons" to replace it.

But this was merely a random shot in what seemed to be a general state of truce which set in that summer. Miller had finally returned from Europe, but, still melancholy, he had no taste for combat. He now became the chief apostle of peace and conciliation, and in a short time was able to work out a compromise arrangement in the running of the Yiddish press. He persuaded the Management Board to consider new nominees from among the opposition to be appointed to the *Arbeiter Zeitung* Publishing Association and into its own midst, and to allow both sides to have a voice in the *Abend Blatt,* in an open forum of opinion that would appear as a regular department. In exchange for these concessions, Winchevsky, who had grudgingly remained aloof from the *Abend Blatt* despite the decision of the Board of Arbitration in January that he should work there, would begin to write for the paper. Cahan also agreed to contribute a regular column to the Sunday supplement of the *Abend Blatt*. In general, Cahan, Winchevsky, and Miller were to be granted *de facto* control of the Sunday supplement (which now no longer bore the name *Arbeiter Zeitung*).

This arrangement brought a summer of peace, but not much more. Winchevsky remained difficult to handle at the *Abend Blatt,* and Cahan never even entered the office, sending his weekly column and other contributions by messenger. De Leon's influence over the paper's ruling elements grew still stronger and more obnoxious to the opposition. He seemed more determined than ever to rule the SLP in an authoritarian fashion and enforce a program of a purely radical-revolutionary nature. As for Miller, the sparkplug of the opposition, he suddenly found his fury again that fall. A frequent guest at the apartment of Abraham and Anna Cahan, he met there one evening a friend of Anna's named Helena Rabinovich. A romance developed between them; he proposed marriage, and she accepted. His general state of melancholy quickly vanished. He became the militant oppositionist once again, and was soon filling the pages of *Die Zukunft* with criticisms of the sorry state into which American socialism had fallen.

The annual meeting of the Publishing Association was scheduled for January 7, and as that date approached, Miller prepared a coup. In compliance with the compromise agreements he had arranged the previous summer, the Association was due to elect a number of additional members. Miller planned to enter a large slate of his own; he believed his candidates would be elected, since the opposition was now thought to have enough adherents and sympathizers in the Association to form a slight majority. Then, once his nominees were elected, the Association would move on to its annual vote upon the editorship of the *Abend Blatt*—and Cahan would be entered for an easy victory over Krantz.

When the meeting took place, however, the "clique" proved to be in firm control of the proceedings. The De Leonist chairman appointed three secretaries to record all votes, two of them loyal to the "clique." In poll after poll, the two secretaries loyal to the "clique" counted a slight majority for the De Leonists, while the third, Benjamin Feigenbaum, counted a majority for the opposition. In each case, the victory went to the "clique," who then proceeded to organize on the meeting floor a campaign to disqualify Miller's slate of nominees. The arguments grew fierce and loud, nearly turning into physical violence. Suddenly Miller raised his voice above the din, shouting: "Comrades, come!," and the entire opposition strode out of the hall.

There was no longer any thought of trying to seek reform from within. Gathering together in a nearby meeting hall, Miller, Cahan, Winchevsky, and their allies immediately began laying plans for the creation of a new Yiddish labor newspaper. A meeting was called, for January 30, of all socialist and union leaders who identified with the opposition. At that January 30 meeting, a new Press Association was created, one that was largely sponsored by unions and other labor organizations relatively free of the influence of the United Hebrew Trades; many AFL affiliates were among them. A fund-raising program was mapped out, and a name was given to the proposed newspaper: *Vorwärts* ("Forward"), the name of the great Social Democratic newspaper of Berlin. Miller had proposed this name and it had been accepted enthusiastically; Cahan thought it was too German, but he yielded to the opinion of the majority. Cahan was appointed editor, and plans were laid to begin publication in April.

# CHAPTER 8

# HOW A PUBLICIST BECAME
# A MAN OF LETTERS

A rabbinical-looking man of thirty, who sat with the back of his chair tilted against his sewing-machine, was intent upon an English newspaper. Every little while he would remove it from his eyes—showing a dyspeptic face fringed with a thin growth of dark beard—to consult the cumbrous dictionary on his knees. Two young lads, one seated on the frame of the next machine and the other standing, were boasting to one another of their respective intimacies with the leading actors of the Jewish stage. The board of a third machine, in a corner of the same wall, supported an open copy of a socialist magazine in Yiddish, over which a cadaverous young man absorbedly swayed to and fro droning in the Talmudical intonation.
—ABRAHAM CAHAN, *Yekl, A Tale of the New York Ghetto*

THE ELEMENTS IN ABRAHAM CAHAN'S SPIRIT THAT CAUSED HIM to embark upon a career as a writer of fiction comparatively late in life had already found expression in writing during his earliest years as a publicist and journalist in New York, but in an undeveloped and fragmented form. There were incipient literary elements in his first contributions to the New York *Sun* and other English-language newspapers as far back as 1883; these were descriptions of life in New York's Jewish quarter, which is essentially what his first works of serious fiction were to be a dozen years later. But these early writings were just general sketches of scenes, containing no narrative elements or character descriptions. At that time, Cahan did not even consider himself to be interested in the conventional stuff of novels, things like personal sentiments or amorous relationships, as material for literature. Weaned upon such books as Chernyshevsky's *What Is to Be Done?*, he considered the end of literature to be essentially social; if his passion for Tolstoy also reached out, unconsciously at least, to elements other than the didactic in the latter's work, he did not yet, in the eighties, accord them serious recognition. At best, his enjoyment of literary refinements of the sensibility in this period was a casual, after-dinner pleasure, indulged in at his wife's behest.

If Cahan, in the eighties, had loftier literary aspirations than journalism could satisfy, they expressed themselves in a desire to be a socialist theoretician. Ideological differences aside, Herbert Spencer provided the model of the kind of writing he most wanted to do. In the full grip of the philosophical materialism that was then in force in both Europe and America, especially among Marxists, Cahan thought he had discovered in himself a passion for science. His notion of science was, to be sure, of a rather literary sort, his interest being less in the content of the various scientific disciplines than in the broadly philosophical question of the relationship between the social reality and the material nature of things—one of the central preoccupations of nineteenth-century social theory. Like many of his greater predecessors in this field, young Cahan was convinced that patient inquiry would discover a key to social behavior that applied equally to ants, primitive societies, and the chaotic sophistication of life in a city like New York. It was in this frame of mind that he hoped to write a book working out a philosophical synthesis of Marxism and Darwinism.

His first significant essay on literature, delivered as a lecture for the cultural circle of the Socialist Labor Party in New York, and then printed in the March 15, 1889, issue of the party organ, the *Workmen's Advocate*, came out of these philosophical concerns. Entitled "Realism," it presents its arguments in the excessively lofty tone of a man who clearly feels he must struggle to prove his right to talk on such a subject. "Man," it begins in the most general terms, "is an inquiring, social, imitating creature." Cahan's subject is going to be the third, the imitative aspect of Man's nature, but in an academic flourish, he takes a summary look at the first two faculties mentioned: "The inquiring impulse springs from thought," he says, and "sociality is due to the instinct of self-preservation, which causes us to unite with our fellow men in joint war upon the rest of creation, and which grows, according to Herbert Spencer, into hereditary habit, increasing through the survival of the fittest." This touch of social Darwinism is followed by a physiological definition of the sources of art: "The imitating activity seems to me to be stimulated by the reflective or imitative character of our sensations. . . . For sensation is nothing else than the mental counterpart of our nature." This forms the point of departure for the main part of the essay, which is about art and literature.

Although Cahan's talents were not those of a philosopher, there are nonetheless touches here of fairly sophisticated philosophical argument. Cahan seems to be asserting that sensations are a form of cognition and not merely reflections upon a passive sensibility—this was an idea not yet widely in vogue, and its presence here suggests that he had been reading William James. By formulating the nature of sensations in this way, Cahan is able to free his theory of realism from notions of mere photographic representation: "The end of imitative activity," he goes on to say, "is not so much to copy the outside nature as to stimulate the sensations which it evokes in us." This is putting it rather broadly, especially for a man whose personal tastes in literature and painting did, in fact, lean to the photographic; indeed, one is led to wonder if such a statement necessarily constitutes an argument for "realism" at all. But Cahan was, of course, not speaking in a cultural context in which any significant school of non-representational art yet existed; his claims in favor of "realism" were being made against something else altogether. This becomes clear when, further on, he repudiates the "fallacious proposition that the sole end of art is to afford pleasure and has therefore to be limited to the province of the beautiful." Cahan was writing these words during a period of extreme aestheticism in the arts, and it was against this trend that he was defining his concept of "realism." His arguments were pertinent in New York above all, where there was not even a Swinburne or a Wilde to exemplify the trend, but only the merest Victorian chromo-sentimentality.

For Cahan, whose sensibility owed its primary allegiance to the printed word, questions of artistic form were not so important as those of subject matter. Among American novelists, he liked both William Dean Howells and Henry James, but he liked Howells better, for being the more "socially conscious" author. James' celebrated innovations of form and style meant nothing to him. As a Russian realist *cum* Yankee journalist, he was inclined to see only one proper way of telling a story: the most straightforward one. It was therefore quite in keeping with his views that his favorite painter, the chosen exemplar for this essay on "realism" in the plastic arts, was the Russian Vassily Vereshchagin, a painter of subjects of social import in a photographic style. There had recently been a Vereshchagin exhibition in New York, and Cahan and his wife had gone to see it several times. Essentially a romantic, Vereshchagin had begun his career traveling through Russian Central Asia and the Middle East, drawing and painting the exotic scenes and personalities he encountered. This passion for turbans and minarets later found social significance with the outbreak of the Russo-Turkish War in 1877. Vereshchagin went to the front, and from the sketches he made there he painted scenes of battles and of wounded soldiers that became celebrated as antiwar documents. His interest in exotic types became focused upon such suffering Near Eastern minorities as Serbs and Jews, and his paintings of them came to be seen as statements of social and political principles. When he visited the United States on the occasion of his first New York exhibition in 1888, he painted American Negroes. "Having a greater susceptibility for the sufferings of the oppressed classes than for anything else," Cahan writes in this essay, "Vereshchagin takes more delight in painting gibbets and hospitals than he derives from his landscapes." (The demand for "beautiful landscapes" had come to symbolize the artistic tastes of the New York bourgeoisie at this time.)

It seems more than an accident of personal taste that Cahan, in many ways so Russian in sensibility, goes on from here to cite Tolstoy as his ideal model of a novelist; for, setting aside the immense difference in quality between the works of Tolstoy and those of Vereshchagin, the two artists had remarkably similar—and significantly Russian—qualities of the sensibility. The two traveled a similar path—along the Black Sea littoral, as it were—from youthful adventurous romanticism to mature social concern, passing through a common preoccupation with the problems of war (it is noteworthy that Vereschagin ultimately went on to do a series of paintings illustrating *War and Peace*). It might even be possible to say that the sensibility of Vereshchagin was that of Tolstoy applied to painting, for it is conceivable that a vision which achieves greatness in one medium may only achieve mediocrity in another. Tolstoy's epic realism was better suited to literature than to painting at that moment in the history of Russian culture, which was a moment of extreme literalism in the arts. Cahan points up this quality when he says in his essay: "And yet Tolstoy, the greatest of realists, affords us more pleasure by the pedantic truthfulness and impartiality to nature than any of the polished and sifted novels which are especially devoted to the delight of the reader." Pedantic truthfulness, indeed; this scarcely even seems a compliment to us today. It is the outlook of "socialist realism," which was shared, *mutatis mutandis,* by Tolstoy, Vereshchagin, and Cahan.

The final compliments of the essay are reserved for William Dean Howells, the foremost American representative, in Cahan's opinion, of the realist tradition. "Mr. Howells is not a socialist," Cahan writes, "and yet, unconsciously, free from the pressure of partisan passion, merely at the bidding of his realist instinct, he accentuates in his works . . . and brings into high relief a fact in American life which lays bare the fictitiousness of American equality." Cahan thus uses Howells as another example of his thesis that a genuinely realistic perception of the world leads inevitably, as with Tolstoy and Vereshchagin, to an art of social protest—in other words, in Cahan's view, to an argument in favor of socialism. "The same public-spirited American citizen," he points out, "who sets down critical socialism for the cranky babble of foreigners 'unacquainted with our institutions' takes pride in the great American novelist, whose pen makes a more dangerous assault on the present system than the most eloquent speeches of the most rabid 'foreign socialist.'" This was to prove to be a prophetic insight on Cahan's part, for Howells went on to become a professed socialist a few years later. The essay ends with a vision of realism and socialism marching hand-in-hand "with gigantic strides on the path of progress and happiness."

The general outlines of this essay suggest the Marxian literary critic that Cahan was eventually to become—"the critique of good novels," he was to write a few years later, "is a social as well as a literary study"—but they indicate little of the budding novelist. Indeed, they suggest the outlook of someone more committed to theorizing about fiction than to writing it. Nor do any of his other published writings at this time suggest he was preparing to become a novelist. His only sustained work in the vein of creative realism thus far was his journalism. Yet this was not at all insignificant, for newspaper writing was at that time a more creative endeavor than it has usually been since, for better or for worse. Indeed, in the pragmatic atmosphere of late-nineteenth-century America, the journalist's "true-life" account of what happened tended to play the role that fiction played in other cultures. "Someone has said that newspapers are the characteristic literature of Americans," Samuel Gompers wrote. Perhaps a mute, inglorious Tolstoy or two really was buried somewhere in those clattering editorial offices, his vision squeezed under the pressure of deadlines and chopped up into daily fragments of "copy." This atmosphere rarely produced literature by any aesthetic criteria, but it unquestionably produced something closer to Cahan's Russo-Yankee notion of "realism" than most American novels did at the time.

In the easygoing, experimental atmosphere of the *Arbeiter Zeitung,* where Cahan was able to dabble in an immense variety of literary genres—including even poetry—under different pseudonyms, it was inevitable that he should try his hand one day at writing a formal work of fiction. Informally, of course, he had already tried out all the various elements of a finished work of fiction, scattering them through his different writings. In particular, he had done this in his many feuilletons—that most intimate, direct, and flexible of literary forms, the most characteristic one in Yiddish journalism. The essence of the Yiddish feuilleton was always to make a point—very often a socialist one—by plunging into the heart of a situation and conveying it to the reader through anecdote and free-style reflection. The most characteristic feuilleton was told in the first person, the author being clearly one and the same with the protagonist; sometimes, however, the protagonist might be some third person, real or imagined. Very often, then, a feuilleton became almost imperceptibly a short story.

During the *Arbeiter Zeitung*'s first year, this transition was beginning to happen with growing frequency in Cahan's weekly *Sidra,* the most feuilleton-like of his regular features. In January, 1891, for example, *Der Proletarishker Maggid* takes off one day from the text, "I am Joseph your brother, whom ye sold into Egypt," into reflections upon the irony of the fact that rich and poor, masters and slaves, can exist among the same people—Jewish sweatshop owners and Jewish workers are the example here—and even sometimes within the same family. This leads to a more extended story than was usually found in the maggid's discourses. It tells of a rich man who gives some money every day to a certain beggar woman in the street, but who one day arrives at the spot to learn that she has died; his look of great anguish upon hearing this news gives rise to the rumor, in the days that follow, that he is, in fact, the old woman's son. This story was undoubtedly either factual or a piece of authentic Lower East Side folklore, and Cahan's desire to tell it clearly came out of his old instinct to be a chronicler of life in the Jewish quarter. But now, unlike in his old sketches for the New York *Sun,* specific characters and lines of dramatic action were beginning to come to the center of the stage. The instincts of a writer of "realistic" fiction were now all at play.

It was later that year, in June, that Cahan took the final step into writing a formal piece of fiction. This was an unlikely moment in some respects, for he was busier with his labor-movement activities than he had ever been before. He was preparing to take up his temporary post as a replacement for Joseph Barondess—then heading for prison—in charge of the cloakmakers' union, and he was getting ready to leave for Europe as a delegate to the Second International. But it is probably just because the practical side of his life had become so full that his inner, contemplative side, stimulated by all this activity, began to yearn for expression. Cahan was the sort of man whose productivity in one area of activity increases under the stimulus of several activities at once. Furthermore, the highly informal, often slapdash, quality of Yiddish journalism was helpful here; for if Cahan felt stimulated to write a short story, he nevertheless did not have the time or the inclination to polish it—nor did he have to for the *Arbeiter Zeitung,* as he well knew. Indeed, when he placed the first installment of his story in the June 5 issue in the column of *Der Proletarishker Maggid,* under the heading "Instead of a *Sidra,*" he had not yet even finished writing it. He assumed it would be finished in the second installment; instead, it went on for five issues.

Like Cahan's feuilletons, the story seems to be based on a real incident. Entitled "Mottke Arbel and His Romance" (*roman,* in Yiddish, means both "romance" and "novel"), it tells the story of a young immigrant whose low social origins—in the old country he was a cart driver, or *balagula,* a word which is also virtually a synonym for "crude person"—are reflected in his boorish manners. The nickname *arbel,* which means "sleeve," was given him in honor of that part of his clothing to which he usually assigned the functions of a handkerchief. As a peddler in New York, he has begun to accumulate the beginnings of a personal fortune, and is now, at the age of twenty-six, eager to find a store to buy and a woman to marry. One day he learns that his former employer back in the Lithuanian *shtetl* of Khropovetz (this fictitious place name suggests snoring) has fallen upon hard times, and that the latter's daughter Hannah, whom Mottke had in the old days adored with all the longing that social inaccessibility can provoke, is still unmarried and now dowerless at the age of twenty-five. Mottke obtains the services of a matchmaker from Khropovetz who now lives in New York, and sends an offer of marriage to Hannah; the terms include steamship passage to New York for both her and her father. Back in Khropovetz, Hannah receives the offer with revulsion; her father, however, after much deliberation, reluctantly accepts. A few weeks later, Mottke is seen awaiting them at the pier. Hannah appears walking arm-in-arm from the ship with a young man, whom she introduces to the stunned Mottke as her fiancé. They had met on the boat, and their romance had blossomed under "the moon, which is the best matchmaker of all, especially on board ship." The young man is an intellectual, a gymnasium graduate who plans to study law in America.

This story might have been nothing more than a crude anti-capitalist morality tale, were it not for the fact that its parvenu protagonist comes across with a certain pathos: he is shy and bumbling, and "he had never, in his whole life, been acquainted with ladies." Also, the story's descriptions of Lower East Side immigrant life—Cahan's first literary specialty—are quite good, especially in the detailed rendering of the anatomy of the peddling career. Cahan was a shrewd and sensitive observer, whatever his ideological predispositions. These qualities came through when Cahan read the story aloud in Russian one evening, painstakingly translating it sentence by sentence, to an older friend whose literary opinions he greatly respected, a non-Jewish exiled Russian revolutionary named Zhuk. Greatly impressed, Zhuk said that though this particular story could not be considered a serious literary work, it showed talent, and he urged Cahan to continue writing. He suggested that Cahan read Chekhov, then still a relatively new name on the literary scene. Cahan obtained a volume of Chekhov's stories and read it with growing astonishment; these were not stories in the traditional sense at all, but carefully drawn scenes from life. He saw them as a new advance in "realism," and also as something closer than he had ever imagined fiction could be to what he had been doing all along, another link between his now converging notions of feuilleton and of short story. He began rereading the great Russian authors with a new eye, that of an aspiring writer. A chance occurrence at around this time served to further the growth of Cahan's literary aspirations. One evening, at the end of a day's work at the *Arbeiter Zeitung,* he went down to Sussman and Goldstein's Cafe and found a note waiting there for him: it was from William Dean Howells. Cahan still considered Howells to be the greatest living American author, but he had never met him, nor did he ever dream that he would. What had happened was that Howells, like many a Yankee man of letters living in New York, had begun to discover the Lower East Side as a fascinating source of material for his books, and was now making frequent excursions there. In the course of his wanderings, he had been interested to learn of the existence of a Yiddish-language socialist newspaper, and had gone to the *Arbeiter Zeitung* office in the hope of meeting its editor. But Cahan had not been there at that moment, nor was he at Sussman and Goldstein's, where Howells had been told he would find him. Howells had thereupon left him this note, asking for the pleasure of making his acquaintance. Cahan promptly went back to his office and wrote a reply.

A few days later Cahan received an invitation to come to Howells' home. "The Dean of American Letters" then lived in a brownstone on East 17th Street near Second Avenue, facing Stuyvesant Park; Cahan's visit here provided him with his first glimpse of the upper-class life of an established American writer. In general, Cahan was eventually to be somewhat disapproving of the bourgeois sanctimoniousness that characterized the life style of many successful American writers at that time; they had none of the Bohemian disarray and cultivated unpretentiousness that he admired in Russian writers. But Howells had a quality of innocence, also characteristically American, that caused Cahan to warm to him quickly that afternoon all the same. Howells, for his part, was astonished and delighted to learn that Cahan had read all his novels. This was not only an honor rarely accorded him by his fellow Yankees, but it was not at all something he had expected from a labor leader; for, before their meeting, he had supposed that Cahan was going to be a Yiddish-speaking version of the tough, pragmatic American-style union organizer, who had little time or inclination to read fiction. Instead, he found sitting before him a full-fledged Russian intellectual, a type for which he felt the greatest admiration. As Cahan might well have expected, Howells turned out to be passionately fond of Russian literature; only recently, he had closed one installment of his regular literary column in *Harper's Weekly* by suddenly saying, without preliminaries: "I will close with a name, which is the name of the greatest of all literary artists: Tolstoy." Their conversation ended in a long discussion of Russian novelists. Cahan suddenly was given an opportunity to see his own literary inclinations in a new light: for how many writers in New York, men capable of writing in English, were as well qualified as he was to discuss—to *represent,* for that matter—the spirit of Russian literature among Americans?

Still, preoccupied with his established round of activities, he hesitated to take the next step. It was not until the melancholy summer of 1893, the season of his meeting with his parents, that his mind began turning again to thoughts of serious literary endeavor. Cahan was accompanied on this trip to Europe by a friend, a man named James K. Paulding. A descendant of early New York Dutch settlers, and grandson of the writer of the same name who had been one of Washington Irving's collaborators on the journal *Salmagundi,* Paulding was himself a leisured dilettante and something of a literary dabbler. Along with some other Yankee literati, Paulding had come to the Lower East Side, whose cultural life fascinated him, through the social work projects of the University Settlement. With Cahan's old mentor Edward King, and another young American named Charles B. Stover, Paulding had established a flat on Forsythe Street, where the three men regularly held evening readings and literary discussions for residents of the Jewish quarter. Cahan's activities as a lecturer brought him on occasions both to the University Settlement and to the Forsythe Street apartment, where he had met Paulding.

Curious to see the world through the eyes of a genuine European socialist intellectual, Paulding had decided to go along as Cahan's traveling companion in the summer of 1893. Thus all of Cahan's doings that summer, from the meeting with his parents to the social-ist Congress, were accompanied by a running conversational play of sensibility with Paulding, a commentary on passing events. In all these discussions, Paulding kept urging Cahan to begin writing stories and novels about his experiences. By the time they got back to New York, Cahan was sure that he would take Paulding's advice immediately. His first feuilleton after his return was a lyrical and nostalgic descrip-tion of autumn.

But the factional combats coming to a head that fall proved, for the moment, to be too demanding to permit him the leisure to write fic-tion. His literary propensities satisfied themselves, for the time being, with essays in literary criticism for *Die Zukunft,* which he took over as editor starting with the February, 1894, issue. He also worked at that traditional intermediate solution for writers eager to keep their pens flowing while they are momentarily unable to tap the sources of their own creativity—translation. Starting with the December, 1893, issue, the *Arbeiter Zeitung* ran a serialization of Howells' *A Traveler From Altruria,* translated into Yiddish by Cahan.

Essentially Cahan's impulse to write—even in the case of *Mottke Arbel*—was always a didactic one, and it was therefore natural that Cahan's breakthrough into the writing of serious, extended works of fiction, when it finally occurred, was achieved within the framework of a purely didactic intention. In the July 24, 1894, issue of the *Arbeiter Zeitung* there appeared the first installment of a long, episodic moral fable, written by Cahan under a pen name, called *How Raphael Na'aritzokh Became a Socialist*. Basically an extended illustrative anecdote out of the repertory of the Proletarian Maggid, it tells the story of a poor Jewish carpenter who comes to America and is confronted by a vast, hostile world of technology and capitalism that robs him of his innocence and leads him, through the logic of his own spiritual simplicity, to a vision that is socialist or proto-socialist in character. Then one day Raphael attends a public socialist lecture of the sort that Cahan used to deliver, and he finds his ideas to be confirmed by the views of learned men. Through his conversations with the lecturer, he is gradually converted from his own simple Utopianism to a clearly defined Marxism. The unabashed didacticism of this tale, told in the simplest Yiddish, is clear in every line; but one can also perceive a certain charm in the telling, a vividness in the depiction of character and scene, that shows the hand of an incipient novelist. Many details are fondly recounted for their own sake. Indeed, the series ends on a purely novelistic level, with Raphael's teacher telling his pupil the story of his own early marriage and divorce; as with *Mottke Arbel* and virtually all his fiction that was to follow, Cahan had come up with the theme of frustration or failure in love when his novelist's pen was being brought into play.

Cahan was pleased with this work; but it was still considerably less than the real thing for him, above all because it was in Yiddish. By this time, Sholem Aleichem and Isaac Loeb Peretz were already demonstrating the capacities of Yiddish literature for excellence— Cahan had himself been the publisher of one of Peretz's greatest stories, "Bontshe the Silent," which appeared in print for the first time in the *Arbeiter Zeitung* of March 9, 1894—but Cahan could never rid himself of his innate prejudice against *zhargon* as a vehicle for serious writing. Also, he realized that, for the sake of his own development as a writer, it would be better for him to separate himself by a psychological Chinese Wall from the atmosphere of disarray in which he produced his Yiddish journalism. *Raphael Na'aritzokh* had given him precisely the catapult he needed over that wall; now he would write a story in English.

But not entirely without some initial propping-up from the equipment in his safely familiar old Yiddish workshop—for he chose to begin his English fiction-writing career by simply doing a new version of his lone short story to date, *Mottke Arbel*. In the transition, Cahan made some efforts at tidying the house: "Mottke," for example, became "Rouvke" (a nickname for "Rouven," or "Reuben"), just a shade less inelegant and more accessible to the Anglo-Saxon ear. Yet, for the most part, the story's crudeness did not diminish, but became accentuated in the journey from Yiddish to English. Not only did Rouvke lose much of Mottke's charm, but the anticapitalist portrait of him came perilously close to being an anti-Semitic one in English. This weakness was subsequently accentuated in the presentation of the story when it was published—for Cahan got it accepted on the first try—in the February, 1895, issue of *Short Stories* magazine. Ironically entitled "A Providential Match," it was accompanied by a set of illustrations that pushed heavy-handed irony into the realm of anti-Semitic caricature, full of greasy, aquiline, viciously acquisitive faces that would have satisfied the prejudices of the most rampant American nativist of the time. In this effort in English, Cahan seems to have been unable to find the proper control of his own ambivalences about Jewishness; for he himself provided in places ample material to support the spirit of the illustrations, as in this closing of the final scene on the pier, not to be found in the Yiddish version:

But at this juncture a burly shaven-faced "runner" of an immi-grant hotel, who had been watching the scene, sprang to their rescue [i.e., of Hannah and her fiancé, the young man she met on the boat]. Brushing Rouvke aside with a thrust of his mighty arm, accompanied by a rasping "Get out, or I'll punch your pock-marked nose, ye monkey!" he marched Hannah and her fiancé away, leaving Rouvke staring as if he was at a loss to realize the situation, while Reb Feive [the matchmaker], violently wringing his hands, gasped, "Ai! Ai! Ai!" and the young peddlers [standing all around] bandied whispered jokes.

The accompanying illustration was more than equal to the spirit of this scene.

The story, which, despite its crudenesses, was not below the aver-age quality of American fiction in the mid-nineties, aroused some interest; for "local-color" writing was reaching a height of popu-larity at this time, and Cahan was the first "local colorist" of the New York Jewish quarter. Shortly after its appearance, the editor of *Short Stories* invited Cahan to his office to discuss ideas for more stories. They decided that Cahan's next contribution would deal with that already mythic Lower East Side institution, the sweatshop. Cahan went quickly to work, and his next story, "In the Sweatshop," appeared in the June issue. It repeated the distillation that had char-acterized his earlier efforts at fiction: socialist didacticism combined with an undercurrent, steadily growing from story to story, of a his-tory of unhappy love.

Beginning with a vivid description of a sweatshop—the story's selling item—it goes on to tell of a romance that has been brewing between two of the workers: Beile, a pretty young "finisher" (seam-stress), and Heyman, a shy sewing-machine operator. Heyman has thus far been as timid in his relations with Beile as he is known for being in his relations with the boss; he has regularly been going out with her after work, but she has had to wait with growing impatience for his expected proposal of marriage. Today, at last, he has brought a watch to the shop with him, and he intends to present it to Beile at the right moment as a token of their engagement. But he has not yet found the courage to take it out of his pocket, and instead sits by quietly while David, the shop's baster, carries on a mildly flirtatious conversation with Beile.

Then the crisis occurs. The boss, Leizer Lipman, and his shrewish wife, Zlate—both of them vintage portrayals of Cahan's crude immigrant parvenu type—return from their morning's expedition in search of contracts at the Pig Market. They are accompanied by two old acquaintances, a husband and wife, whom they have just met on the street. "Zlate's visitors," Cahan carefully points out, "had recently arrived from her birthplace, a poor town in Western Russia, where they had occupied a much higher social position than their present hostess, and the latter, coming upon them on Hester Street, lost no time in inviting them to her house in order to show off to them her American achievements." Seeing there are no refreshments in the house, Zlate, in full swagger, hands Beile a nickel and tells her to go downstairs and buy some soda. Beile, shocked at being treated like a servant, hesitates; then David leans toward her and whispers: "Don't go, Beile!" Encouraged by this show of support, the girl refuses to budge; Zlate grows livid, and as the confrontation becomes more intense, David rallies openly to Beile's side, while Heyman, frightened and dismayed, hunches over his machine. David and Beile are fired on the spot; the two prepare to go immediately, without protest, David consoling Beile with promises to help her find another job. "And as she [Beile] stood in her new beaver cloak and freshly trimmed large old hat by the side of [Zlate] her discomfited commander, Basse [the woman guest] reflected that it was the finisher girl who looked like a lady, with Zlate for her servant, rather than the reverse." In silent anguish, Heyman watches David and Beile leave together.

Two weeks go by before Heyman can summon up the courage to go see Beile and find out what has happened to her. As he walks up the tenement-house stairs toward the flat in which she has been living with her mother, he hears the sounds of a celebration within. Listening through the door, he discovers that it is the wedding of Beile and David!

Years later, Cahan was to admit that this ending was "childish." From the point of view of his socialist morality tale, Cahan was indeed laying it on here rather thick. But on the level of Cahan's deeper-lying—and not, as yet, fully conscious—intentions as a writer of fiction, this ending was thoroughly pertinent and not at all contrived. For the Proletarian Maggid was already yielding place to a less didactic and more mournful inner self, which was beginning to find its characteristic expression in a tragic vision of love.

Meanwhile, destiny was taking a hand in Cahan's literary career, and once again through the medium of William Dean Howells. One day in February, Howells' wife, while waiting for a train on the platform of an elevated railway station at Sixth Avenue and Central Park South (where the Howells now lived), had been browsing at the newsstand there and had spotted Cahan's name on the cover of that month's issue of *Short Stories*. She bought a copy and brought it home to her husband, who read "A Providential Match" and then wrote a letter to Cahan inviting him for another visit.

"It is not a serious work, of course," he told Cahan when the latter came to see him. "But it convinces me that you must write. It is your duty to write."

A young author could scarcely ask for better encouragement, but the force of Howells' words was especially great, because they had come at a time when the strains of controversy at the *Arbeiter Zeitung* were getting to be almost unbearable. Things had reached such a pitch that Cahan, the paper's editor, contrived not to be present at its fifth anniversary celebration on Sunday, March 3. His excuse was sound enough: he went to Mount Sinai hospital that day for a minor operation—although the appointment could in fact have been arranged for any time. It had come about one day when he had gone to see a doctor about an inflammation in one of his eyes. The doctor, a German-Jewish American and a well-known eye specialist, looked at his patient a moment and said:

"Why aren't your eyes even? In America, it's a crime to go around with eyes like that. They can be fixed by a minor operation."

"I never thought of that," Cahan answered. The cross-eyes that had tormented his youth were something that he now rarely thought about.

"A crime, a crime," the doctor persisted, "for a man to go around with such eyes in the modern world! They could be fixed, one, two, three!"

Cahan gave in, and that is why, on the day of the *Arbeiter Zeitung*'s fifth anniversary celebration, he was in the hospital having cocaine dropped into his crooked eye. The operation took only a few minutes, but he had to stay in the hospital several days. When he left, his eyes were considerably straighter than before, though not perfectly straight. He had fulfilled the doctor's prescription for becoming an American; perhaps this would now even enable him to see the America around him in sharper outline than before.

Cahan decided that the time had come to write a more extended work in English than he had done so far. He discussed his plans with his friend Paulding, who proposed that Cahan jot down several of the plot ideas that most interested him at the moment—by this time, he had on notepaper and in his memory a large stock of real-life stories he had collected as a journalistic chronicler of the Jewish quarter—and let Paulding decide which one looked the most promising. Cahan heeded this advice, and Paulding in fact made the decision as to what was to be the subject of Cahan's first novel. Taking advantage of the summer break from his evening-school English classes, Cahan rushed home from the *Arbeiter Zeitung* office every night for several weeks to work on his new project. The result was a short novel, not much longer than thirty thousand words, which he called *Yankel the Yankee*.

The novel's protagonist is a burly young immigrant named "Jake" (his name had been "Yankel" in the old country), a former blacksmith who now works in a New York sweatshop. At work, he spends most of his slack time—used by more serious-minded workers for intermittent study—boasting to his comrades of his profound knowledge of such "goyish" institutions as boxing and baseball. He is proudly and ardently a "Yankee," and wishes to impress everyone with this fact—especially the girls who work in the shop. What they do not know is that he is also a married man, who had come to America ahead of his wife and small child three years before, promising to send for them as soon as he had earned enough money for their passage. The pleasures of life in New York have dulled the edge of his desire to send for them. But one day news arrives from home of his father's death, and Jake is told that it had been his father's dying wish that he send for his wife and child as soon as possible. Guiltily, Jake borrows some money and buys the long-awaited steamship ticket.

When Gitl arrives with their child at Ellis Island, Jake is dismayed at the sight of her: she is a frumpy, old-fashioned, pious Jewish wife. He is impatient with her from the outset, and grows all the more so even as she tries, in the weeks that follow, to learn some techniques of American-style grooming. Their estrangement grows, and Jake gets increasingly involved with one of his flashy "American" girl friends, Mamie, who, it turns out, has saved up a considerable dowry out of her earnings. Finally, Jake and Gitl are divorced, and Jake goes off with Mamie, the two planning to start a business together with her savings. The hollowness of Jake's aspirations is suggested in the very last scene of the novel, as he is shown being led pell-mell to a City Hall wedding by the shrewish Mamie; he is suddenly filled with gloomy forebodings. Gitl, on the other hand, is about to be compensated for the sufferings she has undergone at the hands of the crude and illiterate Jake, by marriage to Mr. Bernstein, a scholarly and gentle young man.

The basic patterns in this novel are the ones established in Cahan's two short stories: like them, it is a morality tale built around the theme of failure in love. Jake is more or less equivalent to Mottke Arbel, Bernstein corresponds to the gymnasium student Hannah finds on the boat, and Gitl, though she is not the modern, "Russian" type that Hannah and Beile represent in the two short stories, is nevertheless akin to them in the ideal of old-country purity that she embodies. The heavy-handed ironies—the weapons of a conscientious didacticism—are present in the novel as they were in the stories, but they are no longer applied with quite the same conviction; a more highly developed tragic sense seems to be displacing the predominantly moralizing spirit of the two short stories. In fact, the essentially socialist theme of the stories has all but vanished here; there are no capitalists in the novel at all. To be sure, the lure of the dollar is shown in Jake's attraction to Mamie's dowry; but he has, in fact, already been attracted to her for other reasons before he learns of her fortune. It is not specifically the dollar that is corrupting in this novel, but something that it represents. The corrupting force seems to be nothing less than America itself, or at any rate some vision of America that captures the souls of immigrants like Jake and Mamie. Cahan has thus moved on to a larger, more interesting, and more perilous theme. For if America itself is the cause of a deterioration of the spirit among his immigrant characters, then we are passing beyond the realm of didactic fable into that of tragedy. No immigrant, capitalist or proletarian, can be immune to the moral disaster he is now attempting to describe.

Cahan brought the completed manuscript to Paulding, who read it and was delighted. Then he brought it to Howells, and a few days later received an invitation to dinner at Howells' home. Howells was enthusiastic about the novel; an inveterate discoverer of new literary talent, he had now found a budding "Russian" realist right here in New York! At dinner, Howells discussed the book's prospects with Cahan. He suggested starting with magazine serialization before publishing the novel in book form, and he offered to keep the manuscript a while and show it around to magazine editors. But he urged that the title be changed; *Yankel the Yankee* seemed much too artificial and undignified. "That's all right for vaudeville," he said, "but not for a story like yours." Cahan fished for other Jewish equivalents of "Jake," and came up with "Yekl." Using this, they soon arrived at a new title: *Yekl, A Tale of the New York Ghetto.* This would draw the growing audience for stories of New York Jewish "local color." But Howells warned Cahan not to raise his hopes too high about finding a publisher quickly. "Our editors have their own ideas about literature," he said. "They can't be blamed for this. They have to keep their reading audience in mind, and the taste of the public at large is not the same as yours or mine." Then, before Cahan left, Howells took him aside, opened a bureau drawer and pulled out a letter. He proudly handed it to Cahan to look at: it was an old letter from Turgenev, complimenting Howells on his writings.

Howells' warning proved to be well founded. He first submitted Cahan's manuscript to *Harper's Weekly,* for which he wrote his regular literary column, but it was returned to him with the comment that life on the Jewish East Side would not be of interest to the American reader. Cahan's short stories had been one thing for the American market, but a novel, appearing in installments in issue after issue, was something else again. A second magazine was tried, and a second letter of rejection came, this time from the editor's wife. "But you know, dear Mr. Howells," she wrote, "that our readers want to have stories about richly dressed ladies and gentlemen, and love that develops between them in the countryside, while they are playing golf. How can they be interested by a story about a Jewish immigrant, a blacksmith, who has become a tailor here, and whose ignorant wife becomes repulsive to him?" Cahan was receiving an object lesson in those same American attitudes toward "realism" that he had criticized in his lecture and article on the subject back in 1889.

The manuscript was next sent to *McClure's Magazine,* the most popular periodical of the day. This time Cahan decided to go and hear the editor's response in person. He was shown into the office of an associate editor, John S. Phillips. The two men soon became engaged in a heated debate about literature.

"You describe only Jews," Phillips said. "Someone who reads your novel is likely to think that there are no other kinds of people in America than Jews."

Phillips went on to expound his view that art should deal with beautiful things. Cahan's novel about sweatshops, slum tenements, and ignorant people had nothing beautiful in it; what, then, did it have to do with art? Cahan answered by giving examples from Russian literature, pointing out that even the most beautiful works by Russian writers described the lives of poor, unwashed peasants.

"Ah," Phillips replied, "but around the peasants stretch beautiful meadows, magnificent fields, and woods!"

"Do you believe," Cahan asked, "that a flower is more beautiful than the noble soul of a peasant?"

"Your Yekl has a noble soul, then?"

As Cahan got up to leave, Phillips assured him that he had definite talent as a writer. All he had to do was apply this talent to the description of beautiful things, and he would certainly do well.

Fearing now that his novel would never be published in the American press, Cahan began translating it into Yiddish. The first installment appeared in the *Arbeiter Zeitung* on October 18, while Howells was away on a trip. Cahan gave it, for this version, its more Yiddish-sounding original title: *Yankel der Yankee*. Letters in praise of the story soon began streaming in from *Arbeiter Zeitung* readers. Many of them wondered how the author knew the experiences of this or that person whom the story was presumed to be about. There was also a widespread apprehension on a certain point: wasn't the story doing a disservice to the Jewish immigrants by presenting them in such an unflattering light? Cahan was often to encounter this response to his writings.

When Howells got back to New York, he was dismayed to learn that Cahan was running the story in the *Arbeiter Zeitung*. He feared that editors would not want a story already published, in whatever form. But then he and Cahan decided to renounce the idea of preliminary publication as a magazine serial. Howells now sent the manuscript directly to a book publisher, his own, R. Appleton and Company. Appleton had at this time a literary adviser of notable imagination and taste, Ripley Hitchcock. Only a year ago, Howells had given Hitchcock the manuscript of Stephen Crane's *The Red Badge of Courage,* which Appleton published. Inclined to be persuaded by Howells' opinions of new authors, Hitchcock read Cahan's manuscript sympathetically, and decided that he liked it. Cahan's novel came in this way to be published by the company that had put out *Appleton's English Grammar,* the book from which Cahan had taken his first lessons in the language in which he now was writing.

*Yekl* appeared in July, 1896, simultaneously with Stephen Crane's new novel, *George's Mother,* which was about Irish immigrants on the Lower East Side of New York. Cahan's book received decent reviews in New York, Chicago, and other cities; the best one, however, came from Howells himself. One day, posters appeared, announcing that in the literary section of the New York *World* of Sunday, July 26, William Dean Howells was going to "discover" a new literary talent. The review appeared that day under the headline: "The Great Novelist Hails Abraham Cahan, the Author of 'Yekl,' as a New Star of Realism, and Says that He and Stephen Crane Have Drawn the Truest Pictures of East Side Life." The text asserted that what Crane's book had done for the Irish immigrants, Cahan's had done for the Jewish immigrants, in a new type of realistic fiction about life in urban America. "As Mr. Cahan is a Russian," Howells wrote, "and as romanticism is not considered literature in Russia, his story is, of course, intensely realistic."

The "Russian" soon got his first taste of what it was like to be a literary lion in America. Reporters came to him for interviews; articles about him appeared in the newspapers. Now the magazines flooded him with invitations to contribute stories. That fall, he was invited to a banquet one evening at the Lanthorn Club, an exclusive New York literary society, where he shared the rostrum with Stephen

Crane and Hamlin Garland as the honored guests for the occasion. Soon he received word from England that *Yekl* was going to be published there, by Heinemann and Company. The door had now suddenly opened wide to a career in American letters. How could the relatively obscure world of the Yiddish press, with its stifling factional squabbles, hold on to him much longer?

# CHAPTER 9

# INTERLUDE: WITH YANKEES

What we [Americans] need ... is a spiritual unity. ... We need
something similar to the spirit underlying the national and religious
unity of the orthodox Jewish culture.
— HUTCHINS HAPGOOD, *The Spirit of the Ghetto*

Responding to a reported suicide, we would pass a synagogue where
a score or more of boys were sitting hatless in their old clothes,
smoking cigarettes on the steps outside, and their fathers, all dressed
in black, with their high hats, uncut beards, and temple curls, were
going into the synagogues, tearing their hair and rending their
garments. ... It was a revolution. ... Two, three, thousand years
of continuous devotion, courage, and suffering for a cause lost in
a generation.
— *The Autobiography of Lincoln Steffens*

THE *FORWARD* BEGAN PUBLICATION ON APRIL 22, 1897, IN AN
atmosphere of excitement akin to that which accompanied the founding of the *Arbeiter Zeitung* seven years before, but not in the same
spirit of unity; for tensions had already begun to arise among the
staff of the new paper in the weeks preceding the appearance of its
first issue. The brewing conflict revolved around the question of how
the *Forward* should deal with the enemy that had, in effect, created
it: should it fill its pages with attacks upon the *Abend Blatt* and the
De Leonist "clique," or should it ignore that old fight and concentrate
on building a personality all its own? These questions, which went

to the very heart of Yiddish journalism as it had thus far been understood, were complicated by the human relationships out of which they
emerged. For, this time, the battle lines were drawn, not between two
factions of roughly equal size, as had been the case in the *Arbeiter
Zeitung* controversy, but between Cahan alone on one side and the
rest of the *Forward* staff on the other.

An established American novelist, Cahan was by now far and
away the leading figure of the Lower East Side literary world, and he
saw himself as having a more profound grasp of the American experience than any of his colleagues. He was filled with ideas about how
a newspaper—whether in English or in Yiddish—should be run in
America. In general, the populist in him that had been born in Russian
Narodnism and nurtured in the pragmatism of the New York press
and the lecture platform was losing patience with the dogmatic
approach to journalism and the theoretical view of society that characterized the thinking of most of his fellow Jewish intellectuals. Added
to this now was his increasingly literary turn of mind, which made
ideological abstractions about the lives of men all the more intolerable
to him. In his last years at the *Arbeiter Zeitung* and the *Abend Blatt*,
he had written a regular feature called "The Hester Street Reporter,"
in which he described scenes of life gleaned in his ramblings through
the Jewish quarter. Here in the streets were things that Cahan found
more interesting, more complex, and more true than were dreamed of
in the socialist philosophy. Cahan now wanted his journalism to relate
to that world in two ways at once: to reflect it as richly and as accurately as possible, and to reach out to it and be read—for knowledge,
for self-understanding, for sheer entertainment—by as many of the
Jewish immigrants as possible. What, after all, was socialism about,
if not the people? And what did the people care about the partisan
disputes of the socialist intellectuals?

The member of the *Forward* staff most inclined to be annoyed
by these attitudes and accomplishments of Cahan's was Morris
Winchevsky. Four years older than Cahan, and his predecessor in lit-

erary fame by a good deal more, Winchevsky was not prepared to be overshadowed by him or by anyone else on the Lower East Side. Not that the editorship itself was ever an issue between him and Cahan; Winchevsky's lyrical turn of mind was in no way suited to the hectic chores of running a daily newspaper, and he was satisfied simply to be a distinguished regular contributor. But he had not envisioned the *Forward* as a place in which there would be a hierarchy of authority in the fashion of the *Abend Blatt* anyway; editor and staff were, in principle, to be perfectly equal. His conception of the paper belonged to that happy era of London in the eighties, the passing of which he could never accept. He wanted the *Forward*, for example, to be an embodiment of the ideal of a socialist "free press." By this he meant not only a completely cooperative administering of the paper by its staff, but also a free expression of a wide range of socialist opinion—a kind of daily forum—on its pages (this policy would allow anarchists to have a voice on the *Forward*, as Winchevsky saw it; De Leonists, of course, were not welcome). But there was also, in Winchevsky's eyes, one overriding duty that had to be performed: a relentless critique of the *Abend Blatt* and the De Leonists. For they aroused in him all the excessive rage that sometimes occurs in such a normally unworldly and uncombative spirit as his when its peace has been disturbed.

Essentially, then, Winchevsky conceived of the editorship as the merest technical position, as that of a kind of middleman between the staff and the printer. Such a conception was hardly suitable for Cahan, however, whose old impulse to be at the top was now strengthened by a touch of authoritarianism in him, the outgrowth of the demagogic mystique that was gaining control of his spirit. The old thunderous ovations from the simple Jewish workers who crowded the lecture halls, who could touch these off better than he? Who understood so well as he did the souls of the Yekls or the Raphael Na'aritzokhs of the world? In a sense, the makers of the *Forward* had created the "House of Commons" Cahan had once advocated, in their rebellion from the *Abend Blatt*'s "House of Lords"; and Winchevsky was parliamentarianism's most passionate advocate. But Cahan was already seeking to be its Caesar. In this aim, it was natural that he be opposed not only by the parliamentarians, but by any other potential Caesar as well. This is why a sudden and unprecedented rivalry also arose between Cahan and Louis Miller.

It is not at all unusual for friendships founded in the atmosphere of solidarity provided by a common disenfranchised and visionary young manhood to begin to break down under the first shocks of oncoming middle age. Miller was now thirty-one years old and Cahan almost thirty-seven—the moment at which the crucial sense of being "younger" and "older" that a six-year difference in age had once signified begins to disappear. Miller had finally married, and was no longer the forlorn young bachelor hanging around in the warmth of the Cahans' hearth; indeed, the very fact that he had once been so, and that he now had found his bride there, made it all the more necessary that he establish his new sense of well-being and emotional independence with a clear break from this outward symbol of his previous condition of abject immaturity. He and the Cahans quite naturally drifted apart.

Miller's new state of mind reflected itself in a growing sense of his own powers in the world of Yiddish journalism. Miller had traditionally been regarded as second only to Cahan in a number of things, above all in lecturing and editorial writing. He had none of Cahan's or Winchevsky's talent for the feuilleton or for the other more literary forms of journalism, but only Cahan could compose an argument in Yiddish prose as well as Miller could. And Miller's talent for flamboyant polemics was only just coming into its own. Yet this type of journalism was precisely what Cahan now wanted to eliminate from the pages of the *Forward*. To Miller, this could not but seem to be a pointed challenge to the spiritual and emotional independence he felt he had just won from Cahan. It seemed as if Cahan, who had no children of his own, could not resist the impulse to be a domineering father in some of his relationships, especially in the Yiddish-speaking world.

The tensions at the *Forward* came to a head that summer, when De Leon succeeded, under the guise of a routine administrative realignment, in purging the *Forward* group and all its followers from the Socialist Labor Party. Thus freed from the compunctions of lingering party loyalty, Miller, Winchevsky, Zametkin, and others sought to launch a full-scale campaign of vilification against De Leon on the pages of the *Forward*. Cahan, who was now firmly convinced that he wanted simply to create a popular workers' newspaper, and that the printing of dull and intricate intramural polemics was no way of doing so, resisted their aims. The issue was forced one day when Zametkin submitted a long article denouncing the *Abend Blatt*. Cahan did not want to print it at first, but as the pressure upon him to do so mounted, he offered a compromise: he would publish it as a "communication." Cahan's opponents saw through the subterfuge: this would be as if to wash the *Forward*'s hands of responsibility for Zametkin's statement. They demanded that it be published as a regular article. A special meeting of the Press Association was called to deal with the question, and Cahan found himself severely criticized on all sides. Winchevsky was the most voluble of his critics; Miller simply sat in silence throughout the meeting. Cahan knew that there was no chance of having his way. He agreed to print the piece as a regular article, and a few days later he submitted his resignation. By the end of August, he had left the *Forward,* and Miller had been appointed editor in his place.

Cahan felt as if a millstone had been lifted from him; now he could devote all his daytime hours to his own writing. Anna, too, was glad to see her husband turn his full attention to occupations more befitting a Russian intellectual than Yiddish journalism had ever seemed to her to be. But there were now financial problems to be faced, for Cahan not only had to do without the fifteen dollars a week he had been earning as editor of the *Forward,* but was suddenly confronted with the loss of the traditional foundation stone of his income as well. For one day, in September, he realized that he had not received the usual annual letter inviting him to teach another year of English classes at the evening school for immigrants. He made inquiries, and learned that one of the school's trustees had spotted him on a street corner the previous fall, giving a speech for the candidates of the Socialist Labor Party. He had thereupon been deemed unsuited to teach there. Cahan was now flung back entirely upon his own skill and productivity as a freelance writer.

But it was clear from the outset that the exclusive pursuit of belles-lettres was not going to bring him sustenance. *Yekl,* for all its respectable critical reception, had earned him next to nothing. True, his short stories were now commanding as much as fifty dollars each, and he had no trouble placing them; but he found he was utterly incapable of producing fiction at a rapid enough pace to turn his fees for stories into a regular income. There was no choice; he had to go back to his old activity of hustling for freelance newspaper assignments. This was easy enough to do: he was a thoroughly experienced journalist, and he was soon able to become a regular contributor to such papers as the *Sun* and the *Evening Post.* But it was a nuisance to have to spend so much time in a round of journalistic potboilers, not only because they took time away from his serious writing, but because they often violated his Russian-bred intellectual and ideological integrity.

One day, for example, Cahan had gone on recommendation to the office of Henry J. Wright, the new editor of the New York *Commercial Advertiser,* to solicit an assignment. To his dismay, Wright suggested that he cover a rally to be held that evening for Benjamin F. Tracy, the Republican candidate for mayor.

"But I'm a socialist," Cahan protested.

Wright looked at him in bewilderment. Cahan explained that, as a socialist, he considered it to be against his principles to write about a bourgeois candidate.

"But I only want you to describe how he looks," Wright explained, "how he speaks, what kind of impression he makes—and also, to write a few lines on the meeting. Do it any way you want."

Reluctantly, Cahan took the assignment. He went to the rally, wrote an article unfavorable to Tracy, and brought it in the next morning for that afternoon's edition. It was not printed. Cahan went up to see Wright the next day, and asked what had happened.

"Belles-lettres is one thing," Wright said, "and newspaper writing is another."

Cahan now felt confirmed in his scruples. "I cannot write political articles or descriptions for your paper," he said. "I'm a socialist. I can give you other things."

Wright seemed amused. He pointed out that it was quite common in American journalism for reporters to work for papers whose political opinions were different from their own. Cahan made it clear that he was not opposed to working for the *Commercial Advertiser,* which was nominally Republican, but that he would not do political assignments. Wright gave in.

Despite these initial difficulties with Wright, Cahan became a regular contributor and eventually, a salaried member of the *Commercial Advertiser* staff. Wright did not at all represent the conservative Republicanism of William McKinley, then President of the United States, but was rather of that progressive school of Republicans who were increasingly to identify their aspirations with the figure of Theodore Roosevelt in the years to come. Wright's recent arrival at the *Commercial Advertiser* was itself a phenomenon of this new Progressivist trend. Until now, he had been city editor of the stolid and conservative *Evening Post;* but he had pooled his resources with that paper's business manager to buy the nearly defunct old *Commercial Advertiser*—which, as its name indicated, had hitherto been devoted primarily to business news. He hoped to bring about a new departure in New York journalism, one that would reflect the new spirit of reform that was in the air, generated by such recent local phenomena as the Reverend Parkhurst's personal crusade against crime and vice and the Lexow Crime Commission. The New York Yankee upper-crust, descendants of Mrs. Archer, of Edith Wharton's *The Age of Innocence,* were now at last becoming aroused to the urban jungle that had come into being around them, and they needed to have their newspaper. Wright's notion was a paper that not only would give them the information they sought, but would satisfy their cultivated tastes. He envisioned a kind of "daily magazine," in the European (and, incidentally, the Yiddish) fashion. This would fill a gap that was being created at that very moment by an unfortunate polarization taking place in the New York daily press: on the one side, Hearst's *Journal* and Pulitzer's *World* were pioneering new realms of irresponsible sensationalism, while on the other, papers like the *Evening Post* and, subsequently, the *New York Times,* were moving in the direction of the merest dry, factual reporting of "the news." Something was needed between these two extremes, to interpret the passing scene intelligently and even colorfully, but without sensationalism. "We were not dreaming of a huge circulation," Norman Hapgood later wrote of Wright's new staff at the *Commercial Advertiser* at the time he joined it. "Our hope was to pay our way by pleasing people who enjoyed the things we enjoyed, and there were plenty of them in New York."

The things enjoyed by this new, youthful staff were perhaps best exemplified by its city editor, brought over from the *Evening Post,* Lincoln Steffens. Now thirty-one years old, Steffens was in the midst of a spectacular ascent in the world of New York journalism, to which he had applied himself with the breathless energies of a schoolboy, injecting into its established atmosphere of worldly wisdom and corruption an intellectual high seriousness which was his own special distillation of Yankee innocence and several years of study in German philosophy. His journalistic technique was that of an intellectual who once had aspired to be a novelist: instead of settling for mere "news," he tried to trace every story to its origins. His work thus became a series of exercises in practical sociology, and a series of revelations that the nature of reality was not to be found in books of philosophy after all, but in streets and smoke-filled rooms. As a Wall Street reporter, he found himself exploring the anatomy of capitalism in all its hidden intricacies; switched to Police Headquarters, he embarked upon a quasi-Russian inquiry into the structure of the lower depths. Burglars and business manipulators had more to tell him about life than professors after all: this discovery was made by Steffens with the jubilation of one who, in his student days, had been intimidated by an exalted notion of Culture. It made him, for the rest of his life, an ardent exponent of the reality principle to those who had not learned its lessons—especially to those members of his own class who had not broken through the wall separating them from contact with the harsh experience of lower-class America, as he had done. And for him, as for Cahan—another penetrator through intellectual categories in pursuit of a vision of American reality—there was really no book, no form of literature, that seemed so adequate to reflect the urban world he had discovered in a way that would be true to his ideal of "realism" than the newspaper, the only novel that raced to the presses day after day to keep up with the life that was ever unfolding around it.

This was why Steffens decided that he wanted novelists, or young men who aspired to be novelists, on his staff in the city room of the *Commercial Advertiser*. "In the main," he wrote in his *Autobiography*, "the *Commercial* reporters were sought out of the graduating classes of the universities, Harvard, Yale, Princeton, and Columbia, where we let it be known that writers were wanted—not newspaper men, but writers." For Steffens, creative journalism was going to come out of that same postgraduate revelation that he had undergone; he wanted none of the tired, cynical eyes of the average professional reporter, and when such a man came to Steffens for a job, he was usually turned down. "When a reporter no longer saw red at a fire," Steffens wrote, "when he was so used to police news that a murder was not a human tragedy but only a crime, he could not write police news for us. We preferred the fresh staring eyes to the informed mind and the blunted pencil."

Cahan, whom Steffens had met in the offices of the *Evening Post*, and whose novel, *Yekl*, he had read and admired, was a natural inclusion in this elite circle. Like Howells, Steffens admired the "Russian" realist that he saw in Cahan, but he went further: for, whereas Howells viewed Cahan's Jewish side merely as a representation of the oppressed social orders from which he came, Steffens passionately embraced the Lower East Side Jewish culture itself. Like many another educated Yankee who longed for a European culture—especially one who, like himself, had been attuned to the possibilities of Yiddish by some acquaintance with the German language—he had been delighted by his discoveries, made as a city reporter, of sweatshop poets, cafe-table philosophers, and Yiddish audiences who responded to what was happening on the stage with a passion that often broke out into violent quarrels right in the theater. What polite "uptown" audience ever took drama so seriously? Not even the well-to-do German-Jewish families who lived uptown could compare in spiritual quality with their unruly, poverty-stricken coreligionists on the Lower East Side. Once Steffens had to answer a complaint from "a socially prominent Jewish lady who had written to the editor [of the *Evening Post*] asking why so much space was given to the ridiculous performances of the ignorant, foreign East Side Jews and none to the uptown Hebrews. I told her. I had the satisfaction of telling her about the comparative beauty, significance, and character of the uptown and downtown Jews. I must have talked well, for she threatened and tried to have me fired, as she put it." The incipient radical had combined with the touch of the aesthete in Steffens to cause him to embrace the colorful culture of the lower-class Jewish immigrants. "I at that time was almost a Jew," he said; he even nailed a mezuza to his office door and tried to fast on Yom Kippur. "I had become as infatuated with the Ghetto as eastern boys were with the wild west"—Steffens had been born in California.

Steffens therefore had many interesting and exciting cultural lessons to learn from Cahan, who was, by the way, six years older. But Cahan also had much to learn from Steffens. Cahan was practically an old man relative to the group of recent college graduates Steffens had assembled along with him in the city room, but he was still only a novice to many of the ways of American life. On one of his first assignments, for example, Cahan had to make his first acquaintance in life with an already well-established tool of American journalism—the telephone. But most of what he had to learn was at once more difficult and more elementary than this, for he found himself regularly encountering for the first time in his journalistic career the problems of ferreting out a story and writing it up. This pure but difficult process of "getting the news" was something with which Yiddish journalists, who were primarily polemicists and feuilletonists, had rarely concerned themselves. For Cahan, the realm of unvarnished fact came like a revelation; he was being made to discover that there *was* a way of writing about such things as the rally for Benjamin F. Tracy without injecting one's political opinions, that news coverage and argumentation were two different spheres. In his first weeks at the *Commercial Advertiser* he learned this in that veritable university in which Lincoln Steffens, and Jacob Riis before him, had obtained their journalistic education: Police Headquarters. Following police wagons and ambulances, he learned the humility of confrontation with the depths of human misery and depravity, and in the process acquired enough material for a potential lifetime of realistic writing.

From Police Headquarters, Cahan moved on to a round of general assignments, at a moment highly advantageous to his journalistic education, for this was a time of rapid and dramatic movement in American public life. Just around the time when Cahan went to work at the *Commercial Advertiser,* the city of Brooklyn was incorporated as one of five boroughs into a newly created municipality of Greater New York. The city was no longer exclusively identified with Manhattan Island, and this meant, among other things, that the supremacy of Tammany Hall, the Manhattan Democratic organization, was being threatened by supersession. In general, the spreading mood of reform and a newer mood of expansionism seemed to be going hand in hand, sometimes in pursuit of common aims, often harbored by the same public figures. In April, 1898, such widely differing exponents of reform as Theodore Roosevelt and William Randolph Hearst both saw their respective visions of a militant crusade for righteousness fulfilled with the outbreak of war against Spain over the issue of Cuban "independence." Before Cahan would leave the *Commercial Advertiser* he was to witness the peculiarly American phenomenon of Theodore Roosevelt in the White House, fighting the excesses of Big Business on the one hand and turning the United States into an imperialist power on the other, all at once. Cahan was learning, as Steffens had learned before him, that a clear understanding of the workings of power in America was a challenge indeed to one's philosophical predispositions.

And Cahan had ample opportunity to see these workings up close in the course of his assignments. He got to meet Theodore Roosevelt just before the latter became governor of New York, he took part in a group interview of President McKinley, he discussed politics with Tammany boss Richard Croker, he spoke with underworld leaders. During the Spanish-American War he covered training camps and hospitals, interviewing soldiers of all ranks from private to general. He also interviewed a wide range of public personalities, such as Buffalo Bill, and the millionaire Russell Sage ("Why do you have to have so much money, Mr. Sage?" Cahan had asked him, and Sage replied: "Just for the fun of making it."). He went to prisons and covered murder trials. At Madison Square Garden, he watched a cakewalk, and wrote it up for the paper. He became an habitué of Ellis Island, where he witnessed the arrival and first American experiences, not only of masses of Jews, but of Italians, Rumanians, Czechs, Croats, and innumerable other nationalities as well. Here Cahan learned to see the world of the immigrant objectively and with purely American eyes for the first time. Once again it came home to him—what were the quarrels of a few socialist intellectuals alongside this teeming reality?

Not that Cahan completely lost his identity as a Russian intellectual during all this. Sometimes, when he was cast adrift in the furthest reaches of Yankee ways and attitudes, his old elitism would come bursting forth with sudden fury. On the occasion of Peter Kropotkin's visit to New York, Cahan took part in a group interview of him in his stateroom. Kropotkin was, of course, an ardent apostle of peace and brotherhood among men, but to many Americans the word "anarchist" had a different meaning. Inevitably, one reporter suddenly posed the question: "Tell us, Prince, how you make a bomb." A hush filled the room. A few reporters smirked, but all of them lifted pencil to pad in the expectation of a reply—all but one. Cahan, indignant, turned to the questioner and informed him haughtily that the question was absurd. The reporter glared at him and grumbled, "It would make a good story."

It was above all among his youthful colleagues at the *Commercial Advertiser* that Cahan played his role as Russian intellectual to the hilt. A small group of them used to gather around him at about three o'clock every afternoon, after the paper had been "put to bed." These were, in the main, young men who were deeply interested in literature and were searching for a commanding philosophical vision, some principle of high seriousness, that they felt they could not find in American culture. Cahan, who liked to think of them as the "spiritual aristocracy" of the paper's staff, was of course most impressive to them, not only as a published novelist and a European intellectual, but as a man whose broadly socialist conception of the world gave him a framework of values that enabled him to judge one novel or another with a vigor that astonished their easygoing and pragmatic Yankee sensibilities. Not only had they not hitherto realized that literature could be taken so seriously, but they had also never assumed that literary judgments could claim any but purely subjective grounds.

Cahan easily gained disciples in his discussions with them. One of them, Edwin Lefevre, the paper's Wall Street reporter, was inspired enough by Cahan's example and personal words of encouragement to begin writing short stories about what he observed on Wall Street; these eventually were published in book form.

If Cahan acted as something of a literary midwife among certain of his younger colleagues, he was never quite so successful in this role with anyone else as he was with Hutchins Hapgood. The brothers, Hutchins and Norman Hapgood, both members of Steffens' brain trust at the *Commercial Advertiser,* were as truly Yankee as could be; though they had been born and raised in a suburb of Chicago, their parents had migrated from New England, where their ancestry went back to the seventeenth century. Norman and "Hutch" had both studied at Harvard and, like Steffens, had done some graduate study in Germany. Also like Steffens, their knowledge of German had provided them with a means of access to the Yiddish culture of the Lower East Side—Norman Hapgood was the *Commercial Advertiser*'s drama critic, and he often covered the Yiddish theater—of which they had become passionate devotees. This was especially the case with Hutchins, who was, in general, the more casual and Bohemian of the two. As fully in the grip of the romance of teeming New York as Steffens was, Hutchins Hapgood enjoyed no greater pleasure than the serendipitist's ramble through the city's streets, or the unexpected and amiable encounter, on park bench or adjacent bar stools, with some forlorn stranger eager to pour out his troubles to a sympathetic ear. One of his best articles for the *Commercial Advertiser* was a biographical sketch of a bum he had engaged in conversation on a park bench.

As Hapgood became more and more drawn to the Lower East Side, Cahan found himself once again—as he had with James K. Paulding—playing host to an interested Yankee in excursions through its streets, cafes, and, on occasion, homes. Like Steffens, Hapgood saw in the life of the Russian Jews a cultural integrity and vitality that he considered to be wholly lacking in the Yankee civilization from which he came. Only when he was in Europe had he encountered the excitement of the kind of Bohemian cafe life that he found again on the Lower East Side, a typical scene from which he described thus:

> Four men sat excitedly talking in the little cafe on Grand Street where the Socialists and Anarchists of the Russian quarter were wont to meet late at night and stay until the small hours. An American, who might by chance have happened there, would have wondered what important event had occurred to rasp these men's voices, to cause them to gesticulate so wildly, to give their dark, intelligent faces so fateful, so ominous an expression. In reality, however, nothing out of the ordinary had happened. It was the usual course of human affairs which kept these men in a constant glow of unhappy emotion; an emotion which they deeply preferred to trivial optimism and the content founded on Philistine well-being. They were always excited about life, for life as it is consti-tuted seemed to them very unjust.
>
> It was nearly midnight, and the men in the cafe, although they had drunk nothing stronger than Russian tea, talked on, seem-ingly intoxicated with ideas.

As Hapgood saw it, America was a land of practical achieve-ments that had dispensed with the kind of cultural matrix which governed the thoughts and behavior of the typical European society. In a country like France or Germany, the smallest practical details in the life of a farmer or of a businessman seemed to contain the essence of the same aesthetic culture that dominated the activities of the country's writers, painters, or composers. In America, on the other hand, there was no vital link between the practical concerns of every-day life and the preoccupations of artists. An American with aes-thetic interests was forced to feel irrelevant in his own country, a mere dilettante. But, if this was the sad truth about the predominant American culture, it was nevertheless not true, as Hapgood was now discovering, of every culture on American soil. The Russian Jews possessed precisely the kind of cultural wholeness that Hapgood had admired and yearned for while in Europe, and here they were right in New York, just a few blocks from his office or from his flat on Washington Square.

From the gleanings of his excursions through the Lower East Side, Hapgood wrote a series of sketches for the *Commercial Advertiser.* Eventually these were to appear assembled in a book, with illustrations by a young Lower East Side artist, Jacob Epstein, who used his earnings for this assignment to go to Paris and then London, where he was to become one of the celebrated sculptors of his generation. Such a discovery of Ghetto talent was characteristic of Hapgood, whose portraits, in this book, of Yiddish-speaking poets, novelists, playwrights, actors, journalists, spiritual leaders, and ordinary men and women, turned out to be the richest description of the life of New York's Jewish quarter that had ever been written in English.

But *The Spirit of the Ghetto,* for all its admirable objectivity, was also a record of its author's spiritual strivings. At this time, the Jewish quarter had become a prominent leisure-time attraction to many New Yorkers from the middle and upper classes, and "slumming" there was a favorite pastime. They would come on Saturday evenings and Sunday afternoons, and "aristocratically scrutinize the poor neighborhoods with 'artistic' curiosity," as Cahan wrote. "In this way, two restaurants grew up in the poor East Side, in which millionaires would spend their evenings. This supposedly meant that they were scrutinizing the poor 'other half.' But in reality they were just scrutinizing one another." What is most noteworthy about Hapgood's sketches is the obviously sincere effort on the part of their author to avoid any of the undertones of slumming. In places, Hapgood even bends over backward to show his own dilettantish leanings in an unfavorable light, as in this description of an encounter:

One day an American [Hapgood] dined with four Russian Jews of distinction. Two were Nihilists who had been in the "big movement" in Russia and were merely visiting New York. The other two [Abraham and Anna Cahan] were a married couple of uncommon education. The Nihilists were gentle, cultivated men, with feeling for literature, and deeply admired, because of their connection with the great movement, by the two New Yorkers. The talk turned on Byron, for whom the Russians had a warm enthusiasm. The Americans [sic] made rather light of Byron and incurred thereby the great scorn of the Russians, who felt deeply the "tendency" character of the poet without being able to understand his aesthetic and imaginative limitations. After the Nihilists had left, the misguided American used the words "interesting" and "amusing" in connection with them; whereupon the Russian lady [Anna Cahan] was almost indignant, and dilated on the frivolity of a race that could not take serious people seriously, but wanted always to be entertained; that cared only for what was "pretty" and "charming" and "sensible" and "practical," and cared nothing for poetry and beauty and essential humanity.

Hapgood's book is, in effect, a search to awaken that "poetry and beauty and essential humanity" within himself. He is always present, testing the quality of his own responses, although not always so explicitly as in the encounter with the Cahans and their "Nihilist" friends, or in this one with Eliakum Zunser:

One of the two visitors [Hapgood and Cahan] was a Jew, whose childhood had been spent in Russia, and when Zunser read a dirge which he had composed in Russia twenty-five years ago at the death by cholera of his first wife and children—a dirge which is now chanted daily in thousands of Jewish homes in Russia—the visitor [Cahan] joined in, although he had not heard it for many years. Tears came to his eyes as memories of his childhood were brought up by Zunser's famous lines; his body swayed to and fro in sympathy with that of Zunser and those of the poet's second wife and children; and to the Anglo-Saxon present this little group of Jewish exiles moved by rhythm, pathos, and the memory of a faraway land conveyed a strange emotion.

But if Hapgood strove, in these explorations, to transcend his own impulses toward dilettantism, he did not necessarily seek to eschew the responses of the aesthete within himself. It is significant that, among the serious writers who had begun to write about the Lower East Side at this time, Hapgood was the only one for whom the passion for social reform did not overwhelm the capacity for pure enjoyment of a rich and interesting culture. Such a capacity is not to be found at all in Jacob Riis, whose descriptions of Jewish life, like his descriptions of all non-Nordic groups, convey more than a touch of bigotry:

> The jargon of the street, the signs of the sidewalk, the manner and dress of the people, their unmistakable physiognomy, betray their race at every step. Men with queer skull-caps, venerable beard, and the outlandish long-skirted caftan of the Russian Jew, elbow the ugliest and the handsomest women in the land. The contrast is startling. The old women are hags; the young, houris.

Where Hapgood sees qualities of cultural richness, Riis, the slum reformer, sees only habits that lead to filth and disease:

> It is said that nowhere in the world are so many people crowded together on a square mile as here [in "Jewtown"]. . . . Here is [a tenement] seven stories high. The sanitary policeman whose beat this is will tell you that it contains thirty-six families, but the term ["family"] has a widely different meaning here and on the avenues. In this house, where a case of small-pox was reported, there were fifty-eight babies and thirty-eight children that were over five years of age. In Essex Street two small rooms in a six-story tenement were made to hold a "family" of father and mother, twelve children, and six boarders. The boarder plays as important a part in the domestic economy of Jewtown as the lodger in the Mulberry Street Bend. These are samples of the packing of the population that has run up the record here to the rate of three hundred and thirty thousand per square mile.

As for the spiritual life of the Jewish immigrants, Riis does not care to venture very far beyond the observation that "Money is their God." There is nothing here of Hapgood's learned rabbis or conscience-racked socialist intellectuals.

But the profound difference of approach on Hapgood's part from that of Riis and others of the reformist type is made clear in the preface to *The Spirit of the Ghetto.* "The Jewish quarter of New York," Hapgood says there, "is generally supposed to be a place of poverty, dirt, ignorance, and immorality—the seat of the sweatshop, the tenement house, where 'red-lights' sparkle at night, where the people are queer and repulsive. Well-to-do persons visit the 'Ghetto' merely from motives of curiosity or philanthropy; writers treat of it 'sociologically,' as of a place in crying need of improvement. That the Ghetto has an unpleasant aspect is as true as it is trite. But the unpleasant aspect is not the subject of the following sketches. I was led to spend much time in certain poor resorts of Yiddish New York not through motives either philanthropic or sociological, but simply by virtue of the charm I felt in men and things there." Years later, Hapgood was to characterize the lifelong attitude expressed here as a preoccupation with "how individuals and groups who represent what might be called the underdog, when they are endowed with energy and life, exert pressures towards modification of our cast-iron habits and lay rich deposits of cultural enhancement, if we are able to take advantage of them." Shortly after *The Spirit of the Ghetto,* Hapgood was to make a similarly passionate anthropological inquiry into the life of the working-class, in a book called *The Spirit of Labor.* Then he hoped for a while to do a study of Negroes similar to the one he had done on the Jews, but W. E. B. Du Bois, who was to have been his Abraham Cahan for the occasion, discouraged him. By this time he had become a radical socialist, even though he had not been a socialist at all when he wrote *The Spirit of the Ghetto.*

There is, in this respect, a significant similarity between Hutchins Hapgood and Lincoln Steffens. Both men were essentially aesthetes who had made their way into the art of real-life social observation. For both of them, the vividness and authenticity of lower-class immigrant life, which appealed at first mainly to their aestheticism and passion for European culture, eventually gave rise to an antibourgeois—or rather, an anti-*American*-bourgeois—attitude. In the end, this process turned both these previously unpolitical men into radicals. They were, in other words, quite different in temperament and development from the reformer type that dominated the progressive politics of their generation. The reformers were practical and political spirits to their very core, who, like Jacob Riis, did not see anything beautiful in a culture that flourished amidst dirt and poverty. In a sense, the reformers were simply more liberal and conscientious versions of that uptown Jewish lady whom Steffens had chided for not understanding her coreligionists on the Lower East Side. Indeed, "uptown" Jews were by this time flooding the immigrant Jewish quarter with their philanthropy: their contributions had created such social-work projects as the Educational Alliance and the Henry Street Settlement, and from their ranks came one of the great figures in the history of settlement work in America, Lillian Wald. But just as Cahan and the other Russian-Jewish socialists were inclined to view these uptown Jewish charities with contempt, so also did Steffens and Hapgood come to look down upon mere reformist efforts as manifestations of the kind of bland establishmentarianism which they had always sought to shake off from their own lives.

It was inevitable that careers yet more brilliant than those they were then enjoying should begin to beckon to some of the talented young men of the *Commercial Advertiser* staff. The first major loss was Norman Hapgood, who left the paper in the early part of 1901 to accept the post of editor of *Collier's Weekly*, the most popular magazine of the day. In the fall of 1901, Steffens himself left to take a job with *McClure's Magazine*. It was in this post that he was to begin, a few months later, the series of exposés of urban corruption in America—eventually published in book form under the title *The Shame of the Cities*—that would make him nationally famous. With Steffens gone, his circle at the *Commercial Advertiser* disintegrated rapidly. Hutchins Hapgood, independently well-off like his brother, quit to devote himself full-time to his writing. Another member of the group, Pitts Duffield, left and started his own publishing company.

Cahan quickly lost interest in the job after Steffens left, and he, too, quit before the end of 1901. His prospects for freelancing looked better now than they had four years earlier; not only was he commanding higher fees and getting assignments of a better quality—from such magazines, for example, as the *Atlantic Monthly*—but he had also resumed writing for the Yiddish press on a freelance basis. There seemed to be a chance to make ends meet financially while he devoted himself full time to his own writing. The time had come to see where he was heading as a writer of serious fiction. Since *Yekl,* he had published a volume of short stories and had done many more stories for magazines besides. But his newspaper work had left him no time for a long work of fiction. The scattered fragments of a novel had been accumulating on his desk for quite a while, and now he had to see if he could finish it.

# CHAPTER 10

# A "RUSSIAN" BEMOANS
# HIS EXILE IN AMERICA

⌒

Cleisthenes made proclamation to the Greeks that all who aspired to the hand of his daughter [Agarista] should assemble at Sicyon.... At the end of the year he would decide who was most worthy of his daughter. Then there came to Sicyon all the Greeks who had a high opinion of themselves or of their families.... Cleisthenes... tried them in gymnastic exercises, but laid most stress on their social qualities. The two Athenians, Hippocleides and Megacles, pleased him best, but to Hippocleides of these two he most inclined. The day appointed for the choice of the husband came, and ... the wooers competed in music and general conversation. Hippocleides was the most brilliant, and as his success seemed assured, he bade the flute-player strike up and began to dance. Cleisthenes was surprised and disconcerted at this behavior, and his surprise became disgust when Hippocleides, who thought he was making a decisive impression, called for a table and danced Spartan and Athenian figures on it. The host controlled his feelings, but, when Hippocleides proceeded to dance on his head, he could no longer resist, and called out, "O son of Tisander, you have danced away your bride." But the Athenian only replied, "Hippocleides careth not," and danced on. Megacles was chosen for Agarista and rich presents were given to the disappointed suitors.

—J. B. BURY, *A History of Greece*

WITH THE WRITING OF YEKL, *A TALE OF THE* NEW YORK GHETTO, Cahan had brought to light themes that were more disturbing than those which had originally impelled him to write stories. Now that his earlier socialist morality tales had yielded place to a tragic history of spiritual decline on American soil, the easy lines of distinction between heroes and villains that he had once established were bound to become blurred. For if America itself was a source of the spiritual decline, then the noble Hannah and her gymnasium student, for example, were as much in danger of falling victim to the malaise as Mottke Arbel was.

It is precisely the equivalents of Hannah and her gymnasium student who suffer the tragic American fate in Cahan's very next story after *Yekl*—"Circumstances," which appeared in *Cosmopolitan* of April, 1897. This story comes much closer than any of its predecessors to depicting qualities of Cahan's own life experience, for it is about an intellectual "Russian" couple in New York, who have never quite recovered from the shock of being driven by anti-Semitism from their beloved native land. The dreariness of their life in America—the husband, a law graduate in Russia, is forced to make his living in New York as a worker in a button factory—weighs down upon their marriage and finally causes it to crumble. (As the story develops, its "autobiographical" elements become less definite, but it seems quite clear that Cahan's marriage, though it ultimately survived, had known a good deal of crisis by this time.) At the end, Boris and Tatyana have separated.

The editor of *Cosmopolitan,* apparently hoping for a reconciliation between Boris and Tatyana, asked for a sequel to this story, but the one Cahan wrote turned out to be so gloomy the editor rejected it. In his next story, solicited by the *Atlantic Monthly,* Cahan tried for a lighter vein. He had just left the *Forward*—a step which Anna Cahan wholeheartedly approved—and was in a better frame of mind than he had been in for a long time. He was returning to his old vocation of writing sketches of Lower East Side life for the English-language press, and the local colorist was again active in him, obscuring for the moment the gloomier part of himself. The result, which appeared in the February, 1898, issue of the *Atlantic,* was a bittersweet romance called "A Ghetto Wedding," which described the frustrated efforts of an engaged immigrant couple to have a large and splendid wedding ceremony despite the ravages of the depression of 1893. The joy of their love ultimately transcends the squalor of their surroundings.

The *Atlantic*'s editor, Walter H. Page, was delighted with the story, and he immediately asked Cahan for another. Cahan responded euphorically, writing a narrative that turned out to be nearly as long as *Yekl* when it was finished. It was, in fact, too long for publication in a single issue, and Page did not want to serialize it. But he did want it to see print, and he suggested that Cahan use it as the keystone for a volume of short stories which could be published by the *Atlantic*'s own house, Houghton, Mifflin and Company. This was too good an offer to turn down, even though Cahan was a bit dismayed at first by the realization that such a volume would have to be filled out by all the stories he had written so far, including even "A Providential Match," which he no longer regarded very highly. Nevertheless, this story, too, was included in the volume, which appeared in April, 1898, under the title *The Imported Bridegroom and Other Stories of the New York Ghetto*.

The novella which occasioned the publication of this book and which gave it its title proved to be Cahan's best work to date, the most successful marriage thus far between his deeper-lying subjective concerns and his calling as a New York Jewish local colorist. The narrative begins by focusing upon the character of Asriel Stroon, who is Cahan's vulgar immigrant parvenu *à la* Mottke Arbel seen thirty years later; middle-aged, prosperous, the father of a grown daughter, a widower, Stroon is no longer the crude caricature drawn by the socialist propagandist of more than six years before. Cahan is now able to perceive touches of the charming old roughneck in Stroon's type. Better still, he is able to perceive something of himself: for both Stroon and Cahan, whatever might be the other differences between them, have had the American immigrant experience in common, and they share, in fact, a similar nostalgia for the simple pieties of their *shtetl* boyhoods in Russia.

Overcome by a nostalgia that is even beginning to turn him into a religious man—something he had never been before—Stroon takes a trip back to Europe and to the village of his youth. He enters his native Pravly the way he had left it, on the back of a cart, and during this ride all the emotional ambivalences of his life's experience are awakened in him. For a moment, he feels like the child he had once been in this village, as if time had not passed at all, but "then he relapses into the Mott Street landlord, and for a moment he is an utter stranger in his birthplace. Why, he could buy it all up now! He could discount all the rich men in town put together; and yet there was a time when he was of the meanest hereabout." This pattern of vacillation fills his spirit during his entire stay in Pravly, and brings him into conflict one Saturday morning, in the synagogue, with Reb Lippe, the town's leading citizen. Stroon tries to obtain the honor of reading the main section of the week's Torah portion by offering a large contribution to the synagogue. But Reb Lippe, who was due to read the main section this week because of his daughter's forthcoming marriage, demands that the honor be auctioned off. The bidding begins, but when Reb Lippe sees that Stroon is about to obtain an easy victory, he uses his influence to get his own highest bid recognized as final.

Stroon is incensed at this defeat at the hands of the same old *shtetl* establishment whose airs of social superiority had driven him to America years before. "It was as if, while he was praying and battling, the little town had undergone a trivializing process. All the poetry of his thirty-five years' separation had fled from it, leaving a heap of beggarly squalor. . . . The only interest the town now had for him was that of a medium to be filled with the rays of his financial triumph." That afternoon he suddenly realizes what the form of his revenge will be, when the maggid's sermon reminds him that, according to Jewish tradition, it is a good deed to marry one's daughter to a scholar. Reb Lippe is about to marry his daughter to a Talmudic prodigy; this choice match had of course been obtained on the basis of Reb Lippe's ability to pay what seemed, in Pravly, to be a substantial dowry. Stroon decides that he will use his superior wealth to obtain Shaya, the Talmudic scholar, as a husband for his own daughter. He challenges Reb Lippe to another auction, this time for a bridegroom, and now he does not lose. Triumphantly he heads back for New York, his young prize in tow.

The focus of the narrative now shifts to Shaya, and to Stroon's daughter, Flora. In many ways a reflection of her father's driving ambitiousness, Flora is an aggressively "American" girl, who reads novels and dreams of marrying some elegant, "uptown" doctor. She is therefore horrified when her father first presents Shaya to her and announces that she is to marry him. But Stroon decides to be patient, confident that she will learn in time to like her imported bridegroom, who is to remain in the house as a boarder and receive English lessons from her. And indeed, she does begin after a while to feel an attraction to her pupil, whose modernization at her hands takes place with astonishing rapidity. Shaya has already become American in dress and outward appearance; soon, he becomes American in thought as well, eagerly reading secular literature and beginning to have doubts about his old religious convictions. Flora persuades him to study medicine, for she still wants to marry a doctor; he agrees to do so in secret—for Stroon still imagines his prospective son-in-law to be the Talmudic scholar he had bought in Pravly—and the two young people exchange vows of love.

Now Flora, despite her pretensions, is not the picture of enlightenment and elegance her unworldly lover imagines her to be. All her vaunted love of culture focuses merely upon elegant-looking exteriors, whereas her own cultural accomplishments are in fact questionable. Despite her self-proclaimed interest in writers like Dickens, for example, her own English is rather crude. In one ironic scene, she comes in on Shaya bent over his English grammar and says: "I'll bet you was singing in that funny way you have when you are studying the Talmud." Shaya, despairing of his own English, replies, "I so wish I could speak it like you, Flora." Shaya is of course supposed to be speaking Yiddish, like Stroon throughout the story, and so his speech is rendered in the text in faultless syntax; it is only Flora's speech—she alone is always speaking English—which appears as marred before the eyes of the reader. By this device, Cahan places Flora at the center of the stage as a new version of the American vulgarian that has often figured in his stories. It suggests clearly that things are not going to work out perfectly well between her and Shaya.

On the surface, the story ends in a triumph over paternal bigotry that is reminiscent of the ending of *The Merchant of Venice*—and as full of somber undertones that compromise the joy of victory. Stroon finally discovers that his Talmudic prodigy has become a heretic, and he threatens to cancel the wedding; but Shaya and Flora run off and are married at City Hall. Stroon learns of this when his daughter returns to the house to get her things right after the wedding; the news comes to him as a moral awakening. "I know you are not to blame," he says to Flora. "America has done it all." He proposes marriage to his housekeeper, a pious Jewish woman, and decides that he and his bride will settle in Palestine. Flora, meanwhile, goes to rejoin her new husband at his apartment. Meeting her in the hallway, Shaya tells her he has a few friends upstairs visiting for the afternoon. The visitors turn out to be a group of intellectuals, Jews and Gentiles, who meet every week at a different home to discuss some book or philosophical topic. Flora enters and gazes in dismay upon the shaggy, Bohemian assemblage gathered in her bridal apartment; this "was anything but the world of intellectual and physical excellence into which she had dreamed to be introduced by marriage to a doctor." Shaya soon becomes deeply involved in the discussion, arguing secular ideas with the same style and fervor he once used to apply to his discussions of Talmudic law. There the story ends.

The ironies against Flora are so heavy that one is tempted to surmise that Cahan had a pointed revenge against someone in mind. But there is another level of irony to this ending which Cahan may not have consciously intended. For, if Shaya has unwittingly shown up his wife's vulgarity and pretentiousness in this final scene, there is nevertheless something rather unsettling in the fact that he has done this on their wedding day. There are intimations of impotence in this triumph, which echo ambiguously in the story's very title. Cahan's American tragedy of unfulfilled love suddenly comes to seem endless and remorseless in its ramifications, for now it has, unexpectedly, reached out to Shaya, too. In him, even the Talmudic spirit has not escaped the American taint, for the New World seems to have galvanized that spirit into a driving ambition to realize itself that brings Shaya beyond the capacity to love. Cahan's themes have now exploded with terrifying reverberations.

The new implications here come into sharp focus in Cahan's next story, which was not written until about a year later. Perhaps Cahan needed this long to recover from "The Imported Bridegroom"; but, in any case, his job at the *Commercial Advertiser* was making it hard for him to find the time for his own writing. In another respect, however, this job was advantageous for his fiction, for it provided him with a far wider range of experience than his work in Yiddish journalism had yielded, and thereby gave him a richer store of subject matter for his fiction. Howells, in a review of *The Imported Bridegroom,* had flung something of a challenge at his erstwhile prodigy by saying: "It will be interesting to see whether Mr. Cahan will pass beyond his present environment out into the larger American world, or will master our life as he has mastered our language." The man who had designated him the "Russian" realist of American letters was now suggesting that he was in danger of becoming the merest local colorist. Cahan was therefore eager to venture afield somewhat with all the "American" material he was amassing at the *Commercial Advertiser.* When he took his next step after a year, however, he made it only a half-step outward, writing a story about a marriage between a Jew and a Gentile.

"The Apostate of Chego-Chegg," which appeared in the *Century Magazine* of November, 1899, takes place in a Long Island village populated mainly by Polish Gentile immigrants: "A local politician had humorously dubbed the settlement Chego-Chegg (this was his phonetic summary of the Polish language), and the name clung." The apostate of the title is a young woman who now calls herself Michalina. Her name had been Rivka, but in her hometown in Poland she had abandoned Judaism in order to marry a young peasant. To escape the opprobrium of her family, she and her husband, Wincas, have emigrated to the United States and settled in this village, where Wincas works as a farm laborer. But Michalina, who now has a small daughter, is beginning to have great misgivings about her apostasy, which had been provoked, it turns out, more by a desire to take revenge upon a hated stepmother than by love for Wincas. She looks with growing longing to a small Jewish community that has recently sprung up in an adjacent village (Michalina is unaware of the origins of this community: it was established by sweating contractors seeking to escape the sphere of influence of the New York garment unions). She even goes there from time to time to do her shopping and to wander through its streets, and though she is known there to be an apostate, she eventually comes to be grudgingly tolerated by the community.

Among the townspeople is a certain young Rabbi Nehemiah. Known for an extreme religious orthodoxy and zeal that makes him something of an outcast, he presents to Michalina's eyes an image of Jewish integrity that fascinates her. One day, however, to her great surprise, she is confronted by a clean-shaven young man, almost unrecognizable to her at first, who announces to her that he is that same Nehemiah. He has lost his religion, and is now known among the townspeople as Nehemiah the Atheist. "Nehemiah was an incurably religious man," we are told, "and when he had lost his belief disbelief became his religion." There are intimations that he was at least partly lured into this conversion by an attraction to Michalina, to whom he had never spoken until this moment. Michalina's reaction is mixed: "Another sinner!" she says to herself with a momentary thrill of pleasure, but then finds herself "bemoaning the fall of an idol."

Her idol soon proves to be mere flesh and blood. She and Nehemiah begin seeing much of one another during the daytime hours, when Wincas is at work, and he does a great deal of talking. "All she understood of his talk was that it was in Yiddish, and this was enough. Though he preached atheism, to her ear his words were echoes from the world of synagogues, rabbis, purified meat, blessed Sabbath lights." But one day he tells her the story of Petrarch, and of how he was inspired by Laura, a married woman. Then, suddenly:

> ". . . Laura mine!" he whispered.
> "Stop that!" she cried, with a pained gesture.
> At that moment he was repulsive.

Yet Nehemiah continues to attract her as a link with her lost and lamented Jewish past. She begins to keep a kosher home and to light candles every Friday evening. One day she goes to New York and visits a rabbi to get his advice. She learns from him that she and her daughter are both still legally Jewish, and that her marriage does not exist in the eyes of Judaism. She is, of course, a married woman according to American law. A plan forms in her mind: she will marry Nehemiah secretly in a Jewish ceremony and escape with him to England. The Jewish women of the village are delighted when she tells them of her plan, and they organize a wedding in one of their homes and raise the money for two steamship tickets. But, as the ceremony is about to begin, Michalina looks out the window and sees her husband, still unaware of what is about to happen, on his way home from work. Something pierces her heart and she rushes from the house, takes her husband's arm, and goes home with him; the story closes as they walk down the road together.

This story is another manifestation of the way in which more than one level of alienation, of American exile, is beginning to emerge in Cahan's fiction. Michalina's alienation and longing are the main focus of the narrative, but they do not constitute its sole thematic level. Less sharply in focus, but deeper and more disturbing, is the story of Nehemiah. He is Shaya of "The Imported Bridegroom" seen in a clearer light, dominated by an overwhelming drive to idealize and intellectualize what is essentially an amorous impulse. Why can't he simply love, without these excesses of self-consciousness and sublimation? That is his mystery. No matter what he embraces or seeks to embrace—Judaism, atheism, Michalina—there is always something bloodless about him, just as there is always something profoundly human and sensual about Michalina, no matter what her mistakes and inner torments.

In his next major story, "The Daughter of Reb Avrom Leib," which appeared in the May, 1900, issue of *Cosmopolitan,* Cahan brings the Shaya-Nehemiah figure to the center of the stage, and shows his kinship with Mottke Arbel by making him a businessman. Zalkin is Cahan's summary statement of what had hitherto been expressed in only scattered and fragmented form throughout several characters. It is clear from the outset that the search for a wife on the part of Zalkin, who had been a Talmudic scholar when he was a boy in Russia, is fused with a longing to recover the spirit of a way of life he has lost in becoming an American businessman (in this way he foreshadows Cahan's major protagonist of many years later, David Levinsky). He spends his free hours taking sentimental rambles through the streets of the Jewish quarter and wandering into synagogues. It is in one of these synagogues, on a Friday night, that he becomes captivated, not only by the singing of its cantor, but by the beauty of the latter's daughter, whom he spies sitting in the women's section in the balcony breathlessly watching her father sing the traditional welcome to

"Sabbath, the Bride." Zalkin makes the acquaintance of both father and daughter after the service, and though he finds the girl somewhat less attractive when viewed up close than she had seemed from a distance, he begins to court her.

Sophie turns out to be something of a Flora Stroon, full of cultural pretensions—she plays the piano ardently, but badly—combined with touches of vulgarity: she "was a good girl, but she knew it and talked too much." Zalkin is not terribly much in love with her, but she appeals profoundly to his nostalgia—largely through the aura of her deeply pious father—and seems to be the salvation he has sought from his loneliness. Sophie's feelings toward him are even more ambivalent: "As long as Zalkin, like the bashful Talmud student that he was, held himself at a respectful distance, Sophie took his presence and his love-lorn eyes as part and parcel of the great change which was coming over her. When, with throbbing heart, he finally ventured to take her by the hand, however, her whole being revolted." Zalkin is far more successful with her father, Reb Avrom Leib; on the first evening they met, Zalkin had demonstrated his thorough knowledge of the Talmud, and "Reb Avrom Leib fell in love with his daughter's suitor on the spot." In the end, it is the force of the old man's spirit that proves to be the decisive factor in the vacillating courtship; he dies, and Sophie, in her grief, becomes reconciled with Zalkin—with whom she had just broken up—out of nostalgia for her father. She agrees at long last to marry him. "And as if afraid lest morning might bring better counsel," the story concludes, "she hastened to bind herself by adding, with a tremor in her voice: 'I swear by my father that I will.'"

By this time, Cahan felt confident enough in his skill as a writer of fiction to try some non-Jewish subject matter. He remained close to home in another respect, however, for he continued writing about immigrants, using the material he had gleaned as a reporter at Ellis Island. "A Marriage by Proxy," which appeared in the December, 1900, issue of *Everybody's Magazine*, is about Italian immigrants, and tells of a man's difficulties in getting his imported bride to come and live with him. Another story, "Dumitru and Sigrid," published in the March, 1901, issue of *Cosmopolitan,* is about a Rumanian man and a Swedish woman who strike up an unusual romance during several days' detention at Ellis Island. They have no common language, but they have two dictionaries—one Rumanian-English, the other Swedish-English—and are thereby able to communicate to one another by composing notes in nonsyntactical English ("I not joke, Sigrid. Know not where I be and where thou be, but I eternal remember thou."). They then go their respective ways into the New York melting pot, and Dumitru, lonely but ambitious, learns photography and begins a successful career. He begins to resemble the now traditional lonely young expatriate of Cahan's fiction. Dumitru had been of the aristocracy in Rumania, from which he had been forced to flee because he had slapped a superior officer in the army for insulting his sister; but in America he gradually becomes quite bourgeois in dress, manner, and outlook. The Sigrid episode alone remains the touch of romance in his otherwise prosaic American experience, and he longs to meet her again. Then one day—four years after his arrival in America—he chances to see her, sitting on the steps of a tenement, a baby in her arms. She is matronly in appearance, and the English she speaks seems less romantic to him than her painfully written patois of Ellis Island. She introduces him to her husband, a Swedish piano-maker, as "de gentleman vat mashed me" at the immigration center. Dumitru takes his leave and hastens away, the four-year romance of his daydreams at an end.

It is a new but significant variation upon Cahan's traditional theme that his lonely young man has made an appearance, in this story, as an East European aristocrat. Until now, the alienated immigrants of Cahan's stories had usually mourned the loss of their *Jewish* roots. This was clearly a way of representing Cahan's own experience of uprootedness, at least in one aspect; but there was always another aspect to be considered as well. For Cahan's roots in the Russian revolutionary tradition were even more important to him than his roots in Judaism, and that tradition was essentially an aristocratic one, in its ideals and spirit of selfless dedication, and in its very social composition, made up, as it was, of a considerable number of young men and women from noble families. This was the background that he now longed to deal with more and more. But he knew that it was not yet going to be easy to get some bourgeois American magazine to print a story about the Russian revolutionary movement—for the time being, he confined that material to his manuscripts for potential novels. Nor did he choose to write explicitly yet about the theme that was closer to his heart than any other, the "embourgoisement" of the Russian revolutionary spirit on American soil. The moral complexities of this theme would be alien to the American fiction-reading public. What he *could* write about, however, was the problem of what happened to the Russian aristocratic spirit in America—and this would be essentially the same thing.

The story he produced as his definitive statement on this theme is as incredible as its title. "Tzinchadzi of the Catskills," which appeared in the August, 1901, issue of the *Atlantic Monthly,* is about a Georgian nobleman—as if to reflect the marginality of his own Russian identity, Cahan persists in seeking out his East European noblemen in cultures that *border* on Russia—who has come to America and made his home in the Catskill Mountains. To the American sensibility today, such an idea seems to come out of Jewish vaudeville comedy. First perceived from the veranda of what is clearly a Jewish resort hotel, Tzinchadzi is described as wearing "a long coat, gathered in at the waist by a narrow girdle of leather and Caucasian silver. A white fur cap shaped into a truncated cone, its top covered with red satin and gold lace, was jauntily tilted back on his head. A shirt of cream-colored silk trimmed with gold shone through an opening at the bottom of the cassock, and dangling from the girdle were a dagger and a sabre. The silver tips of what looked like two rows of cartridges glistened at his breast." This strange figure lives somewhere in the woods and comes out from time to time, on horseback, to sell oriental goods to the tourists.

It should be pointed out that the tradition of comic Jewish folklore associated today with the Catskill Mountains was as yet only barely in existence in 1901. Nevertheless, the Catskills had by then already become established as a popular summer vacation area for New York Jewish immigrants who could afford it. Cahan, after he had begun working for the *Commercial Advertiser,* had taken to going there with his wife for two weeks every summer. There he took up the hobby of bird watching, and began in general to enjoy some of the pursuits of leisure that he had never known before. For him, as for many other Jewish immigrants, the Catskills were a symbol of prosperity and of a growing range of bourgeois comforts. It therefore did not take long for Cahan's sense of irony—the main spiritual faculty of many disillusioned romantics—to be struck by the contrast between the physical magnificence of the Catskill Mountain setting and the prosaic way of life that was coming into being there. It is precisely in a moment of contemplating this contrast that the unnamed first-person narrator of "Tzinchadzi of the Catskills" first sets eyes upon the story's main character: "I was gazing at the mountain slopes," the story begins, "across the ear-shaped valley, unable to decide whether they were extremely picturesque or extremely commonplace, when a queer-looking figure on horseback dived out of a wooded spot less than a mile to the right of me." The intention here certainly is comic, even though comedy is rarely to be found in Cahan's writings; furthermore, it is comic in a way that foreshadows the American-Jewish humor of a later generation.

The comedy of the story does not last long, however; but even after it subsides, a surrealistic atmosphere continues to prevail, marking a clear departure from the resolute realism of Cahan's earlier works of fiction. Learning the location of Tzinchadzi's forest home, the narrator goes to visit him one day. "He welcomed me with joyous hospitality, and presently we sat on a fallen tree by the road, chatting of Russia." Their conversation has a ceremonious, dream-like quality:

> When I asked him if he thought the Catskills pretty, he raised his clear eyes toward the peak looming blue between the trees, and he said condescendingly, "They are good."
> "Of course, they don't come up to your mountains."
> He smiled and held out both his index fingers and said: "A butterfly is pretty, and the sea when sprinkled with sunshine is pretty. These mountains are a butterfly; ours the mighty sea."

Tzinchadzi soon warms to his fascinated listener, and reveals to him the reason for his exile:

> "I loved a dark-eyed maiden, and that's why I am now roaming about these strange mountains. . . . Will you hear my tale, sir?"
> His speech seemed to me oddly stilted, but, strange to say, I was beginning to feel its effect on my own.
> "Even if it takes you three days and three nights," I answered.

Tzinchadzi tells of his native town in Georgia, and of Zelaya, the girl he had loved there. Zelaya was a great equestrienne, in a country where, Tzinchadzi points out, the passion for horses has always been extreme. "I never saw a girl," he says, "who could ride like Zelaya." Now, another young man, named Azdeck, had also been in love with Zelaya, and since she was equally fond of both suitors, her father had decided that they should compete for her hand in a horserace. Describing his preparations for this race, Tzinchadzi, carried away by the excitement of his recollections, suddenly leaps onto his horse and performs some turns. He refuses to return to his story until the astonished narrator applauds him for his riding skill. Then he goes on to tell of his victory in the race. "I am yours," Zelaya had said to him at the finish line as the defeated Azdeck headed sadly home past the jeering onlookers.

At this point, Tzinchadzi's narrative becomes strangely garbled and incoherent. "And yet," he suddenly exclaims, "it was Azdeck who got her, not I, and all because of that accursed victory of mine!" Then he adds: "There are many ways of bewitching a maiden, but beware of casting the wrong spell. I thought I should kindle her blood with admiration for my victory, but I only kindled it with pity for Azdeck." Tzinchadzi explains that he should never have let the villagers jeer at Azdeck the way they did. The upshot of the story is that Zelaya had suddenly decided to give herself to Azdeck, hurling at the victor the final and scornful remark: "You are without a heart, Tzinchadzi." For all Zelaya's horsemanship, compassion had been the key to her heart, after all.

Tzinchadzi goes on to describe his life in the months that followed. "My horse," he says, "was the only friend I had." Riding furiously to console himself, he would cry out to his horse: "Fly like an eagle, my love!" And "so I flew over mountains, and flying I sobbed." Eventually he had reached Batum, where his riding skill was discovered one day by the American consul, who thereupon invited him to perform at the Chicago World's Fair. Tzinchadzi had accepted the invitation, and had thus come to America. At the fair he had met another Georgian, a merchant, who "was homesick like me, only he had a wife and children at home, and I—there was a maiden who would not let me love her." Upon returning homeward, the Georgian merchant had sold all his wares to Tzinchadzi, who, on the advice of a Jew of his acquaintance, then went to the Catskills to become a merchant himself. "I sell all kinds of goods now," Tzinchadzi concludes. "The Americans are kind: they like my horsemanship and buy my trinkets. I make plenty of money, but can it buy me Zelaya? Can it turn the Catskills into the Caucasus? Oh!"

The two men part, but the story does not end here. One day six years later, the narrator meets Tzinchadzi again by chance, on a New York ferryboat. He does not at first recognize the Georgian. "His beard was gone, and instead of his picturesque costume of yore he wore an American suit of blue serge, a light derby, and a starched shirt-front with a huge diamond burning in its centre. He had grown fat and ruddy; he glistened with prosperity and prose." He is now, he tells the narrator, a wealthy merchant and owner of real estate, and has changed his name to Jones, which is "easier for Americans to pronounce." The two men converse in a mood of nervous revelation:

> "Are you still homesick?" I joked him.
> "I wish I were," he answered without smiling.
> "And Zelaya?"
> "She married Azdeck. They are happy, but I bear them no grudge."
> "Are you married?"
> "No, but my heart is cured of Zelaya. I bear her no grudge."
> "So you are all right?"
> "Yes. America is a fine place. I expect to go home for a visit, but I won't stay there. A friend of mine went home, but he soon came back. He was homesick for America."

But Tzinchadzi admits he is not happy, "because I yearn neither for my country nor for Zelaya, nor for anything else. I have thought it all out, and I have come to the conclusion that a man's heart cannot be happy unless it has somebody or something to yearn for." In the Catskills, his heart had ached, "but its pain was pleasure, whereas now—alas! The pain is gone, and with it my happiness." Then he says:

> "I am yearning for—what shall I call it?"
> "For your old yearnings," I was tempted to prompt him.

The story ends with the forlorn Georgian's final injunction: "If you want to think of a happy man, think of Tzinchadzi of the Catskills, not of Jones of New York."

This odd story is clearly a dialogue between Cahan and an imaginative projection of himself. At one point, the intellectual's identity lurking within Tzinchadzi reveals itself when, in the narrative about Georgia, Zelaya's father says to him: "You talk too much, my lad, and your talk is too fine. Sift it through a sieve and out of a dozen words one will be to the point." The whole story is a gradual revelation of Tzinchadzi's identity as a kind of Jew—his inclination toward the Catskills, his mercantile career and interest in real estate, the parvenu image he offers in the last scene on the ferryboat, the change of his name to a more pronounceable American one, all point to this. One need only perceive the horses as symbolic of the revolutionary movement and the story of the Jewish immigrant intellectual becomes clear, even down to his postimmigration period of sojourn—Tzinchadzi's forest retreat in the Catskills—in a never-never land of revolutionary nostalgia, lived out in Hester Street cafes and meeting halls as yet impervious to the din of pushcarts and Pig Market negotiations, the American reality, just outside the door.

But what about Zelaya? "There was a maiden who would not let me love her"—this figure of a scornful, proud and unattainable woman has now become a major recurring image in Cahan's writings. If, as is possible, she represents someone specific in Cahan's own life, her identity will ever remain a mystery; there is, of course, a touch of Anna, Cahan's ultimate *barishnya,* about her, but this does not tell the whole story. Clearly, in this narrative as in others to come, she represents Russia, that visionary land of Cahan's past with which his relationship has indeed been that of a failed lover. Zelaya is like Sophia Perovskaya herself, of whom the exiled revolutionary Sergey Kravchinsky ("Stepniak") had written: "She knew how to preserve intact the sacred spark. She did not wrap herself up in the gloomy and mournful mantle of rigid 'duty.' Notwithstanding her stoicism and apparent coldness, she remained, essentially, an inspired priestess; for under her cuirass of polished steel, a woman's heart was always beating." One is tempted to contrast her with the American female vulgarian, Flora Stroon, or Sophie, the daughter of Reb Avrom Leib, who also recurs in Cahan's stories. But, on second glance, the matter seems more complex than that; for one can see touches of the bitch even in Zelaya, the taunting *barishnya* who encourages or rejects her lover's advances on a whim. It will become clearer still in Cahan's subsequent writings that these two sides of his feminine ideal are not cleanly separated from one another by the distance which separates Russia from America. If only Russia were simply the figure of Perovskaya, then her aloofness would be more easily acceptable. Unfortunately for Cahan's spirit, however, his Russian ideal has her craven side as well; but isn't she thereby all the more like Russia itself, that home of noble revolutionary acts, that Jew-hating land?

Cahan's literary development had now fallen precariously astraddle of two sides of his personality. In the latter part of "Tzinchadzi of the Catskills"—the scene on the ferryboat—Cahan is, as in most of his earlier fiction, that "Russian" realistic observer of New York immigrant life that Howells had praised in 1896. But, as the first part of the story reveals, Cahan's most profoundly "Russian" side is not the prosaic New York realist at all, but a romantic dreamer about the past. When examining the dreary present, he was able to bring to bear all the power of his honest and ironical reporter's eye; this critical faculty tended to dim, however, when he looked at the idealized past. It was somewhere in the past that his soul lay, he now felt; the New York milieu with which he had established his literary reputation was a fine subject for journalism, but it no longer seemed adequate to what he was pursuing in his fiction. Yet he could not get a grip on the past adequately, either; it was too blurred, emotionally ambiguous, and painful.

The gap that was growing between these two sides of his spirit severely affected the novel he was trying to write. Significantly called *The Chasm*, its title seems to have represented Cahan's psychological dilemma, just as its story focused upon that dichotomy in his life's experience: for it was to be an epic novel of Jewish emigration from Russia to America. Yet, appropriate as this projected novel evidently was to its author's frame of mind, Cahan could not get it going. Even after leaving the *Commercial Advertiser* he was unable to finish it; instead, he spent more and more of his time roaming through the streets and cafes of the Lower East Side. He was, to be sure, in search of material for stories and articles on these excursions; but he was above all engaged simply in a restless quest for some realization he could not define. There was something about this kind of anonymous immersion in the teeming life of the streets of the New York Ghetto that satisfied the *Narodnik* in him; this flinging of himself upon the masses had almost the quality of a Russian-revolutionary style self-immolation. It provided relief from the pains of subjectivity, and intimations of a fulfillment yet unknown.

## Chapter 11

# Cahan Returns to the *Forward*;
# or, The Fable of the Birds

Der Vogelfänger bin ich ja,
stets lustig heisa hopsasa!
Ich Vogelfänger bin bekannt
bei Alt und Jung im ganzen Land.
Weiss mit dem Lokken umzugehn
und mich auf's Pfeifen zu verstehn.
D'rum kann ich froh und lustig sein,
denn alle Vögel sind ja mein.

Ein Netz für Mädchen möchte ich,
ich fing' sie dutzendweis' für mich.
Dann sperrte ich sie bei mir ein,
und alle Mädchen wären mein.
　　　　　　　—*The Magic Flute*

AS FAR BACK AS THE SUMMER OF 1900, WHEN THE SCARS OF battle were already three years old, Cahan had become a frequenter of Herrick's Cafe on Division Street, where the staff of the *Forward*, then located only a few doors away, used to congregate. By this time, only Winchevsky among the *Forward* staff harbored any continuing rancor toward Cahan, and Winchevsky rarely appeared in person at the office. Tensions between Cahan and Louis Miller had disappeared, and the two were exchanging social visits at one another's homes once again. There were, furthermore, still people at the

*Forward* who were absolute enthusiasts for Cahan's cause. Foremost among these was the poet and political columnist Abraham Liessin, one of the bright young lights of the staff. Cahan had discovered Liessin when the latter was still living in Russia and sending his first contributions to the New York Yiddish press by mail; his name was Abraham Wald, but since prudence had then required that his work appear over a pseudonym, Cahan had concocted one for him out of the Russian translation of his last name, which means "forest": *lyess.* Cahan had also introduced Liessin to Hutchins Hapgood, who included an enthusiastic sketch of him in *The Spirit of the Ghetto.*

An atmosphere of cafe-table good fellowship easily revived between Cahan and his former colleagues, and he soon became a regular visitor at the *Forward* office itself. There he quite naturally began picking up an occasional freelance assignment. Then, in November, 1900, B. Holtzman, who was the paper's editor at that moment—the post was being rotated—asked Cahan if he would like to contribute a series of articles. The idea appealed to Cahan, for this was just when he was beginning to feel the symptoms of an incipient writer's block; he was still turning out short stories, but at very long intervals, and his projected longer works were getting nowhere at all. His old careless ease in dashing off things in Yiddish could now serve him in good stead; an extended piece of writing for the *Forward* could loosen him up, set the juices flowing once again. Also, this was a chance to get back to the psychological source of his creative energies, for in doing a piece for the *Forward* he could write with conscious didacticism once again. What Holtzman had in mind was a series of *articles,* however, whereas Cahan had in his files a mass of notes for potential *stories,* and he wanted to use them. All right, then, the solution was to do a synthesis, a didactic serial in the vein of *Raphael Na'aritzokh.* The very idea struck chords deep in Cahan that had long lain quiet.

Cahan chose as his main narrative subject a plot idea he had jotted down in his notebooks shortly after writing "The Imported Bridegroom." That story had been about the rupture with religious orthodoxy that takes place on American soil—now, what about socialist orthodoxy? His note had prescribed: "A disappointment like Asriel's [Stroon], but instead of an Asriel, a Jewish worker, a crude and simple man, but with a deeply religious nature. Socialism occupies the place of religion for him. He is happy with his son-in-law, because the latter is a 'comrade.' But the son-in-law repudiates the movement and makes fun of it. And his own son, whom he had tried to educate as a socialist, turns into a Tammany-Hallnik. A tragedy." He would weave this plot into a series of sketches describing "a few other former socialists, and also a few other unswervingly faithful ones, like the disappointed father-in-law." His series would thereby be a kind of miniature epic canvas showing the condition of Lower East Side socialism at that moment.

At the time Cahan started to work on this—writing some installments at home, dictating others in the *Forward* office—the American socialist movement was still in disarray. De Leon's reckless and authoritarian personality had caused a mass flight from the Socialist Labor Party. Many of the dissidents had already reorganized their ranks under the banner of the Social Democratic Party that had been created two years before around the figure of the Illinois labor leader, Eugene V. Debs. Now a second wave of dissidents seemed to be forming in the SLP. Known to De Leon's loyal followers as the "Kangaroos" for their apparent ability to hop easily from one party commitment to another, this new group of dissidents was being assiduously cultivated by Debs. On the *Abend Blatt,* Philip Krantz and Benjamin Feigenbaum were leading the "Kangaroo" forces; the *Forward* had, of course, long been affiliated with the Debs party. The following summer would see a major attempt on the part of Debs to bring together this and other dissident elements into a single, new Socialist Party of America; but for the moment the general atmosphere in American socialism was still chaos. For Cahan, the ways in which this chaos manifested itself in the lives of the Jewish intellectuals was further proof of his growing conviction—reinforced by several years of experience in pragmatic Yankeedom—that the purity of socialist orthodoxy was not nearly so important as any method for the betterment of mankind's lot that worked.

For example, one of the sketches in Cahan's series is about a certain Dr. Bunimowitz, a socialist comrade of former times who is now a successful physician and who has invested some of his earnings in real estate. Thus, he is now a capitalist; and yet, as Cahan points out, a decent and charitable man. "When I was a fool, a socialist," Bunimowitz says to an old comrade whom he has met on the street, "I used to talk a lot and do nothing. But now I don't tell stories, and I know full well how much good I do—and so do the hundreds of people I help." Cahan, always in the forefront of those who criticized the condescending charity of uptown Jews, considers that he must nevertheless give credit where it is due. "The doctor's heart is a good one," he writes, "even if his spirit is not that of an eagle flying amid the stars and looking down from a great height, from which all of mankind can be seen; it is, alas, nothing more than an ordinary hen, his spirit. . . . [His old comrade] demanded an eagle-like nature of him. . . . But it is better to have a nice hen than a bad eagle." This observation holds throughout the entire series of sketches. It applies to the son-in-law in the main plot, who is depicted as essentially a decent and honest man even though he mocks socialist ideas. It applies even to the apostate, the son who has gone over to the side of Tammany Hall—an act equivalent, in the eyes of a Lower East Side socialist, to what conversion to Christianity is to a religious Jew—but who, at the end, goes repentant to his father's graveside.

These sketches, which appeared roughly once a week from November, 1900, to January, 1901, were crudely written, but they constituted nevertheless the richest and liveliest piece of work Cahan had done in a long time (it was only after this that he wrote "Tzinchadzi of the Catskills"). They were well received by the *Forward* audience, and almost overnight Cahan's name once again became a byword on the Lower East Side, as it had been years before. Cahan was delighted, and he began contributing articles and feuilletons to the *Forward* regularly. It was quite natural, after his resignation from the *Commercial Advertiser* in the fall, for some members of the *Forward* staff and the Press Association to begin talking about the possibility of his returning to the editorship.

One afternoon in March, 1902, Cahan was walking along East Broadway in the direction of Division Street, where he planned to make one of his frequent calls at the *Forward* office. To his right were the ruins of an entire block of tenements, being cleared to make way for what was to be Seward Park. The spirit of reform, which was now going full steam in New York, had thus reached the hitherto dank corner of Essex Street and East Broadway and was demolishing whatever stood in its way. This was America: progress, boundless optimism, the wrecker's ball; and once again, a whole fragment of history, the relics of struggle, suffering, and human aspiration had been destroyed without a murmur. To be sure, who had not wanted to see those urine-smelling hallways collapse? Yet, some of these foundations—which ones, again?—had held up meeting halls and living rooms within which some of the great struggles of Cahan's youth had taken place. Many of the stones of Vilna had, for better or for worse, been exactly where they were for centuries; yet here was a mere twenty years of one's life—the twenty years of youth—vanished without a trace.

Cahan looked up and saw William Lief and Albert Feller, the two advertising managers of the *Forward*, approaching from the opposite direction. Both these men, in their early thirties, were representatives of a new, more moderate and pragmatic "American" spirit that was being brought into the *Forward* organization by a younger generation; this was true even of Lief, who had been one of the ardent anti-De Leonists who had urged Cahan's departure in 1897, but who had had a considerable change of heart since then. In recent months Lief and Feller had welcomed Cahan's return as a contributor, viewing this hopefully as a step away from the old parochialism and backbiting and towards the more eclectic and entertaining Yankee style of journalism that Cahan represented and that the *Forward* needed as an antidote to its dangerously falling circulation. Indeed, the *Forward* was in danger of extinction. The audience for Yiddish newspapers seemed to be dwindling steadily, for immigration had declined sharply in recent years, and many of the older immigrants had been turning to the English-language press for their news. The *Abend Blatt,* now suffering from the recent defection of the "Kangaroos" as well as from the general crisis of the Yiddish press, was clearly on its last legs. Some members of the *Forward* staff thought the days of their own paper were also numbered, for it had undergone two major financial crises in the past few years. This feeling was shared even by Louis Miller, who, through the years of the rotating editorship, had held the principal reins of editorial power at the paper.

The three men stopped to talk, and the condition of the *Forward* quickly became their subject of conversation. Things were looking bad, they all agreed; of course, Lief and Feller both went on to observe, the paper's prospects would greatly improve if Cahan were to become its editor once again. Wouldn't he give this some thought? Well, Cahan replied, for one thing, there was the problem of the old antagonisms toward him and his policies. With special emphasis, Lief assured him that the situation had changed completely in that respect. Cahan looked at him. Lief, along with Winchevsky, had been his most ardent opponent five years before. But now Lief had clearly changed his views, and as for Winchevsky, he simply did not come to the office any more. All right then, Cahan went on, but there was also the problem of his own work; he could not possibly take an editorial job unless he was free, say, by two o'clock every afternoon to go home and write. Lief and Feller hastened to assure him that this would be possible; the paper went to press at around two o'clock every day, and an editor could certainly then leave the office. The three men had by now forgotten about their respective destinations and were walking together, slowly circling the block of ruined tenements.

"I'm afraid you're making a mistake, Lief," Cahan said, after some deliberation. "The comrades at the *Forward* are just the same as they used to be, but I'm not."

Warming to his subject, Cahan decided to get off his chest some of the criticisms of Lower East Side socialist parochialism that he had been wanting to make for a long time. "I've been out in the world," he went on, beginning to slip unconsciously into the intonations of the lecture platform, "and I've found out that we socialists don't have a monopoly on honesty and wisdom. The outside world is more tolerant of us than we are of it. It tries, at least, to understand us. You and your comrades are utterly parochial in your outlook. But if the *Forward* remains what it is, it won't get very far. It won't get to a very large audience because it doesn't interest itself in the things that the masses are interested in when they aren't preoccupied with their daily struggle for bread. I'm telling you, Lief, it's as important, say, to teach the reader to carry a handkerchief in his pocket as it is to teach him to carry a union card. And it's as important to respect the opinions of others as it is to have opinions of one's own." Cahan paused; he had just given a spontaneous little sermon on American liberalism—but what had been its purpose? Was he giving his reasons for rejecting the offer, or his conditions for accepting it?

Lief recognized the ambiguity. "I'm not the one who's making a mistake, Comrade Cahan," he said. "You are. I'm sure we all want exactly what you want. But we don't quite know how to give expression to our inner aspirations, which are still inarticulate, not yet clearly defined. What we need is, precisely, someone who can put it all into words for us, translate it into acts."

He had said precisely the right thing. Cahan made no further words of protest, but continued quietly to reflect upon what was happening.

"Let me present your name at the next meeting," Lief urged, "as candidate for the editorship. Then you'll see that, in reality, neither of us is mistaken."

They reached the front steps of the building in which the *Forward* was located, and stopped. "I want to think about it," Cahan said at last. "An editor should have unlimited authority. I don't know if that idea is ready for acceptance yet in our circles."

Cahan took his leave of them and walked away. As Lief and Feller gazed after his departing figure, they sensed that they had won their battle. At that moment, Liessin appeared in the doorway, and they told him what had happened.

"You shouldn't have let him get away," Liessin said.

As Cahan headed home, his spirit was in a turmoil. Back to the Yiddish press! Only a few months ago, he would never have dreamed of such a possibility. For years he had been "out in the world," just as he had said, a distinguished resident of the broader realms of American culture, a writer and journalist of good reputation and good prospects. How could he consider leaving all this for a return to the provinces, to the narrow, stifling, backbiting world of Yiddish journalism from which he had been emancipated almost five years ago? Of course, he had to admit, after those four years of illuminating experience as an American reporter, the prospect of running a newspaper of his own was exciting. He had learned much, and his head was already brimming with ideas for the kind of paper he would create. But he would brook no opposition from any of those narrow ideologues assembled in and around the *Forward;* a jot of interference from them, and he would quit.

What about his writing, though? Would he really be able to wind up each day's editorial work at two in the afternoon, and if he could, would he then be able to get to work at his own writing table? For the fact was, he was not getting much writing done even now; how would he do, then, after a hectic two-thirds of a day in an editorial office? This was a crucial problem, for he sensed it as a potential forthcoming test of his determination to go on being a writer of fiction. In a way, he dreaded the confrontation. And yet, there was the possibility that the whirl of activity at a newspaper office would be just the stimulus that his writing needed, as had often been the case in the past. He needed worldly activity and the externally imposed imperatives of the newspaper deadline to make his blood flow. He was like some literary Antaeus who, in order to be strong, had to have his feet planted in the flux of news-getting, in the depths of that seething, ever-unfolding, daily "living novel" that had also quickened the blood of Lincoln Steffens. To write a book, one had to step out of this flow, to enclose oneself in a container of the sensibility that passing events would not disturb; Cahan was temperamentally unable to live his life exclusively in such a container.

By the time he got back to his apartment on East 7th Street, just off Second Avenue, he was persuaded of the virtues of the offer he had just received. His wife, however, felt differently when he told her about it. Anna had never been thoroughly pleased with her husband's involvement in Yiddish journalism in the old days, and she now very much enjoyed thinking of him as an American writer. The financial difficulties of his present situation did not worry her.

"Here, you've made a name for yourself in the literary world," she said. "You have a fine future ahead of you—and you have peace of mind. Do you want to throw that all over now and get mixed up in the movement again, with all its internal 'politics'?"

She reminded him of how bitter the old conflicts had been, and repeated to him a rule that he had himself made in recent years: that it was better to be a "Sunday socialist" than to take up any official party position. Since the creation of the Socialist Party of America the previous summer, Anna and Abraham had enjoyed the luxury of just being ordinary members, attending meetings, making occasional proposals, but otherwise staying out of party affairs. Wasn't this preferable to the political tornado he was now thinking of reentering? Furthermore, Anna warned him, the two-o'clock rule would never work; he would never get home in time to do his writing each day. Cahan was plunged into gloom.

Still another gloomy prospect connected with the *Forward* job came up a few days later, when Cahan ran into Louis Miller. With an air of forced insouciance, Miller asked him if the rumor of his imminent return to the *Forward* was true. Cahan told him that he would probably return, but only on condition that he have the complete authority he sought over editorial policy, and that he be able to leave the office at two every afternoon. Miller assured him that, should he want to take the job, these conditions would certainly be fulfilled. Miller then went on to speak animatedly about how good it would be if his old friend returned to the editorship. But Cahan sensed that something rang false in these remarks. He knew full well that Miller had been the constant power behind the endless round of successions to the throne, a power that would be utterly subordinated by his own return. The conversation between the two old friends remained cordial, but there was a distinct and unpleasant undercurrent of tension between them.

In a few more days, Cahan learned that the fateful meeting of the *Forward* Press Association had been held, and that he had been elected editor. All his conditions had been accepted, including a third one that he had attached in the meantime, in some ways the most difficult of all to fulfill. He had insisted that the paper, which was six pages in length, be expanded to eight; he felt that only this greater length would give him space enough in which to accomplish anything. Even Lief and Feller were a trifle dismayed at this request; they well understood the paper's economic problems, and wondered if this extra load could be supported. On the other hand, they also well knew that this was the best time of year to make such a move if it was going to be made; for Passover was approaching, and this was when advertising always increased in the Jewish quarter. For the time being, the two extra pages could carry enough ads to pay for themselves; what would happen after Passover was another question.

Nothing remained now but for Cahan to go to work, and he did so, with the fit of enthusiasm and boundless energy that he always brought to some new and profoundly appealing project. The first issue to be published fully under his auspices was scheduled for March 16, only a few days after his arrival. It was a Sunday, and Cahan was determined to fill that day's *Forward* with the widest possible range of feature material, to signal a new departure. "There will be much more to read than there has been so far," he told his readers in an announcement that appeared on Saturday, "and bit by bit improvements will be made in every department. The news and all the articles will be written in pure, plain *Yiddishe Yiddish,* and we hope that every line will be interesting to all Yiddish-speaking people, big and little." The announcement then presented a list of headings for the articles that were to appear the next day. Much of the material had been written by Cahan himself, who worked well into the evening each day to create the new paper that he wanted. The two-o'clock quitting schedule had vanished almost before he thought about it. When he did get around to thinking about it, he promised himself he would return to his literary work at a later date. For the moment, there were more pressing tasks.

The paper that Cahan was about to transform had been a serious but drab six-page sheet, three pages of which were regularly filled with advertisements. Its heart had been the fourth and fifth pages, which embodied the old formula of a "daily magazine," containing poems, sketches, serialized fiction, articles on a great variety of subjects, and, above all, the editorial, or "lead article," as it was called by Yiddish journalists. The "lead article" was the keystone of the Yiddish socialist newspaper; more often than not of a theoretical nature, it constituted a daily forum for the discussion of socialist ideas. The rest was largely trimming: the news on page one was not distinguished by anything but its particular luridness of presentation. In fact, the front page was the one part of the *Forward* that had an American, rather than a European, character: like its English-language counterparts on Park Row, the *Forward* tended to favor local "police" news over national and international affairs, and to stress the sensational aspects of murders, thefts, fires, and the like. This was the *Forward*'s, only concession to the principles of mass appeal prior to Cahan's return. But Cahan was now going to set loose his instinct for the "American" and the popular upon every department.

His first issue was a dramatic demonstration of his intentions. Knowing full well that socialist theoretical discussions, for all their talk *about* the worker, meant very little *to* the average worker, he was determined to appeal to a broad readership through that time-honored element of American journalism, "human interest." Indeed, one of the pieces he included in this issue was a translation of a "human interest" article he had done for the *Commercial Advertiser*. Called "In Love With *Yiddishe Kinder*," it was an assortment of anecdotes about Christian boys or girls who had fallen in love with Jews and, in some cases, married them. One story tells of a Jewish girl who had married an Italian barber on condition that he convert to Judaism. He had done so, and from then on she had watched sternly to see to it that he did not neglect to put on his phylacteries and say his morning prayer each day. But one day, years later, the barber observes that their teen-aged son, Joe, does not have to per-form the same ritual. Why is that?, he asks his wife. "Because," she replies, "Joe is a Jew." This material was clearly designed to appeal to the uneducated immigrant Jewish housewife—a person to whom Yiddish socialist journalists had hitherto never dreamed of address-ing themselves. Cahan knew there was a vast audience of women readers to be tapped, and he was making his bid for it.

He did not completely neglect the paper's more purely socialist purposes, but for these, too, he sought more popular formulae. For this same issue, for example, he had Abraham Liessin write a piece, entitled "Protzentniks in Sweatshops," about bosses who readily grant advances on wages to needy workers in their shops, but who then deduct interest (*protzent*, i.e., "per cent") on the loan from the following week's wages. Nobody could question this article's ideo-logical purity of intentions; but it also happened to be written in an unusually vivid anecdotal style. On the other hand, there were signs in this first issue of his that Cahan was inclined, not merely to ignore socialist concerns—as he had done in his article about love and marriage between Christians and Jews—but even perhaps to challenge them. In a column of miscellaneous anecdotes, observations, riddles, and sayings, he had placed the following description of "the three stages in the life of a freethinker: (1) when he passes a synagogue and gnashes his teeth; (2) when he passes a synagogue and smiles; (3) when he passes a synagogue and, though inclined to sigh because the world is still in such a state of ignorance, nevertheless finds himself taking an interest in such moments as these, when men stand together immersed in a feeling that has nothing to do with the egoistic life." One can hear the voice of Zalkin and other nostalgic heroes of Cahan's fiction speaking. This is undoubtedly a genuine utterance of Cahan's feelings on the subject. It also is clearly a step toward reconciliation with the sensibilities of that average Jewish workingman who, though he may have become a loyal member of a union, had nevertheless remained pious enough still to prefer the orthodox *Tageblatt* to the fiercely anticlerical *Forward*. "It's as important," Cahan had told Lief and Feller that day on East Broadway, "to respect the opinions of others as it is to have opinions of one's own." Even as far back as his last years at the *Arbeiter Zeitung* and the *Abend Blatt,* he had begun to advocate a more tolerant attitude toward the feelings of religious Jews than socialists usually were inclined to show. He had always been, for example, an ardent opponent of Yom Kippur balls, which were popular for a time even among the social democrats. Clearly, he was now preparing for a revival of his old anti-anticlerical crusade.

But the most striking example of Cahan's new policy in this inaugural issue of March 16 was offered in his editorial, or "lead article," which stood forth like a return of the Proletarian Maggid after years of wandering through the *goles* of American journalism. A complete distillation of Cahan's aims and techniques, the editorial's aggressively down-to-earth character was summed up by its title, or heading: "Send your children to college if you can, but don't let them become disloyal to their own parents and brothers!" It begins:

> On Second Avenue at around eight o'clock every morning, one can see hundreds of Jewish boys from fourteen to eighteen or nineteen years old walking with books under their arms. They are walking uptown from Houston Street or Chrystie Street. They walk in pairs or in groups, conversing merrily. Their clothes are mostly poor and old, but their Jewish faces often shine with spiritual joy and bear the stamp of lively, active minds.
>
> These are Jewish college boys, children of immigrants.

Nothing like this had ever been seen in the Yiddish press before. Here was a "lead article," about to address itself to a question of principle as "lead articles" always had done; and yet it was beginning with a scene, as if from a story. This was a striking departure from the traditional "abstract-theoretical" plane, as Cahan put it, of Yiddish socialist editorials.

But the popularizing form of presentation and style is not the only new departure represented by these opening lines. For Cahan is also making a frank appeal here to Jewish nationalist or chauvinist sentiments, another traditionally forbidden course in Yiddish socialist journalism. This appeal is given a socialist legitimacy, however, by being couched in proletarian terms in the ensuing lines:

> From the various corners of the Jewish quarter they come, from the poor, narrow tenement houses. And they go to 23rd Street, where City College is—a pleasant-looking red building on the corner of Lexington Avenue. This college is maintained by the city; one doesn't pay there, and the government also gives the students books and all necessary writing materials free. But even so it is still hard for poor people to send their child to college, it is hard for them to keep their children provided with shoes and clothing and—quite simply—to keep them properly fed. A worker or ped-

dler or poor storekeeper is, for the most part, forced to take his ten year old child out of school. The child must go to work, there to break and scrape his little ten year old fingers—what can you do? You have to pay the rent.

You don't find many German, Irish or Italian children in City College. About ninety per cent of the boys there are Jews, and most of them children of Jewish workers.

The Jew undergoes privation, spills blood, to educate his child. We know of a poor Jewish worker's family in which the father earns barely eight dollars a week and the mother is ill. But when the boy wanted to go to work, his parents absolutely refused to let him. In another such home, an aunt (the mother's unmarried sister) works sixteen hours a day—the luster of her eyes has already dimmed—to keep her nephew in college. There are hundreds of examples like this. . . . In it is reflected one of the finest qualities of the Jewish people. It shows our capacity to make sacrifices for our children (perhaps this is one of the reasons it is so hard to make the Jews disappear), as well as our love for education, for intellectual effort.

No more welcome compliment could have been paid to the average Jewish immigrant parent. Here, suddenly, in their workers' newspaper, was a bit of concern for their real struggles and hopes!

Now the editorial takes a sudden change of direction. For Cahan not only recognizes the family virtues he has just described, but also is aware of the problems that result from these manifestations of virtue. In general, what arises is a gap between the generations, wider than the traditional one to begin with because of the immense differences in experience between an immigrant and his American-born children, and widened further still by the superior education those children are obtaining. And so now the preacher steps to the fore:

Most of these children are loyal to their parents and a joy to them. But there are also bad examples, and, indeed, many such examples in the land of hustle and bustle and of dollars and cents. It often happens that the over-educated son (or daughter) of a poor family is ashamed of his father and mother who have toiled and

Abraham Cahan in 1883, aged twenty-three, a year after his arrival in the United States. *The Jewish Daily Forward*

Anna Bronstein in 1885, at the time of her marriage to Abraham
Cahan. *The Jewish Daily Forward*

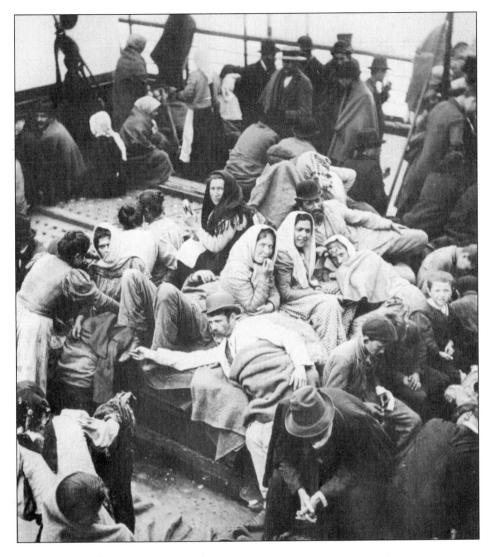

Jewish immigrants on their way to America. *Brown Brothers*

Young Russian Jews arriving in New York. *Brown Brothers*

Hester Street, westward from the corner of Essex Street.
Down the street is the site of the "Pig Market." *Brown Brothers*

A typical sweatshop in a contractor's apartment. Photograph by Jacob A. Riis, The Jacob A. Riis Collection, Museum of the City of New York

Preparing for the Sabbath in a Ludlow Street coal cellar. This picture illustrates why Abraham Cahan, among others, perceived that socialist intellectuals were mistaken in ignoring the workingman's attachment to religious traditions. *Photograph by Jacob A. Riis, The Jacob A. Riis Collection, Museum of the City of New York*

Education in the New World, traditional and modern. ABOVE: A *kheder* (religious elementary school) on Hester Street. BELOW: A classroom in the Essex Market Public School, Essex Street. *Photographs by Jacob A. Riis, The Jacob A. Riis Collection, Museum of the City of New York*

Louis Miller in 1892.
*The Jewish Daily Forward*

Philip Krantz in 1891.
*The Jewish Daily Forward*

Morris Hillquit in 1901.
*The Jewish Daily Forward*

Joseph Barondess, some years
after his time of leadership in
the Jewish labor movement.
*YIVO Institute for Jewish Research*

Morris Winchevsky, about the time of his arrival in the United States. *YIVO Institute for Jewish Research*

Jacob Gordin at the height of his career. *YIVO Institute for Jewish Research*

Police reporters on Mulberry Street. (The man in the rear is peering through the door to see if any "news" has developed at Police Headquarters across the street.) Jacob Riis, Lincoln Steffens, and Abraham Cahan all served part of their journalistic apprenticeships in this room. *Photograph by Jacob A. Riis, The Jacob A. Riis Collection, Museum of the City of New York*

The excavation for William H. Seward Park, looking from Essex and Hester Streets toward East Broadway and Jefferson Street, about 1900. The large building in the right rear, with the American flag on top, is the Educational Alliance; at the extreme right is the four-story building housing the *Tageblatt*. The *Forward* was later to be located a few doors farther right, out of the range of the photograph. *Photograph by Jacob A. Riis, The Jacob A. Riis Collection, Museum of the City of New York*

Samuel Gompers addressing the shirtwaist makers in the Great Hall of Cooper Union, during the general strike of 1909. *Brown Brothers*

The Triangle Shirt Waist Company after the fire, 1911. *Brown Brothers*

Members of the United Garment Workers in Union Square, March 1, 1913, protesting the settlement made by the union's leaders and endorsed by the *Forward* the day before. The sign reads: "Unzere leaders zogn: Strike gesettled—ober diezen demonstratzion tzeigt andersh" ("Our leaders say: strike settled—but this demonstration indicates otherwise"). *Amalagamated Clothing Workers of America.*

Abraham Cahan at about sixty-five years of age. The *Forward* editor at the height of his power and influence. *The Jewish Daily Forward*

The *Forward* Building, circa 1968. *Photograph by Sol Zaretsky.*

saved in order to send him to college. It is not unusual nowadays to hear of a poor Jewish college boy who goes on to become a flatterer of the rich and a toady to the politicians, enemies of the people, of the college boys' parents. . . . Such college boys are traitors to their own parents!

The orthodox socialist theme of the editorial seems to be emerging: fancy college boys who betray their working-class parents with *arriviste* snobberies. For a moment here, Cahan seems to have struck the chord that sounds a perfect harmony between his search for themes of mass appeal and the traditional socialist aims of the *Forward*. But something goes wrong in the next paragraph:

A story is told in Russia of a general who came to a Jewish doctor's house and found there a Jew with sidelocks and a long gaberdine. The doctor turned red. "This is my tailor," he said to the general. In reality the Jew with the sidelocks is the doctor's father. This doctor, then, was ashamed of his own father.

Reading this passage, one cannot but reflect on the probability that the strictly orthodox old father of many a Jewish socialist and freethinker—Cahan's own case cannot be excluded—would not have even been present in his son's household, much less be an embarrassment to him in front of his associates. Cahan is veering dangerously here in the direction of describing a kind of filial snobbery that cuts across the lines normally dividing socialist from capitalist. This slip may have been unconscious on his part, but one thing is clear: it is the result of drawing upon folk attitudes rather than socialist principles as his source. As Cahan the novelist well knew, the tensions between an uneducated father and an educated son have, at bottom, nothing whatsoever to do with ideology. Cahan is really using the cloak of a discussion of socialist principles to address a visceral appeal to the everyday experience of the uneducated masses. Beneath the aspect of the ideologue, the demagogue was emerging.

This first issue of the *Forward* under Cahan's editorship was an immediate sensation. Letters poured into the office, most of them praising the new features, others condemning the vulgarity of such articles as the one about Jewish-Gentile marriages, and many asking the question that was already being asked by a large part of the *Forward's* staff and Press Association: what was a socialist newspaper doing writing about such things? Another socialist editor might perhaps have been driven to write a series of furious replies to many of these criticisms; but Cahan had been to America, and he knew that all this was just grist for his mill. Whether the responses were favorable or not, the more of them the better. Circulation was bound to grow as a result; the flow of letters coming in was like a bloodstream connecting Cahan's desk with that living organism, the folk life of the Jewish quarter. He had entered upon a new phase of the relationship between his inner self and the seething streets of the Lower East Side. And in the process, he had begun to move imperceptibly from the liberal frame of reference of Steffens or the Hapgood brothers to the demagogic one of those other journalistic contemporaries of his, William Randolph Hearst and Joseph Pulitzer. For Cahan was beginning already to have glimmers of their prophetically American vision of the newspaper as an instrument for creating a realm of charismatic power.

As if consciously applying the techniques of Hearst and Pulitzer, Cahan announced a competition in his second issue. Readers were invited to contribute a sentence or short paragraph on the theme: "What Is Luck?" (in Yiddish, what is *mazzel?,* a term extremely rich in folk associations). Cahan could not have made a better choice for a simultaneous incentive and barometer to growing circulation and reader interest. Only two days after the competition was announced the *Forward* had enough responses to fill two columns with them, and to be able to do so every day thereafter for weeks to come. The responses were as varied in character as Cahan could have wished. Some of them were orthodox enough from the socialist point of view (e.g., "*Mazzel* is something that the rich have, but not the poor"), but often enough they were the utterances of despairing businessmen (e.g., when one man opens a store and fails, and another man, no more talented than the first, does so and is successful, this is the second man's *mazzel*), and many of them had a frame of reference which went beyond ideology, such as this one: "*Mazzel* is the silken blouse in which the lucky person is born, I have tried to make friends with *Mazzel*. 'Ah, how I would like to be your friend,' *Mazzel* once said to me, 'if only my brother, your enemy, *Shlim-mazzel* ("bad luck") weren't always following you around." The *Forward* asked its readers to write letters judging which was the best of these contributions; the winner would receive a cash prize. The honor went to the author of the laconic observation: "*Mazzel* is somebody else's *shlim-mazzel*."

Features of this sort soon bore fruit in a new type of relationship between newspaper and reader. Suddenly the *Forward* was the immigrant's friend and confidant—nay more, it was a patient and omniscient father, wise in the ways of America, to whom one wrote seeking counsel. Letters seeking advice came in constantly, and though they were not all dealt with on the pages of the newspaper, Cahan's journalistic sense knew which of them could profitably be accorded prominent treatment. One day, for example, a letter came in from a high school boy, the son of Jewish parents who had immigrated from a small village in Rumania. Having become thoroughly steeped in American ways, the boy was finding himself constantly in distress over the boorish peasant manners of his parents. In particular, he was troubled by the fact that dishes were unheard of in his house, where the entire family gathered around the table every evening and ate dinner from a single bowl. Now, the father was a proud man, who had struggled hard to see his son through school, and he was always deeply resentful of any attempt on his son's part to tell him how to behave. The boy had therefore written to the *Forward,* of which his father was a devoted reader; for he was certain that his father would heed the *Forward*'s advice if it told him to use dishes at the dinner table. Cahan sat down and wrote an editorial on the subject, which began by complimenting the father for having given his son such a fine education, and then went on gently to suggest, in the name of the excellent progress that the younger generation was making, that he let his son buy some dishes for the household. A few weeks later, a grateful letter came from the boy: a set of fine new dishes adorned the family dinner table. Cahan immediately used this as material for another editorial, entitled: "Now there are dishes in the house!"

This was more than men like Winchevsky and other high-minded associates of the *Forward* could bear. Cahan was beginning to find himself the center of a furore, in the *Forward* editorial offices, in the Press Association, in the labor unions, and among the readership of the paper in general. Where was he taking the *Forward?* The circulation was growing rapidly, there could be no question about that—and this made men like Lief, Feller, and others associated with the business side of the *Forward* enterprise Cahan's staunchest allies—but how far would he go in compromising the paper's dignity in order to bring about such results? Cahan answered all these questions of principle with statements of principle. He constantly reiterated his view that the paper should be an organ of "socialism" and not of "socialists," and that this meant it should not confine itself to a narrow circle of true believers, but should reach out to the masses and be a genuine "folk paper," reflecting broadly human concerns. "When Karl Marx gave us to understand," he argued in one editorial, "that real socialism is the struggle of the working class and the emancipation of the worker through his own power, he did not mean to construe the working class as some fanatical, selfish little Hasidic circle." How, he asked, was the ordinary, unlearned, sometimes barely literate worker to become a socialist in the first place, if a group of socialist intellectuals simply talked to each other in an abstruse language that that worker was unable to understand?

Cahan's critics conceded that the masses had to be won over somehow; but, they argued, Cahan always "lowers himself to the masses instead of lifting them up." To this Cahan replied: "If you want to pick a child up from the ground, you first have to bend down to him. If you don't, how will you reach him?" This became one of his favorite arguments, along with his claim that his opponents were like Talmudists overly attached to the tradition of *Halacha*—of legalistic intellectual analysis—at the expense of that of *Haggadah*—of storytelling for the purpose of spiritual instruction. Himself a representative of the latter tradition, Cahan summed up his own position in a story which echoed both with the traits of Talmudic *Haggadah* and with his recently acquired passion for bird watching. Once upon a time, the story went, there was a city that had no birds in it who could sing. The inhabitants longed to hear the singing of birds. Then one day a Jew came into the city and proposed a remedy: he knew a certain way of chanting the Holy Name of the Lord (a traditional method for healing and working miracles in Jewish folklore) which would bring forth melodies from birds that had never sung before. He proceeded to try out his method on the birds of the city; but every time he approached one of them to make his incantation, it would fly away. Unable to get close enough to any of the birds to work his miracle, he became heavy-hearted with despair. Then one day another Jew came to the city and said to him: "Scatter some corn! If the birds have something to peck at, they won't fly away so quickly. And while they're pecking, you can make your incantation." Cahan's colleagues got the point; but some of them wondered, in effect, whether the Holy Name could really be heard amidst all the din of pecking, or whether the Jew, for that matter, wasn't really too busy feeding the birds to be trying to chant it at all any more?

What troubled them, indeed, even more than the vulgarity of much of Cahan's material, was the feeling that his search for wide popularity, his consensus journalism, was leading to a weakening of socialist principles. This seemed to be the case particularly in the matter of religion. Anticlericalism and even atheism were virtually fundamental principles of the socialist ideology of most of Cahan's generation of Russian-Jewish intellectuals, for they had fought their way to their beliefs against the stifling orthodoxy of a centuries-old religious establishment. Cahan's tendency toward toleration of religious pieties was, in their eyes, as much a heresy as their own views were to orthodox rabbis. From the moment he returned to the *Forward,* many of them anticipated a struggle over this question, and they were right. In one of Cahan's earliest issues, he published an editorial entitled "Freethinkers, Don't Be Fanatics!" Then the impending conflict hung fire for a few weeks.

But one day a letter came from a young socialist seeking advice. His father had recently died, and his mother was now imploring him, the only surviving son, to recite the *Kaddish,* the traditional Jewish prayer for a dead parent. Now, as a socialist and a freethinker, he did not believe in this ritual and his mother knew it. Nevertheless, she was in despair at her son's refusal to say this prayer for his dead father's sake. The young man had therefore decided to ask the *Forward:* should he comply with his mother's wish in order to soothe her troubled heart, even though it meant doing something in which he did not believe? This was the opportunity Cahan had been waiting for. With all the solicitude for parental feelings that could be mustered by a man who was himself a guilty son, Cahan wrote an editorial saying yes, the young man should recite the *Kaddish.* He argued that this would not be hypocrisy, because everyone—the young man's mother, and now all his comrades reading his letter in the *Forward*—knew what his true feelings were. His mother would know that he was doing this only for her peace of mind; and bringing peace to a mother, Cahan pointed out, was as important a moral duty as maintaining one's agnostic principles.

This article aroused the expected storm of criticism, but Cahan was able to hold his own in the editorial office because he had firm and influential allies there. Two of the most important figures on the *Forward* staff, Louis Miller and Abraham Liessin, were on his side, and Miller even wrote an article defending Cahan's views on religion. At heart, after all, Miller had always been as much a Yankee pragmatist as Cahan was. But his support for Cahan at this time was especially remarkable in light of the fact that, since the latter's return to the paper, tension between the two men had grown sharply. They were, in fact, no longer on speaking terms with one another. One day Miller had come up to the *Forward* from his law office—he had been in private legal practice now for many years—and begun talking to Cahan at length about a case he was working on, with the idea of sounding out its possibilities as material for an article in the *Forward*. To Cahan, never one to brook interruptions when he was busy, as he was at this moment, this lengthy intrusion apparently seemed like an overweening effort on Miller's part to assert the continuing priority of his interests over all other matters at the *Forward* office. It smacked of the old careless, unworkmanlike dilettantism that had prevailed at the *Forward* before Cahan's return—this was a trait Cahan had never liked in his colleagues and that he even often thought he saw, to his dismay, lurking within himself. Cahan suddenly found himself brusquely interrupting Miller's long discourse, saying he was not interested in the idea and had no time now to discuss it further. Miller was stunned; this was exactly what he had always feared would happen. He left the office and never spoke to Cahan again.

The jealousies and rivalries that Cahan was beginning to incur against himself in abundance were aggravated by the fact that the circulation of the *Forward* was now leaping skyward. By the middle of May, two months after he had taken over, the average weekday circulation had gone up from six thousand to eight thousand; by the middle of the summer, the *Forward* was selling nineteen thousand copies a day. The birds were coming in great numbers to peck at his corn, and Cahan, jubilant hobbyist, began again to ramble through the streets of the Jewish quarter and to observe the life there, as of old, but now with greater energy and a new purpose. For this time he wanted to hear the voice of the Yiddish folk not only making the spontaneous utterances of its soul, but answering the specific question: "What do you think of the *Forward?*" Though his name, as editor, was becoming well known, his face was not yet, and he was able anonymously to engage people in conversation on street corners, in stores, in barber shops, always working his way with apparent casualness to the central question. It was as if all his years of wandering those streets had achieved fulfillment at last. The epic he had been trying to write all that time had suddenly become the epic he was living, the *Forward* itself a central dramatic element in the "living novel" it was recording each day. What book that he could write could ever be adequate to this flow of reality that now surged through his eyes and ears, his brain, and his newspaper?

In this rush of vitality and power, Cahan found that he was able to push the dark side of his spirit into the background along with his novelist's quill—and indeed, along with the English language. The Yiddish language—to which and within which he never ceased to feel a lurking sense of superiority—brought out the paternalist in him, the old instinct of the lecturer striving for the simple phrase or anecdote that would instruct the Jewish worker. This in turn brought upon him a mien of fatherly goodwill and optimism. Who had time for the kind of brooding that had emerged in his later fiction when the immediate and pressing reality around him was the task of instructing Mottke in the use of the handkerchief? Indeed, Cahan devoted one of his editorials precisely to that task.

If his old novelist's sorrows did occasionally break through somewhere in his journalistic writings, they did so in the context of his role as a fatherly counselor. This took place one day, for example, when a letter from a reader inspired him to write a feuilleton on the subject of "yearning." "When I read recently," he wrote, "a letter in the *Forward* from a 'greenhorn' [a newly arrived immigrant] saying how he yearns for home, I too began to yearn—but not for home. . . . It's already quite a long time since I became *oysgegreent* ["de-greened," adjusted to the ways of America], a long time since I've yearned." Like Tzinchadzi in his business suit, Cahan invokes the lost happiness of those days, twenty years ago, when he was a greenhorn and still had the capacity to yearn for his European past. But the mournful spirit of Tzinchadzi belongs to Cahan the novelist and not to Cahan the fatherly counselor, who eschews crying over spilt milk here and tries to provide a philosophical balm to the soul instead, incidentally offering a sermon on his own pragmaticized socialist beliefs:

> My heart broke in disappointment a thousand times, until it became *oysgegreent,* and now it's stopped breaking and suffering disappointment. "If you can't fight 'em, join 'em"—this is the Scriptural lesson it has learned. "You mustn't be a foolish dreamer," it has told itself. "You have to look reality in the face, and instead of getting excited over the fact that everything doesn't become what it should in a single stroke, you should find out what to do about it. Instead of gnashing your teeth over the muteness of the masses and not doing anything because you'd rather do things as they would have been done once, a long time ago, you should spend your time doing what you can." . . .
>
> I have become *oysgegreent*—practical, as they say. I no longer gnash my teeth over the foolish world.

But the confidence of this resolution does not quite accommodate the overflow of the author's feelings. The fact is that a deeper chord has been struck than the sermon writer can handle with ease, and the piece turns into a tormented soliloquy after all:

> My thoughts, my wish about how men should live in the world, my belief, my firm belief that it will someday be so—this has remained unaltered, it has stayed within me and will stay for as long as I remain in the world. How terrible my life would be if these rays were not to glow in my heart, if my idea did not glow! My dear, my sacred idea! You are as young to me as I myself was twenty years ago; you give me light in my darkest moments, you give me a shred of self-respect when, in the humdrum course of things, I sometimes lose faith for a moment in my own decency. You warm me when my soul feels chilled, you are often my only

consolation—my idea, my precious idea! Deep down, my heart knows the purity of my faith in you, and because it knows this, it retains a shred of self-esteem. But—

Oh! But now I am a practical man; I am no longer a greenhorn! I no longer think of my home town. . . . I sleep in peace and look peacefully upon the world; I do not yearn. . . . I know that I am right in being like this, that twenty years ago I was too green, but nevertheless . . . I yearn for my greenness of old . . . I yearn for my yearnings of twenty years ago.

Normally, Cahan was prevented by his busy schedule from having time for broodings of this sort, but before the end of the year he was to have ample opportunity to indulge them again. For in September he resigned once again from the editorship of the *Forward*.

This came about, ironically, as a result of a financial crisis that had been created by Cahan's very success. For the *Forward* had grown too rapidly for its own capital. The increase in the number of pages from six to eight, and the trebling of the number of copies printed for distribution each day within a four-month period, had brought on heavy additional printing costs. These costs would, of course, eventually be met by the increased advertising and the raised advertising rates that came of this expansion, but for the moment there was a time lag, and the margin of funds with which to meet current expenses was perilously narrow. Matters were made worse toward the end of the summer, when a strike broke out at the American Tobacco Company, the *Forward*'s biggest buyer of advertising space. As a gesture of solidarity with the striking workers, the *Forward* had to refuse to carry its vital revenue-producing ads.

The dying *Abend Blatt*, making a last grab for life—it was not to last out the year—continued to carry the American Tobacco Company ads, claiming justification for this in the fact that the striking union was not affiliated with the Socialist Trade and Labor Alliance. This move caused considerable controversy among the Lower East Side intelligentsia and a further defection from the De Leonists' sink-ing ship. Philip Krantz and Benjamin Feigenbaum, who had already resigned from the *Abend Blatt* a while ago, and who, in the previous year, had had a brief, unsuccessful fling at publishing a Yiddish newspaper of their own, decided that the time had come to throw in their lot with the flourishing *Forward* enterprise. From private investments, they had accumulated a fair amount of capital for their own short-lived paper, and they had managed to rescue a good deal of it. They now proposed to merge their resources with the *Forward*—on certain conditions. Opposed to Cahan's policies, they demanded that the paper be made more "socialistic" once again, and that an editorial board be established to have a hand in the making of policy. This latter demand, in particular, represented a complete violation of the major condition on which Cahan had resumed the editorship. The *Forward*'s Press Association, troubled by its financial straits, saw no choice but to accept Krantz's and Feigenbaum's offer, on their terms. Repelled by the prospect of thus submitting to Krantz's influence, Cahan submitted his resignation instead.

The heavy heart Cahan felt upon taking this step contrasted significantly with his mood of elation at the time of his first resignation from the *Forward,* five years earlier. At that time he had just been beginning as a novelist and was eager to confront his possibilities. Now the luster of his literary career had long since faded, and the creation of a new sort of Yiddish-American newspaper had become the prospect that fascinated him. But trying to carry out that task under anyone's thumb, above all that of Krantz, was out of the question for him. So now, wearily, he had to try to gather his manuscripts together again and get to work on the literary projects he had never finished.

His wife was determined to force him back onto the literary path he had so precipitously left a few months before. Their relations had evidently become strained, for Anna now proposed, as an effort to deal with both her husband's difficulties in writing and the financial problems they faced without the income from the *Forward,* that they live separately for a time. By giving up their relatively expensive apartment they could cut costs; she would live in a modest furnished room and he could fulfill an old wish to spend some time in the country, working there in peace and quiet. They agreed to do this, and Cahan decided to set himself up in Woodbine, New Jersey, the site of an experimental Jewish agricultural community that he had long wanted to write about. He proposed a series of articles on this subject to Henry J. Wright at the *Commercial Advertiser;* Wright agreed, and Cahan went forth in search of his happy rural seat.

In Woodbine, he wrote a lot of journalistic pieces, both for the *Commercial Advertiser* and for the *Forward,* to which he again became a regular contributor after tempers had settled a bit. But, on his more serious literary endeavors he made little progress. He tried to get back to work on *The Chasm,* the epic novel of the Jewish migration from Russia to America that he originally had hoped to finish more than two years ago, but he could not make it work. His stint at the *Forward* had made him restless physically as well as spiritually; he yearned for the constant and hectic movement of the editorial office. Instead of Manhattan streets, he now wandered the New Jersey countryside, going either from town to town to observe the life in them, or through the fields, binoculars in hand, to gaze at birds. In this way, Cahan passed the late fall and winter.

With the spring came swarms of mosquitoes, and Cahan decided to go elsewhere. At the beginning of April he bought a new pair of binoculars and went up to New Milford, Connecticut, where he began his bird watching in earnest. Every morning at five o'clock, the townspeople were presented with the sight of this oddly foreign figure of a man, with his mustache, spectacles and great shock of hair, heading out to the countryside armed with field glasses and a bird manual. Usually he was not seen returning until quite late in the afternoon. Thinking him to be an ornithologist by profession, many New Milford residents took to referring to him as "The Bird Man."

"In New Milford," Cahan later wrote of these days, "I felt the true taste of spring for the first time." Spring is the best season for watching birds. "A heavenly pastime!" Cahan went on. "The American birds are not such gifted musicians as the European nightingale or canary. But there are lots of other types here worth hearing. The few notes of the American thrush or red-breasted grosbeak say more to my fancy than does the whole concert of the nightingale or the canary (perhaps this is because I never heard the European songbirds up close), and there are several American birds from whom you get a melody that is truly magnificent." In particular, Cahan loved the experience of practical confirmation that this hobby provided to the patient observer, the satisfaction of finally seeing in reality something which had originally been presented only as a concept to the mind. "In the bird manual you would read (and see the picture) of types of birds that you had never yet seen in reality. . . . When you recognized one of these birds [in the field], your heart would pound with joy."

Cahan recalled how, when he had studied English in a public school class back in the fall of 1882, he had been puzzled one day during a discussion of something called a "bobolink." Now, "in New Milford I saw and heard live bobolinks for the first time. And with what joy did I recognize them! They are not richly colored; but they are interesting all the same, and their notes"—here Cahan recalled the tones of an instrument he had briefly tried mastering when a student at the Vilna Teachers' Institute, the homely but powerful wail of which had always appealed to something deep within him—"their notes are like those of a clarinet. I chased after them like a man who had been hypnotized. But they become silent in mid-June." In this way, he became acquainted with some fifty varieties of American birds; "many of them were richly dressed, some of them beautiful in a merely sensational way, others more genuinely beautiful." All this somehow helped to confirm his hard-earned intimacy with the country he had adopted, and in which he had now spent nearly half his life. "In my native land the birds had been strange to me. I knew their names from Russian literature, but how this or that one looked or what kind of songs they sang—of this I had no idea."

Shortly after Cahan set himself up in New Milford, news reached America of a vast pogrom in Kishinev, in which some forty-five Jews were killed and more than a thousand injured. This was the worst outburst of violence against the Jews of Russia to have occurred since the pogroms of 1881. The entire Jewish world was enraged at the news. Upon hearing it, Cahan took a train back to New York and rushed to the *Forward* office, eager to talk about the event and become part of the response to it. He contributed an editorial, one of several about the pogrom written in a succession of days by various staff members and collaborators. For a few days, he was thus back in the thick of battle. Then he returned to New Milford, where his wife joined him a few weeks later; together they spent the rest of the spring and summer there. Life became a bit pleasant for them again, although Cahan remained unable to finish his novel.

By the time they returned to New York, where they settled for the time being in a furnished room on East 17th Street near Stuyvesant Park, pressure was mounting in the *Forward* organization in favor of Cahan's return to the editorship once again. Krantz, Feigenbaum, and the other "Kangaroos" who had come to the *Forward* had not made their influence felt there so profoundly as had been expected. Such friends and allies of Cahan as Abraham Liessin, in the editorial office, and Charles (Chaim) Rayevsky, Cahan's old collaborator in the *Neie Zeit* venture of 1886, now a successful physician and a member of the Press Association, had been able to keep Cahan's policies fairly intact after his departure. Even Louis Miller, always amenable to Cahan's influence when the latter was not actually sitting in the editor's chair, had shown support for this trend as against the old, hard-line socialist policies represented by the "Kangaroos"; when Rayevsky had led a small delegation down to Woodbine the previous fall to ask Cahan to begin contributing to the *Forward* again, Miller sent word through them that he had voted "with both hands" for the proposal to contact Cahan. Nor was Miller the only rival who seemed for the moment to have come around to him. One day, Cahan responded to a knock on the door of his furnished room and opened it to see Joseph Barondess standing in front of him. By this time Barondess, now a lawyer and an insurance agent, had completely removed himself from labor-union organizational work, but he was still politically active as a member of Debs' Socialist Party of America—his flirtation with anarchism was over, but he remained as hostile as ever to De Leon and the SLP—and he had recently been given the token position of labor editor of the *Forward*. The presence of the "Kangaroos" at the *Forward* had driven even him to become a supporter of Cahan's cause, and so now he had come in person to register his plea that Cahan return to the editorship. Cahan, in a confusion of personal inclinations, and uncertain as to what, precisely, was happening at the *Forward,* could only say that he would give the matter some thought.

Krantz and Feigenbaum had clearly brought about a polarization of attitudes at the *Forward* that was now working in Cahan's favor. But conflicts of personality and ideology were not the only factor at work there for him. The *Forward* was losing circulation again, and the men who governed its business affairs were reemerging as the voices to be heeded. Albert Feller had recently died at the age of thirty-four, but William Lief remained a strong force at the paper, and he was now more determined than ever that Cahan return for once and for all.

Cahan was now at last beginning to get somewhere in his writing again, having started a novel about Russia inspired by the Kishinev pogrom; nevertheless, he was amenable to going back to the editorship of the *Forward*. His finances were in a poor state, and he knew furthermore that he was eager to pursue the destiny which had opened up at the *Forward* the previous year. He was forty-three years old, and the time had come to give some clear definition to his life, a clearer one than his literary work had been able to give him thus far. He balked only at the prospect of a recurrence of the same sort of opposition to his policies that had occurred the last two times. This time, he made it clear to his allies at the *Forward* that he had to have "absolute full power" if he was to return. They assured him that he would have this, subject to review only once each year at the Press Association's annual election or confirmation of the paper's editor. On this condition, Cahan finally agreed to let his name be submitted in nomination, and he was elected editor of the *Forward* once again. This time he returned to his old desk there for good.

# CHAPTER 12

# YIDDISH THEATER, I: THE BEGINNINGS

In dem Beys-Hamikdosh in a vinkel kheyder,
Zitzt die almonah Bas-Tzion alleyn,
Ihr ben-yokhidel, Yidele, viegt zie k'seyder,
Un zingt ihm tzu shlofen a liedele sheyn:
   "Unter Yideles viegele
   Shteyt a klor-veisse tziegele,—
   Dos tziegele iz gefohren handlen—
   Dos vet zein dein beruf;
   Rozhenkes mit mandlen,
   Shlof-zhe, Yidele, shlof!"

"In a remote corner of the ruined Temple of Jerusalem
sits the forsaken widow, Daughter-of-Zion,
rocking her only son, little Judah,
and singing him to sleep with a sweet lullaby:
'Under little Jew [Judah]'s cradle
stands a dazzling white kid—
now the kid has gone forth to be a tradesman—
this will be your calling, too;
raisins and almonds,
sleep, little Jew, sleep!' "
     —FROM ABRAHAM GOLDFADEN's *Shulamis*

WHEN CAHAN BEGAN TRANSFORMING THE *FORWARD* INTO AN
instrument of mass appeal among the Jewish immigrants of New
York, there was only one serious rival for the kind of influence he
hoped to achieve: the Yiddish theater. If the *Forward* was becoming

a kind of running Talmudic text for the secular cultural life of the Yiddish-speaking masses, the theaters on the Bowery were serving as that culture's temple. In a sense, there could be no rival to the immediacy of the stage's appeal to a public which tended to adore its stars in a way that its ancestors had once adored their favorite cantors, and even Cahan's populist imagination could provide no match for the vulgarity of which Yiddish entertainers were capable. Cahan and his fellow socialist intellectuals could never hope to displace the influence of the Yiddish theater—even though it was an influence that most of them had found questionable in its early days—and they did not try. Rather, what they hoped to do was to use their own growing influence in order to have some effect upon the standards of Yiddish drama. For they, as men of the written word—the secularized offspring of a rabbinical culture for which the written word was the holiest of human forms of expression—saw themselves as the guardians of Yiddish literary values, and they were determined to impose such values even upon the spoken culture of the stage. This is why the writing of drama criticism had an importance at the *Forward* second only to that of writing editorials, and why Cahan increasingly found himself taking on that job as part of his round of chores.

The Yiddish theater owed its origins to a marriage between East European Jewish folk sources and the Haskalah, the nineteenth-century Hebrew Enlightenment. A close ancestor to Yiddish drama can be perceived in the traditional Purim play, the culminating event of the holiday celebrating the triumph of Queen Esther and Mordecai over the evil Haman that comes closer to exhibiting pagan elements than any other occasion marked by the Jewish calendar. On this one day of the year, good Jews are permitted to roister unabashedly, get drunk, play practical jokes, and even violate the ancient injunction against masquerading in the clothing of the opposite sex. It was therefore customary in the annual Purim play, which dramatized the Book of Esther, for men to play women's roles. For centuries, East European

Jews got their public entertainment only under the aegis of religious occasions such as this. But by the eighteen-fifties, certain communities in which normative traditions were relaxing, most notably in Rumania, were becoming accustomed to seeing regular performances in Yiddish that were unattached to religious occasions of any sort. Usually the performers at these entertainments were singers and instrumentalists, who gave color to the atmosphere of the cafes and wine cellars in which Rumanian Jews of all classes were fond of gathering.

These first Yiddish entertainers tended to be of Hasidic background. More than any other factor in the history of East European Jewry, Hasidism had succeeded in implanting a truly visceral Yiddish culture, a culture of the sort that can dispense with religious or ideological props and still maintain its vigor. Indeed, the Rumanian cabaret singers of the eighteen-fifties were known as "Brody singers," a name which came from the town in Hasidic Galicia from which they were said to have originated. The first Brody singer seems to have been a Galician Jew named Yakovka, who had discovered the art of cabaret singing in Vienna while doing military service in the Austrian army. After his release, he organized a small troupe of his own in Brody, composed songs for it, and took it around to perform in various locales. Inspired by this example, other Yiddish singing groups came into being; in some cases the founders of the new groups were former members of Yakovka's company. Some of the new groups grew more ambitious in their use of material. Ephraim Broder, for example, incorporated Hasidic folk material into his performances, something that Yakovka had not done. Other singers and groups began to accompany themselves with musical instruments. Soon these troupes were to be found traveling a wide circuit, and making their way with increasing concentration into the towns and wine cellars of Rumania.

Some of these troupes eventually developed skits as settings for their songs. At first, the skits may have been just a few lines of introductory dialogue, but they sometimes grew more elaborate. Audiences were delighted by them, and some troupes began devoting themselves to the refinement and elaboration of them as much as to their songs. Rudimentary costumes were worn and, in the fashion of the Purim play, men played women's roles, since the participation of women in these entertainments was still unheard of. The favorite subject matter was Hasidic life, and the favorite costume the thick beard, side-locks, and huge, fur-edged hat, or *shtreymel,* that the Hasid traditionally wore. Perhaps because humor requires a degree of detachment, the most successful performer of these sketches was, as it happened, a Lithuanian Jew. Israel Grodner, who became the ruling favorite of the Rumanian-Jewish cabarets in the early seventies, was the only outstanding non-Galician entertainer of this epoch. Grodner regularly performed an elaborate, three-character sketch with songs, really a rudimentary musical play. All the rudiments of incipient Yiddish drama were present in this sketch, which depicted the marital quarrels of a Hasid who gets drunk when he is supposed to be studying. Nothing but an informing spirit, a playwright, a *metteur en scène* was needed to transform its elements into a real play. This spirit came from the Haskalah.

As far back as 1825, a Lemberg physician and Haskalah writer named Shlomo Ettinger had written a play in Yiddish. Like many a maskil of that period, Ettinger wrote his serious works in Hebrew and merely amused himself in Yiddish; his jottings in *zhargon* were not intended for publication, although they were rarely without didactic purpose. He wrote *Serkele,* with its female main protagonist, as a criticism of the ways in which Jewish traditions subordinated women in courtship, marriage, and domestic life. The form of the work was, of course, a mere literary device. Ettinger did not write his play for production—who would perform it, and where?—although he undoubtedly meant to have it read aloud in his home, the guests taking various parts. *Serkele* thus came to be known to a small coterie of maskilim, among whom it circulated in manuscript copies, and in this way it passed from one generation to the next.

Perhaps the first attempt ever made at staging a production of *Serkele* took place in the early eighteen-sixties, long after Ettinger's death, at the Zhitomir Rabbinical Seminary. This school was the companion to the seminary in Vilna—both of them were later to become Teachers' Institutes—created by the government to train a Russified rabbinate. At this time, both schools were major centers of Haskalah culture. The director of the Zhitomir seminary, Haim Selig Slonimsky, was a well-known maskil, who had the further distinction of being married to a Russian-Jewish woman of learning and advanced ideas. It was Madame Slonimsky, long an admirer of *Serkele,* who decided to stage a student production of it. The result was strictly an amateur theatrical, but it made a strong enough impression upon the student who played the role of Serkele that he tried writing a similar play himself shortly thereafter; his name was Abraham Goldfaden.

Born in the town of Starokonstantinov, in southern Russia, in 1840, Goldfaden was a maskil to the core. His father, a watchmaker, had been an admirer of Haskalah culture, and had sent his son to the secular "people's schools" that the Tsarist government had recently established for Jews, many of which were gathering places for Haskalah teachers. Young Goldfaden had studied with one of the greatest of these teachers, Abraham Baer Gottlober, who had also taught the young Sholom Abramovich (later known as Mendele Moicher S'forim). Gottlober was one of the first of the maskilim to sense the cultural importance of Yiddish, and he imparted this sense to his students; Goldfaden, while studying with him, would come to his house evenings and the two would sing Yiddish songs together. After finishing his studies, Goldfaden also became a teacher, and gave his time to composing poems and songs in Hebrew and Yiddish. The Yiddish play that he wrote was meant, like *Serkele,* to be read at private gatherings, and it, too, remained in manuscript.

After some eight years of teaching, the pressures of marriage and fatherhood caused Goldfaden to conclude that the spiritual satisfactions of his chosen calling were insufficient compensation for its small financial rewards, and he decided to go into business instead. He was now living in Odessa, and here he embarked upon a new career, first obtaining a position as a cashier in a millinery store in order to learn business from the ground up. Then he opened a store of his own; but it quickly ended in failure. For a while he thought of studying medicine; then he heard that an old friend and fellow Haskalah poet named Joel Linetzky was planning to start a humorous Yiddish weekly in Lemberg, and he decided to join him there. Together they launched a journal called *Yisrolik,* which lasted only a few months. His appetite now whetted for journalism, Goldfaden moved to Bukovina, where he gathered the resources to found a paper which he called the *Bukoviner Israelitishe Folksblatt;* but this, too, stood at the brink of failure after only a few issues. At the last minute, however, a letter arrived from a well-to-do subscriber in Jassy, Rumania, who offered to support the paper if Goldfaden would move it there. Goldfaden accepted, and arrived in Jassy in the spring of 1876.

As it happened, Israel Grodner's troupe was performing in a garden cafe in Jassy at this very time. Grodner was at the height of his popularity, and was even doing engagements in Bucharest music halls, as well as in large cafes like Mark's in Jassy. Goldfaden, a Russian and an intellectual, had never heard of Grodner, and did not know that his own Yiddish compositions formed an important part of Grodner's repertory. There were no copyright laws in Rumania, and all literary works, domestic or foreign, were for anyone to use there as he liked. Grodner never dreamed of paying for any of the material he used, and he assumed that a writer would simply be satisfied with the glory of having his works performed on the stage: it was Grodner's practice to announce the name of the composer of every song he sang. It was therefore a pleasant surprise for Grodner to hear that one of the men whose names he most often announced was now in Jassy. He decided to pay Goldfaden a visit.

When Grodner came to Goldfaden's quarters one morning and explained who he was, Goldfaden, ever on the alert for business opportunities, immediately offered to sell him some new songs. Grodner explained that it was not customary for him to buy the material he used. But he had an idea: since Goldfaden's songs were so popular with the audience at Mark's Cafe, why couldn't their author perform them there one evening in person? He would certainly be paid well for this. Goldfaden, who had already given numerous public readings of his poems in Odessa cafes, was delighted by the idea.

Grodner proposed the idea to Shimeon Mark, who agreed to set aside one evening for Goldfaden at his cafe. The poet's name was well known to Mark's clientele. Goldfaden's appearance was billed as a major event, and prices for that evening were raised accordingly. On the evening of the scheduled reading, the cafe filled to capacity. Goldfaden had decked himself out for the occasion in his best platform suit, complete with frock coat and white gloves. Grodner made the brief introduction and then, as the audience applauded, Goldfaden rose, walked ceremoniously to the platform, and began to declaim his first poem.

When he finished, Grodner applauded, and a few other scattered admirers joined in; but, to Goldfaden's astonishment, most of the audience remained silent. Concluding that they must have been a little awestruck, Goldfaden decided to warm them up by reading his most charming and popular work, "Dos Pintele Yid." He began to recite again. When he finished, the response was the same: scattered applause, but mostly silence. What was the matter? He would try a humorous poem this time. He recited it, and when it was over the audience began to whistle and boo. Goldfaden was incredulous. Then Grodner leaped onto the stage.

The audience burst into applause, but Grodner silenced them. Sternly, he chided them for behaving this way before a great poet; when he was done, they applauded him again. Grodner took Goldfaden aside and explained to him what was happening. These people, he said, were in the habit of hearing the songs sung, of watching them performed, and they had expected the author to do this. Goldfaden's Russian, declamatory style of presentation had been an utter disappointment to them. Then Grodner illustrated his point. He stepped off the stage, hurriedly donned his old *shtreymel* and sidelocks—he forgot the beard—leaped back onto the stage, and proceeded to dance and sing Goldfaden's "Dos Freylakhe Hasid'l"; the applause and cheering were thunderous. Grodner performed a few more pieces, and got the same response; he had rescued the evening. When he was done, Goldfaden tried again; this time he sang his songs. He did not do brilliantly, although the audience was appreciative this time. He was cut out to be a creator of material, not an interpreter of it. But that was good enough—his head was already brimming over with ideas. By the next morning, he was ready to propose to Grodner a whole theatrical project.

At first, it occurred to Goldfaden that he might try persuading Grodner's troupe to do a performance of *Aunt Sosia,* the play he had written under the inspiration of Ettinger's *Serkele* years before. But on second thought he realized that this would be to miss the point of the lesson he had just learned in Mark's Cafe. His play, like Ettinger's, had been written to satisfy the tastes of a small, educated coterie. Its wit was subtle, and it was not meant to include any singing or dancing. The audience he had encountered last night would be bored to tears by it. But that audience was nevertheless unquestionably the nucleus of a potential audience for real theater in Yiddish; they were hungry for such a thing. They only needed the right kind of fare to wean them from the desultory and miscellaneous diet of song, dance, and sketch they had been receiving, and to educate them to real drama. It was unquestionably an educational task: the old teacher and maskil in Goldfaden came once again to the surface. The transition from wine cellar to theater had to be made patiently, step by step.

Goldfaden's first theatrical effort in collaboration with Grodner was an elaborated version of the old skit about the drunken Hasid and his wife. This was expanded into a two-act play with several musical numbers, and although a considerable element of ad-libbing was retained—there was no written script at all—the scenario was much more complex and exacting in conception than it had ever been before. For all the crudeness of the piece, it was now palpably no longer a mere skit, but a play, a whole evening's theater in itself. It was performed at Mark's Cafe with Grodner and Sacher Goldstein playing their usual roles of the Hasid and his wife, and it was a great success. Goldfaden immediately arranged a tour of towns in the vicinity. Thus began the career of a traveling theatrical troupe, consisting of two actors (supporting players were picked up, an evening at a time, along the way), and of Goldfaden, who was producer, director, writer, composer, and set designer all in one.

This happened at the time when Russia was making preparations for the war against Turkey that was to break out in a few months and bring about the complete emancipation of Rumania from Ottoman hegemony. In Russia, many Jews were being drafted into military service, and Goldfaden chose this as the subject for his next production, a farce, which he put down in writing this time and called *The Recruits*. It depicted two Jewish recruits getting themselves into various scrapes and so upsetting the military order that they are finally discharged from the army. There were many musical numbers in it, and many scenes of soldiers marching to music. Goldfaden filled the stage by hiring soldiers from the local garrisons where he performed.

Eventually, Goldfaden's policy of hiring extras in the communities where he performed led to a few permanent acquisitions of actors for the company. By the spring of 1877, the troupe consisted of four permanent players. Goldfaden thereupon wrote a four-character play, *Die Bobba mit dem Eynikel* ("The Grandmother and the Grandchild"). It was a return to the reliable old tradition of domestic comedy. This genre appealed to the audiences, in which there were increasing numbers of women, and it also satisfied Goldfaden's maskilic inclination to be a critic of manners and mores. The new play depicted an elderly woman's efforts to marry off her orphaned granddaughter to a pious young Jew, a dull person whom the girl does not love. Instead, the girl falls in love with her teacher, a "modern" young man of the maskilic type, and she runs away with him. The old grandmother dies broken-hearted. This charming play thus had it both ways with the audience: there was something for the rebellious younger generation, and something for those who preferred to cry over the plight of the pious, well-meaning grandmother.

The outbreak of the Russo-Turkish War and the Russian occupation of Rumania that spring found Goldfaden's troupe in Bucharest, doing its first stint in the capital. Goldfaden's sojourn there resulted in a major leap forward in the growth of his theatrical enterprise. Bucharest was a city of considerable worldliness and gaiety, in which the theater arts were flourishing. Its Jewish community was somewhat more sophisticated in secular matters than most East European Jewish communities were at the time. Quite characteristic of Bucharest Jewry was the fact that there existed a small circle of young cantors at its synagogue whose true ambitions lay in the direction of the theatrical world, and who occasionally sang on the Rumanian music-hall stage. When a group of these young men went to see Goldfaden's productions, they were delighted, and decided to audition for his troupe. Goldfaden thus found himself hiring several young Bucharest cantors of considerable theatrical talent. In particular, he was impressed by the abilities of two of them, one a young man named Lazar Zuckerman, the other a seventeen-year-old boy named Zelig Mogilevsky who had appeared on the Rumanian stage under the name Sigmund Mogulesco. These two had had considerable experience in the music halls, at weddings, and even in a church choir—a fact which they had carefully concealed from the chief cantor of the Bucharest synagogue. At his audition for Goldfaden, young Mogulesco had done a scene from a popular Rumanian comedy, *Vladescu Mamu*, about a spoiled child; his interpretation of this role had been so good that Goldfaden, after hiring him, immediately wrote an adaptation of the play as a vehicle for him. The result, the first of a long line of offspring of the collaboration between Goldfaden and Mogulesco, became the most popular piece in the repertory. Called *Shmendrick* after its main character, its title was eventually to enter the Yiddish vocabulary as the term for a spoiled ninny.

Mogulesco also soon made a specialty of the role of the grand-daughter in *Die Bobba mit dem Eynikel,* sharing the spotlight with Grodner's charming old *bobba.* He was, in fact, beginning to take too much of the spotlight, and was finding too much favor in Goldfaden's eyes, for Grodner's taste. One day Grodner resigned in a fit of jealousy. Going back to Jassy, he organized his own troupe, and proceeded to stage his own productions of Goldfaden's plays. Mogulesco went on to become the unrivaled star of Goldfaden's company. He was of great value to the troupe, moreover, not only because he was a brilliant natural performer, but because he had great musical abilities and an intuition for Yiddish folkways even more profound than that of Goldfaden. His collaboration with Goldfaden therefore produced songs of greatly improved quality. Goldfaden, who was never more than an amateur musician, had usually picked up old folk melodies as settings for his lyrics; but with Mogulesco, he became more ambitious about attempting original compositions. The texts of the plays themselves also became, as it were, more musical through this collaboration, more Yiddish in their rhythms. Many of Goldfaden's phrases and lyrics came eventually thereby to pass for genuine folklore.

But it is rare when two men of large and overlapping talents can stay together for long. Seeking independence from his mentor, Mogulesco quit the troupe before the end of 1877, though he was then still only eighteen years old. After casting about a while for the next turn to take, he went to Jassy and formed a surprising partnership with Grodner. Evidently, a common desire to shake off the influence of the increasingly overbearing Goldfaden was sufficient to enable the two of them to overcome their own differences. Goldfaden, meanwhile, made Zuckerman his star, and hired a theater in Bucharest to serve as his permanent headquarters.

At the beginning of 1878, then, there were two Yiddish theatrical troupes in existence, one in Bucharest and the other in Jassy, and both of them were flourishing. The circumstances had been propitious. Large numbers of Jewish merchants and contractors had come into Rumania with the Russian occupation troops. These well-to-do Russian Jews were eager for the kind of entertainment the Yiddish theatrical companies had to offer, and they could more easily pay for it than could the poorer clients of the wine cellars in which it had all begun two years before. Furthermore, they were, on the whole, better educated and more sophisticated intellectually than the audiences at Mark's Cafe had been, and could be given plays of a subtler quality. The two troupes responded to the demands of this new audience, and the developing Yiddish theater moved onto a higher qualitative plane.

The increased demand for new and interesting theatrical productions, and the pressure of rivalry, made it impossible for Grodner and Mogulesco in Jassy to go on relying exclusively upon Goldfaden for their texts. Searching for another writer, they found one in their own prompter's box, a twenty-four-year-old native of Jassy named Joseph Lateiner. A former rabbinical student, Lateiner had been won over to Haskalah in his youth, and had already long been dabbling in the writing of plays after the fashion of *Serkele*. A talented student of modern languages, he had become thoroughly familiar with the drama of various countries. This knowledge served him in good stead when he responded to the call for new plays; he adapted with facility whatever he had read. His work was greatly inferior to Goldfaden's but this was not important. A text was the merest grist for the mill of Yiddish actors, especially for one like Mogulesco; its virtues consisted simply of the number and variety of opportunities it gave them to show what they could do. They also freely injected material of their own.

The cultural organism that Goldfaden had sired had by now already shown its fissiparous tendencies, and these were to go on being active in the future. But now, its capacity for mutation suddenly also emerged. Somehow, at the beginning of 1878, the right moment had arrived to start including women in Yiddish theatrical performances. What still had seemed unthinkable at one moment—what "nice" Jewish girl would go onto the stage?—suddenly became an obvious and overdue next step, for why should the Yiddish theater, in this respect as in any other, be different from the European theater in general? This realization spread so swiftly that it subsequently became impossible to recall which actress had been the first to begin performing regularly on a Yiddish stage. Possibly it was Rosa Friedman, who joined Goldfaden's troupe in the first weeks of 1878, having already so broken with Jewish traditions that she had worked for a time as a dancer in a Constantinople cafe. Or perhaps it was Lazar Zuckerman's wife, who began doing the role of Shmendrick's fiancée at around this time. On the other hand, Grodner was always to claim that his own wife had preceded either of these two women as a Yiddish actress.

Actually, there was one young woman who had performed with Goldfaden's troupe as far back as the late winter of 1877. This had occurred in Galatz, a small town in Rumania; there, an eighteen-year-old girl named Sarah Segal, a native of the town, had approached Goldfaden before the performance and apprised him of her passionate desire to become an actress. Since it was Purim, the day when much was permitted, Goldfaden thought that no one would object to there being a woman in the cast, and that evening he placed her in the role of the granddaughter in *Die Bobba mit dem Eynikel*. The prompter undoubtedly had a lot of work to do that night, but Goldfaden was impressed by the girl's performance. The following year, when the rush for women began, Goldfaden asked Sarah if she wanted to join the troupe. Sarah, of course, had the problem of convincing her mother, who was a widow, that this was all right for a proper girl to do. Her mother insisted that so long as she was responsible for her daughter's welfare, she could not permit such a thing, but finally conceded that once Sarah was married, the girl could do as her husband saw fit. Upon hearing this, Goldfaden decided that Sarah would become the wife of one of the bachelors in his troupe. The choice fell upon Sacher Goldstein, Grodner's old partner in the Hasidic act. In this way Sarah, who adopted the stage name of "Sophie," became Sophie Goldstein, the first regular female member of the Goldfaden troupe. (Naturally, the marriage did not last. A few years later, Sophie-Sarah divorced Sacher Goldstein and married another Yiddish actor, Moshe Karp. It was under the name Sophie Karp that she subsequently became famous to the Yiddish theater audience in New York.)

New splits took place. In the late spring of 1878, a group of Yiddish actors, dissidents from the two existing troupes, were organized into a third company by an aspiring Yiddish playwright named Moshe Horowitz. Born in Galicia in 1844, Horowitz had also started with a traditional Jewish education—he had been destined to become a ritual slaughterer—and had then become converted to Haskalah. He had settled in Jassy as a Hebrew teacher in 1862, and had tried for a while to put out a newspaper in Hebrew and Rumanian. From there he went to Bucharest; in later years he claimed that for a while he held the post of Professor of Geography at the University of Bucharest. In honor of this claim, he chose always to be known as "Professor" Horowitz. Whatever the truth of this claim, it is certain that he was also the director of a Jewish school in Bucharest for a time. But for unknown reasons he was dismissed from this post and was left destitute; at this point, according to rumors of later years that he never tried strenuously to deny, he took out his wrath at the Jewish establishment that had rejected him by undergoing a formal act of conversion to Christianity. It was, however, a conversion more in form than in fact. The attractions of Yiddish theater eventually brought him back into the bosom of Jewish culture. Somehow, he raised the money to organize this troupe of his own. The plays he wrote were as filled as Lateiner's were with skillful borrowings from the world's dramatic literature.

But Horowitz's company folded a short time after it was formed, mainly because Goldfaden succeeded in enticing its chief actor back into his own troupe. At the same moment, the inevitable break between Grodner and Mogulesco took place. Mogulesco maintained his hold upon the troupe, and Grodner, searching for another home, joined forces with Horowitz. The company they formed also failed after a short time. This round of splits and new alliances went on with increasing rapidity and complexity. The troupes thus formed were often unstable; but the sum total of it all was a steadily growing pool of new talent and new plays.

The end of the Russo-Turkish War in the summer of 1878 brought Rumania's war prosperity to a sudden end. The wealthy Russian-Jewish merchants went home, and the large audience for Yiddish theater disappeared. In a few months, Mogulesco's troupe in Jassy was forced to close down for lack of business. Goldfaden, holding his company together on a shoestring, went in search of fresh fields of endeavor. If Russian Jews had formed the core of the Yiddish theater audience in recent months, then why not bring Yiddish theater to Russia? Goldfaden sensed that a good audience was to be found in the city of his youth, Odessa; many of his merchant clients had come from there, and its Jewish life was permeated with a cosmopolitanism that was not to be found among Jews elsewhere in Russia. In fact, a small group of semiprofessional actors, most of whom held other jobs during the day, was already performing regularly in a private club there, and was getting good audiences. This group had been organized by one of Goldfaden's former actors. In the spring of 1879, Goldfaden brought his own troupe to Odessa and established it in this club, absorbing the semi-professional group. His expectations of success proved to be correct, for he did so well he was soon able to engage a large theater, the Maryinsky, as a permanent home for his troupe. He also took to the road again, leading his company on regular tours through southern Russia.

This period became the most fruitful one of all for the acquisition of new talent. As had been the case in Rumania, many young actors were recruited on the road: in Kishinev, Goldfaden hired David Kessler and Moshe Haimovich (later, Heine), who were to achieve fame as tragedians, and in a small town called Smileh he discovered the girl who was eventually, under the name Keni Liptzen, to become widely regarded as the greatest Yiddish actress of her generation. In Odessa itself, Goldfaden had inherited from the semiprofessional group that had preceded him there a young businessman and part-time actor named Jacob P. Adler. A native of the Odessa slums, Adler was the type of man who, having obtained his first lessons in life under the harsh imperatives of the city streets, never could find any satisfaction in what formal education had to offer. He had left school early and gone into business; but his deepest inclinations were artistic and, like many such men, he one day discovered the theater to be his university. It was, of course, the Russian-language theater that had attracted him at first; Yiddish theater, at the time of its arrival in Odessa, struck him as a mere curiosity. But Yiddish theater proved to have one advantage from his point of view: being semi-amateur in nature (this was before Goldfaden's arrival), it was the one place in which he was free to try out his secret ambition to become an actor himself. Starting with nonspeaking roles, he worked his way up slowly, only gradually giving up on the idea that he would make his way into the Russian theater. Unlike Mogulesco, he did not take to the stage as a fish to water, and he had to develop his craft painstakingly from unpropitious beginnings. But this fact added force to an innate desire on his part to see the high seriousness that prevailed in general European drama introduced onto the Yiddish stage. He did not sing or dance well, and since no Yiddish play was without music as yet, he naturally longed to see an element of straight, nonmusical drama introduced into the repertory. Eventually he was able to pioneer a genuine Yiddish tragic theater, and to become its greatest actor.

The old pattern of splits and rivalries was transplanted onto Russian soil. The owner of the Maryinsky Theater, a Greek named Omer, tried to prevail upon his tenant Goldfaden to form a partnership with him, but he was rebuffed. Piqued at this, Omer heard one day of Mogulesco in Rumania, and sent for him. Together with some other embittered former colleagues of Goldfaden, Omer and Mogulesco formed a new company. Omer then ejected Goldfaden from the Maryinsky and set up his new company there. Goldfaden retreated to the provinces, drawing warm receptions wherever he went with his troupe.

As in the past, vigorous rivalry brought new developments in the growth of the Yiddish theater. While touring the provinces, Goldfaden heard that Lateiner, working for the Maryinsky troupe, was composing an operetta set in Biblical times. Thus far the Yiddish playwrights had pretty well restricted themselves to contemporary material, usually domestic comedy. The idea of going back to the ultimate Jewish folk source for material had been thought of before—Goldfaden and Mogulesco, while still together, had started working on a Biblical operetta—but there had not hitherto been any need to try it out, since the public had seemed quite satisfied with what it was getting. But now that Goldfaden's plays were no longer available at all to Mogulesco—for he was now in Russia, and subject to its copyright laws—Lateiner had decided to make a bold plunge after new material in order to rival the supremacy of Goldfaden's texts. What was particularly annoying to Goldfaden was to learn that Lateiner was using the very material that he, Goldfaden, had started to work on with Mogulesco two years before.

Goldfaden and Mogulesco had drawn the original idea from two Haskalah novels about Biblical times, Abraham Mapu's *Love of Zion* and Elijah Mordecai Werbel's *Trusty Witnesses, or Well and Weasel*. Lateiner was stressing elements in the former for the play he was now working on, which he was going to call *Love of Zion*. Goldfaden decided he would beat him to the punch. Drawing upon the Werbel novel, Goldfaden wove an incredible tale of a girl wandering alone in the desert who becomes stranded in a well and is rescued by a high-born young man; the two exchange vows of love, invoking as their witnesses the well and a passing wildcat (Goldfaden's variant on the original weasel). Later, the young man breaks his vow and marries a noblewoman; but the children of this marriage die violently, one by falling into a well, the other at the hands of a wildcat! Recognizing the omen, the repentant Absalom travels back across the desert to be reunited with his predestined love, Shulamis. The utter absurdity of the story is part of its charm, for Goldfaden had a rare ability to tell a naive story with genuine naiveté. Despite its Biblical subject matter, *Shulamis* is utterly Yiddish in presentation and style, and elements in it—most notably the lullaby "Raisins and Almonds"—could pass for pure folklore.

Goldfaden did beat Lateiner to the punch, and *Shulamis,* a great success, became the first Biblical—and, in general, the first historical—operetta to appear on the Yiddish stage. But it was by no means the last. The passion for historical and Biblical operetta soon became so great that plays of this type threatened, for a time, to engulf the Yiddish theater. Lateiner made this line his specialty, and Horowitz eventually followed suit; gradually they turned their approach to historical subjects into a formula for the mass produc-tion of plays (Horowitz reached the point where he could write a play in a night), and the quality of Yiddish theater was threatened as a result. But the interest in history thereby awakened also provided the first opportunities for the Yiddish theater to turn to the kind of serious drama to which men like Adler aspired. In Odessa a writer and theatrical entrepreneur named Joseph Lerner, who had bought the Maryinsky Theater when the Omer-Mogulesco company dis-banded in internal strife, began trying out a new type of material. From the repertory of general European drama, he selected plays which, though usually written by Gentile writers, were on Jewish subjects, and he translated them into Yiddish. These proved to be excellent vehicles for straight dramatic actors like Adler; Lerner's two greatest successes were his adaptations of Augustin Scribe's *La Juive* and Karl Gutzkow's *Uriel Acosta* (this latter became a permanent part of the Yiddish repertory). The advent of this type of drama persuaded two of the foremost writers of Yiddish prose fiction—Shomer (N. M. Shaikevich) and Mendele Moicher S'forim—to try their hand at writing plays. But these first efforts to make Yiddish drama, like European drama, part of a literary tradition were still only rare and desultory.

Goldfaden's successful entry into the new field of historical and Biblical operetta also led, indirectly, to a major disaster for the fledgling Yiddish theater. This was, ironically, the result of a major triumph. In September, 1883, Goldfaden completed a play about Bar Kochba, the celebrated false messiah and leader of the Palestinian Jewish revolt against the Romans in the year 135. This was mounted in a lavish production at the Maryinsky Theater, to which Goldfaden had returned in a partnership agreement with Joseph Lerner and N. M. Shaikevich. Its star was Mogulesco, with whom Goldfaden had by then had a reconciliation, and with whom he had collaborated in writing the play. *Bar Kochba* was as successful as *Shulamis* had been; it was not quite so unworldly, however, and its hero spoke a number of rebellious speeches against the Romans. This did not please the Tsarist authorities, who were in any case coming to regard the Yiddish theater to be a more rambunctious cultural phenomenon than they liked the Jewish community to have. Shortly after *Bar Kochba* opened, a Tsarist ukase announced a ban on Yiddish theater in Russia. After four years of work, a flourishing community of artists and their craft suddenly had to find a new home.

In the first wave of shocked response among the Yiddish players, there took place a splintering and scattering more extreme than usual, a kind of cultural diaspora. Mogulesco formed a troupe and went back to Rumania, Lazar Zuckerman formed another one and took it to Germany, and Jacob P. Adler brought a company of his own to

London. Although the trend of mass Jewish emigration was already clearly in the direction of the United States, most of the Yiddish actors hesitated to make the long journey there, feeling the traditional reticence of European-bred artists toward the cultural desert that America seemed to be. Eventually, they were to follow the trend of emigration there anyway, but for the time being only one troupe went to America. Led by Moshe Silberman, it included Sacher and Sophie Goldstein (still married to each other at this time), Moshe and Sarah Haimovich-Heine, and Joseph Lateiner as its prompter and playwright. Arriving in New York in the summer of 1884, it gave its first performance—of Goldfaden's *Die Khishuf-Makherin* ("The Witch")—in the German Turner Hall on East 4th Street near Second Avenue.

This marked the beginning of professional Yiddish theater in America, but it was by no means the first Yiddish production the Lower East Side had seen. Two years earlier a group of amateur players had begun staging regular performances of works by Goldfaden and others. Prominent in this group was Pinchas Thomashevsky, a former cantor from Kiev who had lost his religion and come to America with the *Am Olam* movement. A passionate participant in the amateur theatricals in Turner Hall, he also regularly brought his children with him to serve as actors. One of his sons, Boris, who was fourteen years old when he began acting in 1882, soon achieved some prominence playing the feminine leads. Seeing a potential family business, the elder Thomashevsky hired a theater on the Bowery near Canal Street, planning to administer there a permanent company of his own. A brief flurry of Yiddish theatrical activity ensued on the Bowery, presaging times to come, in two theaters that had formerly housed German companies: Pinchas Thomashevsky's National Theater, and the Old Bowery Garden across the street, where a succession of amateur groups performed. But both of these enterprises had collapsed by the time the Silberman troupe arrived. The Bowery, however, had not ceased to be a magnet for Yiddish theater. Looking for a permanent home, the Silberman troupe rented the Old Bowery Garden and changed its name to the Oriental Theater.

Although New York could hardly provide as yet the kind of sophisticated theater audience that had been cultivated in Bucharest and Odessa, the Silberman troupe had proved that it was nonetheless a viable place in which to work. In the early part of 1886, when the Oriental Theater was well into its second year of thriving activity, two young Jewish producers decided to summon Mogulesco to New York. Things had not been going so well in Jassy, and Mogulesco gladly responded to the call. His troupe eventually obtained the National Theater and renamed it the Rumanian Opera House. A reunion of the Yiddish theatrical family, and a redeploying of its old battle lines, was now taking place on the Bowery. The process was completed when Jacob P. Adler arrived from London. He had first reached New York in 1887, but finding competition on the Bowery rather too intense, he had decided to try to establish his company in Chicago. The audience for Yiddish theater was not sufficient there for him to make a go of it, however, and he left, returning to London for a while, and then finally settling permanently in New York in 1889. In spite of everything, he found himself on the Bowery after all, in the Germania Theater, a few blocks north of the other two companies.

Only Goldfaden did not rejoin the family he had sired. The ban on Yiddish theater in Russia had immobilized him completely, and he was never able to recover his stride as a playwright. He did go to New York for a short while, from 1887 to 1889, but he had nothing to do with the Yiddish theater there. Rather, he tried to publish a Yiddish illustrated weekly, and when it failed he sailed back across the Atlantic and settled in Paris. He was eventually to return to New York, to stage productions of his old plays, in 1903.

It did not take long for a lively Yiddish theatrical culture to come into being in New York. The immigrant audience, if somewhat primitive in its tastes, was nonetheless passionately fond of going to the theater as a way of life. Hutchins Hapgood observed that the nights of Yiddish performances presented "a peculiarly picturesque sight. Poor workingmen and women with their babies of all ages fill the theater. Great enthusiasm is manifested, sincere laughter and tears accompany the sincere acting on the stage. Peddlers of soda-water, candy, of fantastic gewgaws of many kinds, mix freely with the audience between the acts. Conversation during the play is received with strenuous hisses, but the falling of the curtain is the signal for groups of friends to get together and gossip about the play or the affairs of the week. Introductions are not necessary, and the Yiddish community can then be seen and approached with great freedom." Many a Jewish immigrant theatergoer, Hapgood wrote, spent as much as half his meager earnings for tickets, not only out of love for the plays themselves, but out of a desire to meet friends in the audience and, above all, to see the actors. "With these latter he, and more frequently she, try in every way to make acquaintance, but commonly are compelled to adore at a distance." The actors, who "take themselves with peculiar seriousness," respond to "the enthusiasm, almost worship, with which they are regarded by the people . . . with sovereign contempt." The typical Yiddish star "struts about in the cafes on Canal and Grand Streets, conscious of his greatness," and "refers to the crowd as 'Moses' with superior condescension or humorous vituperation." These were the princes and princesses of the Ghetto.

Goldfaden's pieces continued to be the principal favorites of the Yiddish repertory, but no Lateiner and Horowitz (who had reached New York in 1886) achieved a virtual monopoly in the supplying of new material. Together they brought Yiddish theater to a new low. The New York theatergoers could enjoy Goldfaden's works, because Goldfaden's unique skill had been to write in a way that cut across the lines which divided the cultivated from the uncultivated. But Horowitz and Lateiner had no such skill, and they simply pandered to their audience's lowest common denominator. The result was a seemingly endless succession of cheap historical operas, written in swollen *Deitshmerish,* and constructed out of stock plots and speeches—very often, Horowitz or Lateiner would present the merest sketch of a manuscript and let the actors fill in the lines, which were already well known from previous plays. These productions were of a tawdriness that was enhanced by the enormous pomposity of the presentation. The Yiddish-speaking intellectuals coined the term "Horowitzism" as a characterization of everything that was wrong with Yiddish drama in New York at this time.

Indeed, the intellectuals tended to regard the Yiddish theater as an alien cause. A few years later, they would be eager to criticize the faults of the Yiddish theater, because by then they were to believe that it was a place in which the intellect could reside; but at the beginning of the nineties, no such thought had yet entered their minds. Only Jacob P. Adler worried over the gap between serious art and the New York Yiddish theater. At the Germania, he had started out doing productions of his own type of vehicle, such as *Uriel Acosta* and Yiddish translations of Shakespeare, but the audience responded to them as if he were deliberately driving people away from the theater. It was no use trying to get them to swallow wholesale something that was alien to them. There had to be some way of weaning them to serious drama, just as Goldfaden had weaned his audience to theater in the first place. What the Yiddish theater needed was an original serious dramatist of its own, a Goldfaden of tragedy. This was the vision that was haunting Adler in 1891, when, one evening in a Lower East Side restaurant, Mogulesco and Philip Krantz introduced him to a writer who had just arrived from Russia named Jacob Gordin.

# Chapter 13

# Yiddish Theater, II: The Feud
# Between Cahan and Jacob Gordin

"Mirele Efros" gedarft keyn prolog nit
Rikhtig tzu shatzen ihr vert, ihr gevikht,
Punkt vie men darf far dem likhtige tog nit
Kinstlikhe flammen tzu veizen zein likht;
Un vie men zeyt ohn dem shvimmers ertzeylung
Dem okeyans ungehoyere makht,
Punkt azoy tzeigt zikh ohn fremde empfeylung
Unzer ferfassers talant heint bei nakht.

"*Mirele Efros* needs no prologue to evaluate its worth and importance properly, any more than the bright day needs artificial flames
to display its light; for, just as the ocean's enormous might can be
seen without the swimmer's account, so also does our author's talent
stand out tonight without need of introduction."
—From Morris Winchevsky's Prologue to *Mirele Efros*

Like many Lower East Side intellectuals, Jacob Gordin,
who was born in the Ukraine in 1853, had largely renounced his
orthodox Jewish legacy early in life in favor of a more Russian culture. Starting at the age of nineteen, when he contributed his first
articles to Russian newspapers, he embarked upon an adventurous
period of traveling and working at such odd jobs as that of farm
laborer, longshoreman, and traveling actor, all of which represented
a conscientious attempt on his part to exorcise the ways and occu-

pational preferences traditional to the Jews of Russia. When he did finally settle down, married, to a job as editor of a small newspaper in Elizabethgrad in 1880, he made something of a return to Jewish concerns, but accompanied by notions of physical and spiritual regeneration that had been derived from his experiences on the road. Organizing a "Spiritual Biblical Brotherhood," he sought to promote a program that would ultimately make the Jews over again into the peasants of the Bible. This resembled Labor Zionism in all fundamental respects but one: Gordin, with his own utterly personal, unique, mystical blend of Narodnism and heretical Biblical fundamentalism, was opposed to Jewish settlement in Palestine and to all other manifestations of Jewish nationalism. This is why the pogroms of 1881, which originated in the very town in which he was living, did not drive him out of Russia at first; still believing that the Jews could and should become a part of the Russian peasantry and working class, he was inclined to place much of the blame for the pogroms upon the Jews themselves, who, he said in his editorials, had brought the wrath of the peasantry down upon their own heads by their persisting commercial role in society. The local authorities clearly appreciated this view of the matter, for in 1883 they allowed Gordin to reestablish his Brotherhood, which had momentarily vanished in the upheavals.

This peace could not last, however, for Gordin's organization had radical tendencies; it was finally banned in the spring of 1891. Gordin then decided to emigrate to the United States, where many of his friends and admirers were now established; he arrived in New York with his wife and eight children on July 31. Philip Krantz, who had been a friend of Gordin's in Russia, was at this time still the editor of the *Arbeiter Zeitung*, and he invited Gordin to become a contributor. Financially hard-pressed, Gordin set to work immediately, and produced an article describing a riot that had broken out between peasants and Jews in Elizabethgrad just before his departure. This was the first article he had ever written in Yiddish. Like Krantz, Miller, and others who were writing for the *Arbeiter Zeitung,* he had found this return in maturity to the language of his childhood to be rough going. What was especially hard, of course, was the task of having to execute an exact prose description—like this news story—in a tongue that had been associated, in one's own experience, exclusively with conversational utterances. Indeed, Gordin sensed right away that the genius of the language—and his own best possibilities in writing it— lay in the realm of dialogue. And so dialogue is what he wrote for his second contribution to the *Arbeiter Zeitung.*

"Pantole Polge"—the title is the name of the protagonist, whose first name is an anagram of the Hebrew spelling of Naphtali—was, in effect, a short story; although Gordin, who kept its narrative elements down to a minimum, simply intended it to be a specimen of that classic form of feuilleton often referred to as "imaginary dialogue," a debate between the representatives of various moral viewpoints. Pantole is a simple Jewish tailor, illiterate but full of zest for life, who has just died and is now appearing before the celestial court for a decision as to whether he should go to heaven or to Gehennum, the nether world of Jewish folklore. Pantole concedes in advance that he should be sent to Gehennum, for his life has fallen far short of the strict requirements of Jewish piety. But, as his story unfolds, the simple purity of his soul begins to emerge; he relates incident after incident in which, without his even being aware of it, superficially more pious people than he have taken advantage of his naive generosity and capacity for self-effacement. The judges are deeply moved by the time he finishes speaking, and one of them offers the astonished tailor his chair. Pantole is, of course, sent to heaven.

This little story bears clear resemblances to I. L. Peretz's more celebrated tale, "Bontshe the Silent," which also made its first appearance in the *Arbeiter Zeitung,* more than two years later; most Lower East Side intellectuals consider Peretz's story to have been inspired by Gordin's. But Pantole, unlike Bontshe, was anything but silent, and it was the richness and authentic folk quality of his speech that gave

Gordin's story its special merits. No less an ear than that of Sigmund Mogulesco spotted these merits in Pantole's discourse, even before the piece was published. Apparently Krantz had shown the manuscript to Mogulesco, who had decided upon reading the story that he wanted to perform a dramatization of it. Pantole was a perfect vehicle for his own style of acting, which ran the whole gamut from comic to pathetic to tragic, and was capable of moving a Yiddish audience from laughter to tears in an instant.

Mogulesco was eager to have a meeting with the man capable of writing such dialogue, and he asked Krantz to arrange it. The get-together took place in a Canal Street restaurant one evening in early September; Krantz brought Gordin, and Mogulesco arrived accompanied by Jacob P. Adler. By this time, Adler had also seen the manuscript of "Pantole Polge" and, having heard of Gordin's writings and activities in Russia, was impressed that a man of such intellectual stature could write good dialogue in Yiddish. This was a most unusual combination of qualities, and Adler had therefore begun to hope that Gordin might be the man he had been looking for. The conversation of the four men quickly turned to the problems of the Yiddish theater and its great need for a good writer of serious dramas. Would Gordin like to try his hand at writing a play in Yiddish?, Adler asked. Gordin was amenable to the idea. Adler suggested that he try doing an adaptation of a German drama, after the fashion of Joseph Lerner. Gordin said no, he would write a *Jewish* play, not a German one in Yiddish words. He pulled out his copy of the *Arbeiter Zeitung* and spread it open on the table; he would find his Jewish story in there. He came across an article about a Jew who had escaped from Siberian exile and settled down under an assumed name years before, and who had now just been caught by the Russian police: this, he said, would be the subject of his play.

A few days later, on September 11, "Pantole Polge" appeared in the *Arbeiter Zeitung,* and on September 14 Mogulesco performed it at the Union Theater on East 8th Street, as part of a benefit evening for the newly created monthly, *Die Zukunft*. It was well received, and Mogulesco arranged to give further performances of it. Gordin, in the meantime, was already at work on his proposed full-length drama. He had never written for the stage before in his life—even "Pantole" had been adapted for Mogulesco's performance by another writer—and he had to have a great deal of technical help from Adler. Still, he was determined to write something in an entirely different sphere from that of the standard New York Yiddish theatrical fare of the moment, which he had already discovered to be "far from Jewish life, cheap, unaesthetic, false, debased and corrupt." By early October he had finished his play.

*Siberia*, as Gordin called his play, tells the story of Reuben Cohen, who, in his young manhood, had been sent to Siberia for a minor infraction of the law, and had escaped. Changing his name to Rosenkrantz, he had brought his wife and children with him and settled in a town far from his original home. There he had become a wealthy business-man and a pillar of the community. The play depicts what happens when a jealous business rival discovers the secret of Rosenkrantz's past and turns him in to the police. The final scene shows him saying farewell to his despairing family as he is taken into custody.

This drama had a range of emotional dynamics suitably wide for the Yiddish theater and provided an appropriate vehicle for the tragic style of Jacob P. Adler and his wife, Sarah, who cast them-selves in the roles of Rosenkrantz and his wife. When rehears-als were begun, however, some of the other actors in the company turned out to be less persuaded than the Adlers were of its virtues. The play did not include much singing or dancing—what little there was had been inserted by Gordin and Adler as an afterthought, a concession to popular tastes—and it seemed perilously dull. Even Mogulesco, for whom Gordin had written a lush, comic-pathetic role as Rosenkrantz's servant, had his doubts. For one thing, he was worried about Gordin's anticlerical zeal, which had led to portrayals of the good people in the play as relatively lax in their pieties and of such scoundrels as Berl Taratutya, the business rival and informer, as rigorously observant Jews. Mogulesco was hardly a model of pious observance himself, but he knew his audience. It was a common thing for Friday night audiences in the New York Yiddish theater—many of whose members had bought their tickets before sundown so as to persuade themselves that they were not violating the Sabbath—to hiss and boo whenever an actor on stage, in the course of performing his role, would commit such a Sabbath violation as lighting and smoking a cigarette. Mogulesco feared that the play had tendencies he chose to describe as "anti-Semitic." He also objected to its relative lack of musical material. Then one day, during a rehearsal, he suddenly broke into a song and dance that he had inserted into the middle of a scene without Gordin's prior knowledge. Gordin, who was not familiar with the ad-libbing propensities of Yiddish actors, interrupted him, and a quarrel broke out. "Anti-Semite!" Mogulesco shouted at the playwright, and stormed off the stage. He refused to return until Gordin agreed to stay away from future rehearsals. Adler persuaded Gordin to do this.

Nervous and at odds with the actors, Gordin also stayed away from the theater on the play's opening night, November 1. It was probably just as well for his peace of mind that he was not present in the theater during the first two acts. As many of the actors had feared, the audience became restless, inattentive, and noisy. This was indeed not the kind of play they were used to. Then, after the second-act curtain, Adler stepped out onto the stage. It was not unusual at this time for Yiddish actors to address the audience during some break in the performance—or sometimes, for that matter, in the middle of a scene. The relationship between actor and audience had some of the air of browbeating intimacy that frequently characterized the relationship between rabbi and congregation in a *shtetl* synagogue. Authoritative thundering from a stage, as from a pulpit, often had a dramatic effect upon one's listeners. Adler imperiously informed the crowd that the play which they were showing their incapacity to appreciate was a "masterpiece," the work of an eminent Russian-Jewish author. They listened in respectful silence. By the time the third act began, they were thoroughly attentive. The timing was opportune, for the play now reached its moments of greatest emotional intensity. During the scene in which Rosenkrantz begs Taratutya to have mercy and not to reveal him to the police, some members of the audience began to weep audibly. When, in the final scene, Mogulesco as the servant cried out: "Master, they're taking you from me!," there was a violent general outburst of sobbing. *Siberia* was a success. During the enthusiastic applause that greeted the curtain calls, somebody went out and fetched Gordin, who was met with a thunderous ovation when he stepped into the theater. Mogulesco begged his pardon, and the two became friends once again.

The Lower East Side suddenly became awakened to a new phenomenon. Horowitz and Lateiner both dismissed Gordin's success as a passing fad, pointing out that numerous attempts had hitherto been made to bring "literature" onto the Yiddish stage, and that all had failed in the long run. Indeed, many Yiddish theatergoers continued to have mixed feelings about what Gordin had done, for they still thought of the theater as a place to provide them with relief from their everyday cares and sorrows. Life was tragic enough, who needed tragedy on stage? But one group was unanimous in its praise of Gordin's achievement: the intellectuals.

It was Cahan who served official notice that Gordin's *Siberia* had been admitted into the radical intelligentsia's universe of concerns. He wrote a lengthy critique of the play that appeared in two successive issues of the *Arbeiter Zeitung*. "We believe," he said, "that this play . . . will bring about a complete revolution on the Yiddish stage." The Yiddish theater had long been blessed with a group of excellent actors, he pointed out, but until now most of the vehicles they had found for their talents were like "second-hand Bowery melodrama." Intelligent people had despaired of Yiddish drama. But now something almost unhoped-for had taken place: an average Yiddish audience, made up mostly of simple working men and women, had responded warmly to a play that "belongs to real literature."

Once he had bestowed this endorsement, however, Cahan went on, in his second installment, to deal with the play's faults. After stressing once again that the play, to its credit, deserved to be judged by genuine literary criteria, he then said that "as a real literary work, Mr. Gordin's first play is not of the best." Mentioning numerous structural weaknesses, Cahan also delivered a passing blow at the title. He thought it to be sensational and false, referring as it did to something outside the play's action altogether. Such arbitrary methods of getting attention, he said, could only happen in the Yiddish theater. Despite Cahan's earlier praise, these criticisms must have rankled with Gordin, who was never able to accept any kind of criticism with equanimity.

Meanwhile, Gordin pursued his bright new career. Boris Thomashevsky, who, upon entering young manhood, had embarked upon a professional acting career, now presided over the company that resided at the Rumanian Opera House. Like Adler, he had ambitions to do serious drama, and he commissioned Gordin to write a play for him. Gordin's second play, like the first, was about Jewish life in Russia, and was called *The Pogrom*. By this time Gordin had found in his efforts at playwriting the self-assurance which had marked anything else he had ever done. Confirmed in his view of the high literary standards of his own efforts by the reception that had been accorded *Siberia,* he was determined to apply rigorous literary criteria in the writing and staging of his dramas from now on. In this second play, for example, since he was as ardent a "Russian" realist as Cahan ever was, he placed in the mouth of one of the characters, a Russian police inspector, speeches that were entirely in Russian rather than in the customary Yiddish. What Russian police inspector ever spoke Yiddish? But, on the other hand, how many Yiddish actors spoke good Russian? Certainly not the man whom Thomashevsky had chosen for the part, as it turned out; refusing to compromise, Gordin thereupon took the part for himself. Similarly, a Ukrainian peasant appears in the play, and Gordin wrote the part in Ukrainian. The actor originally slated for the role, a Hungarian Jew, thought it would be sufficient to the purpose if the character spoke "goyish"—i.e., any non-Jewish tongue—and he began, during rehearsals, to inject Hungarian into his speech whenever he could not remember something in the Ukrainian text he had tried to learn by rote. Gordin would not stand for this, and he hired a non-Jewish Ukrainian immigrant to play the part.

But Gordin's notion of high literary standards was applied most rigorously of all in his demand that the integrity of the written text not be violated. In respectable theater the world over, actors did not simply do what they wanted with the text of Ibsen or Shakespeare; Gordin would permit no ad-libbing of his own plays either. As it happened, this demand was a particularly difficult yoke for Yiddish actors to bear, since it went to the very foundations of their craft. What was theater, if not the spontaneous emanations of their spirits in front of an audience? The problems inherent in Gordin's demand showed themselves in the opening-night performance of *The Pogrom*, during its very first scene. In this scene, the lady of a well-to-do Russian-Jewish home, played by Bina Abramowitz, opens the door to a Russian police inspector, played by Gordin himself, who is paying a surprise visit. Unruffled in her cordiality, the lady welcomes him, invites him to sit down at the table, offers him wine and fish, wishes him a good appetite; suddenly, at this point, Miss Abramowitz turned to the audience and said in a loud aside: "He should choke on it!" Gordin's fist slammed down on the table. "Stop it!" he said, forgetting where he was. "That's not in the script!"

Despite such vagaries, Gordin's second play went over as successfully as the first. His reputation now assured, Gordin was hired as the resident playwright of Jacob P. Adler's troupe at the Union Theater. In the months that followed, he turned out a rapid succession of plays of greatly varying character, trying out his new craft in as many different veins as he could explore. He studied the masters of classical and modern drama, and used their plots as well as their techniques for his own works. When, in the fall of 1892, he considered that the time had come for him to try his hand at doing a major play, he went to the very top for his source, and wrote a drama candidly entitled *Der Yiddisher Kenig Lear* ("The Jewish—or Yiddish—King Lear"). It tells the story of David Masheles, a rich Jew who tries with lavish gifts to bribe his three daughters into making loud protestations of love for him; two of them do so, the third refuses—the rest is literary history. But unlike his royal counterpart, David Masheles does not die in the end; he is simply left sick, blind, poor, broken by old age, forsaken by two of his children—this is tragic ending enough for the Yiddish audience, which had no Elizabethan appetite for blood and violence. Jacob P. Adler's performance in this role became a historic moment in the development of the Yiddish theater.

Many objections were made, however, to the play's heavy dependence upon Shakespeare. Can a play be considered a work of art, some of the Jewish intellectuals asked, when its plot has been so liberally borrowed? Gordin replied in written articles and on the stage—for he had taken to addressing his audiences, and answering his critics, in speeches delivered between the acts of performances of his plays—saying that Shakespeare himself had borrowed his plots, so why couldn't Gordin do the same thing? Originality, he argued, was a false criterion for art; it was the rendition that counted. He was backed in his views by the respected voice of Morris Winchevsky, still in England at this time, who wrote a learned defense of Gordin's use of Shakespeare as a source. Winchevsky had probably not yet read or seen any of Gordin's plays, but he was familiar with his other writings, and was overjoyed at the idea that a high literary tone was being introduced into the Yiddish theater. This was all the backing Gordin needed, and he went on writing plays that leaned heavily upon their sources in world drama. Once, a few years later, he escorted a friend into his study, showed him shelves filled with the works of the great playwrights of ancient and modern times, and said: "These are my masters. From them I take my plots, subjects and actions." He went on to add that his characters, however, were taken from life: they "speak their own language, propagandizing my own ideas all the while."

Gordin had found a good working formula for his own talents, and one that furthermore seemed to be a way of weaning the Yiddish theater audience away from historical operas to something more like serious drama. In a fashion parallel to that of the *Arbeiter Zeitung* intellectuals writing popularizations of Marxian theory, Gordin was providing his public with popularizations of the themes of the great playwrights. Like the socialists, "propagandizing my own ideas all the while," he was more teacher than anything else, and the teacher's occasional note of condescension was not absent from his writing. In *The Jewish King Lear*, for example, there is a point at which David Masheles is told the story of Shakespeare's play and warned that he might be heading for a similar fate; far from being bashful about his heavy reliance upon Shakespeare, Gordin is here, as in the title, making sure his unevenly educated audience knows exactly what he is up to. He is giving them a lesson in literature, and is also preparing them to enjoy his ingenuity in adapting his source to a Yiddish milieu. Something similar occurs in a play Gordin wrote a few years later, which became one of the most popular dramas in the Yiddish repertory, *God, Man and Devil*, a retelling of the Faust story. The play has a prologue in heaven, with a dialogue between God and Satan; and sure enough, at the end of the scene Satan turns to the audience and announces that he has previously had similar dialogues with God concerning both Job and Faust. Such instances of "cluing in" the audience, along with the heavy-handed didacticism, forced loftiness, and formula-writing quality of the plays all clearly bespeak a quality known today under the name "middlebrowism." It is not at all surprising that Gordin was not able, for example, to perceive the charm of Goldfaden's plays (as Cahan did, incidentally), but regarded them to be as much an example of the low state of Yiddish theater before his own arrival as were those of Horowitz and Lateiner.

Certain of Gordin's achievements were unquestionable, however. For one thing, he had introduced a debate over aesthetic principles, salutary for any cultural milieu, into the hitherto predominantly music-hall atmosphere of the Yiddish theater. "The Ghetto and the Russian Jews," Lincoln Steffens wrote of this era years later, "a disputatious lot, were splitting just then into two parties over the question of realism in the arts. Cahan took us, as he could get us, one by one or in groups, to the cafes where the debate was on at every table and to the theaters where the audience divided: the realist [pro-Gordin] party hissing a romantic play, the romanticists [supporters of Horowitz and Lateiner] fighting for it with clapping hands and sometimes with fists or nails. A remarkable phenomenon it was, a community of thousands of people fighting over an art question as savagely as other people had fought over political or religious questions, dividing families, setting brother against brother, breaking up business firms, and finally, actually forcing the organization of a rival theater [formed by Gordin at the Thalia] with a company pledged to realism against the old theater [Lateiner's company at the Windsor], which would play any good piece."

Another of Gordin's achievements was that he had at last created native vehicles for the tragic powers of the greatest actors of the Yiddish stage. Through Gordin's works, Jacob P. Adler was able to attain the eminence he deserved. David Kessler, who came to be regarded as second only to Adler in the interpretation of Gordin's male roles, was an even more characteristic phenomenon of the milieu Gordin had created. Kessler was an uneducated and largely inarticulate man, whom the Gordinian culture enabled to rise to a state of princeliness in the world of the arts. This was even more the case with Keni Liptzen, a woman of little learning who became a symbol of artistic and spiritual aristocracy through her performances of Gordin's plays. Indeed, a special artistic relationship evolved between her and Gordin, who was, like Shakespeare his teacher, assiduous in the creation of characters tailored to the personalities and requirements of his actors. With Madame Liptzen as his surrogate of the proscenium, Gordin ranged through the whole history of drama from Aeschylus to Ibsen gathering heroines to represent his favorite theme: the need for woman to become emancipated in society. The plays he produced on this theme readily made Gordin the target of the wrath of orthodox Jews and prigs, a fact which won over to his cause those intellectuals who might otherwise have had second thoughts about the quality of his work.

Gordin's association with Madame Liptzen culminated in the writing of his best play, in 1898, a return to and reworking of his favorite old source: *Die Yiddishe Kenigin Lear* ("The Jewish Queen Lear"). By now a much more accomplished playwright than he had been when he wrote his *Jewish King Lear,* Gordin felt free to venture further from Shakespeare's plot. Mirele Efros, the Jewish "Queen Lear," is a rich widow with two weakling sons, one of them well meaning, the other something of a charlatan. The main conflict, a struggle for control of the household, occurs between the aristocratic Mirele and the low-born girl that the well-meaning son has married and brought home with him. In the end, it is Mirele's aristocratic haughtiness that is the victor; the old woman has left the house and gone off to live in proud poverty until, ten years after her departure, on the day of her grandson's bar mitzvah (religious confirmation), her repentant daughter-in-law arrives and begs her to come home. After much persuasion and mutual self-examination, she does so, in one of Gordin's few "happy endings." Although the rights to this play were owned in America by Madame Liptzen, who made the lead role her trademark for several years, it was performed by other actresses in Warsaw, where a revival of Yiddish theater was then taking place, and where the play soon became a favorite in the repertory under the title *Mirele Efros*. There, the foremost interpreter of the role at the turn of the century was Esther Rachel Kaminska, whose daughter Ida subsequently began her own acting career in the role of Mirele's thirteen-year-old grandson in the last act. (In later years, Ida Kaminska went on to play the willful daughter-in-law, and eventually inherited the role of Mirele. Most recently, her own daughter, Ruth Kaminska, has played opposite her mother in the role of the daughter-in-law. The splendor of this family tradition overshadows the mere adequacy of Gordin's play.)

*Mirele Efros* completed Gordin's rise to the cultural high priesthood of the Lower East Side. Although the plays of Horowitz and Lateiner still drew the larger crowds, Gordin's works were nonetheless commercially successful, and no other Yiddish writer in New York could rival his claims as a creator of serious literature. He bestrode the Jewish quarter like a colossus. Physically a great bear of a man, with a large black Assyrian beard and an air of flamboyant yet aristocratic Bohemianism that was often characteristic of Russian artists, he made a legend-provoking impression upon the public imagination. "I still see him walking through the streets," wrote one of his fellow Yiddish playwrights, Leon Kobrin, years after his death, "straight as a palm, his princely beard solemnly covering his broad chest, his eyes like two points of fire, sharp as daggers. In his right hand he carries a cane; in his left one of his plays. He is going to the theater to read it to the actors. People who know him say, 'That is Jacob Gordin.' Those who do not know him stop and remark, 'What a fine man!'" Hutchins Hapgood saw Gordin as the representative of what was best in Yiddish theater, his plays as "realism worked out consciously in art." And realism, as Hapgood saw it, was the artistic essence of the spirit of the Ghetto, the lesson that it had to teach to the American public in general. Was not this, after all, the lesson that Abraham Cahan was already teaching to his Yankee readers and colleagues?

Cahan undoubtedly had been the first to herald Gordin before the Hapgoods and his other Yankee friends; but, in private, he continued to have reservations about Gordin's talents. To be sure,

Gordin had brought the spirit of literature to the Yiddish theater, as Cahan had pointed out in his review of *Siberia* back in 1891, and furthermore, there could be no doubt that he stood head and shoulders above any American playwright of the moment. But the extreme touting of Gordin that was going on among some Lower East Side commentators, who often did not blush at comparing him to Ibsen, Chekhov, and Shakespeare, was too much for Cahan's critical judgment. Cahan's objections to some of the shortcomings of Gordin's writing had even led to a personal rivalry between the two men. This had broken out in 1895, during the run of one of Gordin's first plays about life in the New World, *The Russian Jew in America*. The play was a scathing comment about the state of the human soul in America, and it presented a large portrait gallery of corrupt and opportunistic types. Among these was a Jewish labor leader named Huzdak, a man who was perfectly willing to compromise abstract socialist principles in order to obtain concrete gains for his union. Throughout the play, Huzdak kept repeating the line, "What do I need brains for when I've got a Constitution?" Upon first hearing this, Cahan leaped up from his seat and cried out in Russian, "That's a lie!" In the ensuing weeks, there was an angry exchange between Gordin and Cahan on the pages of the *Arbeiter Zeitung*.

The result of this episode was a lasting coolness between the two men. At the time the *Forward* was founded in 1897, Gordin still needed to do newspaper work to supplement his income; being anti-De Leonist, he had no choice but to work for the *Forward*, even though Cahan was its editor. But he and Cahan managed to maintain a professional decorum in their relations at the office until, one day, Gordin handed Cahan the manuscript of a review he had written of Cahan's novel, *Yekl*. Cahan had heard from Jacob P. Adler that Gordin was reading the book and that he liked it. Upon reading the review, however, Cahan discovered it to be a violent denunciation. Without commenting on the review, Cahan suggested to Gordin that since he, Cahan, had just submitted his resignation, it might be more discreet if it were not published until after his departure. Gordin replied: "Jacob Gordin is not in the habit of making conditions over an article he has written." Cahan turned and walked out of the room. The article was published shortly after he left the *Forward*.

In the months that followed, his vantage point in the realm of American journalism and literature, far from the strife and the jealousies of the Yiddish world, enabled Cahan to look upon Gordin somewhat more serenely and objectively. It was not hard for him to sing Gordin's praises to Hapgood, Steffens, and other American friends. Gordin soon responded in kind, and even paid Cahan a compliment in person—although the two men were not on speaking terms—at the "Russian" colony's traditional party on New Year's Eve of 1900. Cahan was then writing his series of sketches for the *Forward* on the disarray of the Lower East Side socialist community, and Gordin, sitting at the opposite end of a long table, held forth about the virtues of these articles loudly enough for Cahan to hear. Cahan could not but feel better disposed toward Gordin after that, and a short time later, when a friend brought them together at a party, they carefully resumed cordial relations with one another.

But this was to prove to be merely a truce. There was a natural incompatibility between these two men, both of them populists by instinct, both of them—after Cahan's return to Yiddish journalism in 1902—seeking cultural supremacy over the selfsame public, and yet so different temperamentally. Gordin was completely the dashing, sentimental Russian life force that Cahan, outwardly the dry, reserved, cerebral Litvak, felt himself to be in his heart and was never able to be in his person. Gordin could not bear Cahan's intellectual meticulousness and seemingly ignoble capacity to master the requirements of Yankee practicality, and Cahan could not bear Gordin's heroic but often thoughtless thundering. They returned to battle against one another after a few months, when Cahan attended a performance of Gordin's *The Slaughter* at the Thalia, which now housed Gordin's own company. Backstage after the performance, Cahan told one of the actors that he thought Gordin had not been successful in the creation of one of the main characters, a simple *shtetl* girl, into whose mouth Gordin had placed speeches which Cahan thought to be improbably intellectual. Gordin heard about this comment, and a short time later Cahan was astonished to hear that Gordin had stepped out on stage between acts one night to make one of his celebrated denunciations of his critics—this time of Cahan, whose word-of-mouth remarks had not even appeared anywhere in print. Gordin had never mentioned Cahan by name, but his *ad hominem* attack had left no doubt as to the identity of his victim. Angrily, Cahan went to the actor to whom he had spoken the criticism and told him to "assure Gordin that I won't have any more opinions about forthcoming works of his." Cahan vowed never to see another Gordin play.

By the time Cahan returned to the *Forward* for good in the fall of 1903, a number of the most prominent members of the staff were ardent supporters of Gordin and his work. Foremost among these, as it happened, were the two men who were now Cahan's leading rivals at the paper, Morris Winchevsky and Louis Miller. Their steadily growing enthusiasm for Gordin seemed to work roughly in direct proportion to their increasing hostility toward Cahan. This was especially the case with Miller. Winchevsky had been Gordin's fan without letup since 1892; Miller, on the other hand, had once been as critical of Gordin's shortcomings as Cahan was. But, at around the time when tension first arose between Cahan and Miller, during Cahan's first stint as editor of the *Forward* in 1897, Miller was beginning to manifest a warm-hearted appreciation of Gordin's works. Only a few months after Cahan had left the *Forward,* when Miller was editing the paper, it carried a series of six articles praising *Mirele Efros* by the staff drama critic, M. Katz.

This alignment of forces between Cahan and his opponents on the *Forward* staff over the question of Gordin's abilities as a playwright gradually turned into a major intramural policy question. The first signs of the brewing conflict emerged less than a month after Cahan's definitive return to the editorship in 1903. A new play by Gordin, *The Orphan,* opened at the Thalia on the evening of October 12. This did not present an immediate problem for the *Forward:* Katz wrote a favorable review of the play, and Cahan did not go to see it—a working arrangement that satisfied everybody. But a complication arose when a severe criticism of the play appeared in the *Forward's* ancient rival, the orthodox *Tageblatt.* A few nights later, during a repertory performance of another of Gordin's plays, the author stepped out on stage between acts to make his traditional spirited reply to his critics. Suddenly he spotted the *Tageblatt* critic sitting in the audience with a colleague, the editor of a newly founded orthodox Yiddish paper called the *Morning Journal,* which was also opposed to Gordin's notions about feminine emancipation. "There they are," Gordin cried, pointing his finger at them, "sitting there, the two scroungers—they haven't even paid for their tickets!" With every eye in the audience turned upon them, the two men rose silently and walked out of the theater. The expected counterattack appeared in the *Tageblatt* a few days later, this time denouncing not merely Gordin's irreverent plays, but his person, his ideas—and socialism in general.

This was all the provocation Louis Miller needed. During the years of Cahan's absence, when he had been effectively in command of the *Forward,* Miller had devoted much of his time and energy to writing denunciations of the *Tageblatt.* His annoyance at that paper's consistently higher circulation had been compounded by his anger at its false religious piety—false, because while preaching strict observance of the Sabbath and the dietary laws to its readers, some of its editors completely ignored such proprieties in their own lives. The popular myth among socialists was that the typical *Tageblatt* editorialist would write such preachments on a Saturday, when Jewish law prohibits writing, and while eating a ham sandwich. One accusation apparently was factual: that one of the *Tageblatt* editors had undergone a formal conversion to Christianity years before going to work for the paper. For this reason, Miller's anti-*Tageblatt* articles had always employed the ironic phrase "cross and skullcap" to characterize the paper's hypocrisies.

Miller now wanted to rally to Gordin's defense on the pages of the *Forward,* and, in the process, resume his old campaign against the *Tageblatt;* still not on speaking terms with Cahan, he conveyed these wishes to him through a colleague. Now, Cahan did not yet feel any more eager than he had ever been to return to the old Yiddish style of vituperative combat, certainly not for the sake of Gordin, whom he did not consider to be entirely blameless in the matter. Furthermore, his Yankee-nurtured spirit was not so troubled as those of Miller, Gordin, and Winchevsky seemed to be about *Tageblatt* hypocrisy; he had seen worse forms of charlatanism in American public life. But considerations of intramural diplomacy finally forced him to yield: his tensions with Miller and his dislike of Gordin were too well known for him to be able to refuse Miller without uncomfortable repercussions. And so Miller went to work. First, he submitted a long diatribe against the *Tageblatt* and its views of Gordin, called "Cross, Skull-Cap and Art." Then he organized a mass meeting in support of Gordin in a Clinton Street hall; Cahan did not attend. Miller wrote up the meeting in a long article for the next day's *Forward,* in which he included demands that both the owner of the *Tageblatt,* Kasriel Sarasohn, and its editor leave the Jewish quarter immediately.

Now politics entered the picture. The November elections were coming up. Edward J. Ahearn, the Tammany boss of the Lower East Side, had long come to terms with the fact that his bailiwick was no longer virtually an Irish province, and was now striving to maintain his power over the growing Jewish population. Since 1900 the Congressional representative of the Ninth District—which roughly corresponded to the Jewish quarter—had been a New York-born German Jew named Henry M. Goldfogle, Tammany's offering to the Jewish voter. But outside of Goldfogle, Lower East Side Jews had not shown much favor to the candidates of Tammany Hall, which was associated in the minds of many of them with images of young Irish toughs and brawls on neighborhood streets, and they tended, in this era of patrician progressivism, to vote for Republican reform candidates. One problem, from Ahearn's point of view, was that Tammany had still not obtained any support in the Yiddish press. The socialist press was, of course, out of the question; Tammany Hall represented precisely the kind of capitalist "boodle-politicking" that the socialist intellectuals despised. But the *Tageblatt* was something else again. One day during the first week in November, while feelings about the *Tageblatt*'s attacks on Gordin were still running high, the *Forward* came into possession of a copy of a letter written to Ahearn by Hatzkel Sarasohn, one of the sons of the *Tageblatt*'s publisher, promising that his traditionally Republican paper would campaign for Tammany candidates provided that his younger brother, a lawyer, be nominated for a judgeship.

The letter was, of course, grist for the *Forward*'s mill, and Cahan was as eager to exploit it as any of his colleagues were. He therefore permitted Miller to have his way with it for the time being; the letter was reproduced in the *Forward* with an editorial by Miller at its side, compounding the usual vituperations against the *Tageblatt* and invoking Gordin's cause once again. But once the elections were over, Cahan decided that the time had come to separate Gordin's case from the issue of the Sarasohn letter, which he wanted to pursue. On November 10, he published an editorial which asserted that the *Tageblatt* had used Gordin merely as a pretext to denounce socialism in general. From then on, Cahan avoided mentioning Gordin again, while he pursued a campaign of denunciation of the *Tageblatt* that lasted for weeks. This was a quarrel that Cahan didn't mind entering into now, for the *Tageblatt* was a major rival for circulation and was at this moment extremely vulnerable. By the time he was done, Cahan had pushed ahead of the *Tageblatt* in the race for circulation. He had also succeeded in outflanking Gordin and Miller. His conflict with them hung fire for nearly a year.

On Friday evening, September 2, 1904, the Thalia company produced a play that Gordin had written to expose the hypocrisy of *Tageblatt* orthodoxy. Its ironical title, *The Purity of Family Life,* was a traditional Jewish phrase that the *Tageblatt* pietists had often used against the sympathetic portrayals of extramarital love that were sometimes in Gordin's plays. This new play, which is no longer extant, presumably set out to show the violations, in secret, of this and other canons of traditional morality by a Jew who claimed to be pious and who sought to impose his hypocritical standards upon others. Since the *Tageblatt* affair of the previous year had become celebrated, the play's opening was treated as a major event, and all the socialist eminences of the Jewish quarter were invited to attend. A superficial cordiality prevailed in the relations between Gordin and Cahan by this time. Cahan could not refuse the invitation; as far back as the previous December, when M. Katz had gone, as usual, to cover the opening of a Gordin play for the *Forward* and had written an adverse review of it, sentiments were beginning to grow that Cahan, who reviewed all other playwrights for the *Forward,* should start reviewing Gordin as well. So Cahan went to his first Gordin play in five years. Perhaps he had genuinely believed for a moment that he would seek peace by pointing up in his review all the virtues of the play he could find. Unfortunately, he could not find any. The play contained in superabundance what he had long considered to be the worst fault in Gordin's writing: a tendency to place sermons in the mouths of his characters, to make them spokesmen of the playwright's ideas rather than dramatic representations of them. Cahan thought it was the worst Gordin play he had ever seen.

What was he to do? He thought for a moment of remaining silent and assigning Katz to review the play. But it was no use; everyone had seen him at the performance, and they would be expecting his review. He had no choice but to go through with it. The next morning, he sat down to write the article. By this time, despite his scruples about the matter, he was beginning to feel a certain satisfaction at this opportunity to put Gordin in his place. He decided to open his piece with a little lecture about *Tageblatt* hypocrisy, a matter which he increasingly regarded more with amusement than moral outrage, the more the *Forward*'s rising circulation left that of the *Tageblatt* far behind:

> Hypocrites and pious frauds exist in Russia, too. But there, at least, they behave as such. Here in America, in the topsy-turvy world we have here, it's a completely different story. . . . Here the hypocrite doesn't even behave like one. He eats pork and he often smokes on the Sabbath, at the same time that he preaches Judaism to the world at large. Everybody knows that his articles about observing the Sabbath are often written on Saturday, but this is nothing unusual here in America. "Business is business"—that's the way people see everything here, always keeping this rule in mind. In fact, the religious hypocrite is not really a hypocrite at all here. He is nothing more than an example of American gall (*hutzpah*).

Having thus got off his chest a dismissal of Gordin's concern over the issue of hypocrisy that could have been written even if the play had been a good one, Cahan proceeded to the matter at hand. Pointing out that Sarasohn's newspaper was an outstanding example of the sort of mercantilistic gall he had just described, Cahan went on to recall how the *Tageblatt* had really come to its day of reckoning a year ago, when the controversy with it broke out on the pages of the *Forward,* after which "hundreds of articles were written" denouncing the *Tageblatt*'s hypocrisy. The implication here was that the matter had really been settled months before. Editorial after editorial had familiarized Yiddish readers with the faults of *Tageblatterei,* until there was virtually nothing more to be said; since then, the matter had almost been forgotten. But now that the playwright Jacob Gordin had come forth with what was presumed to be a *dramatization* of this theme, Cahan wrote, everyone went to the theater eager to see how Gordin would *portray* the kind of hypocrisy that had been thoroughly *denounced* a year before. Alas, they were disappointed, for they did not see it portrayed; it was merely denounced again. "The audience obtained an expression of protest from the play, but unfortunately this came in the same form that it was expressed in a year ago in our speeches and editorials." The characters were not real people, but mere vehicles for ideas:

> The leading feminine role was not a role at all, but a collection of propagandistic speeches. Madame Liptzen, who played this role, had nothing to play. Her task on stage was to propagandize; instead of an actress, she had to be a speechmaker.

Only the male lead seemed reasonably interesting, Cahan said, and this was because of an excellent performance by Mogulesco, not because of any virtue in the part that had been written for him. As for the secondary roles, there were two which Cahan deemed to be "of the variety-stage type that we are used to seeing from the pen of Mr. Lateiner—not one jot better." As for the general outlines of the play, there was "no interesting dramatic development." Cahan ended the review with a pious hope that Gordin, whose talent was well established, would write better plays again in the near future.

The article, which appeared in Sunday's edition, the next day, was like a renewed declaration of war. Gordin and Miller were convinced that this was not an aesthetic opinion judiciously arrived at, but a pure case of personal animosity revived. In fact, they were sure that the article had been written before Cahan had even seen the play—how else did he get it out so fast? Yiddish reviewers were usually not so prompt. Miller sat down and wrote a reply to Cahan's review. Never referring to Cahan specifically by name, he said among other things:

> The critic says that he had expected Gordin to *portray* his ideas, and that since they were uttered rather than portrayed, the play is a failure. In other words, the critic is saying that the drama is a failure because Gordin has provided not what the critic wanted, but only what Gordin wanted.

> This is a new notion in drama criticism. If it's correct, then one can condemn not only every play of Gordin's, but every writer, every painter, every artist.
>
> A drama, like any work of art, is to be treated not from the standpoint of a critic, but from that of the author himself. The first question the critic must ask himself is: what has the author sought to express in his work? The second question is: has he succeeded? If the author succeeds in reaching the goal he has set for himself, then the task has been fulfilled and the work is a success.

Granting that the characters in this play had not been "brought out so well" as in some other Gordin plays, Miller said that this was not the point. There are lots of great plays in which the utterance of ideas predominates over the development of character, Miller argued, claiming *Hamlet* as an example. Gordin's purpose, after all, was not merely to *portray* a battle on the stage, but to *fight* it from there. "I would not even have written this critique," Miller concluded, "if this were merely a question of the right way to create a work of art. Unfortunately, the question at hand here has a much greater and deeper meaning in the Jewish quarter than the success or failure of a play. What is involved is an issue that has provoked a storm which has had a purifying effect upon the moral atmosphere of our quarter. The *Forward* has no right to destroy the work to which so many people have sacrificed themselves just because its critics feel that it is better to portray a battle on the stage than to fight it from there."

Miller placed over this essay the title "A Critique of a Critique," and sent it to the *Forward*. Cahan sent it back, with the reply that it was a policy of the *Forward* not to publish criticism of drama criticism. Miller relayed the word back to Cahan that he was "declaring war." He took the article to Gordin, who published it in the September 15 issue of *Dramatishe Velt* ("Drama World"), a journal he had just founded.

In the same issue, Gordin also included a reply of his own to Cahan's criticism. Like Miller, referring to Cahan as "the critic" but never using his name, he wrote:

> I cannot reach any accord with him, because he is my principal detractor, because whatever I build he tears down, because whatever I've been doing all my life he negates. It is clear that we are working for the sake of the selfsame people. But I want to lead them forward, and he drags them backward through the *Forward*. I say to them, a man must be upright and defend his principles unequivocally. He teaches them to be politicians. I say, a revolutionary should not be two-faced. . . . He says, you have to keep the circulation in mind. I say, an honest man should never kowtow to anybody. He says, you've got to make friends. . . . I say, you have to lift the masses up to your level. He says, you have to stoop down to the level of the masses, cater to them and accommodate yourself to their basest instincts.

The battle lines had been drawn for all-out war. The very next month was the time of the first annual election for the editorship of the *Forward* since Cahan's return the previous fall. Miller, with Winchevsky as his staunch ally, was determined to use this occasion to oust Cahan. Their only problem was where to find a strong candidate to replace him. Neither of them was a possibility: Miller had too many enemies, and Winchevsky simply was not temperamentally inclined to take the job. It was not until the Press Association meeting itself on the evening of October 6 that Miller and Winchevsky decided upon their candidate: Michael Zametkin, the most resolutely radical of the old guard. Zametkin had not been too outspoken of late, but Miller was sure he would be ready to stand up in opposition to Cahan. Unfortunately, Zametkin was not present at the meeting. Miller tried to press for an adjournment, but he was unsuccessful; instead, a committee was sent out to find Zametkin. The potential candidate was not at home, and the committee members scoured the cafes until they found him in one of them, playing chess. When told that he had been nominated for the editorship, Zametkin replied that this was a superfluous gesture, since the *Forward* already had an editor, Cahan. He went back to his game, and the committee returned empty-handed to the meeting hall. Cahan was reelected by all but three votes; Miller and another member voted against him, while the peaceable Winchevsky abstained.

Neither Miller nor Winchevsky ever appeared at another *Forward* meeting. While Cahan further consolidated the power that had now been assured him, Miller and Winchevsky gradually withdrew from participation in the paper's affairs. By the end of the year, they had decided to seek backers and try to found a newspaper of their own. As for Gordin, he and Cahan had again reached a momentary cease-fire. Gordin's fortunes were on the wane. The Depression of 1903, which redounded to the *Forward*'s benefit by decreasing printing costs and bringing to it more readers in search of a labor-newspaper's counsel (it now cost only one cent a copy), had not had such a salutary effect upon the theater. People could not afford tickets so easily, and when they did go they preferred lighter fare than what Gordin had to offer; Horowitz and Lateiner continued to do reasonably well, and Goldfaden, who had now returned to New York and was mounting his old productions, was enjoying a sudden new burst of success. Gordin seemed to have passed the height of his powers as a playwright and was returning to his old career as a journalist and polemicist. Cahan no longer had to think about him, at least not for the time being.

CHAPTER 14

# 1905

In our friendship, personal feeling has played . . . a secondary part—
though we are united forever. In the name of the cause? Yes, in the
name of the cause!

—IVAN TURGENEV, *Virgin Soil*

WITH THE *FORWARD* NOW WELL ON THE WAY TO A BRILLIANT
success, one might have supposed that Cahan had come to terms with
his American destiny at last. But he had still not succeeded completely
in exorcising the ghost of his Russian revolutionary dream, the haunting recollection of a nobler life he might have lived but had left behind
forever. This remained with him even though he had established,
as far back as 1899, the terms of a possible reconciliation between
the visions of the past and the realities of the present, in a feuilleton
that he wrote for the *Commercial Advertiser.* Called "Back to Dear
Old Russia—the Disillusionment of Sonia Rogova," it described one
of the annual New Year's balls of the New York "Russian" colony,
and a special tribute that was paid that night to one Sonia Rogova,
who had just returned from a sentimental journey to the old country.
Expecting to share in some fond reminiscences, Sonia's friends are
dismayed to hear her tell them instead that Russia is far less splendid
than they remember it to be. The streets seem small and tawdry, she
says, after one has become used to American ones. Furthermore, her

trip has reminded her of something she and her friends had forgotten altogether too easily: that Jews are badly treated in Russia. It is simply impossible for her to feel at home in Russia any longer under these conditions, Sonia says, although she must admit that she does not feel perfectly at home in America, either. She is an exile in both countries. Why must this be? "Perhaps," she reflects, "it is because we are Jews—a persecuted, wandering people without a home."

There it was, clearly stated at a time when Cahan had been far less engaged in the ramifications of his Jewish identity than he subsequently became with his return to the editorship of the *Forward*. It was the implicit answer to Tzinchadzi's plight; for, if Cahan's outward circumstances had, like those of his fictional Georgian, become cast hopelessly adrift in the doldrums of the American bourgeois experience, his inward spirit had found justification for his condition in the Jewish identity that had unconsciously manifested itself even in his portrayal of Tzinchadzi. Unlike the Georgian, his own spiritual exile had really begun, not on the day he left Russia, but some eighteen hundred years earlier. If he was a Jew, then exile was part of his very nature; it was this fact that gave him a present and a future. It was also what made him profoundly an American. For even Hutchins Hapgood, more than two hundred years a Yankee, keenly felt the pain of his exile from Europe; who, then, represented that American condition of exile better than a Jew?

But such a conclusion was persuasive to Cahan only in moments when he was convinced that no reconciliation had ever been possible between his Russian identity and his Jewishness. Sonia Rogova believed it, experience seemed to have proven it in the pogroms of 1881, and then again in the pogrom at Kishinev in 1903. But were these really the terms on which he had broken his ties with the revolutionary movement and left Russia forever? Had he really departed as a Jew submitting to his destiny—or simply as an individual who preferred exile to a Tsarist prison? He had been given a chance to reflect upon this question later in the year in which he had done the feuilleton on Sonia Rogova, when two exiled Russian revolutionaries arrived in New York. Natan Bogaraz and Vladimir Yokhelson—the two Russians whom Hutchins Hapgood described in his anecdote about Anna Cahan and the discussion of Byron—were both Jews, and yet they had stayed with the *Narodnaya Volya* even after the pogroms of 1881. Which is to say that they had stayed with the organization even after it had become extremely dangerous to do so. They had both finally been arrested; Bogaraz served three years in the dungeon of the Peter and Paul Fortress, and then he and Yokhelson spent ten years together in Siberian exile. There they passed the time by collecting observations of the life of the tribes living north of the Arctic Circle. After their escape, they settled in Paris and published their findings. Now reputed as ethnologists, they had come to New York for a visit at the end of 1899 at the invitation of the National Museum of New York (later the Museum of Natural History), for whom they had published some treatises.

Bogaraz had heard about Cahan and his writings (some of his stories had been translated into Russian), and wrote him a letter upon arriving in New York. The two men got together often during Bogaraz's stay, and they became good friends. Once, as they strolled along Second Avenue, Bogaraz told Cahan the story of his arrest and imprisonment. He explained how, at the moment he was sent to the dungeon, he thought he would never see daylight again.

"Tell me how you felt," Cahan asked. "What was your state of mind when you thought that the bright world was being shut off from you forever?"

Bogaraz smiled. "Only a man of letters, interested in the human soul," he said, "would ask a question like that." He proceeded to give a detailed account of his inner experiences during his first days in prison. When Cahan got home he wrote it down as well as he could remember it, and put it among his piles of notes.

A short time later, during one of their literary conversations, Bogaraz suggested to Cahan that he write an account of his own experiences, and call it "Memoirs of a Russian Emigré." An interesting question: was he a Russian emigré or a Jewish immigrant? Cahan said he would give the idea some thought. The fact remained that if Bogaraz had been able to be so completely a Russian revolutionary, he had to have achieved this at the expense of his Jewish identity. Somewhere in the darkness of the Peter and Paul Fortress, he had purged himself of this identity, and of an American fate. So it seemed to Cahan; these were the alternatives as they had presented themselves to his and Bogaraz's generation, at least.

However, there now existed in Russia a new generation of young Jewish radicals for whom it seemed to be an entirely different story. In 1897, the year that the *Forward* was born, an organization had been founded, called the Jewish Workers' Federation (*Yiddishe Arbeiter Bund*) of Russia and Poland, or simply the "Bund" for short. It was the outgrowth of activities, primarily centered in Cahan's home city of Vilna, that had been going on ever since Aaron Lieberman—Morris Winchevsky's tragic comrade—had begun propagandizing socialist ideas in Yiddish in the eighteen-seventies. By the nineties the onset of industrialization had largely proletarianized the Jews of the Vilna region, and this combined with the strong Yiddish cultural tradition in that area brought an unprecedented phenomenon into being: a modern-minded, European working class for whom Yiddish was its primary medium of expression. The powerful educational traditions of East European Jewry imparted to this class an intellectual level unusual among proletariats, and produced among them a genuine proletarian intelligentsia. For the typical Lithuanian-Jewish worker, Marx's writings replaced the Talmud of his childhood religious schooling; the result was a viscerally socialist culture, as spontaneously Yiddish as his religious culture had been. This was the kind of synthesis that had occurred earlier on American soil, but that had once seemed impossible in the homeland of the Yiddish and the revolutionary cultures. The Bund was founded by precisely the type of men who, in Cahan's day, would have repudiated their Jewish origins and become completely assimilated Russian revolutionaries.

This had happened because, for a moment at least, Marxism—with its affirmation of a proletarian identity and its repudiation of the peasantry—had provided a myth within which Jewish particularist cultural aspirations seemed in no way inharmonious with the general aims of the revolutionary movement. In its Bundist form, Yiddishism was simply the culture of one wing of the world-wide proletariat. The first days of the Bund were a time of intimate relationship between its own leadership and that of the Russian Social Democratic movement. The idea for organizing the Bund, for example, had originated in a speech delivered in Vilna in 1895 by a twenty-two-year-old radical named Lev Tsederbaum who only a short time later, under the name Martov, was to be one of the preeminent leaders of the Social Democratic Party of Russia (before the Bolshevik-Menshevik split). The Bund was actually created under the initiative of Arkady Kremer, a Russian-Jewish intellectual who had once been almost totally assimilated but had made his way back to a Jewish self-identification, and who, by 1896, was the leader of a loose federation of Jewish social-democratic unions in Lithuania. That year, Kremer made a trip to Geneva to visit the founders and spiritual leaders of Russian Marxism, Georgy Plekhanov, Vera Zasulich, and Paul Axelrod (himself an assimilated Jewish revolutionary of the old type), who were then editing the underground newspaper *Iskra* ("The Spark"). Kremer had come to ask them about the possibility of propagandizing the activities of the Jewish labor movement through their journal; they replied by suggesting that he organize the Jewish unions into a single movement. Kremer did so the following year. The Bund was so completely identified, at the time of its inception, with the aspirations of Russian Social Democracy in general that it led the initiative in organizing the conference in Minsk in March, 1898, that created the Russian Social Democratic Party.

But this harmony between Bundist particularism, and the general Russian Social Democratic movement was coming to an end by the time of the party's second congress, which took place in Brussels and London in 1903. The flowering of Yiddish literature and the impact of the Zionist movement—which had also created its own political organization in 1897—had provoked a powerful spurt of Yiddishist nationalism among socialists and nonsocialists alike. This had led the Russian Social Democratic movement to begin to regard Bundism as being dangerously tainted with the kind of bourgeois-chauvinist attitudes that had produced Zionism, which the Bundists nevertheless denounced as vigorously as any Marxian socialist group did. But by the time the dust of the Kishinev pogrom had settled, it had indeed become extremely difficult for a Bundist to prove even to himself that he was more socialist than Jew, and it was this ambivalence that the Social Democratic Party held against him.

Matters reached a head on the floor of the 1903 Congress, when the Bundists put forth a demand for cultural autonomy within the party organization. A generation younger than that *Iskra* group which had urged Kremer to organize the Bund in the first place was now coming to the fore in the party. Led by Lenin, these younger men would not tolerate separatism of any kind within the party ranks, and they were determined to repudiate the Bundist demand. In order to avoid charges of anti-Semitism, this group gave the task of repudiating the Bundists to the two foremost Jews among its leadership, Lev Martov—who had by now completely renounced his Jewish-autonomist ideas of 1895—and Leon Trotsky, who delivered a scathing denunciation of Bundist separatism on the floor of the congress. The Bundists promptly withdrew from the party. This outcome undoubtedly did not surprise Cahan.

There were numerous links naturally connecting the Bund with the *Forward*, its exact contemporary. Both had their roots deep in Jewish Vilna, for Cahan was far from being the only *Vilner* in the *Forward* organization. In particular, the links were strong through the person of Abraham Liessin, who had been born in Minsk but had spent part of his youth in Vilna. He had been closely associated with Arkady Kremer, and would undoubtedly have been one of the founding members of the Bund had he not gone to the United States just before it was created. One of the *Forward*'s regular features was a roundup of Bund activities, usually written by Liessin. But the communion between the Bund and the *Forward* did not merely go in one direction, from Russia to America; the spiritual exchange was reciprocal. The formation of a Yiddish-speaking labor movement in New York had been a major source of inspiration for the founding of the Bund in the first place. The *Forward*'s own moderate social-democratic stance had also undoubtedly been of influence in the evolution of a similar attitude among the Bundists.

The strength of this relationship gradually led the *Forward* to assume the role of the Bund's chief representative in the United States. If the *Forward*'s Bundist comrades still lived where the soul of the revolution was, the men of the *Forward* lived where the money was, and fund raising for the Bund became one of the latter's principal activities. Every so often, a Bundist leader would himself come to the United States on a fund-raising tour, and the *Forward*—or, more specifically, Cahan himself—usually served as the welcoming committee. Cahan thus found himself involved again in Russian revolutionary actualities, as the middleman between the heroes from the homeland and the coffers of America. He relished his privileged association with these emissaries, but he could not help feeling a certain resentment toward them. He found faults wherever possible. For example, he thought that their theoretical approach to the ideal of a Jewish revolutionary nationalism, though it was in principle like the view developing within himself, was too abstract and bloodless: it did not vibrate with the mystical sense of communion with the Yiddish-speaking masses that he felt within himself. That was why the Bundists could be more ideological and less pragmatic than he; they could thus lay a claim to greater purity of soul, Cahan felt, while they conveniently neglected some of the morally compromising claims of reality. It gave him a secret satisfaction to discover, when he welcomed Kremer himself to the United States at the end of 1904, that the founder of the Bund spoke Yiddish rather poorly.

Would the Bund really achieve, after all, that reconciliation of Jewish and Russian revolutionary identities that Cahan had been unable to discover in his own day? The Russian Social Democratic Party seemed to have willed against it; above all, the Kishinev pogrom had perhaps shown its realization to be hopeless. For his part, Cahan had been astonished at the accuracy with which the lesson of 1881 seemed to have been reiterated in 1903. In fact, the selfsame forces seemed to be at work in both years. This is the view Cahan presented in an article on the "Jewish Massacres and the Revolutionary Movement in Russia" that he published in the *North American Review* in July, 1903, just after the Kishinev pogrom:

> About three weeks after the Kishinev massacre, the governor of the province of Ufa, M. Bogdanovich, was assassinated by two Russian revolutionaries as a result of a scene of carnage which had taken place in the town of Zlatoust, of that province, where forty persons, including children, were killed and two hundred were wounded in less than two months before the anti-Semitic outbreak in the capital of Bessarabia [Kishinev]. Ufa lies outside the "Pale of Jewish Settlement," and the victims of the slaughter for which Governor Bogdanovich was held responsible were all Gentiles; nevertheless, the two massacres are linked by ties of logical affinity. This becomes apparent when the Kishinev atrocities are considered in the light of recent developments in the progress of the revolutionary movement in Russia, on the one hand, and of the situation surrounding the epidemic of anti-Jewish riots which followed the assassination of Alexander II in 1881, on the other. Indeed, at the time of those riots, M. von Plehve, the present Minister of the Interior, was at the head of the police of the Empire.

Cahan goes on to analyze the events of 1881, demonstrating how the Tsarist police had then played upon the anti-Semitism of the Ukrainian peasantry to create a diversion for outbursts of energy that might otherwise have had revolutionary force. And now, once again, the Tsarist police—under the experienced guidance of von Plehve—was using this tried and true technique for channeling off potentially revolutionary discontentment. The energies of the *masses,* not merely those of two lone assassins, ought to have been turned against men like Bogdanovich and the regime he represented; instead, those mass energies and resentments were being diverted against the Jews. "Is it not a rather significant coincidence," Cahan points out, "that it was shortly before May 1st"—a regular date for skirmishing between Russian workers and police—"that M. von Plehve's subsidized favorite, the editor of the *Bessarabetz,* launched those rumors of a ritual murder by the Jews of Kishinev which brought about the terrible massacre?" And he concludes: "The meaning of all this, according to the interpretation of the revolutionists, is that the authorities are determined to set the various elements of the population against each other as a means of demoralizing the movement for constitutional reform."

Cahan did not say if he foresaw any solution to this problem, which was, after all, the tragic paradox of his own life's experience. It was not a problem to be solved by some simple act of social engineering; rather, it was one to be contemplated and described by the poet or the novelist. Cahan wrote this article while he was still in New Milford, Connecticut, struggling to articulate his next step as a writer of fiction. *The Chasm,* the fictionalized version of those "Memoirs of a Russian Emigré" that Bogaraz had proposed to him in 1899, was still not working. His effort at synthesizing the two main elements of his life's experience in personal, realistic terms was bringing him to irresoluble cross-purposes, between his impulse to project an ideal past and his unerring skill at perceiving an unflatteringly real present. If realism was to be his vein, that present was the only element he could portray successfully; for, beyond one fleeting and sublime glimpse, he had not really experienced the Russian revolutionary movement at all. Yet that movement was what he wanted to write about; now more so than ever, for the Kishinev pogrom had awakened in him the desire to confront that old problem of 1881 for once and for all. He had no choice, then, but to abandon the realism that had been his strength. Setting *The Chasm* aside once again, he started to work that summer on a new project, and gathered up enough momentum to be able to finish his "novel of revolutionary Russia" by the fall of 1904, even though he had by then spent a year engaged in full-time editorial duties.

*The White Terror and the Red,* as it was called, turned out to be a fabric woven of literary sources, touches of personal experience, and a great quantity of Tzinchadzi-like fantasy. Its models clearly were Chernyshevsky's *What Is To Be Done?* and Stepniak's novel, *The Career of a Nihilist,* both of these being books characterized by an inordinately stilted romantic tone. There are also to be found in it echoes of Turgenev, but not of his best side. Cahan readily falls into the hushed exaltation these writers take on when they are talking about noble deeds, without the compensations of Turgenev's genius or of the solid foundations of experience and suffering upon which Chernyshevsky and Stepniak stood. His narrative suffers above all from his evident desire to dream out a course he had never followed, and thereby somehow achieve vicarious justification for his troubled soul.

The novel begins with an account of the early life history of its main protagonist, a Russian nobleman named Prince Pavel Alexeyevich Boulatoff. When we first discover him, at the age of eighteen, he is a reactionary and an ardent lover of the Tsar. But he is subsequently converted to the revolutionary cause by a means traditional to the heroes of Cahan's fiction: an idealized passion for a woman. The process of his conversion begins when Pievakin, an elderly gymnasium professor who is beloved by all his students, including Pavel, is dismissed for having inadvertently digressed too far on the subject of constitutional government one day during a geography lecture. On the day of the teacher's departure, the students amass at the railroad station to see him off, and the police, fearing a demonstration, start to clear them away. Suddenly, a girl's voice rises above the din of the crowd, urging the students not to move. There is some scuffling, but a riot is averted, and the students remain to say farewell to their teacher. This is the early eighteen-seventies, and for many of the students in Miroslav (Cahan's fictitious rendering of Vilna) this first act of resistance to the police is the beginning of their involvement in the revolutionary movement.

Pavel is not present at the railroad station when this incident occurs; "he had not been informed that such a gathering was in contemplation at all." But when he hears about the incident, and about the heroic girl, he is troubled: "Everybody had been there except him. But what tantalized him more than anything else was the fact that a girl was the only person who had taken a brave and noble stand in the old man's behalf." At first, it seems to be only his nobleman's pride that is ruffled: "This hurt his knightly sense of honor cruelly. He should have been on the scene and done exactly what the girl had done." But the deeper, erotic nature of his feelings emerges in the ensuing weeks, when "the only gleam of light [upon his troubled conscience] was the veiled figure of that gymnasium girl." He tries to learn her name from some of the radical students whom he knows, but they refuse to tell him because he is a noble and a nephew of the reactionary governor of the province. Suddenly, his social position has made him an outsider. "At the gymnasium he felt his loneliness more keenly than ever. Wherever he saw a cluster of boys, he felt sure they were whispering about the gendarmes and the girl who had made the 'speech' at the railroad station. His pride was gone. He now saw himself an outcast, shut out of the most important things life contained."

The Jewish element in the story now makes its first overt appearance. Miroslav, like Vilna, is about one-third Jewish in population, and its gymnasium has a number of Jewish students. They are, of course, at the very center of the radical student circles. Pavel, still trying to learn the identity of that "pretty girl boldly raising her voice" (it is not indicated how Pavel found out she was pretty), approaches Elkin, an "underfed Jewish youth" with a chalky complexion, whom he knows to be one of the radical leaders. He begins his inquiry with the bravado of a reactionary Russian nobleman addressing a Jew, but declines precipitously into guilty abjection (such dynamics of mood are an instance of one of the novel's genuinely Russian qualities):

> "Look here, Elkin, I want to know who that girl is and all about the whole affair, and if you think I ought not to know it because— well, because I am a Boulatoff and my uncle is the governor, I can assure you that if I had been there I should have acted as she did. What's more, I hate myself for not having been there."

Elkin of course refuses him, with a sneer. This drives Pavel to try, in his own thoughts, to take out his agonies of conscience upon the Jew:

> "What did *he* do there?" he would say to himself. "To think of a lot of fellows running away when they are told they can't say good-bye to their martyred teacher, and a girl being the only one who has courage enough to act properly. And now that she has done it this coward has the face to give himself airs, as if he were entitled to credit for her courage. If I had been there I should not have run away as Elkin and his crew did."

Now the lines had been properly drawn:

> This placed Elkin and his followers on one side of the line and Pavel and the girl on the other. So what right had that coward of a Jew to place himself between her and him?

So far, Pavel has represented a fairly accurate projection of his author's own identity and feelings, in a nobleman's guise. Now begins the projection into realms of conscience-soothing fantasy. Pavel goes to the University of St. Petersburg, where he tries to become part of the student revolutionary circles. These continue to resist him, until one day he makes contact with a student radical from his own social class: none other than Sophia Perovskaya, the daughter of the former governor of St. Petersburg. This attempt on Cahan's part to introduce a real-life revolutionary personage—it is to be repeated later in the story—has a curious, shadowy effect, the result of Cahan's unsuccessful grafting of fantasy upon real history. Perovskaya gives Pavel some underground literature, but then, in an instant, she "disappeared from St. Petersburg and Pavel found himself cut off from the 'underground' world once more." Pavel resorts once again to trying to make contact with the revolutionary movement through Jews, and it is in this way—an odd one for a Russian nobleman, but a more accessible one to Cahan's imagination—that he eventually becomes a part of it.

Years pass. It is 1879. The "return to the soil" phase of the movement has played itself out and is being gradually replaced by terrorism. Pavel, now twenty-three years old and a full-fledged member of the revolutionary movement, is back on a visit to Miroslav to deliver a talk before a student gathering. In the audience he sees Elkin; it is a moment of triumph for Pavel. "When Elkin discovered who the important revolutionist from St. Petersburg was the blood rushed to his face." Their respective claims to high revolutionary credentials, as it turns out, have shifted considerably since their last confrontation. Elkin "had been expelled from the University for signing some sort of petition. Since then he had nominally been engaged in revolutionary business. In reality he spent his nights in gossip and tea-drinking, and his days in sleep." But Pavel does not care to turn the dagger of his triumph; he simply wants an answer to the old question: who, where is she? Elkin, who for some reason does not give her name at this point, says she is well known and beloved in radical circles in Miroslav, and promises to introduce Pavel to her next time he comes.

Enthusiastically, the ever ingenuous Pavel tells Elkin of the influence she has had upon his destiny. " 'I see. It needed a little girl to make a convert of a great man like you. Well, well. That's interesting,' Elkin remarked, with a lozenge-shaped sneer." But Pavel does not even notice this display of scorn, for his heart has been carried away once again with the old romance:

> The student girls of the secret movement, their devotion to the cause, their pluck, the inhuman sufferings which the government inflicted upon those of them who fell into its hands—all this was the aureole of Pavel's ecstasy. His heart had remained spotless, the wild oats he had sown during the first weeks of his stay in the capital notwithstanding. The word Woman would fill him with tender whisperings of a felicity hallowed by joint sacrifices, of love crowned with martyrdom, and it was part of the soliloquies which the sex would breathe into his soul to tell himself that he owed his conversion to a girl.

It would seem that Pavel's old problem of love and conscience is about to achieve its resolution; there are ominous forebodings, however:

> But these were sentimentalities of which the Spartan traditions of the underground movement had taught him to be ashamed. Moreover, there was really no time for such things.

Conscience, the offspring of love, now proceeds to become its adversary, and love's realization is soon to become as problematic for Pavel as entry into the revolutionary movement once had been. When Pavel finally meets the girl, the narrative is curiously muffled, as if the author himself, sharing Pavel's sense of guilt, has shied away from the self-indulgence of this literary consummation. Her name had been mentioned earlier in a casual way, as if it were not being mentioned for the first time, and as if its obvious Jewishness should come as no surprise: "in the evening he was to make the acquaintance of Clara Yavner, the heroine of the Pievakin 'demonstration.' " That evening he does just that, he simply meets this "fair-complexioned Jewish girl of good height," as if he were being introduced to just another woman at a party. But gradually, a dense air of suppressed, Victorian eroticism begins to gather about the scene. At one point, Clara steps outside for something: "The men followed her out of the room with fond glances. More than half of them were in love with her." There is a tendency on the part of the men present to ruffle the feathers of their revolutionary convictions in front of her. Pavel feels the impulse to do so as well; but he also senses a deeper truth as he contemplates Clara from across the room:

> If I became a revolutionist it was the result of a gradual develop-
> ment, through the help of conditions, books, people; whereas this
> girl acted like one, and in the teeth of grave danger, too, purely on
> the spur of the moment and long before she knew there was any
> such thing as a revolutionary movement; acted like one while I was
> still a blind, hard-hearted milksop of a drone.

It is the old familiar voice of Nehemiah the Atheist or of Tzinchadzi of the Catskills despairing at his own bloodlessness; will he have a chance to redeem himself through Woman this time?

Well, Pavel does have some advantages. Taking Clara aside, the celebrated speaker from St. Petersburg is able to tell this wide-eyed provincial girl a thing or two about what the revolutionary movement is like at its center. "Pavel's unbounded faith in the party instilled new faith into her"—a partial repayment of the debt, at least. This enables him to feel momentarily worthy of the passion that is now coursing through his heart, and permits him to seize his exquisite and soulful pleasures on the quiet: "He took to scanning her afresh . . . and as he looked at her . . . it gave him pleasure to exaggerate her instrumentality in his own political regeneration." He can contain himself no longer: "he poured forth the story of his awakening and how he had all these five years been looking forward to a meeting with her. As he spoke his face bore an expression of ecstatic, almost amorous grimness."

What ensues from this moment on is not so much a love affair as a painful groping in the realm of the Holy Ghost, a seemingly unrealizable striving to make an orgy of spiritual passion into a real love of the flesh—the agony of the Cahan hero. From the outset, Pavel is racked with guilt about his love for Clara, about the implication in it that his life's work is governed by merely an erotic passion—this fear is unuttered, but it is present at every moment when he is with Clara. It manifests itself, for example, in the moment when he first fully realizes that he is in love. He and Clara have taken a spring walk through the countryside—a rare moment of pure self-indulgence!—and are having lunch at a farmhouse. He gazes at her over the table:

> He was sensible of sitting in front of a pretty, healthy girl full of modest courage and undemonstrative inspiration. The lingering solemnity of his mood seemed to have something to do with the shimmering little hairs which the breeze was stirring on Clara's neck, as she bent over her earthen bowl, with the warm coloring of her ear, with the elastic firmness of her cheek, with the airiness of her blouse. A desire stirred in him to speak once more of the part she had unconsciously played in his conversion.

But suddenly he remembers a friend of theirs, a comrade in the revolutionary movement, who is now in prison. How can he be so frivolous as his thoughts are being now, when their comrade is suffering so? Thus the revolution itself becomes the justification for an ecstasy of painfully suppressed eroticism: "Her absence was darkness; her presence was light, but pain and pleasure mingled in both." What surer sign could there be? "And he knew that he was in love."

Then, for an instant, there takes place another one of those shifts to a real, historical frame of reference that mark the novel from time to time:

> He had never been touched by more than a first timid whisper of that feeling [of love] before. It was Sophia [Perovskaya], the

daughter of the former governor of St. Petersburg, whose image had formerly—quite recently in fact—invaded his soul. He had learned immediately that she belonged to Zachar [Andrey Zhelyabov], and his dawning love had been frightened away. Otherwise his life during these five years had been one of continuous infatuation of quite another kind—the infatuation of moral awakening, of a political religion, of the battlefield.

Thus Cahan, Homer-like, invokes the Russian revolutionary goddess appropriate to the passion of exalted love he is describing. One wonders if he had not once intended to write more about Perovskaya, but had, like Pavel, been frightened away.

When Pavel finally blurts out a confession of his love to Clara, she promptly becomes the outward form of his conscience, the same reluctant woman who has been seen in Cahan's fiction many times before. "Well," she tells him, "when the Will of the People has scored its great victory and Russia is free, then, if we are alive, we shall announce it to my poor parents." Clara's love thus becomes, like the Revolution itself, a messianic promise. "I simply don't feel like being married—yet," she says. "I want to give my life to the movement, Pasha. I am enjoying too much happiness as it is." Pavel tries lamely to offer a protest in the name of reason, but bogs down in the logic of his own passion: "The question of giving our lives to the cause," he tells her, "has nothing to do with the question of our belonging to each other. Or, rather, it's one and the same thing." An inadvertent admission of guilt, a revelation of the nature of a passion whose very unrequitedness is its fulfillment.

A momentary glimmer of a solution presents itself in a scene that is another sudden juxtaposition between Cahan's protagonists and real historical personages. Pavel and Clara go to the party held on New Year's Eve of 1880 in St. Petersburg by the leaders of *Narodnaya Volya*—this is a real historical event. Although Clara and Pavel do not know it, plans for the assassination that would take place the following March 1 are now well under way. The feeling of strain among the conspirators manifests itself, on the part of some of them, in an air of untrammeled gaiety, a last fling before the final confrontation. One of the merriest of the participants is the Jewish girl, Hessia Helfman, the movement's goddess of warm, earthly love; she is already pregnant with the child of Nikolay Kolotkevich, who is by her side at the party. For an instant, Clara sees Hessia as the outward representation of her own birthright. "As she now looked at Hessia and her husband, she said to herself, with a great sense of relief: 'She is as good as I, anyhow. If she could marry the man she loves I can.'" Is this the end of Pavel's agony, then? Wait a moment: in another part of the room sits the austere and exalted Sophia Perovskaya. Looking upon her, Clara's "joy in this absolution from her self-imposed injunction soon faded away. To sacrifice her happiness seemed to her the highest happiness this evening. She would surpass Hessia. If there was a world in which Platonic relations were called for theirs was that world." That was the last chance; no hope remains now for love's fulfillment but the messianic one.

But Pavel and Clara live in a messianic era. For we are now entering 1881, the year which Cahan entered as a Russian revolutionary and departed from as a Jew once again and for all time, but also the year in which the protagonists of Cahan's fantasy may ascend the brightest heavens of fulfillment. Cahan now sets his characters momentarily aside and turns to an interlude of pure historical narrative, describing the assassination of Alexander II and the subsequent arrival of the news of the first anti-Jewish disturbances. We are now entering full force upon the book's central but hitherto understated problem: the relationship between Jewish identity and the revolution. So far, Cahan has been able to skirt the issue somewhat by making his protagonist a Gentile, and a nobleman at that. Jews and Jewish problems have been seen almost exclusively through the eyes of this "outsider." And he, despite an occasional early manifestation of peevishness toward some of Elkin's Jewish traits, has shown his true humanity in the long run by passionately embracing a whole Jewish milieu. He has come to the revolutionary movement through Jews, his dearest comrades in it are Jews, and now the love of his life is a Jewish girl. Furthermore, through Clara, he has even come to take an interest in some of the elements of her Jewish heritage, things which do not interest her in the slightest. In one passage of rare vindictiveness, the author reflects upon the irony of Clara's concern for a Russian peasantry she knows only through novels, and her unconcern for the Jewish sufferings that surround her in her everyday life: "Her peasants . . . were so many literary images. . . . The Jewish realities of which her own home was a part had nothing to do with this imaginary world of hers." It does not occur to Pavel himself to observe this about Clara, although he is becoming increasingly concerned with the Jewish sufferings that apparently do not bother her. Of course, since he is a Russian nobleman, no one can accuse him of being a Jewish chauvinist.

It is Pavel who is most profoundly troubled by the news of the pogroms: "To Pavel the crusade against Clara's race was a source of mixed encouragement and anxiety." His feeling of encouragement is due to the assurances being given by the revolutionary leadership that the riots are the first rumblings of a general peasant uprising; but his humanity is anxious about the Jewish plight. "As to Clara, she was so completely abandoned to her grief over the death of Sophia and the four men [who have been executed for their complicity in the assassination] that so far the riots (no unheard-of thing in the history of the Jews by any means) had made but a feeble appeal to her imagination." It is through Pavel's eyes that we actually witness a pogrom. A horrified bystander, he rushes about the village to give comfort to the victims. As he helps one woman, "his heart was melting with pity for all the Jews at this moment. He felt a rush of yearning tenderness for Clara, and he wished she could see him taking care of this woman of her race." The awfulness of these events eventually come home even to Clara, and for a moment she feels a pang of conscience: "Why should she, a Jewess, stake her life for a people that was given to pillaging and outraging, to mutilating and murdering innocent Jews?" The central question—but this is ineffable Woman speaking, not Cahan's own more tremulous voice, and the answer comes back in an instant: " 'I shall bear the cross of the Social Revolution even if the Russian people trample upon me and everybody who is dear to me,' she exclaimed in her heart, feeling at peace with the shade of Sophia." We have passed through the messianic moment; from now on, it is Christlike apotheosis on the holy soil of the Revolution for some, and Jewish exile for the nonbelievers.

The denouement now divides itself into two streams, one portrayed with convincing realism, the other a lyrical fantasy. In the realistic vein, Elkin is shown suddenly made aware of his own Jewishness by the pogroms. He has not abandoned his socialism, but, despairing of any way of finding a solution to the Jewish question in Russia, he plans to go to America and participate in the founding of a socialist colony there. Another Jew, Vigdoroff, who has been in love with Clara but whom she has despised for his cravenly bourgeois aspirations, has also discovered his Jewishness in the wake of the pogroms, and he, too, is going to America. Cahan undoubtedly made a special effort to see to it that two of the most despicable characters in the book should be the bearers of this American destiny. But he portrays their illusions about what they are doing with a brutally accurate vindictiveness that could only have been directed against himself. "We don't propose to estrange ourselves from the revolutionary movement," Elkin tells Clara. "We shall support it with American money, and we hope to fit out expeditions to rescue important prisoners from Siberia, and to take them across the Pacific Ocean to our commune." "Dreams!" Clara replies.

As for the vein of fantasy, Clara and Pavel, their messianic catharsis over—Clara realizes that she, too, like Sophia, will soon die for the revolution—are now at last freed from the spiritual bonds which had kept them from marrying. That curious muffling which has taken place throughout the book in moments of relative amorous fulfillment now takes place again, along with the sudden, astonishing glimmer of a touch of Flora Stroon in Clara's personality. The passage reads exactly this way:

> "Now for something to do I feel like turning mountains upside down [Clara is speaking to Pavel]. Indeed, the revolution is a hydra-headed giant, indeed it is. And you are a little dear," she added, bending over him and pressing her cheek against his.
>
> *     *     *
>
> They had been married less than a month when he learned from a ciphered letter . . . that the gendarmes were looking for him.

It is the beginning of the final, joyous agony. Pavel is arrested, and we find him, in the last chapter, in a dungeon cell in the Fortress of Peter and Paul. He soon learns to communicate with his neighbors by tapping messages on the wall of the cell. Messages are relayed thus from cell to cell, so that one may eventually communicate with some fellow prisoner in a distant cell block. In this way, Pavel learns one day that his beloved Jewish comrade in the revolutionary movement, Makar, is in the prison, too, and that he is of course happy to be there. By the same method, he learns a little later that Elkin is also a prisoner there—Elkin! Even he, a good socialist after all, has been spared the American fate; only the bourgeois Vigdoroff has gone there to get what he deserves. There remains only Clara to make the family reunion complete, and soon she too arrives, to join in the symphony of tapping; Pavel's solitary cell is now filled to the brim with the clatter of loving companionship:

> At last, on a morning, the wall brought him a message from her. It had come through walls, floors and ceilings.
> "Clanya sends her love," it ran, "and tells him to keep away from the damp walls as much as possible."
> "Tell Clanya I think of her day and night," he rapped back.

Then a footstep sounded at his door, and with a heart swelling with emotion he threw himself upon his bed and buried his face in his hands.

There the novel ends.

Cahan could not have finished this book at a more significant moment, for, by the time of its publication in February, 1905, revolution had broken out in Russia. Could it be that the revolutionary hope was being fulfilled at last, nearly a quarter of a century after so many had abandoned it? Cahan, when he wrote *The White Terror and the Red,* thought he had put his guilty old dream of revolution to a final rest, and now, no sooner had he done so than it was coming back to haunt him. What could he do, alas, but sing its welcome? "The hand shakes," he wrote, as the *Forward* covered the events in Russia with huge banner headlines each day, "the heart leaps with joy and enthusiasm. Revolution! We have a revolution in Russia! A real, general people's revolution. A proletarian worker's revolution." And his editorial concluded: "Long live the revolutionary proletariat, the great liberator of Russia."

There it was; the dream had apparently been fulfilled for those who had stuck it out in Russia, and for the new generation that had grown up since 1881. Had the Bundists been right, after all, in considering the old problem to have been solved?

In March, the terrible news to the contrary began to arrive. "Is the government making pogroms to blind the public?" inquired a *Forward* headline on March 13, and the next day the answer came: "Nicholas is really making pogroms." The news of the anti-Jewish riots began to stream in: Minsk, Regensburg, Zhitomir, Lublin, then Kishinev itself—the old disease of failed revolution spread once again, fostered and guided, as always, by the Tsarist police. Cahan knew the story well. Now it was simply a matter of the failure of the revolution itself gradually becoming evident. In October the Tsar came forth with the promise of a constitution that placated liberals while granting nothing to socialists, and the revolution lost its energy. The October Manifesto still had to prove itself; in the years to come the parliament promised by it was to turn out to be a succession of failures. None of this was to surprise Cahan, however; his messiah still had not come, and he was now confirmed in his belief that it never would. Calmly, he sat back to await the new flood of exiles, immigrants, and fund raisers that would stream in from Russia, ever ready to be the host of their diaspora, the prophet of the post-revolution.

CHAPTER 15

# A Bundle of Letters

Blessed art Thou, O Lord our God, Ruler of the Universe, Who hast
not made me a woman.

—Jewish Daily Prayer Book

"Rebbe," he then asked, "and my wife?"

"When the husband sits upon a chair in Paradise, his wife is his
foot-stool."

When Chaim got home to make the Sabbath evening blessing,
Hannah was saying her prayers. He saw her, and something took
hold of his heart.

"No, Hannah," he said, throwing himself at her feet, "I don't
want you to be my foot-stool . . . I will bend down to you, and lift
you up and sit you by my side. We will sit together on the same
stool, as always. . . . It is so good when we're together . . . Do you
hear, Hannah, you must sit with me on the same chair. The Lord of
the World will just have to understand!"

—I. L. Peretz, *Domestic Happiness*

A sudden new increase in Jewish immigration had begun
in the wake of the Kishinev pogrom and now, after the disturbances
of 1905, it was reaching its height. The masses of "green" immigrants were larger than ever, and, more so than ever before they were
becoming, on American soil, something like a complete cross-section
of society at large. There were now approximately a million Jews
in neighborhoods throughout Greater New York, the largest Jewish
population of any city in the world, living what had become a highly

complex economic, institutional, cultural, and moral life. Not only were there, in addition to the toiling masses, innumerable business-men, doctors, dentists, lawyers, and other professionals, earnestly seeking to fulfill the American dream, but there were also unprece-dented numbers of Jewish hoodlums, Jewish criminals, Jewish pimps, and Jewish prostitutes. Increasing social mobility had brought with it new opportunities for public vice as well as for public virtue.

Foremost among the public virtues was—despite the element of gangsterism and prostitution that had arisen in the initial shock of transplantation from Eastern Europe to America—a steady revival of the family as an institution in the life of the New York Jewish quar-ter. The family had always, of course, been strong among the Jews of Eastern Europe, but the beginnings of the exodus to the United States had been accompanied by a certain splintering of its structure. In Cahan's day, a rather large proportion of the immigrants had been, like him, individual young men and women seeking their fortunes. They married in America and started families of their own, but they did so as if from the beginning, with no line of continuity extending into their own past. Increasingly, however, the Jewish immigrants had been arriving not only in family groups, but also as individuals who would rejoin family units that awaited them. The typical immi-grant Jewish home had at least one room that was occupied by an unmarried brother, sister, or cousin. The kind of stark loneliness that confronted the young, unmarried immigrant of Cahan's day had since become extremely rare. The new arrival could now often rely upon a helping hand at every step of his adjustment to American life.

The renewed growth of family feeling among the Jewish immi-grants was naturally accompanied by a revival on American soil of organized religion, the close spiritual ally of traditional family life. In the early eighteen-eighties, America had been renowned among East European Jews as a country in which, though there was perhaps less anti-Semitism there than in any other country in the Western world, "Judaism [had] not much of a chance," as one man put it to the newly arrived David Levinsky. This fact had, of course, been perfectly satisfactory to the young Cahan and his fellow "Russian" radicals, while in traditionalist circles of East European Jewry it had, for a time, functioned as a self-fulfilling prophecy: no pillar of the religious establishment would even consider going to America to try to rescue Judaism there. Until 1888, no orthodox rabbi of repute had ever established himself in the United States; organized Judaism in America remained until that time a virtual monopoly of the Reform movement, which the German-Jewish immigrants of earlier decades had imported with them, and which the average East European Jewish immigrant regarded as worse than atheism. The services at the little synagogues established by the first groups of East European Jewish immigrants were conducted simply by the most learned members of each congregation; in many cases, their learning was very little indeed.

Finally, in 1888, the strenuous efforts of a group of prospering and still pious East European Jews in New York persuaded an eminent rabbi, Jacob Joseph of Vilna, to come and accept the handsome salary they offered and assume the title of Chief Rabbi. Although Joseph's career in America proved to be a less than happy one—princes, even when they are rabbis, rarely are accorded in America the treatment to which they have been accustomed—his arrival was an entering wedge for the religious establishment he represented. More orthodox rabbis followed, and in 1896 a training college for rabbis, the Isaac Elchanan Yeshiva, was established on the Lower East Side. Painstakingly, institutions for the proper supervision of kosher dietary laws were set up, and America gradually ceased to be known as a *treyfa* (religiously unclean) land. By the end of 1905, organized religion had solidly re-established itself as a part of American Jewish life. If it did not have quite the overwhelming and virtually monopolistic power that it had enjoyed in certain parts of Eastern Europe, above all in the *shtetl*, it had nevertheless taken on some important new functions in its new home. In particular, the synagogue usually functioned as the main gathering place of the *landsmanshaften,* the societies of immigrants from the same home town. Since the immigrants from any single town in Eastern Europe usually found themselves, under the chaotic conditions of New York, living scattered far and wide throughout the Jewish quarter, the visit to the synagogue provided them, as a rule, with their one regular occasion to get together. The *landsmanshaft* was a major social instrument for the adaptation of the Jewish immigrants to America, and the synagogue gained a new lease on life by being its locus.

In this and in numerous other ways, institutional life had grown so in the New York Jewish quarter since the days of Cahan's arrival that the socialists could no longer dream of having the exclusive control over the destiny of the immigrants that they had once seemed called upon to assume. Cahan, of course, was fully aware of what had happened and was prepared to go along with the tide. If the Jewish quarter was now overwhelmingly dominated by a family style of life, then let the *Forward* be a family paper, addressed to the mother and even, if possible, to the children, as well as to the wage-earner of the household. If the Jewish immigrants were still strongly attached to the synagogue, then let the *Forward* be respectful of this attachment if not necessarily enthusiastic about it. If the social and economic structure of the Jewish quarter was, in fact, more complex than the theory of class struggle implied, then let the *Forward* remember that it was just as much a Jewish paper as a socialist one. In the long run its existence was grounded in the Jewish immigrant reality and not in Marxian ideology. These precepts seemed self-evident to Cahan, who had long since begun to formulate his policies in accordance with them. And his policies were now vindicating themselves in the rapid growth of circulation that accompanied the new surge of Jewish immigration.

Nevertheless, Cahan's troubles as an editor had not yet come to an end. After the failure of the 1905 revolution, many Bundists had decided to give up on Russia and establish themselves in New York.

The *Forward* was a natural refuge for some of them, and both the editorial staff and the Press Association expanded with the new arrivals. Now, as Cahan well knew, the more European a man's outlook was, the more he tended to dislike the *Forward*'s present policies. Consequently, with these Bundist arrivals, a new, younger element of opposition to Cahan was arising in the *Forward* organization, scarcely more than a year after Miller, Winchevsky, and the old opposition had left the paper for once and for all.

Another source of trouble was Miller's journalistic enterprise, the daily *Wahrheit* ("Truth"), which had set up its office on East Broadway, just down the street from the *Forward,* and had begun publication on November 11, 1905. It was clear from the outset that the new paper's principal *raison d'être* was to be vociferous opposition to the *Forward*. The *Wahrheit* made rapid progress in circulation, and for a moment it looked as if Cahan was going to lose ground in his main area of strength against the opposition in the *Forward* organization. For in addition to the stiff competition of the *Wahrheit* in the evening, when the *Forward* came out, there was also a lively new orthodox paper, the *Morning Journal,* on the market to feed the increasing desire for news in the morning. Cahan had to seek effective ways of meeting this new competition for circulation and mollify his opposition within the *Forward* organization at the same time.

He had taken one dramatic measure in September, two months before the *Wahrheit* began to appear. The old socialist monthly, *Die Zukunft,* had just resumed publication after a five-year hiatus, and with Morris Winchevsky as its editor it was moving further than ever in the direction of being a literary journal for the Yiddishist movement that was now in full flower. In response to the growing mood of literary high seriousness in the Yiddish world, the *Forward* began in September to publish a weekly supplement, called *Der Zeitgeist,* to pursue aims similar to those of *Die Zukunft.* It was hoped that this supplement would satisfy the aspirations of Cahan's opponents to restore a more elevated tone to the *Forward* and reach out, at the same time, to intellectual elements in the public at large that the paper might otherwise be in danger of losing. Such a project also conformed perfectly well to Cahan's personal tastes, and, with relish, he took on the job of editing *Der Zeitgeist* himself. The first few issues came out with considerable fanfare, and included contributions by Sholem Asch and Abraham Reisen, two of the foremost younger Yiddish writers of the day. *Der Zeitgeist* got the best contributors by paying well for them—so well, in fact, that the enterprise soon began to sag under its heavy costs.

Something more decisive had to be done to boost the *Forward*'s fortunes and to satisfy the opposition on the staff. By the end of 1905, therefore, the *Forward* organization had decided to enter the burgeoning morning newspaper field with a companion paper to the *Forward* itself. The morning newspaper was increasingly becoming the journalistic response to the accelerating pace of life in a world that now had motorcars and a complex network of telephone and telegraph wires. People wanted to find out what happened yesterday upon waking up in the morning, and journalistic technology now could fulfill this desire. Furthermore, as New York expanded and its residents found themselves living greater distances from their places of work, the demand was increasing for something to read on the train during the long ride to the job. But this demand was not the sole reason that the *Morgen Zeitung* ("Morning Paper") was created by the *Forward* organization. As Cahan saw it, another function of this paper was to serve as an enclave for the radicals and other opponents of his policies on the staff, to be a "lightning rod" for their passions. The radicals, for their part, gladly accepted this opportunity to have their own medium of expression. Benjamin Feigenbaum, who had come to the *Forward* in 1902 with Philip Krantz—Krantz was now back in Eastern Europe, trying to resume a journalistic career there—and who had never ceased to oppose Cahan since that time, was appointed editor of the *Morgen Zeitung*. Michael Zametkin, who was even more radical than Feigenbaum in his political views, set aside his chess board to take up the duties of assistant editor. The *Morgen Zeitung* began to appear on January 15, 1906. For the time being at least, Cahan had a completely free hand again in molding the policies of the *Forward* itself.

He was soon given an opportunity to show what he could do. Cahan had still not completely satisfied his old passion to annihilate the gap that separated his newspaper from the spirit of the folk. He had achieved occasional glimmers of the "living novel" that he wanted the newspaper to be, but not yet the constantly flowing bloodstream of life itself through its pages that would alone constitute a final refutation to literature, which had failed to satisfy the innermost aspirations of his spirit. As far back as 1902, when he had first returned to the *Forward,* he had sought ways of stimulating this flow. This had been the point of such features as the one calling for answers to the question, "What is luck?" This approach, using a specific and poignant question, had the virtue of promoting vivid responses; but it led people to generalize too much, and it did not dig deeply enough into concrete individual experience. Consequently, Cahan had tried asking specifically for autobiographical contributions in December, 1903: "Send us interesting true novels (*emmeser romanen*)," the *Forward* advertised. "In the thousands of tenement houses in which the *Forward* is read, thousands and thousands of life stories unfold, each of them in its own way." As it happened, this notice appeared alongside an article by Cahan on "Realism and Literature," which contained this sentence: "The most important question [about art] always remains the same: does this feel like real life?" What could be more like real life—so much so as to be beyond mere art—than the utterances coming straight from those tenement houses? But, unfortunately, few "true novels" came in, and most of those that did seemed somehow to miss the mark. Cahan knew that the writers were merely telling what they *thought* would be interesting to others, rather than what really *would* be so. Some factor was missing that would guide these people to the significant "true novel" that each of their lives contained. How was it to be found?

Ironically, the hint to a solution was provided by the *Wahrheit*. Miller, too, had long been in search of "true novels" as an element of daily journalism; undoubtedly, he and Cahan had often discussed the matter back in the days when they were still on speaking terms. In this and in more ways than he probably cared to mention, Miller really had journalistic aspirations that were similar to Cahan's. One of the things he had been quick to do in the *Wahrheit*, for example, was to establish a fatherly tone like that of the *Forward*, and to show his paper's readiness to provide advice on all the problems, great and small, that the "green" immigrant faced in America. Letters seeking advice came in abundance, and Miller, like Cahan, would occasionally choose one of them to serve as a point of departure for an editorial on some question of manners or morals.

One day in December, Miller received a letter that was quite unusual in its intimacy and pathos. Its author—a kind of Yekl, as Miller must have wryly observed—told of how he had left his wife behind in Russia two years before and come to America to earn money for her passage, and of how he feared, now that she was coming to rejoin him, that he could no longer love her after all the emotional changes America had wrought in him. The irony was, the letter-writer observed, that it was his wife who had wanted him to come to America in the first place. What should he do? Miller decided to call upon his readers' spirit of socialist fellowship—and also, incidentally, to promote circulation—by publishing the letter and asking for replies.

It was published on December 26 under the heading, "A Broken Heart." Miller added this Cahan-like comment under the title: "Not an invented one, but a *real* tragedy from real life, told in a heart-rending letter to the *Wahrheit* which we invite our readers to answer—whoever feels he can do so." One response came in quickly enough to be printed the next day; written in tones that seemed to echo with personal experience, the letter counseled the man with the "broken heart" to be patient, assuring him that after a month or so he would find himself satisfied to be living with his wife again. By that evening, the responses were streaming in, and Miller realized that he had struck a vein of gold. The next day he assembled all these letters under a new feature which he called "Tragedies, Comedies and Ordinary Troubles From Real Life," and which he prefaced with an open invitation asking more readers to send in letters seeking counsel and answering those who sought it. The feature became an immediate success, and easily obtained enough material to appear every day.

Miller was jubilant, and by the thirtieth he could not resist doing an editorial that gloated over this new success. "The fact is," he wrote, directing his words to the nearby *Forward* offices, "that the *Wahrheit* is beloved by its readers, not as a mere plaything, but as a faithful friend, one to whom you come for advice and open your heart. . . . At the beginning of the week, we printed a letter from one of our readers that told about his family tragedy and asked for advice about what to do. In the few days since then, we have received several hundred letters in reply. Every writer feels for the unhappy man, consoles him, speaks to him from the heart, offers him hope, and assures him that his future will not be as bad as he imagines." Miller went on to claim that what had happened was a demonstration that all the readers of the *Wahrheit* felt like the members of a single family. There was probably some truth to this; meanwhile, in creating this atmosphere of intimate dialogue, Miller had also stumbled upon the factor that could summon the "true novel" into being.

This was dramatically demonstrated only three days later when a letter of astonishing vividness arrived and was printed in that afternoon's edition. Signed simply "Hyman," it read, in part:

> . . . It is now my fourth year in America. When I left the old home I left behind a wife and two children. The whole

time I was here alone I worked and slaved and sent money
home. I'm not like other men who forget their wives and
children once they're in America. I used to send every last
cent. . . .

Last spring I had a good season and I sent for my family. A month ago my wife and children arrived, and I can't
tell you how happy I was—so happy I didn't even care when
it turned out that my wife had used the money I sent her to
bring along her brother-in-law, her sister's husband. He's a
bad sort and I've never liked him, but for my family's sake I
accepted him as an honored guest.

But my happiness didn't last long. I saw right away that
something was wrong with my wife. I began questioning her,
and soon I found out something terrible. Oh, what a shock!
My wife told me she was pregnant and in her sixth month.

Who can imagine how I felt? I don't know where I found
the strength to hold back my fury and not kill her. . . . "Who
is the destroyer of my happiness?" I demanded in a terrible
voice. With tears in her eyes she told me that her brother-in-
law was the guilty man. . . .

Hyman concluded by asking the *Wahrheit* readers what he should
do—stay with his wife and raise a bastard, or leave her? The responses
arrived by the dozens every day for weeks to come. Most of them
advised Hyman to stay with his wife.

Cahan could not but have observed, with consternation, that
Miller's successful formula had evolved out of ideas that he himself
had originated. This sort of thing was his specialty; surely he could
beat Miller at it. The opportunity to do so came on the morning of
January 20, five days after the *Morgen Zeitung* had begun publication, and while the responses to the Hyman letter in the *Wahrheit*
were at their height. Cahan's assistant, Leon Gottlieb, found himself
puzzling over two letters that had just arrived in the morning mail.

They were both quite interesting, eminently printable, but there was no category in the paper into which to fit them. The *Forward* had long had a column in which it gave brief responses to queries from readers; but one of these letters was making a very unconventional sort of request, and the other was asking advice in a merely rhetorical way. Both of them seemed to have been intended for the department called "From the People to the People," which stressed inquiries having to do with labor and union organization. But these were of much too personal a nature for that column. Where did they belong, then? When Gottlieb showed these letters to Cahan, the latter immediately spotted them as two specimens of the "true novel."

It happened that Cahan was at that moment preparing an editorial built around a letter from a reader seeking advice. In his established manner, he was using this letter as the occasion for an editorial on a current question of manners and morals—in this case, intermarriage. The letter was from a young man named Sam Brilliant, who said that he was in love with a Christian girl, and wanted to know if he should ignore his parents' objections and marry her. Cahan's editorial approached Sam Brilliant's particular case with the utmost caution: there were, Cahan wrote, too many factors that the *Forward* could not know about—the depth of the young couple's love for one another, the degree of religiosity of Sam's parents, the girl's attitude toward Judaism, and so on—for the editor to be able to make a specific judgment. He could only take this occasion to observe—and this was, in fact, the purpose of the editorial—that it was possible, from the *national* standpoint (Cahan would not pretend, of course, to speak for the religious point of view), to have a non-Jewish spouse and still be a good Jew. To make his point, Cahan gave examples throughout history of Jews of impeccable nationalist credentials, from Moses to Israel Zangwill, who had non-Jewish wives.

Cahan liked to have such material to work with as Sam Brilliant's letter. It provided a concrete point of origin for a discussion, a source right in the heart of the folk from which to draw a lesson of general and urgent import. This was journalism as he wanted it, intimate and broadly relevant at the same time. But until now, he had had to wait for mere occasions, such as that provided by Sam Brilliant's letter, to enable him to achieve this kind of synthesis. The success of Miller's "Tragedies, Comedies and Ordinary Troubles From Real Life" had now reawakened his old desire to see that synthesis achieved on an everyday basis. But he was not interested in doing it the way Miller had done it. Some of the letters in Miller's column had been excellent specimens of what Cahan would have wanted, but, as far as he was concerned, the context of advice-giving was too narrow a one in which to operate. The feature would inevitably degenerate into a mere American-style "lonely-hearts" column. The problem was, how to capture that atmosphere of intimate dialogue that had brought the "true novel" into being on the pages of the *Wahrheit* without falling into the "lonely-hearts" trap? What was missing in Miller's approach, Cahan felt, was a chairman for the discussion, to participate and supervise in just the way he had done when, as in the case of Sam Brilliant, there was only one other participant. Like the author of a book, the editor must be present to give the "true novel" its shape and direction. When Cahan read, therefore, the two letters that Leon Gottlieb had been puzzling over that morning, he decided to use them as material for a new column, over which he would himself be the presiding spirit.

Cahan's new feature appeared that afternoon on the same page as the editorial on Sam Brilliant's letter. Called *A Bintel Brief* ("A Bundle of Letters"), it opened with a general statement by Cahan: "Among the letters that the *Forward* receives for its 'From the People to the People' department, there are many which have a general 'human interest,' as American critics call it. Starting today we will select these and print them separately, with or without comments, under the name *A Bintel Brief.*" Then followed the first letter, parts of which were deleted in order to conceal the identities of those involved. It was from a woman, a fact which was itself a demonstration of the way in which Cahan had already reached further than his rival into a popular reading public; Miller's letters came almost exclusively from men. This is the entire selection printed in the *Forward:*

> . . . My boy, who's now the breadwinner in the family, is as deaf as the wall; he can't even hear his unhappy parents when they cry. The whole time he's been working he's had a watch and chain, bought with his lunch-money that he saved up, so we can live when slack-time is coming.[1] . . . For how many weeks now we've been able to save our lives whenever slack-time is drawing near, thanks to that watch! And right now, God help us, it's slack-time again, but we don't have a watch and chain! . . . My friend! You're a poor working woman too, how well I know it. . . . I went out of the house for five minutes. I asked you to look after things while I was gone. Alas, you did! . . . And so now the watch is at your pawnbroker's. Not at mine. I give you my honest word and swear to you over the life of my sick husband that I'll go on being the same good friend to you that I've been the whole three years we've lived on the same floor—only mail the pawn-ticket to me! I want to make believe nothing happened. . . . Give me back my bread.

The woman had simply wanted this letter to appear in the *Forward* as a seemingly discreet but authoritative way of urging her friend to return the watch. But Cahan had some comments of his own to add:

> It is not impossible that this suspicion is unwarranted. The woman is nervous owing to her difficult situation. And it could be she has no grounds for accusing her neighbor. But still, what a picture of workers' misery is to be seen in this letter! What artist's imagination could create a situation capable of penetrating into the workers' lot as deeply as these few homely lines do? You may describe how a hundred workers want to kill themselves, but you'll

never convey the picture of humiliation, of constant despair, of fear about what tomorrow will bring, that this little story about the watch and chain succeeds in conveying.

There then followed the second letter that Gottlieb had puzzled over that morning, from a man in Philadelphia:

> I met the man eating breakfast, and when he finished eating I told him he should say grace for us because he had a beard and was a pious Jew. He said he wanted three cents from me first, and then the matzoh he used for his prayer would be mine. I paid him the money and he proclaimed before all witnesses that the matzoh was mine, and then he finished saying grace. Now I ask you, what kind of a man is that? . . .

Cahan suggested in his comment to this letter that the "pious Jew" may have been a practical joker. Other letters followed, some printed in part, others paraphrased; for example:

> A mother asks how she can teach her seven-year-old boy to stop stammering. Our answer is that there are special methods for dealing with this, and specialists who concern themselves with them. But we'll have to write in greater detail about this another time.

This was clearly a practical inquiry of the sort that the *Forward* had always been receiving, now being served up as part of the new "human interest" feature. It was additional bait for more material, along with the column's closing remark: "Answers to other letters next time."

The bait was subtler than what Miller had used with his call for advice to "A Broken Heart," and it was not until the twenty-ninth, nine days later, that Cahan had enough material again to put together a second *Bintel Brief* column. "Another bundle of letters sent to the *Forward* from its readers," he began it, "several more interesting pages from the book of life!" The first letter was one that could just as easily have appeared in the old "From the People to the People" column: it was from a butcher, writing appreciatively of a young customer, a "tsotsialist" as it turned out, who had behaved toward him in an exceptionally honest way; this belied all the adverse things he had been taught about "tsotsialists" as a boy, and he wanted to express his new-found appreciation for them to the *Forward*. The second letter was more in the vein of the kind of domestic drama that had given the first column, with the story of the woman and the watch, its uniqueness; it was from a young girl:

> My stepmother is bad to me and my older brother. She gives us a lot of trouble and always makes us wait a long time at each meal; and when we say that we're going to be late for school, she curses us and tells us to go without eating anything. She says we should starve. . . . We're afraid to tell my father, we just haven't the courage. So somebody told us to write to the *Forward,* because my father reads your paper. He should read this and know how his children have been suffering since our mother died and he brought such a mean person into the house. . . .

The letter was unsigned.

Cahan's idea was already beginning to show a built-in weakness: a tendency toward the banal, or else toward the embarrassingly intimate, as shown in this last letter of the January 29 column, written by a young woman addressing the husband she had run away from:

> . . . It was also your fault—you cast me into the flames yourself. . . . But you're no fool, you have eyes; and yet you kept silent and pretended you didn't know what was going on. . . . And I thought to myself: he wants to leave me, all right. . . . But now I see it was all a bad dream and noth-

ing more. And when L. wrote that you were longing to see me again, I cried like a baby. . . . Believe me, my predestined one, I have never really loved anyone but you. . . . Let's forget everything. . . . The children aren't the reason. . . . Whoever tells you that is my enemy! . . . I've written to you at different addresses and you haven't answered me, so maybe my letters haven't reached you yet.

Cahan's "true novels" were proving to be in danger of becoming "true romances" of the pulp-magazine variety, an early, Jewish form of "soap opera."

In the next day's column—for Cahan was now getting enough responses to begin carrying the feature every day—there was a letter which was somewhat more like what Cahan presumably had in mind when he created the feature. Its problems seemed to have arisen in echo of those that lingered in the depths of his own soul:

Permit me to convey my shattered feelings in our workers' paper. I'm still a greenhorn in America—it's only three months since I came here from Odessa—and now I can't forgive myself for being here. My head and heart grow numb whenever I read in your paper that thousands of workers are standing on the barricades in Russia fighting for their lives. Who can feel this as I can, I, who have just arrived from Russia, from the very ranks of that army which is now fighting? I'm not capable of conveying my feelings. The steam from the factory I work in blots out my feelings until I don't know what to do; I know that I've committed a crime, that I'm a deserter, that I've run away from the field of battle. Oh, how I would like to stand alongside my brothers again in the war! I go around like a lunatic; now, when I hear that the end of Tsarism is near, that it's only a matter of days before the last blow will have been delivered to the Russian regime, oh, how I'd like to be there in battle, standing alongside my comrades and reddening our flag with my blood, too! But the great ocean does not permit us to hurry to the scene without a ticket, and the ship and the railroad know nothing of my thoughts, and they say that without the dollar they won't take me and I have no money for the journey. What shall I do? To round up several dollars is impossible; I earn five dollars a week altogether, and a few days a week I have no work at all. I can't go on living, I spend whole nights without getting any sleep; I don't know what to do.

I beg of you, dear editor, answer me, what should I do? . . .

This, indeed, must have convinced Cahan that life itself had become his novel, as he knew it would. There were no more fictions left for him to invent; his task was now simply to assemble his characters on stage, life's editor. His advice came forth easily in this case: "Well, we can give no better advice than to fight right here in America for a social order in which a man wouldn't have to work like a mule for five dollars a week." It had taken nearly a quarter of a century of inner turmoil and suffering to reach this briefly stated conclusion.

That letter was like a turning point in the history of Cahan's "true novel"; the struggle on the barricades had since been replaced by American trade-unionism, and from now on tragedy was to be soap opera. More and more of the letters streaming in to *A Bintel Brief* came from women—not from revolutionary or progressive-minded *barishnyas,* but from simple Jewish housewives—and more and more of them read like this:

I read in your paper an article in which you tell about what a good life husbands and wives have when the men stay home in the evening, and what terrible scenes of jealousy are acted out in the tenement houses when the men come home twelve and one o'clock at night.

Let me give you my opinion about this. I understand very well what a woman is thinking when her husband comes home in the middle of the night, but the woman, in my opinion, can be of help to herself and avoid "scenes" if she can convince her husband that he should belong to a lodge, union or educational circle. Then she'll at least know where her husband is, and her heart won't break with worry.

Naturally, it could happen that the husband would still sneak away somewhere else and then come home and say: I was at a lecture . . . such men are to be condemned. But not all men are such bluffers. Of course, maybe I don't understand the male mentality. . . .

The tone of the feature was increasingly becoming that of a Yiddish housewife's version of the "lonely-hearts" column, just what Cahan had been trying to avoid. For example:

I must write to you about my situation because I see no other way than through your newspaper. I am one of those women whose husbands spend less time with them than they spend hanging around in the barber-shop. I am certainly not the kind who stays in the grocery store all day. . . . As a matter of fact, my grocer says I must have troubles, because I'm always in tears when I come into the store. . . .

But it was this very trend that soon made the feature immensely popular. From all over the Lower East Side and other Jewish immigrant neighborhoods, ordinary men and women—especially women—flocked to this unprecedented opportunity to be heard and worried over by their eminent newspaper. Many of their letters had to be thoroughly rewritten at the editorial office in order to be made comprehensible; some of the correspondents could not write at all, and dictated their letters to literate relatives or friends. In time, enterprising individuals hung signs over their doors or in their shop windows: "Letters to *Bintel Brief* written here." Occasionally, someone appeared in person at the *Forward* office, asking that his or her letter be written down. The column came to serve as a place in which calls were sent out for long-lost relatives—brothers, sisters or children from whom the writers had been parted by emigration—or even for missing husbands. Sometimes the missing individual was found, and many a reunion was staged at the front entrance to the *Forward's* offices, where huge crowds would gather to witness the event.[2] *A Bintel Brief* became a legend, and its very title passed into American-Jewish folklore: "Oh, that's a real *Bintel Brief* story you're going through, isn't it?" people would say to one another. The column was now the *Forward's* most famous and indispensable feature, and, for better or worse, a central part of the newspaper's identity.

*A Bintel Brief* easily crushed its predecessor and rival, Miller's "Tragedies, Comedies and Ordinary Troubles From Real Life." Having added this new feature to its already superior prestige and circulation, the *Forward* drew away most of the *Wahrheit's* potential letter-writers. Miller tried to respond in kind. *A Bintel Brief* had proven that readers preferred getting their advice from a venerable editor to getting it from their fellow immigrants, and so, on March 7, the *Wahrheit* replaced its old feature with a new one called *Der Ba'al Eytzah* ("The Advice-Giver"). It was an unvarnished copy of the *Forward's* feature. It never got enough responses to appear every day, however, and soon had to give up altogether.

But despite this striking success—the *Forward's* circulation leaped sharply again as a result—Cahan was not going to be let off lightly by his opponents in the organization for this new leap into realms of vulgarity. As early as mid-February, their opposition began to crystallize again, for the *Morgen Zeitung* was by then already foundering. The morning paper had proved not to be as financially viable as everyone had hoped. For one thing, it had been assumed that "want ads"—a very important element in the new morning-newspaper field—would bring in a large part of its revenue. But many potential advertisers, as it turned out, were angry with the *Forward* organization for its socialism and ardent pro-union stance, and so they preferred to restrict their Yiddish "want ads" to the orthodox *Morning Journal*. For another thing, the new paper had unexpectedly cut into the *Forward's* own circulation. It had been assumed that traditional *Forward* readers would go on buying that paper in the evening, and would get the *Morgen Zeitung* in the morning as well—the morning paper for news, the evening one for commentary and entertainment. But it turned out that many people preferred getting only one Yiddish paper a day, and they more naturally made their purchase in the morning.

With the days of the *Morgen Zeitung* clearly numbered, the radical opposition began thinking once again of the *Forward* itself as a potential outlet for their views, and so they sought a renewed confrontation with Cahan. A special conference of the Jewish socialist organizations was due to take place in New York on the weekend of May 3 and 4, and Cahan's opposition focused upon this as a target. Sensing the forthcoming crisis, Cahan ran a series of editorials defending his policies. In answer to the claim that he was watering down socialist principles in order to gain popularity for the *Forward* and power for himself, he argued that socialism must be adapted to the particular conditions of whatever country in which it finds itself. American socialism could not work on principles imported from Europe, least of all from Russia.

The conference was held in a basement hall at 64 East 4th Street. The *Morgen Zeitung* was about to cease publication later that month, and the full force of the radical opposition was once again concentrated upon Cahan and the *Forward* itself. At the crucial final session on Sunday afternoon, when Cahan himself finally appeared in person to defend his policies, a crowd of three hundred persons jammed into the hall; only forty of them were delegates. As it turned out, the large size of the audience was to Cahan's advantage; when he stood up to speak, all his old skill on the lecture platform came into play. He ridiculed his opponents, with their constantly reiterated demand for "more socialism," depicting them as dull, unimaginative pietists, and comparing their litany to the tune of a Salvation Army band. This drew laughter, and Cahan knew before he was finished that most of those present were on his side. A vote was taken on a resolution condemning Cahan's policies; it did not pass. Cahan sensed that he had just leaped over another major hurdle in his career.

Cahan was more than ever the stage manager for the great drama of the Jewish immigration to America. Little time was left now for his old-style literary outpourings. Only one small place remained as an occasional retreat into self-indulgences of this kind, a feuilleton series which he had begun all the way back in his last days at the *Arbeiter Zeitung*, called *Fun a Vort a Kvort* ("From One Word a Whole Quart"—i.e., a story spun from just one word). It was in this series that he had done his feuilleton on "yearning" four years before. The mood of that feuilleton had persisted in this series; several recent pieces, for example, had been devoted to Cahan's favorite opera star of his youth, Adelina Patti. One of them, entitled "Phonograph," dealt with the irony of the fact that though the new Victor phonograph could reproduce the voices of great singers with reasonable fidelity, it had come into being after Patti's voice had passed its peak. Cahan always remembered that moment when, while out selling Leo Hartmann's illuminated tie-clasps, he had stood on the street listening to an organ grinder's tune. Every time he tried to recall that tune he found himself humming the "Intermezzo" from *Cavalleria Rusticana*, one of his favorite operas—which, alas, had not yet been written at the time that incident occurred. In other words, not even his own uncanny memory was as true as the Victor phonograph. Why couldn't he have recorded his feelings at that time, instead of waiting until it was too late to write them down accurately? He had failed to create a monument to the visions of his youth—certainly, *The White Terror and the Red* was a poor substitute. Hartmann was now a businessman, an electrical supplier, somewhere in New Jersey.

It was in the midst of his renewing struggle with the opposition, in mid-February, that Cahan published a feuilleton in this series on the word "clarinetist"—the brief musical calling of his youth. It was about a clarinetist he heard one night when dining in a Hungarian cafe on Second Avenue. "The Hungarians are a lively, flamboyant people," he wrote. "Their spices are full of red pepper, their melodies full of fire and hot tears." Cahan points out that he, a formal, cold Litvak in his outward manner, feels like a foreigner in this atmosphere, and this is why he always goes to the Hungarian cafe. Its contrast to his own outward manner appeals to something deeper and less visible within him. There is an orchestra here which plays Gypsy music; it consists of several wildly playing violins, some other instruments, and a clarinet. The clarinetist is a big, stout man with an impassive manner, whose lips do not even move as he sits awaiting his cue. Then he picks up his instrument slowly, hardly seeming to move as he does so, and begins to play.

"The melody was a genuine Hungarian one. The notes portrayed the most extreme contrasts in a single moment—the wildest joy along with the deepest sadness, great merriment and great sorrow—laughing with the stormy laughter of those who drink deeply of their wine, sighing with the sighs of yearning women, crying with the boiling tears of forsaken children." Cahan wants to cry as he hears this enchanted music floating forth through a room filled with the noise of laughter and conversation, in which hardly anyone even hears it. "I look at the clarinetist's fingers. They barely move over the silver keys. I look at his face, his eyelids closed as if he were asleep . . . no sign of life in his face. I look at the whole of his large, bulky figure—no movement, no sign of an inner world." Stunned at this contrast between the clarinetist's outward appearance and his inner music, Cahan "wanted to ask his forgiveness for what I had thought of him just before." He comes to the conclusion that "not everything that looks asleep and dead is asleep and dead."

From here, Cahan the moralist goes on to draw a broad lesson. The clarinetist, he says, is like Russia, which had seemed to be asleep until the revolution broke out a year ago and which now seems to be going to sleep again, but whose melody ever lies deep within, waiting to be played. So also is he like the seemingly dormant workers of America, who ride to the scenes of their wage slavery every morning reading only the sports pages. But one day, Cahan concludes, the intermission will end and the orchestra will strike up again.

Thus Cahan ends his lesson and sets down his clarinet. Was there anyone in the crowd who had heard his melody?

# CHAPTER 16

# LORDS OF THE PRESS

We must be alarmingly enterprising, and we must be startlingly original. We must be honest and fearless. We must have greater variety than we have ever had. We must print more matter than we have printed. We must increase our force, and enlarge our editorial building.

—WILLIAM RANDOLPH HEARST

THE *WAHRHEIT* HAD BEGUN ITS CAMPAIGN OF OPPOSITION TO the *Forward* on its second day of publication, November 12, 1905. On that day, Miller printed a long communication from a group of former members of the *Forward* Press Association criticizing Cahan's policies. The title Miller placed over the letter, a quote from its text, was an invocation of the memory of old battles and old alliances: *Foyl oder Tzugefoylt?* ("Putrid or Putrefying?")—the title of the challenge that Winchevsky had hurled from Boston against the De Leonist forces back in 1895, happier days, when Cahan, Winchevsky, and Miller had all been on the same side. The letter's point of departure was a typesetters' strike—always an occasion for moral ambivalence among the socialist newspapers—which was then taking place at the *Forward* plant. According to the letter, the *Forward* had responded to the strike by denouncing the typesetters' union as a "trust" and a "disgrace" to the socialist movement because of the fact that it also worked for a newspaper—the *Tageblatt*—that opposed the revolutionary cause in Russia. This denunciation had been answered by Joseph Barondess, who, since his defeat in 1904 as the Socialist candidate for the Ninth Congressional District, had been devoting all his time to selling insurance and working as a labor lawyer and strike mediator. In this latter capacity, he was serving as the typesetters' representative in their strike against the *Forward,* for whom he had been working as labor editor only three years before. Feelings were running high, and the *Forward* had reacted to Barondess' defense of the union by referring to him as "an insurance man who settles strikes for bosses."

The authors of the letter in the *Wahrheit* were now replying to that remark, asking Cahan (who is never mentioned by name): "If Barondess is what you say he is, then why did you support his nomination for Congressman last year and why did you, together with the *Forward,* campaign for him so enthusiastically?" After all, the letter went on, if one is going to raise questions about fundamental loyalty to the cause, then what about the fact that, while Barondess was working for the *Forward,* "suffering through all its problems and helping it to survive every crisis," Cahan was writing for the capitalist *Commercial Advertiser,* which supported McKinley in his campaign for reelection in 1900? Then, invoking Winchevsky's old question as to whether the socialist movement was not putrefying because of the domination of a certain clique, the letter-writers asserted that the *Forward*'s Press Association had become, in its arrogance and lust for power, a present-day equivalent of the *Arbeiter Zeitung* Publishing Association at its worst. Mentioning the resignations that had taken place in recent years, of Miller, Winchevsky, and others, they went on to say:

> When one holds up principles next to the *Forward,* with its flashy editorial and business spirit, and with its editor's despotic character and autocratic methods, then the withdrawal of these comrades can readily be understood.

Then came the *coup de grâce*:

> Yes, history repeats itself. Just ten years ago a certain edi-
> tor of a socialist Yiddish newspaper helped a clique to take over
> that paper—which had been the property of the whole Yiddish
> movement—and drive out most of the Yiddish writers from it.
> The end result was that the offending editor was himself driven
> out from the same clique, and the paper finally collapsed. Isn't
> this remarkably similar to the present relationship of the *Forward*
> with the movement? But there are two differences: that other edi-
> tor published a serious socialist newspaper; this editor publishes
> a paper that makes a mockery of socialism. That other paper col-
> lapsed; the *Forward* hasn't as yet.

In the months that followed, Miller continued to find his issues
in opposition to the *Forward* whenever possible. The result was
that Miller gradually began making his way toward policies, for
opposition's sake, that contradicted principles he once had held.
He had once, for example, despised Barondess even more than
Cahan had, but now he was rallying to his defense. He had also
once been critical of Cahan's tendency to look favorably upon virtually any form of Jewish nationalism, but now he began making
the *Wahrheit* nationalist to a degree that was unprecedented among
Yiddish-speaking socialists. He occasionally even opened its pages
to Zionists—*Labor* Zionists, of course—a heresy that Cahan was
not to commit for many years to come. For several months, Miller
struggled valiantly to achieve a liaison with the Bund. He had
already made his paper a major spokesman for Yiddishist nationalism by opening its pages to Chaim Zhitlowsky, a Russian-born
radical who had managed somehow to reconcile his vision of a
worldwide Yiddish-speaking nationality with allegiance to the
peasant-oriented Social Revolutionary Party of Russia, the non-
Marxist offspring of the *Narodnikii*. In early 1906 Zhitlowsky, who
had been living in New York for a time, returned to Russia to sit in

the Duma as a Social Revolutionary delegate. From there, he continued to write for the *Wahrheit*. The result was that Miller found himself gradually drawn into ardent support of the Social Revolutionary cause—a meaningless position in the American political context—and into bitter opposition to the Bund as they refused to have anything to do with him.

His new attitude came to the surface in the spring of 1906, during the visit to the United States of a widely admired Bundist leader from Riga, S. Klivansky, who called himself "Maxim." This twenty-seven-year-old labor leader had demonstrated, in numerous skirmishes with the Tsarist police and confrontations with anti-Semitic peasants, the kind of physical courage that was becoming characteristic of a new generation of Jewish nationalists, whether Bundist or Zionist. Miller vied for his favors when he arrived in New York, but Maxim remained indifferent to the *Wahrheit*; it was Cahan, rather, who accompanied him wherever he went. The *Forward* had exclusive coverage of his doings and statements, and Miller began to fume. Then one day, the *Wahrheit* printed a report of a rumor that the man presently visiting the United States was not the real Maxim at all, but an impostor. Miller subscribed to the rumor in the ensuing days, and began a campaign of vilification that succeeded in reducing public enthusiasm for Maxim and greatly cut into the sizes of the crowds that attended his public appearances. The *Forward*, which hitherto had tried to remain indifferent to the *Wahrheit*, was forced to publish several editorials, including one by Maxim himself, to answer Miller's arguments. Miller had thus completed his alienation from the Bund in a stroke, and had also begun opening a gap between himself and Winchevsky, who was still a loyal Bund supporter.

As for Cahan, this incident had finally aroused him to a fury that caused him to lower his impassive Litvak mask. Immediately after Maxim's departure from New York, Cahan printed his view of Miller's behavior:

Miller is who he is, as the world well knows. It is hard to imagine an immigrant living in New York more than a year and not seeing—or hearing, at least—that Miller is considerably less honest than he is arrogant, that he has a paltry talent for pulling innumerable fast ones, that he is a little man with a big, dirty mouth and an endless supply of bluffs that never succeed in fooling anybody.

Cahan had descended from Olympus at last—a fact emphasized all the more by his astonishing remark, a few lines later, that "name-calling, even when it comes to someone like Miller, is certainly not in our line."

This was what Miller had been waiting for. He immediately sat down and wrote enough copy to fill half of his editorial page. Among other things, he dealt with Cahan's absurd disclaimer to "name-calling":

Had we the literary taste and journalistic courage of the editor of the *Forward,* we would now be able to tell a joke—in fact, the very one published in the *Forward* not so long ago, about a housewife, a servant-girl, and certain "realistic" language that the housewife said she would use were it not for the fact that her home was sacrosanct, and that cursing and using "realistic" obscenities in it were contrary to the ethics of lady-like behavior. But, since our readers have not yet had much chance to cultivate the spirit of barracks-humor within themselves, we won't tell the joke.

Then, casting aside housewifely proprieties, Miller went on:

Mister "heaven-forbid-that-I-be-caught-using-bad-language" Abe Cahan has forgotten to tell about how, starting with the *Wahrheit*'s very first day of publication, his own newspaper stood on the open market with paint and powder on its face, like those business ladies on Fourteenth Street, protesting its love to anyone who could overcome his inner disgust at the *Bintel Brief* and pay the desired price, which was to boycott the *Wahrheit.*

This first open exchange of blows between Cahan and Miller took place during the summer, setting the scene for the election-time battle in which they were to become engaged that fall.

A turmoil was currently being created in New York politics, on both the state and city level, by the ambitions of William Randolph Hearst. Having by now achieved an unprecedented height of power and influence as a newspaper publisher, Hearst hoped to carry this success to its ultimate American conclusion: the Presidency. As stepping stones to this goal, he had run successfully for Congress in 1902, and in 1905 he had sought to become mayor of New York, first on the Democratic ticket, but then as an independent after Tammany had refused him the nomination. He was narrowly defeated, and became convinced that he had lost because Tammany had rigged the election results. More determined than ever to place himself beyond the reach of the Tammany machine, Hearst was now, in 1906, preparing to run for Governor of New York at the head of his Independence League ticket. A self-styled radical and socialist, Hearst was nevertheless unable to obtain the endorsement of the Socialist Party, which was running its own list of candidates; but he did win the support of a number of wealthy independent radicals like himself, such as the millionaire J. G. Phelps Stokes.

The appearance of Hearst on the political scene had a significant effect upon the politics both of the Socialist Party and of the Lower East Side. The young party had not yet entered the national arena, but it was beginning to make its influence felt in certain localities, such as Milwaukee and New York. The greatest area of Socialist Party strength in New York was the Jewish Ninth District, where it had begun regularly running candidates for Congress, but even here victory had not seemed a real possibility until 1906. Joseph Barondess, who had run for the party in this district two years before, had been merely a token candidate. But now Hearst, who had once tried putting out a Yiddish newspaper among his various enterprises and who had achieved considerable popularity with the Jewish immigrants, was about to run an Independence League candidate in the district against Henry M. Goldfogle, the Democratic incumbent. This meant that a lot of normally Republican and Democratic votes would go to the Hearst candidate, causing a spread in the distribution of votes that might give the Socialists a real chance of gaining a plurality for the first time. With a serious prospect for holding office thus in the offing, the Socialists decided to pass over Barondess this time in favor of a man whom they considered to be more reliable. Morris Hillquit was chosen for his combination of old ties on the Lower East Side and high standing in the party. His candidacy was like a homecoming to the neighborhood, and the *Forward* welcomed him enthusiastically.

As the alignment of forces for the campaign thus shaped up, Louis Miller found himself faced with a problem. Despite all his efforts, he had made no inroads into the Lower East Side Bundist-Socialist establishment over which the *Forward* ruled. But he had begun to suspect that this did not matter; his source of strength was a form of mass appeal that cut across these and other party lines, anyway. Miller was already beginning to feel the pull of the American consensus principle far more strongly than Cahan ever had, despite the fact that he had often in the past professed to identify himself with the critics of Cahan's methods of mass appeal. The question was: should he now carry the mass tendencies of the *Wahrheit* to their logical conclusion and turn against those very Socialist forces whose purity he had so often invoked against Cahan? And if he did, what party should he support? The Democrats were out of the question, for this would mean supporting that Tammany organization against which he had hurled his whole arsenal of invectives through the years, and whose spokesmen on the Lower East Side were his old enemies, the *Tageblatt* and the *Morning Journal*. The Republicans, too, were out of the question, for they were the party of the capitalists. Only Hearst remained, a radical in name at least, whose mass appeal on the Lower East Side—and everywhere else—cut across the established alignments, as Miller's did.

Miller's announcement that he had decided to support Hearst appeared on September 16, the very next day after Winchevsky had published an article in the *Wahrheit* criticizing Hearst's claims to being a socialist. Miller and Winchevsky now had very little to do with one another, even though Winchevsky still contributed to the *Wahrheit* and was nominally on its staff. The editorial announcing for Hearst began with a letter from a reader. "I have always voted for the Socialist Party," the letter said, "but now, seeing the way the *Forward* people have put one over on the Party by pushing through another candidate instead of Comrade Joseph Barondess, it would be a crime pure and simple to vote for the Socialists. . . . So, in the name of myself and of many of my friends, I ask you, how should we vote in the forthcoming election?" Miller's editorial pointed out that the *Wahrheit* had received numerous letters like this condemning the Socialist Party. Many of these letters, it went on, had been urging that the paper support Hearst and his ticket. "We also have friends who say that, though they see eye to eye with the Socialist Party, the party can't do anything for the workers politically at the present time, whereas Hearst can do a lot for them; therefore, as Socialists, we must support Hearst this year."

Miller's political logic received something of a shock the following week, however, when the outcome of the Democratic state convention in Albany became known. Charles Murphy, the astute successor to Richard Croker as the boss of the Tammany machine, had been the bitter opponent who had driven Hearst out of the Democratic Party to form a third party of his own the previous year. But it was only narrowly and by dubious means that the Democrats had been able to defeat Hearst's bid for the mayoralty, and Murphy now perceived that he could not continue in uncompromising opposition to the Independence League with impunity. He therefore made a deal: he would provide Hearst with the Democratic nomination for Governor if the latter would, in return, dispense with the Independence League slate. This meant that, in New York City, Hearst would run at the head of a list of Tammany candidates. The deal was closed, Hearst obtained the Democratic nomination for Governor, and Miller discovered to his dismay that the Ninth District candidate he was now, in effect, supporting was the incumbent Tammany man, Goldfogle. Miller decided to ignore the local contest as much as possible, and concentrate on the gubernatorial election.

The local contest was, of course, the main issue for the *Forward*, its first real entry into the rough-and-tumble of an American election battle. Hillquit was the one real hope of the Socialists that year, a fact which they underscored by making him, the party's most distinguished member short of Debs himself, the candidate in a local district rather than on the state level; the Socialist candidate for Governor was a mediocrity named John C. Chase, whom the *Forward* judiciously ignored. But the *Forward* did not, for all that, ignore the gubernatorial contest. For, whereas Cahan had learned long ago to respect the kind of honest Republican that Charles Evans Hughes, Hearst's opponent, was, he had nothing but the deepest suspicion of Hearst. He was convinced that Hearst's claim to being a socialist was utterly false. Furthermore, Hearst had offended Cahan when he had tried putting out a Yiddish newspaper the year before with the claim that there existed a Yiddish newspaper "trust" in New York, which he would try to break. The offense had been compounded this year at the beginning of October, when Hearst started to publish a Yiddish campaign newspaper. Infuriated, Cahan wrote a long critique of this paper and of Hearst, whom he denounced for lacking a soul, something which the *Forward,* he asserted, possessed in large degree.

At the bottom of this editorial against Hearst, Cahan could not resist appending a jab against Miller. Hearst's Yiddish paper had included, in its first issue, a reprint of one of Miller's editorials, and so Cahan wrote:

> Hearst has reprinted an article by L. Miller in which it is maintained that he, Hearst, is much better than Hughes, the candidate

of the Republican Party. This is not the first article in which Miller
has offered comfort to Hearst, to show his friendship for him.
L. Miller works for Hearst. But he doesn't do this openly . . . but
from behind a fence, in pure Miller fashion, in the same way, for
example, that he works against Hillquit.

It is not clear whether Cahan, in making this statement, meant to
assert that he thought Miller actually was receiving money from
Hearst, but Miller took it that way. "Abe Cahan doesn't come right
out and say that the *Wahrheit* has sold itself to Hearst," he wrote
the next day, in a three-column editorial entitled "The Soul of *Bintel
Brief.*" "He's too sly for that. . . . At the *Commercial Advertiser* the
reporters learned not to attack an opponent openly. Cahan makes his
accusation indirectly, furtively, through insinuations." Then, never
referring to the *Forward* by its own name, but always calling it *Bintel
Brief,* Miller went on to pursue the theme of "soul" that Cahan had
raised in his criticism of Hearst:

> There once were people who believed that Abe Cahan had
> "ability," had a "soul." If that ever was so, it is long, long past
> and forgotten. Among all the dead of the old movement, whose
> shadows hover about in Purgatory waiting for redemption, the
> Almighty God's pity is above all reserved for Abe Cahan.

For Cahan, Miller went on, "gave away his ability for eighteen
dollars a week, and turned over his soul to McKinley and Platt and
against Bryan and Croker [sic!], when the *Commercial Advertiser*
employed him as a reporter."

Cahan could not let this go unanswered, even though he was still
making an effort to be above the battle where Miller was concerned.
Trying to seem casual, he appended his reply to Miller at the end of
an editorial on another subject entirely, as if it were a mere afterthought. This, after all, was the way he had handled Miller in his
remarks of two days before. But now, however, the afterthought grew

unexpectedly to the length of six paragraphs. "To the few lines," Cahan wrote, "that we printed about L. Miller's 'behind-the-fence' work for Hearst and against Hillquit, L. Miller replied in three columns. The three columns were full of teeth-gnashing, gall, nervous tics, feverish lying, and Miller-like bluffs and aspersions. Such a fever, such a convulsion, were called forth by our few lines!" Then he moved to the jugular vein:

> L. Miller cries over the fact that Barondess is not the candidate. Well, two years ago Barondess *was* the candidate. And when Miller was asked why he wasn't working for him, he replied, "I simply cannot lift my hands up to work for such a man. Just imagine if he really were elected—what a disaster that would be!" Today he intones his Jeremiah-like lamentations, not out of love for Barondess, but out of hatred for Hillquit. Only instead of "hatred" it would be more correct to say "jealousy."

At that point, the opportunity to gloat became irresistible:

> And the same word "jealousy" applies to Miller's tears over our *Bintel Brief.* . . . Miller tried to imitate *A Bintel Brief.* He printed letters that we had sent back to their authors because they were too distasteful. He failed. Then he began, in pure Miller-fashion, to complain that the grapes he couldn't reach were really too sour.

For some reason, Miller did not reply to this. Consequently, the battle subsided and the combatants returned to the business of campaigning for their respective candidates.

The *Forward* proceeded to show a talent for creating the kind of carnival atmosphere traditional to American political campaigns. Its efforts produced one genuinely spectacular exploit. Since the spring of that year, Maxim Gorky had been visiting the United States. Until that fall, he had been lionized by literary men and zealots of high culture wherever he went; but suddenly things had changed completely. The New York press had discovered that the woman who had been traveling with Gorky all the while, and whom he had introduced as his wife, had in fact never been legally married to him. Overnight, Yankee Puritanism turned the honored literary guest into an outcast; even Mark Twain joined in the general disapproval and scorn. Gorky suddenly found it extremely difficult even to obtain hotel rooms. Only the Jewish intellectuals of the Lower East Side continued to lionize him in the last disastrous days before his departure from America. Gorky was apparently quite grateful for this, for one night, at the *Forward*'s behest, he appeared between acts on the stages of two of the Bowery Yiddish theaters to make campaign speeches for Hillquit!

The *Forward*'s grandiose approach to campaigning culminated, on election night, in the erection of a large screen in front of the *Forward* building, upon which the incoming returns were flashed by means of a stereopticon. Over sixty thousand Hillquit supporters gathered in Seward Park across the street to watch this spectacle. Every time a return favorable to Hillquit or another Socialist candidate came in, a great hurrah went up and echoed throughout the entire Jewish quarter. Between returns, slogans, anecdotes, and caricatures of Tammany leaders were flashed on the screen. There was constant laughter, shouting, or applause.

This festive gathering, unfortunately, had to witness Hillquit's defeat. But the margin was a small one, and the Socialists claimed a moral victory: since Goldfogle, the victor once again, had been in effect the candidate of two parties—the Democrats and Hearst's now-defunct Independence League—and since Hillquit had tallied many more votes than the Republican candidate, a Jewish immigrant named Charley Adler, the Socialists argued that Hillquit had done better than the candidate of any other *single* party. They therefore braced themselves for victory in the near future. As for the statewide election, the results showed the adroitness of Boss Murphy. Hughes had defeated Hearst for the governorship; but, except for Hearst himself, the entire Tammany slate had won in New York City. By striking his bargain with Hearst, whom he had not wanted to see in office, Murphy had done away with the threat of the Independence League and put his own men in office, effectively getting rid of Hearst as a potential political officeholder into the bargain. In this, at least, the *Forward* rejoiced, noting that Hearst had received some seventy thousand votes less than the average candidate on his own ticket. As for the *Wahrheit,* it had nothing more to say about Hearst, and closed the election year with a final passing grumble, on November 9, about the situation in the Ninth District:

> If only half the energy, a third of the cheating, a tenth of the money and a hundredth of the bluffing used in Hillquit's campaign had been used in Joseph Barondess' campaign, the Ninth Congressional District would have been represented in Washington, not by Henry Goldfogle, but by Joseph Barondess.

If furious argumentation in the Yiddish press had not yet brought victory to any of the Socialist candidates, it at any rate brought the newspapers themselves to new heights of popularity. By the beginning of 1907, the *Forward,* the *Wahrheit,* and the two religious papers all had circulations in the tens of thousands, the *Forward* leading the flock with more than fifty thousand. The crisis of a few years before, which had caused the *Abend Blatt* to collapse and had threatened the *Forward* with the same fate, was now entirely a thing of the past. And yet the *Forward* was not yet entirely out of its financial straits, for it was still expanding too rapidly for its existing capital. In 1904 it had bought a building of its own at 175 East Broadway, opposite the newly built Seward Park, and in January, 1905, it became the first Yiddish newspaper to be produced entirely out of its own printing plant—in the past, the custom had been to send the typeset pages to a separate printing establishment. The paper's staff was also growing rapidly. But the costs of this expansion were still hard to meet because, for the time being, advertisers remained reluctant to buy space in a Socialist newspaper—although the situation had been improving since *A Bintel Brief* had made the *Forward* into a major influence among Jewish housewives. In April, 1907, under the impact of the economic crisis which struck at the beginning of the year, the *Forward* was even forced to declare itself temporarily bankrupt.

An important factor in the paper's destiny at this point was the skill of its business manager. At the beginning of 1907, Marcus Jaffe, one of Cahan's most loyal supporters in the *Forward* organization, resigned from this post which he had held for more than four years, because of illness. The job was then given to a young man named Adolph Held, who had graduated only the year before from the College of the City of New York. Held represented the new, American generation (although born in Europe, he had been brought to America as a child) that Cahan was eager to cultivate at the *Forward*. In years to come, Held was to prove to be an outstanding business manager; but at this time he was only twenty-three years old, and his appointment was considered to be just temporary, until a more mature man could be found for the job. In June, such a man was found: Benjamin Schlesinger, although neither so young nor so American as Held, nevertheless was also a representative of the new generation at the *Forward* and in the Jewish labor movement. Born in Lithuania in 1877, he had come to the United States at the age of fourteen and had settled in Chicago, where he became prominent in Jewish labor activities. His work eventually brought him to New York, where he served for a time as a reporter with the *Abend Blatt*. He soon became an ardent anti-De Leonist, however, and was one of the first to join the *Forward*'s Press Association. His involvement in garment-union affairs brought him to the forefront among the founders of the International Ladies' Garment Workers Union in 1900, and he served for a year as its president, in 1903–04. In the spring of 1907, he had just led the New York "reefer makers"—the makers of children's cloaks—to a major union victory. The strike was as important for the destiny of the *Forward* as it was for the cause of unionism on the Lower East Side, for by taking a prominent role in the strike, the paper had demonstrated itself to be a decisive force in the now-burgeoning Jewish labor movement. The close relationship between the *Forward* and that movement was signaled by the appointment of Schlesinger as business manager.

A traditional quality of the American labor leader is that he is no less a master at business skills than is his counterpart on the management side of the bargaining table. Schlesinger had become such an American labor leader, and he soon demonstrated his business acumen at the *Forward*. Previous business managers had devoted themselves almost exclusively to seeking new advertisers and sources of financial support, and had left the promotion of circulation to the editor's skill at making the paper attractive. Schlesinger, however, decided to go after new subscribers by offering premiums as inducements. For their first premium, he and Cahan chose the Yiddish-English dictionary that had been written by Alexander Harkavy, Cahan's old collaborator on the *Neie Zeit* back in 1886, now a prominent philologist. Harkavy's dictionaries were to become an important instrument in the Americanization of the Jewish immigrants, and Americanization was now a predominant aim of the *Forward,* which gave articles of instruction on everything American from the Senate to baseball. The stock of Harkavy dictionaries vanished quickly in a flurry of subscriptions, and for the second premium, Schlesinger persuaded Cahan to write a history of the United States in Yiddish. By this time, Cahan had taken another major step forward in his own Americanization: he had an ulcer; but despite his great discomfort, he set to work on this project. It fascinated him more than he had expected it to, and before he knew it, he had written several hundred pages, an entire first volume, on Columbus's voyages alone.

In the meantime, the *Forward* had acquired for its staff the young specialist in American history and politics who would eventually take over the completion of the multivolumed history that Cahan had just begun. In the summer of 1906, Adolph Held introduced Cahan to a classmate of his from City College named Hillel Rogoff. In college,

Rogoff had majored in the natural sciences and had never thought of writing seriously in Yiddish, but his involvement in Lower East Side socialist clubs and his friendship with Held had suddenly aroused his interest in the *Forward*. Rogoff had come to America as a small child, and was deeply interested and knowledgeable in the subject of American politics; but he also had a good Yiddish background, having studied in yeshivas for sixteen years. Cahan liked this combination of qualities, including the fact that Rogoff had never seriously written in Yiddish before, and he hired him. He would teach young Rogoff how to write Yiddish from the ground up, so that he would write, not in the manner of Cahan's generation of European-bred intellectuals, but simply and straightforwardly. In the following months, Cahan instructed him to "write just the way you speak." He would hand Rogoff a dispatch in English and tell him not to translate it, but to read it, set it aside, and then rewrite it in Yiddish in his own words. Rogoff became one of the *Forward*'s best writers and one of Cahan's most ardent disciples.

While thus establishing a relationship with a new generation on his own terms, Cahan was cutting his moorings in his own generation more vigorously than ever. A few of the old guard, such as Benjamin Feigenbaum, remained at the *Forward* and began to capitulate to Cahan's increasingly overwhelming authority, but most of them went elsewhere and left the growing *Forward* empire to its younger adherents. Even Abraham Liessin, once a disciple of Cahan and almost fifteen years his junior, had now begun to represent an older generation among Cahan's staff, and was indeed beginning to feel tensions in his relationship with the editor. Liessin had always been inclined to be sympathetic with Jacob Gordin. The controversy between Cahan and Gordin had therefore begun a cooling in Cahan's relations with Liessin, who nevertheless remained on the *Forward* staff for the time being.

By the fall of 1907, Gordin was a sick man, and his thinning, ashen face presented an image of exhaustion and suffering. The previous winter he had gone to Europe and to the Carlsbad baths in an effort to recover, but it had not helped much. He was dying of cancer, but this was not known yet, and many of his friends assumed he had been driven into his present condition by Cahan's relentless onslaughts upon him. Cahan did little to disabuse them of this notion. In November, fighting broke out again between him and Gordin when he published a harshly critical review of the latter's new play, *Homeless.* Gordin replied with vigorous denunciations of Cahan's character in the *Wahrheit* and from the stage of the Thalia Theater. In December, another new Gordin play opened—*Galician Exile,* based on his recent travels in Europe—and it closed after a few days. The *Forward* did not even deign to review this one, but merely published a brief notice with the comment that Gordin had not written a serious play in years. Gordin raged some more against Cahan and the *Forward,* but, for the moment, Cahan did not reply. His ailing stomach had forced him to bed, where he remained for several weeks. Perhaps it was his own physical pain during this time that freed him from any remaining scruples against dealing severely with a man who was deathly ill. Cahan's counterattack began on February 1, 1908.

The article which appeared that day was the first of a projected series, entitled "Gordin's Place as a Yiddish Playwright"; the definitive estimate was to be made at last. Referring to Gordin's most recent denunciation of the *Forward* from the stage of the Thalia, Cahan wrote:

> After he told (with his usual childish boasting) of how he has been applauded now for sixteen years ... he specifically asked why the *Forward* maintains that the public has been mistaken. It is precisely this question to which I now wish to address myself.

First of all, Cahan argued, nobody had ever said in the *Forward* that the public had been "mistaken" in applauding Gordin's dramas. Cahan observed that he himself had always been one of the first to admit that there were many good things in Gordin's works, citing as an example his own warm reception of *Siberia* more than sixteen years before. Even in the case of *The Russian Jew in America* in 1895, Cahan wrote, he had not spoken ill of the play in general, but merely had objected to Gordin's conception of a labor leader as portrayed in the character of Huzdak. The problem, he argued, was not Gordin's critics, but the playwright's intemperate responses to them. Gordin's work had lost its proper direction because of his method of answering criticisms, on stage and off, with "great paroxysms of gall." The result was that effective criticism had been silenced, and Gordin had gone on in his own way, out of control. But now, Cahan concluded, "the ban has been lifted—and better late than never."

The series itself then began the following day, appearing at an average of about twice a week for the next few weeks. In the first two articles, Cahan dealt with history, taking up Gordin's vexed relationship with his critics in one, and retelling the story of the 1903 controversy with the *Tageblatt* in the other. Then he moved on to the corpus of Gordin's works, undertaking a close and not unreasonably critical analysis of the style and structure of the plays. Indeed, Cahan was determined to prove that he meant to be objective despite his personal feelings about Gordin, and in March he published a critique of *Mirele Efros* in two installments which, though it pointed up some flaws, gave a generally high estimate of the play and concluded that it richly deserved the success it had enjoyed through the years. Although other plays were dealt with more severely, the general tone of the articles was becoming fairly mellow.

But during the month of March a deadlier blow was quietly being prepared. Suddenly the *Forward* had begun reprinting a series of articles on world drama that Gordin had written for a Yiddish magazine eight years before. This must have seemed an inexplicable phenomenon to the *Forward*'s readers until, on April 4, the reason for it was made evident. On that day, Cahan began a series of articles which set out to demonstrate that Gordin's pieces on world drama had been plagiarized from an obscure work written some years earlier. With obsessive fury, Cahan's articles appeared every day but one through the course of a week. Never shorter than three thousand words, they examined Gordin's articles with a fine-tooth comb, placing passage after passage alongside corresponding and highly similar ones in the original work from which Cahan said Gordin had plagiarized.

The public was stunned. The anti-Gordin campaign had now opened up in all its fury; it continued into the summer. Cahan, for example, reprinted articles by Europeans severely critical of the Gordin plays they had seen in their own countries. As ever, for Cahan, the European criteria for art and literature were the final court of judgment.

By the time the spate of articles against Gordin subsided later that year, the Lower East Side was left with the impression that Cahan had, indeed, planned a vendetta, a final showdown with the only other Yiddish voice that had rivaled his own for power and influence in America. The fact that he had done so, as it turned out, within the last year of Gordin's life, was ever to be held severely against him by his opponents. Gordin died in April, 1909. The *Forward* carried the news in a black frame, and a front-page article by Cahan called upon its readers to go to the funeral and bring flowers. On the day of the funeral he assigned Liessin to write a eulogy; this was to be one of Liessin's last efforts for the *Forward*.

Gordin was dead, and oddly enough, a part of Cahan's life was gone as well. In recent years, Cahan had been watching death steadily bring the last traces of his youth to a close. Johann Most had died in 1906, a reminder of how long it was since anarchism had ceased to be a significant presence on the Lower East Side. Over the past five years, Cahan had received word of the deaths of both of his parents. And only this past February his younger brother Isadore had died of pneumonia at the age of thirty-five, leaving behind a wife and two small children. Cahan now seemed more alone than ever, standing upon the rock of the *Forward,* increasingly the monarch of the crowded streets that he could see from his office window.

The *Forward* continued to grow, the financial difficulties of 1907 now completely a thing of the past, the threat of competition from the *Wahrheit* becoming more and more feeble. By the beginning of 1910, the circulation of the *Forward* had reached over a hundred thousand. The adjacent building, number 173, had been purchased by the Press Association, and plans were under way to build a new, modern home for the paper, a ten-story skyscraper that would stand high above the surrounding tenements. On Saturday evening, November 12, 1910, a gala fiftieth-birthday celebration (four months after the actual event, at a better time of the year for gatherings) was held in Carnegie Hall for the *Forward*'s editor. The auditorium was filled to capacity; "from the loges," the *Forward* reported the next day, "hung the red banners of socialist organizations and unions that Cahan helped to found and to build with his speeches and writings." Speeches of praise were delivered by a whole spectrum of personalities from Cahan's past and present: Alexander Jonas, Edward King, Morris Hillquit, Lincoln Steffens, various members of the *Forward* organization. The spirit of their remarks was summed up by Benjamin Feigenbaum, former "Kangaroo" and one-time ardent opponent to Cahan on the *Forward* staff, in an article published in the *Forward* the following day. "Colleague and comrade!" he wrote. "You have lived for half a century in this dark world and with all your abilities you have helped brighten it."

How right, and yet how strange! Cahan, after a time of seemingly endless struggles and innumerable moments of despair, had lived out an American success story, after all. He was a fifty-year-old smiling public man; his outer life had become the expression of two generations of Jewish immigrants in America, their beacon and guide. Who could deny that this destiny was the projection of something that had risen from deep within himself? And yet something else remained locked within, as ineradicable as it was inexpressible, which insisted that all this activity, all this success, all this mastery of an American reality, was false, a violation of its own hidden truth. But how, after all, could he have answered to this inner voice? It had already shown him its painful demands, and besides, that way lay mere childishness. He had been a child to his environment for an abnormally long time as it was; now he had become a father to it. If being a father meant to suffer, to achieve a painful control over one's inner self for the sake of external responsibility, then so be it. This was the burden of a life of leadership, the tragedy of his success, and he accepted it. Let this inner tragedy be his Europe, beginning to bend wearily under the weight of a thousand years of civilization and self-knowledge. Outside was America—soulless, perhaps, who knew?—but young, exuberant, and demanding. It had little time yet for tragic introspection.

# CHAPTER 17

# JEWISH LABOR COMES OF AGE

⌒

On this site, 146 workers lost their lives in the Triangle Shirtwaist Company fire on March 25, 1911. Out of their martyrdom came new concepts of social responsibility and labor legislation that have helped make American working conditions the finest in the world.
—ILGWU PLAQUE ON A NEW YORK UNIVERSITY BUILDING

THE TRIANGLE SHIRTWAIST COMPANY OCCUPIED THE UPPERMOST three floors of a ten-story loft building at the corner of Greene Street and Washington Place, a short block away from the elegance of Washington Square. Loft buildings of this type had recently gone up all over the Broadway area from Canal Street to 8th Street; tall, massive, built in sturdy shells of stone or brick, they nevertheless contained wooden frame interiors that were no less susceptible to fire than wooden buildings had been since the beginning of time—only these new structures were more difficult to vacate. They became the homes of the newer type of sweatshop, set up by entrepreneurs more prosperous than the marginal contractors of the eighties and nineties, who could now afford to employ workers by the hundreds. But for all their prosperity, these new entrepreneurs maintained an attitude toward marginal costs similar to that of their predecessors, and the sagging wooden floors of their lofts often bore the weight of workers and equipment well beyond the limits of safety. The three floors of the Triangle factory were clogged with six hundred workers—most of them girls between thirteen and twenty-three years of age, the daughters of Jewish and Italian immigrants—who worked among great piles of cloth and strewn fragments of fabric in loft rooms that were served by inadequate exit facilities.

At five o'clock on the afternoon of Saturday, March 25, 1911, as the workers were preparing to go home, a fire of unknown origin broke out on the eighth floor. In an instant, it turned into a flash fire which leaped to the two floors above, and the entire Triangle factory became an inferno. The screaming girls ran to the exits, to the elevators on one side and the stairway on the other; the stairway doors turned out to be locked. Eventually, some of the girls broke through to the stairway and escaped either to the street or to the roof; others got out by the elevators. But many were overcome by smoke at their machines and died there; others, unable to reach the exits through the volcano that had erupted at the center of each floor, were driven back toward the windows. Then they began to jump.

The crowd that had gathered in the street below gazed up in horror as they leaped from the windows of the eighth, ninth, and tenth floors and fell to their death on the pavement. The fire engines arrived less than ten minutes after the disaster had begun, but the firemen were helpless. Nets were spread, but the momentum of bodies falling from that height was too great; they either broke through the nets, or jerked the firemen holding them inward and onto the ground. The fire-fighting equipment also proved to be inadequate. The ladders reached only to the sixth floor of the building and the streams from the fire hoses only to the seventh. Firemen were further handicapped by the clusters of dying bodies in their path.

"Forlornly [the crowd on the street] stood and watched," Morris Rosenfeld wrote in an account for the *Forward* pieced together from eyewitness reports, "as one girl after another fell, like shot birds, from above, from the burning floors. The men held out a longer time, enveloped in flames. And when they could hold out no longer, they jumped, too.

"Below, horrified and weeping, stood thousands of workers from the surrounding factories. They watched moving, terrible, unforgettable scenes. At one window on the eighth floor appeared a young man with a girl. He was holding her tightly by the hand. Behind them the red flames could be seen. The young man lovingly wrapped his arms around the girl and held her to him a moment, kissed her, and then let her go. She leaped, and fell to the sidewalk with great impact. A moment later he leaped after her, and his body landed next to hers. Both were dead. . . .

"It took a whole hour before the firemen could enter the burning building, and by then it was all over. The sidewalks were full of dead and wounded, and no one could be seen at the windows any longer. The poor girls who had remained inside the building lay all about burnt or smothered to death by fire and smoke. The ambulances and patrol wagons that arrived were not sufficient for the job. Grocers, butchers, and peddlers contributed their wagons and pushcarts. Dozens of stores were transformed into hospitals or morgues."

One hundred and forty-six workers had perished in the fire, all but twenty-one of them girls, the great majority of them Jewish. "The Morgue Is Full of Our Dead," said the banner headline in a special edition of the *Forward* put out that same evening, "The Whole Jewish Quarter Is In Mourning." All through that night and into the next day, the terrible scenes in which the victims were identified by their families took place. Each day thereafter, the *Forward* printed groups of pictures of those who had been identified, with the words: "Tears fall around these pictures." The pages of the paper were filled with tragic accounts, under such headings as: "Funerals instead of weddings"; in one case, a picture of a bride and groom bore the caption: "Becky Kessler, the bride, was burnt to death." Seven of the bodies were never identified.

A mass funeral was held for the victims on April 5. By this time, it was the spirit of organized labor that had been aroused, and the funeral was turned into a demonstration of workers' solidarity.

"Come and pay your last respects to our dead," the *Forward* urged that morning, "every union man with his trade, with his union." It was raining, but a crowd of perhaps a hundred thousand persons marched in silence through the streets of the Lower East Side to commemorate the dead. Morris Hillquit delivered a speech in their memory at Cooper Union, and the Reform rabbi, Stephen S. Wise, spoke on the disaster to a gathering at the Metropolitan Opera House.

It was not only "uptown" German Jews like Rabbi Wise who were suddenly aroused to the plight of the immigrant workers by this incident. In general, many middle- and upper-class Americans of the progressive type, hitherto concerned with the problems of urban reform in a much broader sense, were now made aware of what the specific urgencies of labor were in twentieth-century America. An example of these was Frances Perkins, a young social worker who had been visiting friends in Washington Square when the fire broke out, and who became a shocked witness to it. Subsequently she served on the New York State Factory Commission, which was created in response to the Triangle fire to investigate working conditions; for her this was the beginning of an outstanding career in the service of American labor.

The tragedy also served ultimately to advance the cause of the organization that was now becoming the spearhead of the labor movement on the Lower East Side, the International Ladies' Garment Workers' Union. This was the body that had emerged out of the ashes of the conflict between De Leonists and Gompersists that had destroyed the old cloakmakers' union in the eighteen-nineties. Shortly after the complete breakdown of the various warring union factions in 1896, the old Barondessists had gathered their forces together again—this time without their somewhat discredited leader of past years—and created a new union, the United Brotherhood of Cloak Makers. This union allied itself with the *Forward* when that paper came into being, and with the Debsian socialists, in strong opposition to De Leon and the Socialist Trade and Labor Alliance. By 1900, the greatly weakened

United Hebrew Trades had withdrawn from the Socialist Trade and Labor Alliance, which was beginning to collapse, and in that year the United Brotherhood called a conference to discuss the formation of a national cloak-makers' union. The representatives from other cities were less firmly committed to socialism than were the members of the United Brotherhood, but ideology was placed in the background of this conference, at which the International Ladies' Garment Workers' Union was created. A few weeks later, the ILGWU affiliated with the American Federation of Labor.

The ILGWU continued to be dominated by its socialistic New York component for the most part, so this union remained one of the more "radical" ones in the AFL. There were occasions, however, when the "western" components of the ILGWU sought to establish their more moderate influence over the New York organization. This was how Benjamin Schlesinger came to be elected president of the ILGWU in 1903; since he was originally from Chicago, his presidency was thought to be a concession to "western" opinions. In truth, however, Schlesinger was a more committed socialist than was Herman Grossman, the union's first president, who returned to power after Schlesinger's year in office. It was Grossman who represented the anti-ideological, Gompersist trend in the union, even though he was a New Yorker. The rivalry between the forces represented by Grossman and those represented by Schlesinger reached its height in the reefer makers' strike of 1907, in which Schlesinger functioned as the strike leader and the *Forward* as the chief organ of propaganda. Schlesinger and the *Forward* considered the victory of this strike to be also a victory for the socialist forces in the Jewish labor movement. Grossman, however, attempted to play down the *Forward*'s role in it, and in a speech to the ILGWU convention that fall, he expressed special thanks only to Samuel Gompers and the AFL for the reefer makers' victory. This provoked an angry response among the New York socialists at the convention, who formed a committee which sought to reject the president's report and submit in its place an expression of thanks to the "labor press and particularly to the *Forward,* to the United Hebrew Trades, and to Comrade Schlesinger for ably managing the strike." In the face of this opposition, Grossman resigned from the presidency, Schlesinger did not take up the succession as yet, but he and the *Forward* were nonetheless now effectively in control of the ILGWU.

In the next two years there was something of a slump in ILGWU fortunes, largely because of the Depression of 1907, but by 1909 the union's strength was picking up again. The problems that now confronted the garment unions were of a somewhat different nature from those faced in the old days of the cloakmakers in the early nineties. Union agitation and a succession of legislative acts had effectively eliminated the old tenement sweatshops, and the garment industry was now moving into the factory lofts. Here new sets of unfavorable working conditions were in force, but unionism, on the other hand, had not yet found its strength in these new factories. This was particularly the case in the brand-new shirtwaist industry, which was now flourishing in response to the rage for casual women's wear that had arisen just after the turn of the century. There were two reasons for this. One was the large influx of Italian workers into shirtwaist making, a result of the spurt of Italian immigration that had taken place in the nineties. Hitherto, when New York clothing workers had been almost all Jewish, unions were able to organize on a base of ethnic solidarity; this base had now been somewhat disrupted, and a period of adjustment was needed. The other reason for the weakness of unionism in shirtwaist factories was the fact that their employees were almost all women. Young girls marking time until marriage and motherhood do not easily muster the type of solidarity that is founded upon the notion that one's job is to be a permanent way of life.

By 1909, however, quite a number of immigrant girls of the more intellectual, Bundist type had made their way into the ranks of shirtwaist-industry workers, and a confrontation in the industry took place that fall. The grievances in this industry were primarily concerned with elaborate systems of petty harassment prevailing there: forewomen followed girls into the bathrooms to prevent idling, wall clocks were covered so that the workers could not stare at them during working hours, and, as at the Triangle factory, exit doors were locked during working hours. It was at Triangle that one of the conflicts broke out that were to lead to the industry-wide strike that fall. A company union had been founded there the year before, and its chief activity had been to keep the girls in the shop from falling under the influence of the real union organizers who were clamoring for their attention. But now a strike was taking place in some of the cloakmakers' shops, and the employees at Triangle were trying to use funds from the company union to help the strikers. The manufacturers dealt with the instigators of this plan by dismissing them. The girls who were fired went for help to the United Hebrew Trades, who proceeded to try to organize a protest strike among the Triangle workers. At first the strike call got only a feeble response; but as the company increased its harassment, resorting to such measures as hiring prostitutes to station themselves in front of the factory entrance and fight off the pickets, support for the strike began to grow.

Bernard Weinstein, who was still Secretary of the United Hebrew Trades, began promoting the idea of a general strike in the shirtwaist industry as a way of advancing the cause of unionism and gaining recognition from the manufacturers. A committee, made up in part of young women who had emerged as labor leaders at Triangle and elsewhere, was organized to agitate for a strike in other factories. They soon gained considerable support; the workers of the Diamond Shirtwaist Company, for example, went out on strike when they learned that they were working on garments that had been brought in from Triangle. On November 22, a mass meeting of shirtwaist workers was held in Cooper Union to discuss the question of a general strike. The chairman of the meeting was Benjamin Feigenbaum of the *Forward*. Now something of a moderate, Feigenbaum cautioned his listeners against taking any steps that might be damaging to their own interests. Suddenly, a small, thin girl, clearly only in her teens, stood up and asked to be allowed to speak. Feigenbaum agreed, and she came up to the speaker's platform and began addressing the audience in Yiddish. Her name was Clara Lemlich, and she was a worker at one of the struck factories, where she had been assaulted while on the picket line. "I am tired of listening to speakers who talk in general terms," she said, her voice full of emotion. "What we are here for is to decide whether we're going to strike or not. I offer a resolution that a general strike be declared—now." There was immediately a great commotion in the hall as people stood on their feet shouting, waving hats, canes, handkerchiefs. When the din had died down, Feigenbaum asked if anyone seconded the motion. Almost the entire audience rose to their feet. "Do you really mean this?" Feigenbaum demanded. "Will you take the old Jewish oath?" And some two thousand hands rose as the oath was uttered: "If I forget thee, O Jerusalem, then let my right hand lose its power."

Within a few days, over fifteen thousand shirtwaist- and dress-makers, most of them girls, were on strike; more than five hundred shops were closed. A whole new array of young women, labor organizers, emerged on the scene, exhorting workers in the shops to go out, winning the support of Italian workers, organizing strike activities. The United Hebrew Trades, the Women's Trade Union League, and the ILGWU coordinated the strike activities of the various shops. There were frequent clashes on the picket lines between strikers and girls who had been hired as strikebreakers, and large-scale arrests took place. It eventually became clear that the police and the courts were largely on the side of the manufacturers. One judge, when sentencing a striker, told her: "You are on strike against God and nature, whose firm law is that man shall earn his bread in the sweat of his brow. You are on strike against God." The Women's Trade Union League cabled this statement to George Bernard Shaw, asking for his opinion of it. Shaw wired back: "Delightful. Medieval America always in the intimate personal confidence of the Almighty."

The strike reached a height in early December, when a huge mass meeting organized by its sympathizers took place in the New York Hippodrome. On the twentieth, the general-strike movement even spread to Philadelphia. But by this time the strike was in fact playing itself out. A problem of union organization in the New York garment industry was manifesting itself. A large number of shops, most of them the smaller ones, had made settlements by now, and their employees had gone back to work. But, in other shops, mostly the giants of the industry, no settlements had been made. With large numbers of workers satisfied and back on the job, it became impossible to continue the strike, even though no general agreement in the industry had been reached. The industry was simply too fragmented to permit a uniform victory at this time. On February 15, 1910, the strike was officially declared at an end, even though well over a hundred firms had not accepted union demands, and the manufacturers' association, the Associated Waist and Dress Manufacturers, had not officially recognized the unions at all.

Still, the girls' general strike in the newer branches of the women's garment industry, shirtwaist and dressmaking, had set loose currents which were to have a decisive effect upon the older branches of the industry, particularly cloakmaking, where men workers were predominant and unionism more firmly entrenched. The general-strike mood was now in the air, and leaders among the cloakmakers began pressing for this form of confrontation. By June 28, when a mass meeting of cloakmakers was held at Madison Square Garden to discuss the question, opinion in favor of a general strike was overwhelming. The strike was called for July 7; handbills in Yiddish, Italian, and English were printed and distributed among the workers, instructing them to leave their jobs at exactly 2 P.M. that day. Representatives of the press gathered along with the strike leaders that afternoon in the streets of the ladies' garment center, now on Fifth Avenue. "Among those who were curious to see whether the workers would respond," one strike leader wrote, "were Abraham Cahan and Benjamin Schlesinger, editor and manager of the *Forward*. . . . When at ten minutes past two no worker was to be seen, Cahan asked with irony, 'Well, where are your strikers?' . . . He had barely finished speaking when we saw a sea of people surging from all the side streets towards Fifth Avenue. Every minute the crowds grew larger, and all moved in the same direction. By half past two all the streets from 38th Street down and from the East River westward were jammed with thousands of workers."

This strike was well disciplined, and it brought to bear the resources of an established union organization. In addition to the usual demands concerning wages, hours and working conditions, the union was seeking official recognition from the manufacturers and the right to have a closed, or union, shop. A board of arbitration headed by Louis D. Brandeis was set up to handle the strike. By now a labor lawyer of considerable prominence and an activist in Jewish communal affairs, Brandeis was able to obtain the confidence of the Lower East Side socialists better than could most of his fellow old-stock German-Jewish Americans. Also on the board were Hamilton Holt, representing the cloak manufacturers, and Morris Hillquit, representing the union organizations. The union's counsel was Meyer London, son of the printer Ephraim London who had briefly published the anarchist Yiddish newspaper *Der Morgenstern* in 1890. Now thirty-nine years old, London had run as a Socialist candidate for Congress every Congressional election year since 1904; in that year, and again in 1906 and 1908, he had run in the Twelfth District, adjacent to the more solidly Jewish Ninth, where Joseph Barondess in 1904 and then Morris Hillquit for two election years in a row had been unsuccessful candidates. This year, the Lower East Side had been redistricted so that the Twelfth District now took in much of the old Ninth, and with Hillquit apparently withdrawing from his old candidacy, London was considered the strongest possibility to run for the Socialists in the Twelfth that fall.

By the end of August a settlement was made that came to be known as the "Protocol of Peace"; this agreement was to govern labor-management relations for several years to come. In it, standards were established for wages, hours, and working conditions. The working week in the industry was fixed at fifty hours, with double-time pay for overtime work. The union also achieved official recognition by the manufacturers, although it had to compromise on its demand for a closed shop. In its place, the Protocol provided for the "preferential union shop"—a formula created by Brandeis—which meant that, in situations in which competing job applicants were otherwise equal, preference would be given to union men. This specification was elastic indeed, and the *Forward* characterized it as "the open shop with honey." Nevertheless, the overall settlement was considered the most important victory yet won in the history of the New York labor movement. It brought fame to Meyer London, who that fall came closer than any of his predecessors had to winning the long-sought-after Congressional seat for the Lower East Side Socialists.

The Triangle disaster a few months later, once the shock was recovered from, completed the process of union development that had begun with the general strike of the shirtwaist and dress workers in the fall of 1909. The importance of unionism made itself felt among these girls for once and for all, and the International Ladies' Garment Workers' Union went on soon to become one of the largest and strongest labor organizations in the United States.

The labor organization of the men's clothing industry, the United Garment Workers, though it had once been strong enough nearly to absorb the cloakmakers, was now much weaker than its counterpart in the women's garment industry. The Protocol did not apply to it, and it had fallen far behind the ILGWU in improvements in wages, hours, and working conditions. By December, 1912, therefore, the leaders of the United Garment Workers had decided that the time had come for a test of their own strength similar to that undertaken by the ILGWU in 1910. A strike movement began gaining momentum, first among the UGW leaders, and then among the rank and file. Like the ILGWU, the UGW workers were interested in obtaining not

only the classic improvements in wages, hours, and working conditions, but also full recognition of their union and a closed shop. To
a large extent, the strike movement was directed against the chaotic
conditions that prevailed in the innumerable small shops that had
grown up over the years. Among the workers in the large firms there
was less reason for discontent, and they were somewhat more reluctant to go out on strike than were their counterparts in the small
shops. But, as the *Forward* urged, "in this the whole trade must take
part as one man." A common agreement to strike was finally reached
by December 31, when the men's clothing workers walked out *en
masse* from their shops, large and small. The large manufacturers
were incensed. "We pay top wages to our workmen," one of them
announced to the press, "and the union does not object to our scale.
We must suffer for the deficiencies of the small concerns, it seems."

In the long run, it was the large manufacturers, organized into
the New York Clothing Trade Association, who were to prove to be the
most intractable parties to the dispute. By the beginning of February,
large numbers of the smaller manufacturers had already given in.
In these shops the workers had obtained a fifty-hour week—as good
as the Protocol settlement on hours that the ILGWU had obtained
in 1910, even though the UGW leadership had originally called for
forty-eight hours. In shop after shop, workers were steadily trickling
back to their jobs. On February 16, the *Forward* carried the headline:
"Tailors on Brink of a Complete Victory." But the fact was that none
of the large shops, which accounted for some 25,000 workers—more
than two-thirds of the workers in the men's clothing industry—had
yet given in. The ten thousand or so who had returned to work were
now contributing ten percent of their weekly wages to a strike fund
for those who were still out. But the strain on the striking workers
was becoming great. Pressure for a quick settlement was growing
strong, and the union leadership felt that it was losing control over
masses of workers. T. A. Rickert, the president of the UGW, became
persuaded that the strikers could not hold out any longer, and a

settlement was worked out through a board of mediators. Among other things, this quickly arranged settlement provided for a fifty-four-hour work week and a raise in wages that amounted to about a dollar a week higher than before. On both these points, the workers in the small, settled shops had obtained better terms; but these settlements had been made contingent upon agreements to their terms by the large manufacturers. In other words, the union's present agreement, if enforced, would cause the advantages that had been gained in the small, settled shops to be lost. A crisis was inevitable.

At this point, the *Forward* became the principal actor in the drama that was developing. The paper was now housed in its new, ten-story skyscraper, which had been completed the previous year; it seemed to bestride the Lower East Side like a colossus. Election-night gatherings were held in front of it, and cheering crowds of workers came to its front entrance whenever a Lower East Side union had won a victory. Unions, fraternal workers' organizations, and meeting halls were housed in the new *Forward* Building, which seemed like a huge and powerful nerve center for the activities and aspirations of Jewish labor.

Late in the afternoon of Friday, February 28, Cahan was in his office preparing to close the next day's edition of the *Forward*—it was now a morning newspaper, and it put out a first edition at ten in the evening—when two of the leaders of the UGW strike, Max Pine and Benjamin Schweitzer, appeared at the door. Pine was a member of the *Forward* staff, and he had regularly reported each day's developments in the strike to Cahan in person. This time, however, he had something quite different to say. He and Schweitzer had just come from a meeting of the union's Executive Committee, where Rickert had presented the terms of the proposed settlement. The members of the Committee were inclined to accept the settlement, but knowing that it would be unpopular with the workers in the settled shops, they first wanted to know the *Forward*'s opinion of it. The Committee felt that it could not make its next move without the *Forward*'s support.

Pine and Schweitzer summarized the terms of the proposed settlement for Cahan, and asked what he thought about it.

"Accept the compromise," Cahan said after some reflection. "The *Forward* will stand by you. It's not a good settlement, but this can't be helped. At any rate, it will be a basis for building a real union."

"There'll be some hot-heads who'll cause trouble," Pine warned. "They won't swallow it just like that."

"Don't worry about that," Cahan replied. "They'll understand that there was no other choice."

There was still some space left on the front page of the ten o'clock edition for last-minute news, so Cahan decided to insert an editorial on the settlement. He asked Pine to write for him while he dictated and, pacing up and down the room, he began to compose his article. At that moment, two men appeared at the door of the office. One of them Cahan knew well: he was Ike Goldstein, a leader of an anarchist affiliate of the UGW called the Brotherhood of Tailors. Cahan rather liked Goldstein personally, even though he had little use for his ideas. He did not know the man who stood at Goldstein's side.

"Comrade Cahan, Comrade Cahan!" Goldstein cried. "The settlement is a crime!"

"It's not a good one," Cahan conceded. "We certainly might have hoped for something better. But the first thing to do is save the union. Then you'll have something to build on, and we'll have greater victories."

A debate ensued between Cahan and Pine on one side, and Goldstein and his companion, introduced as Louis Hollander, on the other. Cahan and Goldstein often debated political issues with each other, and their arguments always had a friendly tone. But the tone of this evening's debate was exacerbated somewhat by Hollander, who not only was vehement about continuing the strike, but seemed to have some particular animosity toward Cahan. Presently Goldstein and Hollander left, and Cahan finished dictating his editorial.

Cahan had found a good deal of space on the front page, as it turned out, for it bore a five-column headline announcing: "The Great Tailors' Strike Settled." The editorial began thus:

> The settlement is not as good as it might have been, but for the future destiny of the tailors it is very good. The great tailors' union has been formed.

The terms of the offered compromise settlement were then spelled out. Later, in the morning edition, these words of exhortation were added on the editorial page:

> Bravo, garment workers! The circumstances are such that the settlement will be an excellent foundation for the steady improvement of the conditions of your trade. Don't forget that your great union is a young one. . . . One dollar a week is of course a small increase in wages. Nine hours work is of course too much. But don't forget, this is only a beginning. . . . With such a powerful organization as the one you now have, you will go on increasing your wages and reducing your working hours. Go back to work rejoicing and shouting: Long live the powerful tailors' union!

The workers did not rejoice. On Saturday morning, when they began hearing news of the settlement in the union meeting halls, they surged into the streets and formed a crowd which made its way angrily toward Rutgers Square and the front entrance of the *Forward* Building. There were some moments of jeering and shouting, and then someone called out: "To the *Wahrheit!*" By this time, the *Wahrheit*, just a few doors away from the *Forward*, had become a regular supporter of Democratic and Tammany candidates, and its position in the Lower East Side labor movement was merely a marginal one. Still, when thoughts turned to vengeance upon the *Forward*, the *Wahrheit* was the place to which men naturally repaired. The crowd swelled in the direction of its doorstep, with cries of "Hurrah for Miller!" and "Let Miller speak!" Unfortunately, Miller had not yet arrived at the office that morning—nor had Cahan—but another man, much younger, appeared at the window to address the crowd. It was Louis Hollander, Ike Goldstein's companion of the night before. He gave a brief speech, urging the workers not to accept the settlement and to go on striking. This was the gist of a resolution that he, Goldstein, and other members of the anarchist Brotherhood of Tailors had just drawn up at an all-night meeting. But Hollander was not just speaking for the Brotherhood, as it turned out: for he was a member of a cultural society called the "Gordin Circle," and was therefore an ardent opponent of Cahan and the *Forward*.

Once he had finished speaking, the crowd pressed back toward the front entrance of the *Forward* Building. Angry workers entered the lobby this time, overturned a ta ble, and began smashing windows. The great glass panes of the main doorway broke with a loud crash. Hurriedly, Adolph Held, the *Forward*'s business manager again since Schlesinger's return to the ILGWU, telephoned Cahan at home and told him to come to the office immediately. By the time Cahan arrived—he was now living far uptown, on East 76th Street between Madison and Park—the demonstration was over and the crowd had dispersed. The Executive Committee of the United Garment Workers had already capitulated to the demands of the demonstrators and announced that the strike would continue.

The next morning, the *Forward* and the *Wahrheit* each had its own version to tell of the previous day's incident. "Revolution in Tailors' Strike" ran a banner headline in the *Wahrheit*, with a subheading: "The *Wahrheit* the Center of the Revolution." Miller's editorial inside took up four columns, about twice the usual space. "Don't Go To Work!" was its title, and it ran in part:

> Imagine yourself, reader, amid a great mass of fellow human beings aboard a tiny ship on a raging, stormy sea.
> Now you're heading for the clouds, and now you're plunging into the depths of eternity. Now comes a terrifying mountain of

water, threatening to capsize and drown you, and now you smash against a rock, and everything begins to crack beneath your feet. You think it's all over. . . .

Ten long weeks, ten weeks of dreadful struggle, of strife, of hunger, of need, of bitter cold, of sacrifice and despair, of women's tears, children's wails, the outcries of men—ten long weeks, like ten endless eternities!

And then at last, far away, in the distance—a glimmer, a flicker of light—land!—sweet echoes of life reach your ears—safety—the long-awaited haven—the long-dreamed-of victory—the joyous prospect of an end to the struggle. . . .

You begin to jump up and down for joy. . . . Tears flow from your eyes. . . . You embrace your comrades in the struggle, your friends in sorrow, you kiss them—

But then, O woe, a thousand times woe! No words, nothing, can describe the awful thing that is happening! That glimmering light that had summoned you from afar is the flashing eye of a serpent! Those sweet, heavenly echoes that had reached your ears were the grinding teeth of a monster. . . .

Imagine yourself, reader, in this situation . . . imagine yourself going through all this and you will have some idea, some inkling, of what went on today, Saturday, in the heads, the hearts, the souls of the hundred thousand [sic!] tailors when they were told what they had won after their great ten week long strike.

The *Forward*'s news coverage of the events had little to say about the "revolution" in front of the *Wahrheit* building and much to say about the smashing of the *Forward*'s windows, to which the *Wahrheit* had given only a few words in passing. In both its news columns and in Cahan's editorial, the *Forward* maintained that the demonstration had been led by workers from the settled shops, men who were now at work and collecting their pay, and who were willing to let their co-workers go on striking and suffering to protect a settlement that had been favorable to themselves. "The hungry expressed satisfaction with the settlement under these circumstances," Cahan maintained:

"It's easy for you to complain, you're already back to work," they said to the others. "Our wives and children are getting hungry. We've won a little something—now let's get back to work, let's stick with our union, and it'll bring us better settlements later on."

Cahan held vehemently to this argument that Sunday morning, when he made a speaking tour of several of the union's rallies. The first meeting he spoke to was a gathering of a union branch in one of the halls in the *Forward* Building. His exchange with the audience began good-naturedly. One man spoke up during Cahan's opening remarks, saying everyone agreed that those who had broken the *Forward*'s windows the previous morning were hotheads who should be condemned. Cahan replied by comparing them to "unruly children," who had behaved in a thoroughly typical way. "Why," he asked rhetorically, "didn't they break the windows of other editorial offices? Because those others are strange to them, whereas the *Forward* is their own. It's like their mother, and one makes demands upon a mother, whether they are just or not. And when a bad boy gets unruly and starts breaking dishes, it doesn't matter. A mother forgets." This drew laughter and applause.

But the atmosphere became more heated when Cahan started trying to explain his position. There were frequent shouts and interruptions, and Cahan was soon yelling at the top of his lungs to make his points. He began feeling ill. The next meeting he attended was on another floor of the *Forward* Building, and the discussion there became similarly heated. Cahan emerged from this hoarse, sweating, and exhausted. Some of his co-workers urged him to go home, but he insisted upon attending a large rally taking place at Clinton Hall. He went there, and when he rose to speak, he found himself confronted by a sea of angry hecklers. During his speech, a young man near the front of the audience kept interrupting him and shouting at him.

"Who are you?" Cahan suddenly asked the young man. "Are you a member of the union?"

"Yes, yes, I'm a member of the tailors' union," he replied.

"Perhaps you're from one of the settled shops. Right?"

The young man looked flustered. Cahan asked to see his union booklet. The young man tried to protest, but the audience let up a cry demanding that he show it. At last he produced his booklet; it indicated that he was employed at one of the settled shops.

"So!" Cahan exclaimed triumphantly. "You sit and work and get your wages. You eat three meals a day. It's perfectly all right for you to tell people who aren't eating to go on being hungry and to strike for you!"

By the time he finished speaking, Cahan felt literally as if something had been torn apart inside his stomach. Bent with pain, he had to be helped from the auditorium into a waiting car. He was taken home, where he promptly went to bed and slept ten hours. The next morning, he felt better and went to the office, but he still was not well. On Tuesday, as he sat in his office with a group of colleagues discussing a forthcoming fiftieth birthday celebration for Morris Rosenfeld at which he was to be chairman, he suddenly felt an overwhelming wave of weakness come over him. He promptly announced, to his listeners' surprise, that they would have to find another chairman for the event. Two days later he was in the hospital, and on Friday he underwent an operation for the removal, as one of the doctors put it to him later, of "a duodenal ulcer the size of a half-dollar." The operation was a serious one, and Cahan stayed in the hospital recovering for nearly four weeks. After that, he rested several weeks more, first at home, then in Lakewood, New Jersey, where he tried writing some fiction again for the first time in years.

The strike was settled within a week after Cahan's operation. In these last days of bargaining, the union had been represented by Meyer London and another rising young labor lawyer named Fiorello La Guardia. The dispute had been submitted to arbitration, and the outcome was a settlement that represented a considerable improvement over conditions that had prevailed before the strike, but that was not so good as some of the separate settlements that had been made earlier in the small shops. The work week was fixed at fifty-three hours—only one hour shorter than what had been provided for in Rickert's unpopular settlement of February 28—with the promise that it would be lowered to fifty-two in a year. In general, the union was satisfied with the implicit recognition that had been accorded to it by this settlement. But many of its members remained unwilling to forgive Rickert and the strike leaders for having taken matters into their own hands the way they did. The dissension that ensued produced a weakening of the United Garment Workers so severe that it began falling apart, and was superseded in the following year by the newly founded Amalgamated Clothing Workers of America; this latter organization, under the presidency of the young Sidney Hillman, was to become the equivalent in the men's clothing industry of the ILGWU.

Among the important results of this strike was the emergence of Meyer London as a major political figure. London represented the spirit of moderate socialism that was achieving, largely through the efforts of the *Forward,* ascendancy over the Jewish voters of the Lower East Side. This moderate trend obtained another major victory in the Jewish labor movement in a crisis that took place later that year. Isaac A. Hourwich, a radical intellectual born in Vilna the same year as Cahan, and now a labor lawyer, had recently become the chairman of the New York Joint Board of the ILGWU. This made him in effect the union's leader in New York City, and from this power base he was beginning to agitate against the national leadership, whose policies he considered to be too moderate and conciliatory. In his struggle, he was pitted against the union's national president, Abraham Rosenberg, a veteran cloakmaker who had worked with Barondess in the union's earliest days, and who, though once an anarchist, now represented the cautious spirit of an older generation that had been gratified by the Protocol and was eager to work within its framework. Hourwich, though no youngster himself, made his appeal to impatient younger elements within the union who sought more radical solutions, and he enjoyed considerable popularity for a time among the rank-and-file. But Meyer London and the *Forward* took up Rosenberg's side and organized a solid front of opposition against Hourwich that eventually forced him to resign. The so-called "Hourwich Affair" had also shaken Rosenberg's position among the union rank-and-file, however, and he was forced to step down from the presidency at the ILGWU convention in June, 1914. Benjamin Schlesinger was elected president of the union in his place. The *Forward* coalition, along with the politics that it represented, was now at the height of its power on the Lower East Side.

All that remained was the Congressional prize that had been sought for so many years. In November, Meyer London ran once again for the seat still held by Henry M. Goldfogle, and this time he won. A young Yiddish journalist named Melech Epstein joined the election night crowd in front of the *Forward,* and years later he recalled the scene:

> Stories of Tammany violence and fraud were flooding the neighborhood. At dusk, crowds had been moving towards Rutgers Square, facing the *Forward* Building. They filled Seward Park and the side streets, waiting impatiently for the election returns to be flashed on the screen in front of the *Forward.* For many hours the returns were not conclusive and the results were unknown. Tammany politicians were trying to delay the final count. Tension was mounting. About eleven o'clock, the orthodox *Tageblatt,* a few doors from the *Forward,* published an extra announcing the victory of Henry M. Goldfogle, the Tammany candidate. The crowd refused to accept the finality of this announcement, and thousands remained in the square waiting hopefully. At about 2 A.M., after much bickering, Tammany leaders conceded London's election. The crowd was jubilant; men sang and danced; thousands rose from their beds and came to join the celebration. London was brought to the square at 4 A.M. to head an impromptu demonstration. This writer still remembers the triumphant march through

the streets in the early dawn. Impulsive Michael Zametkin, speaking from the balcony of the *Forward,* lifted his arms to the rising sun and exclaimed, "Perhaps the sun will shine on the East Side from now on!" Marchers carried straw brooms to symbolize that Tammany's rule would be swept out.

A new era had indeed dawned on the Lower East Side. But did this not also mean that an old one was coming to an end? Significantly, Daniel De Leon had died that spring: what were socialism's struggles to be about now, in its Congressional era? And what was to be the effect of the war that had broken out that summer in Europe, the source from which the civilization of the Lower East Side had come?

# Chapter 18

# The Exile Is an American at Last

⌒

Sometimes, when I think of my past in a superficial, casual way, the metamorphosis I have gone through strikes me as nothing short of a miracle. I was born and reared in the lowest depths of poverty and I arrived in America—in 1885—with four cents in my pocket. I am now worth more than two million dollars and recognized as one of the two or three leading men in the cloak-and-suit trade in the United States. And yet when I take a look at my inner identity it impresses me as being precisely the same as it was thirty or forty years ago. My present station, power, the amount of worldly happiness at my command, and the rest of it, seem to be devoid of significance.

—Abraham Cahan, *The Rise of David Levinsky*

In April, 1911, Cahan had written an editorial in honor of Passover which explained how recognition of himself as a Jew had come to him with an acceptance of his American destiny:

In many educated, progressive Jewish families people sat down to the Passover *Seder* last night. Twenty years ago, if anyone had heard that a Jewish socialist was interested in a Jewish religious holiday like that, they would have called him a hypocrite. But today, such a thing is perfectly natural.

Twenty years ago a freethinker would not have been allowed to demonstrate any interest in the Jewish people, but today he can! This right has been bought with the blood of the pogrom victims.

What a change! It can be seen in a hundred different ways. It is a change for the good, too, to a wider understanding, to a more human relationship with one's self and one's own feelings.

And when you think about this change, another one also comes to mind. The educated, progressive immigrant comes here from Europe filled with contempt for America. He steps off the ship with a contemptuous leer and this expression remains frozen on his face. Everything American seems base to him. In Europe it has become the custom to view life in America condescendingly. A land of skyscrapers and yellow journalism, a huge circus of business dealing and bluffing—this is all people there know about the United States.

America is looked upon in Europe in the same way that anti-Semites look upon Jews. Who can deny that Jews have their faults? But the anti-Semites see nothing more in the Jews than their faults. Who can deny that America has in it a lot of bluffing and cheap sensationalism? But the tragedy is that in Europe they don't know of anything else where America is concerned.

And with this one-sided impression the Jewish immigrant intellectual comes to the New World from his old European home.

However, Cahan concludes, the immigrant intellectual learns in time that it is no more shameful to "dress up" for America than to do so for the Passover *Seder*. One learns to shake off one's European prejudices toward being an American and being a Jew.

In the summer of the following year Cahan went on a three-month trip to Europe with his wife, during which he had ample opportunity to observe the ways in which the gap between the European and the American experiences that had obsessed him in his youth now seemed considerably smaller and less consequential. He observed many changes that had taken place in the quality of life there since his last trip to Europe in 1893. New habits, manners, clothing styles, improvements in creature comforts, and advances in the technology of everyday life—the very fact that all Europeans seemed to have adopted the American "hello" as the standard form of salutation on the telephone—all seemed to indicate to him that Europe was getting to be more like America. "In sum," he wrote of this trip, "when I thought about the various changes that had taken place in twenty years, I felt strongly that the different parts of the civilized world were becoming more like one another, that all countries were becoming one." This seemed even more to be the case when, in Paris, he visited his old friend and fellow revolutionist Anton Gnatowski, and discovered him to be living the life of a happy, mellow—and somewhat bourgeois—family man. The term currently in vogue among the more radical socialists of the Second International to describe what was happening to their Revisionist and Reformist colleagues was *embourgeoisement*. So be it, thought Cahan, if this was the only intelligent response to reality; he had discovered it in America long ago.

During this trip he visited a number of the spokesmen of Revisionist and Reformist socialism, such as Jean Jaurès, and his interviews with them confirmed him in the pragmatic convictions he had already developed on the Lower East Side years before. Russia, of course, was still something else again—while visiting Cracow, Cahan had a clandestine interview with Lenin—but Russia, after all, had not yet had the liberal revolution that Western Europe and America had already gone through in the eighteenth and nineteenth centuries. Reform socialism was a pallid notion indeed in a Russia that was still ruled by Tsars; but in Western Europe and America, social democracy could be viewed as a natural and peaceably attainable extension of the established liberal-democratic systems. Why strain, then, after a romantic vision of the barricades that belonged to one's lost youth when the world no longer even required it?

Shortly after his return to New York in the fall, *McClure's* invited Cahan to contribute a series of sketches describing the striking economic successes that Jewish immigrants were now beginning to enjoy in America. Ideology aside, for the Yankee world, Cahan was still the chronicler of Jewish immigrant life in America in all its aspects. He had already shown, in his portrayals of Asriel Stroon or of Zalkin in *The Daughter of Reb Avrom Leib,* that he could describe a Jewish capitalist as intimately and as sympathetically as he could a Jewish worker. Indeed, Cahan had always prided himself on the fullness of his knowledge of the Jewish immigrant reality in America, and he had long ago mastered the details of the way, for example, the New York garment industry worked, from the manufacturer's as well as the laborer's point of view. *McClure's* now wanted a vivid presentation of those details. One of its staff writers, Burton J. Hendrick, a Gentile, was already at work on an article dealing with the general Jewish success story in America. But it was better to have the story told from within, and who was better qualified to do so than Abraham Cahan?

Cahan decided to create a fictitious character who could serve as a composite for numerous success stories in the garment industry. He had no intention of preoccupying himself with a serious work of fiction at this time, for he was too busy; indeed, he barely had time to get two sketches done before he became completely involved in the UGW strike at the beginning of 1913. The fiction form was meant just as a device for conveying a mass of information dramatically. Yet even in these two hurriedly written sketches describing "David Levinsky's" boyhood in Russia, emigration to America, and first efforts as a fledgling garment manufacturer, Cahan had managed to create a character interesting for his own sake. In fact, the sketches contained some of the best narrative passages he had ever written, and *McClure's,* recognizing their worth, asked for two more sketches. Cahan agreed, but he might never have written them if he had not been stricken at Clinton Hall on Sunday, March 2. While in the hospital recovering from his operation, he was visited by Jay Hambidge, the illustrator of his two sketches, which were scheduled for the April and May issues. Discussing some problems of the story with him, Cahan found himself reawakening to the fortunes of David Levinsky, and during the long weeks of recovery that followed he wrote the third and fourth sketches, in time for them to appear in June and July.

Cahan's sketches were not presented as a "story" by *McClure's,* but were given the air of a documentary, which was entitled "The Autobiography of an American Jew" (on the cover it was billed more sensationally as "The Confessions of a Jew"). The narrative was in the first person, as if it were indeed the intimate diary of its protagonist. To reinforce this "true novel" atmosphere, Cahan had sought to personalize David Levinsky, to make him as vivid and convincing a character as the novelist's skill could allow. For this, like any good novelist, he had drawn judiciously upon elements from his own experience. He, too, after all, was a Russian-Jewish immigrant, and if he was not a businessman, he also nevertheless knew something about some of the qualities of the American experience of success. Indeed, in the very opening paragraph, one need only substitute the words "Yiddish press" for "cloak and suit trade," and David Levinsky seems to become Abraham Cahan:

> When I think of my youth in a superficially casual way, it seems to be separated from the present by a wider ocean than the one that lies between my American home and my Russian birthplace. I arrived in this country with four cents in my pocket. That was twenty-two years ago. Now I am recognized to be one of the leading men in the cloak and suit trade in the United States. Surely the contrast is striking enough. And yet, it is not always that the distinction comes home to me. Indeed, whenever I take a look at my inner self, it impresses me as being precisely the same as it was twenty-two, or thirty years ago; and then my present station, power, the amount of worldly happiness at my command, and the rest of it, strike me as something unreal.

In his search for authenticity, Cahan has already sounded the opening chords of a theme far more interesting than his documentary of the garment industry; for one already hears a melancholy note from the inner and contradictory depths of the American myth of worldly success.

Levinsky's youth is that of a poor yeshiva student in Russia. It is likely that Cahan had thought for a moment of making his businessman-protagonist a Mottke Arbel, an uneducated boor of the type that had so frequently elbowed his way up the ladder of business success in America. This would have been an easier approach to his subject, since Cahan intended to take a critical view of capitalism in these sketches. By making his protagonist an educated man instead, he was going to have problems explaining Levinsky's choice of the business career that immigrant intellectuals had usually shunned. But if he was going to write a long first-person narrative convincingly, Cahan had to create a character with whom he could identify.

The young Levinsky is, in fact, so much like the young Cahan—the only major difference is that Levinsky is orphaned at an early age, and is thereby freed of Cahan's own problems of filial piety—that it must have been extremely difficult for Cahan to formulate the crucial point at which Levinsky's life and career diverged from his own. At a certain moment in his own youth in Russia, Cahan had joined the revolutionary movement. Such a course was, naturally, not feasible for Cahan's fictitious budding capitalist; but to depict a young man so like himself as *not* taking this course demanded of Cahan a special effort of imaginative dissociation. He had to reconstruct, from among those elements in his own youthful experience that had contributed to his becoming a socialist, a pivotal moment that chanced to take Levinsky in another direction entirely—or in what seemed to Cahan to be another direction, at any rate. It was perhaps at this moment that he began discovering an even greater identity between Levinsky and himself than he had previously imagined. The result was an odd episode in the story that puzzled Cahan's editors and, undoubtedly, many of his readers as well.[3] Suddenly Levinsky, the shy and awkward yeshiva student, has a brief and thoroughly frustrated love affair with a young *barishnya*.

Sonya, a gymnasium graduate and a divorcee, is the daughter of a kindly and pious woman who brings food to the Talmud students in the House of Study, and who invites Levinsky to convalesce in her home one day when he has taken ill. Levinsky has already heard of Sonya, and his first glimpses of her at the house fill him with a tremulous fascination. She begins to tease him for his extreme piety. One day she offers to tuck his side-locks behind his ears to show how well he could look without them, and he recoils in fright. "The next morning she tantalized me again. My bashfulness, innocence and primitiveness seemed to tempt her. This, at least, is how I interpreted her behavior subsequently, when I was older and had a better knowledge of the world."

In this way an abortive amorous relationship begins to grow between them. She takes to berating him for wasting his native brilliance in religious studies, when he could study subjects like Russian language and literature. She draws him out and he tells her his life story. Soon she is creating a fanciful educational program for him, but he protests, saying that he is in danger of being drafted into the army for five years, and that he has already made plans to go to America. She disapproves at first, saying, in substance, that America is a land of dollars, not of education, and that she wants him to be an educated man. "Still, when she saw that my heart was set on the project she yielded." She offers to raise the passage money for him. Levinsky then begins to realize that his ambition to go to America has "lost its former snap." And he knows exactly why: "I was deeply in love with Sonya."

Levinsky's infatuation becomes increasingly like that of a lovesick child, while Sonya manifests her obvious interest in him in quite a different way: "She continued to treat me in a patronizing, playful way." One day, when she is taunting him as usual about his sidelocks, he lets her tuck them in. She remarks that he looks good without them, that he should cut them off and then "girls might even fall in love with you. But then, what does a pious soul like yours know about such things as love?"

> "How do you know I don't?" I ventured to say, blushing like a poppy.
> "Do you really?" she said in mischievous surprise.
> I nodded.

"Well, well. So you are not quite so saintly as I thought you were! Perhaps you have been in love yourself? Have you? Tell me!"

I kept silent. My heart was throbbing wildly.

"Do you love me?"

I nodded once more. My heart stood still.

"Kiss me, then."

She put my arms around her, made me clasp her to my breast, and we kissed passionately.

In the next moment, Sonya is prancing gleefully about the room, saying, "There is a pious soul for you! There is a pious soul for you!"

Instead of romance blossoming from this episode, Levinsky tells us that "she seemed to be getting a bit nervous about our relations, and when my stay at her mother's house was declared at an end, she was obviously glad of it." She tells Levinsky that she will bring him his passage money at the House of Study. Sadly, he returns there, and one day she shows up in the courtyard with the promised sum. He tries to protest that he is no longer interested in going to America, but she cuts him off impatiently. "I have no time to bother with you," she says. "Go to America. I wish you good luck!"

" 'But I'll miss you. I won't be able to live without you,' I said, all but sobbing.

" 'Are you crazy?' she said sternly. 'You forget your place, young man!' " She walks away, and Levinsky forlornly prepares for his emigration.

It should be pointed out here that Sonya is going to make a brief reappearance later in the story, after many years have gone by, as a socialist. In other words, Cahan has meant this episode to stand as an abortive love affair with the possibilities of Levinsky's own spirit, with his potentialities for socialist fulfillment. From this dual amorous and moral failure is to flow Levinsky's diversion from his proper destiny into a business career. Although Cahan had not yet fully developed his themes at the time he wrote this episode, he is ultimately going to depict Levinsky's worldly success as accompanied by a severe spiritual decline. For, if Levinsky is now going to lose the religion that had consoled his boyhood—his sidelocks are shorn almost as soon as he sets foot upon American soil—he has also failed to discover the socialist credo that might have become the religion of his manhood.

The rest of the first installment and all of the second describe Levinsky's emigration to America, his early struggles there, and the first stages of his rise to business success. Still brooding over Sonya, Levinsky plans at first to get an education, and he saves up his sweatshop earnings for the day that he will have enough money to support himself as a full-time student at City College. But the American business adventure begins to appeal to his lively mind. In the shop where he works, there is a highly skilled designer named Chaikin whose talents, Levinsky notes, are being used unimaginatively by the German Jews who own the shop; furthermore, he is underpaid. Levinsky's mind begins to fill up with business schemes in which Chaikin figures at the center. Finally, he succumbs to temptation. He takes his meager college savings and starts a business in partnership with Chaikin. In some of the best writing he had ever done, Cahan proceeds with a relish worthy of a Balzac to describe Levinsky's rise in business— his chicaneries, his imaginative schemes, his setbacks, his strokes of luck—presenting, in the process, that detailed anatomy of the New York garment industry that the *McClure's* editors had desired.

By the time Cahan, convalescing from a stomach operation and a clash with the rank-and-file of the United Garment Workers, got to writing the second pair of installments of Levinsky's career, he found himself far more interested in his protagonist's soul than in his business dealings. At the end of the second installment, Levinsky had suffered a business setback that is ultimately to prove to be minor, but for the moment, in the first paragraphs of the third, it has caused him to brood about his life: "I was telling myself that it served me right, that I had no business to abandon my intellectual pursuits." He walks mournfully past City College: "This building was the embodiment of my aspirations, the synagogue of my new life, the symbol of my spiritual dignity, a veritable temple of the muses." He considers going back to his original plan of getting an education, and in order to raise money for college he starts giving English lessons to a semi-literate but highly successful businessman named Nodelman. But both teacher and pupil soon become more interested in discussions of business than in the study of grammar. Nodelman gives him a loan, they abandon the lessons, and Levinsky goes back to his career as a cloak-and-suiter.

Levinsky now enters upon the final stages of his climb to success. The timorous Chaikin has withdrawn from the business, but Levinsky goes on using Chaikin's designs by pirating them. Ultimately, poor Chaikin returns to Levinsky's shop—as an employee. In his narrative, Levinsky points out that, along with his own success, the old German-Jewish domination of the New York garment industry has come to an end. The East European Jew has "made it" in America. Now troubles of a new sort appear on the scene: the cloakmakers' union is beginning to make its presence felt. Hitherto, the union had not been strong in Levinsky's shop because the pious, old-fashioned tailors who worked for him were always grateful for the way he accommodated their religious needs, allowing them to say their prayers at work each day, letting them go home early on Friday, making Sunday a workday instead of Saturday, and so on. But now a new type of worker is beginning to arrive, secularist, intellectual, and aware of the values of labor organization. "One of the most active [unionists] was employed in my place," Levinsky records. "I had known him in my native town, where he belonged to a much better family than I. He was liberally educated, and I knew that he was absolutely sincere. . . . In my heart of hearts I liked him, and, what is more, I felt that he was right." But "he made me uncomfortable. He was my living conscience." Finally, Levinsky fires him.

It is now that the long-buried malaise in Levinsky's soul comes to the surface, and in the form in which it had originally expressed itself—the failure to love. The narrative turns into an onslaught of amorous disaster. Soon after his troubles with the union have begun, Levinsky hears that Sonya is in New York. She has, he learns, been a member of the Russian revolutionary movement; having just escaped from prison in Siberia, she is touring America to raise funds for the cause. Levinsky decides to seek her out at a meeting of Russian revolutionaries which takes place one night at Cooper Union. He goes there proudly wearing an expensive fur coat. "Sonya recognized me at once, but my air of prosperity (although there was nothing loud or distasteful in my clothing) had anything but the desired effect on her." She gazes at him, clearly contemptuous of his capitalist success. I had a strong impulse to protest my sincere sympathy for the Russian revolution, to assure Sonya that my heart went out to the heroes and martyrs of the struggle, and to offer a generous contribution." But instead he is overcome by a resurgence of his old timidity under her reproving stare, and he retreats from the hall.

"I received another rebuff about this time," Levinsky's narration goes on. He meets a girl at a Catskill mountain resort; she is a stenographer for a well-known lawyer, and the daughter of an educated family. "I became rather seriously interested in her, but she frankly shunned me and repulsed all my advances." One day, in a rainstorm, they happen to take shelter together in a secluded spot called "Lover's Glen." Levinsky tries to seize the opportunity:

> "Now you can't run away from me," I said gaily, yet timidly.
> "Please leave me alone," she answered, turning away.

The third installment ends with Levinsky, the conqueror of the business world, expressing his determination to win this girl.

Anna Tevkin, as it turns out, is the daughter of a Hebrew writer, and a member of a family in which every ideology dear to Russian-Jewish intellectuals, from Zionism to socialism, is represented. She of course represents that world of the spirit which Levinsky, in his choice of a business career, has denied himself. Ominously, he sets about to win this love of his heart in a manner more befitting the businessman he has become than the man of the spirit lying deep within him. Anna's father, hardly able to make his living in America as a Hebrew essayist, has become a freelance broker for business and real estate transactions, and is mildly prosperous. Levinsky reads up on some of his essays and goes to seek him out in the Lower East Side cafe that he frequents. He gets into a seemingly casual conversation with Tevkin, and then begins to speak flatteringly of the latter's writings; Tevkin, delighted, promptly offers Levinsky some real estate at bargain prices. A huge boom in real estate speculation is going on among Jewish immigrants at this time, and Levinsky, a solidly established manufacturer, hesitates at first to become involved in it. But pleasing Tevkin means getting to his daughter, and Levinsky decides to accept the offer.

Levinsky soon gets a chance to apologize to Anna for his behavior that day at "Lover's Glen," and he becomes a frequent visitor at the Tevkin household. Apparently, however, it remains obscure to everyone whether he is coming as a friend of Tevkin's or as Anna's suitor, until he finally proposes to her on the evening of the Passover *Seder.* She smiles. "I need not tell you," she says, "that I have long since changed my mind about you. You are no more repellent, of course. Far from it. I like you very much. But that is not love. Love is quite another thing. I am very sorry indeed."

Thus ends Levinsky's romance. In the following weeks, the bottom falls out of the New York real estate market, but Levinsky pulls out just in time to avert disaster. The narrative now becomes a long outpouring of melancholy as Levinsky, a wealthy, ageing bachelor, wanders the streets mourning his loneliness. He learns eventually that Anna Tevkin has married. One evening, at the Yiddish theater, he again meets Sonya, who also is married. This time, she greets Levinsky warmly and converses with him all evening. "She was still an active and devoted socialist, but the three or four years she had passed in America had sobered her somewhat, made her more practical and tolerant." She urges him to marry, saying she would be pleased to be invited to his wedding. "I departed in a queer state of mind. Her present identity failed to touch a romantic chord in my heart. She was simply a memory. But as a memory she had rekindled some of the old yearning in me. I was in love with Tevkin's daughter and with the Sonya of twenty years ago at the same time."

On the day of the twentieth anniversary of his arrival in America, Levinsky seeks out Gitelson, the tailor who had descended the gangplank with him twenty years before and who is now, after a brief prosperity, a poor man again. He takes him to dinner at an expensive restaurant. This proves to have been a mistake; the shabbily dressed Gitelson is embarrassed and Levinsky, eager to rectify the situation, offers Gitelson ten dollars in return for a loan he had made of him years before. Gitelson hesitates, then takes the money. Levinsky goes home that night lonely and despondent, muttering to himself over and over: "Such is the tragedy of my success! Such is the tragedy of my success!"

The *McClure's* assignment to write an anatomy of Jewish business success in America had thus led Cahan right back into the depths of his old tragic vision, back to the glimmers of American exile that he thought he had wiped out once and for all with such formulations as that of his Passover editorial in 1911. This was portentous, for, in fact, even that comfortable vision of 1911, of America as a refuge for Jews from centuries of European persecution, began falling apart at the very moment when Cahan's David Levinsky sketches were appearing in *McClure's*. In Atlanta, a Jewish businessman named Leo Frank was arrested at the end of April in connection with the murder of a fourteen-year-old girl in his employ; that summer, a local jury found him guilty of the crime. The *Forward* at first gave more attention to the trial of Mendel Beiliss going on at that time in Russia than it gave to the

Frank case in Georgia; Beiliss, a simple workingman, a victim of Tsarist persecution and of the oldest anti-Semitic weapon in the history of Europe—the ritual-murder charge—was a far more appropriate martyr from the *Forward's* point of view than a German-Jewish bourgeois who seemed at first to have been legitimately found guilty by an American court. But Cahan soon became persuaded, as many liberal Northerners did, that Frank was innocent, and in March, 1914, he went down to Atlanta in person to interview him. It turned out that Frank had been found guilty on no other evidence than the testimony, found to be highly questionable in nature by many reputable outside observers, of a Negro workman named Jim Conley. Even if Conley's testimony had been less dubious, it would still have been quite noticeable in this instance that a white man had been found guilty of a capital offense solely on evidence submitted by a Negro for the first time in the history of the South. Would the Atlanta jury have been so willing to believe Conley if Frank had not been a Jew? Perhaps Cahan's mind heard echoes of Russia in this, where a tyrannical regime also had turned an oppressed peasantry against the Jews in order to keep both groups down. In any case, what Cahan's ears did hear were cries of "Hang the Jew" echoing through the streets of Atlanta; this, then, could happen in America, too! A year later, Frank was hanged by a lynch mob after the governor of Georgia, suspecting his innocence after all, had commuted his sentence to life imprisonment.

By that time, Cahan's recent vision of the Americanization of the world was in ruins. One of the supports of that vision in 1912 had been his conversation with Jean Jaurès; but by mid-August, 1914, Jaurès was dead, killed by the bullet of a French nationalist fanatic who thought he had sought peace with Germany too eagerly, and Europe was at war. Only a short while before, the socialists of France and Germany had been claiming that the workingmen of their two countries would never go to war against one another in the name of a bourgeois nationalist conflict. Now the socialist parties of France and Germany were both ardent supporters of their respective countries' war efforts. Where, then, was that "one world" that Cahan had glimpsed in the summer of 1912? To make matters even more outrageous, the French were fighting their inexplicable war against Germany on the side of the Russian Tsar!

As a socialist newspaper, the *Forward* opposed the war altogether, but as a Yiddish one, it tended to favor the side opposite the one the Tsar was on; this was the feeling of Russian-Jewish emigrants everywhere. For all the anti-Semitism of Germany and Austria, there had at least never been a Dreyfus or a Beiliss in either of these countries. Furthermore, Yiddish-speaking Jews still felt a natural attraction to German culture, and Jewish socialists still looked upon Germany as the capital of worldwide Social Democracy. On the Lower East Side, only the *Wahrheit,* driven as usual to oppose the *Forward* and to favor the sentiments of the American political establishment, supported the side of France and England. But this proved to be a fatal mistake on Miller's part. His paper's circulation plummeted, and angry crowds burned piles of the *Wahrheit* in the streets. Within a year after the outbreak of the war in Europe, Miller was dismissed from the editorship by the paper's financial backers. His successor, Isaac Gonikman, a former writer for the *Forward,* proceeded to change the *Wahrheit*'s orientation to a pro-German one.

In this atmosphere of conflagration, the revolutionary convictions of yesteryear seemed feasible once again, and Cahan was driven still further back into his old, deep-lying second thoughts about the American experience. Even his *Forward* editorials reflected this mood, as did this one in the middle of 1916:

> We have to be Americans. We shall be. . . . We shall love America and help to build America. We shall accomplish in the New World a hundred times more than we could in the Old.
>
> But you will not be able to erase the old home from your heart. The heart will be drawn elsewhere. And in your solitude, images will rise up and stare in your faces with eternal sorrow.

This was the mood in which Cahan went to work expanding and perfecting his David Levinsky sketches for publication as a novel.

From the outset, the final version of *The Rise of David Levinsky* is filled with an even more pronounced melancholy than had marked the *McClure's* sketches in which it originated. Levinsky's opening reflections on the ironies of success are now more severe than they had been and go on at greater length, filled with such asides as "I love to brood over my youth" and "there is a streak of sadness in the blood of my race." The sufferings of his boyhood are described in greater detail than before, but so are its spiritual joys, which now have become embodied in the character of a pious and sweet-souled teacher of Levinsky's named Reb Sender. The Sonya episode is essentially the same, except that her name now is Matilda, and Levinsky's amorous failure with her emerges even more emphatically than before as due to his hopeless, yeshiva-bred shyness. This is novelistically an improvement over the original version, though it is more perplexing in some ways; for, whereas the original, more schematic, version had a certain degree of metaphorical clarity as a representation of Levinsky's failure to discover the real inclinations of his spirit, this new version loses that clarity in its more passionate involvement in what seems to be a personal score that Cahan wishes to settle. We are left more than ever with the uneasy feeling that Levinsky's entire destiny has been decided by the passing whims of a bitchy woman; our hero clearly shows his antecedent in Tzinchadzi of the Catskills.

Levinsky's early immigrant experiences and rise to business success are described in even greater detail than before, and there are a few new strokes that are truly inspired. The City College building, for example, is now referred to by Levinsky as "my temple," and the section in which he suddenly decides to use his college savings to go into business is entitled "The Destruction of My Temple." This crucial decision is more dramatically portrayed than in the earlier version; Levinsky has the same feelings as before about Chaikin and the business possibilities that he represents, but these are now galvanized into action by a significant incident. During lunch hour one day in the factory, Levinsky accidentally spills a small bottle of milk and stains some coats. He is bawled out by the boss, and this causes Levinsky to begin plotting revenge: he will steal Chaikin, become his boss's competitor, and outdo him.

Having found this persuasive way of depicting the pivot that brought Levinsky into a business rather than an intellectual career, Cahan is now better able to stress the alternative destiny that had awaited his protagonist had he remained true to himself. In contrast with the first version, we are told here that Levinsky has been in a "socialist mood," and he asserts at one point that "had I then chanced to hear a socialist speech I might have become an ardent follower of Karl Marx and my life might have been directed along lines other than those which brought me to financial power." That Levinsky's quasi-socialist resentment against his boss could have found the way of taking revenge that it did is perfectly convincing; what is far less convincing, however, is that Levinsky never "chanced to hear a socialist speech." For a young man of his intellectual pretensions living on the Lower East Side in the late eighteen-eighties, it would have been virtually impossible not to have come into contact with socialist ideas. Cahan is stacking his deck at this point.

There now takes place a long episode that is entirely missing from the earlier version. Cahan has apparently decided, for the sake of his naturalistic novel, that Levinsky ought to love at least one real woman in the course of the long years between the bitch-saint Matilda and the shadowy abstraction that is Anna Tevkin. Dora is the wife of a business colleague of Levinsky's, but her feelings toward her husband are dutiful rather than passionate. Her passions are reserved rather for her small daughter and then, after a time, for Levinsky, whose love she nevertheless ultimately refuses out of her sense of duty as a wife and a mother. The episode demonstrates Cahan's ability to give a vivid portrayal of a warm-blooded and appealing woman when he wants to, but it does not fit well into the novel's scheme. Another failure in love on Levinsky's part, yes, but not on the spiritual grounds that Cahan is seeking to portray everywhere else in the novel. This is a pity, for the Dora episode is one of the best sections of the book.

The Anna Tevkin episode in this final version is given greater poignancy than before by the fact that here, at the moment he meets Anna, Levinsky is engaged to be married at last. A successful forty-year-old businessman, he has decided that it is high time he enter into a conventional "good" match, uncluttered by deep and complex amorous yearnings: his fiancée is the spoiled, shallow daughter of a pious and well-to-do Jewish family. But one weekend, while on the way to visit her and her parents at their summer home in the Catskills, he stops off at a hotel and there meets Anna Tevkin. All the romantic yearnings that he thought he had buried deep in his soul come surging back to the surface. Anna rebuffs him as in the earlier version, but he impulsively decides to break his engagement and to pursue her all the same.

Levinsky seeks to make contact with Anna through her father, as before; but old Tevkin has gone through some significant transformations between the first and final versions of the story. This time, Levinsky has heard about Abraham Tevkin as far back as in his boyhood in Russia. One of his fellow yeshiva students, a budding young maskil, had told him the romantic story of the Hebrew poet Tevkin, who courted and won the beautiful daughter of a famous Odessa physician by writing to him a series of letters in Hebrew that were indirectly protestations of love to his daughter. These letters had become classics of Hebrew literature. Levinsky had all but forgotten this story, but he is now reminded of it upon learning who is the father of the girl with whom he has fallen in love. He reads up on Tevkin's *poems*—they are no longer mere, prosaic essays—in the library, seeks out their author in the cafe, and finds, not a mildly prosperous businessman as before, but a shy, unworldly, melancholy man, who has not been able to make much of a go of it in America (he is still a business and real estate broker, but with neither talent nor relish for the calling). His attitude is summed up in a poem of his which he recites to Levinsky:

> "Most song-birds do not sing in captivity. I was once a song-bird,
> but America is my cage. It is not my home. My song is gone."

Levinsky protests that the poem's virtues prove that what it says is not true. "But the idea," he exclaims, "of America being likened to a prison!" The old man overrides Levinsky's objections:

> "It is of my soul I speak," he said resentfully. "Russia did not imprison it, did it? Russia is a better country than America, anyhow, even if she is oppressed by a Tsar. It's a freer country, too— for the spirit, at least. There is more poetry there, more music, more feeling, even if our people do suffer appalling persecution. The Russian people are really a warm-hearted people. Besides, one enjoys life in Russia better than here. Oh, a thousand times better. There is too much materialism here, too much hurry and too much prose, and—yes, too much machinery. It's all very well to make shoes or bread by machinery, but alas! the things of the spirit, too, seem to be machine-made in America. If my younger children were not so attached to this country and did not love it so, and if I could make a living in Russia now, I should be ready to go back at once."

When Levinsky gains entry into Tevkin's home, he finds there an even richer array of Russian-Jewish ideologies than he had found in the first version. Anna's eldest brother, Moissey, is described by his father as "a dentist by profession and a Russian social democrat by religion." Upon introducing Moissey to Levinsky, old Tevkin adds that "Karl Marx is his god and Plekhanov, the Russian socialist leader, is his Moses." Moissey's wife is a Russian-Jewish woman of the modern, progressive sort, who smokes "cigarette after cigarette." Another sister, Elsie, is also a socialist, and Levinsky observes of her and Moissey that "theirs were truly religious natures, and socialism was their religion in the purest sense of the term." It is now considerably more understandable than before why Levinsky, the capitalist, cannot make his way into a family like this. It also is made more clear than in the first version that Anna is repelled by Levinsky's wealth.

*The Rise of David Levinsky* thus emerges as the definitive statement of the conflict that had dominated Cahan's life. Like Cahan, Levinsky has mastered the reality principle in America, coming to terms—as Tevkin refused to do—with the American experience that has, for better or for worse, been thrust upon him. In the process, unfortunately, he has left his heart and his soul back somewhere in that distant, dreamlike Russian past. But what can be done about that? At least, there are a few substantial accomplishments to show for it all. "The average American woman," Levinsky points out, "is the best-dressed average woman in the world, and the Russian Jew has had a good deal to do with making her one." He might have added that he, personally, also had a lot to do with it. As for Cahan, he, too, had worked for the average person, and had done a lot to help in the Jewish immigrant's adjustment to American life. Best of all, he had now written a major novel at last, a summary statement in fiction of the Jewish immigrant experience. In this way, at least, he had come to terms with America after all.

Appropriately, the book was published in 1917, the year in which the hallowed Russian revolutionary dream exploded into grim reality at last. "That which has long been awaited has finally come," the *Forward* said on March 16, after days of tense waiting for some news to break through the silence that had suddenly fallen over Russia. "A Revolution in Russia," it went on euphorically, "a free Russian people, a free Jewish people in Russia! Is this a dream?" On March 18 a *Forward* editorial said, "What a day we are living through! What a golden day!" and two days later a banner headline proclaimed: "Jewish Troubles Are at an End." This event, combined with America's entry into the war on the Allied side a few weeks later, completely transformed the Jewish immigrants' attitude toward the conflict. Overnight, the cause of America and of revolutionary Russia against the Central Powers became that of the average Russian-Jewish American. The Yiddish press soon reflected this change. Although the *Forward* was denied the use of the mail in October because of its old antiwar, anti-Allies stance, it had in fact already begun to open its pages to the opinions of staff members who supported the American war effort. In Congress, Meyer London, who had opposed American entry into the war, proclaimed that his country would have his wholehearted support now that it was in the fight. By April, 1918, a *Forward* editorial reluctantly conceded that "it is no longer a capitalistic war. Neither is it imperialistic or nationalistic. It is a war for humanity." Military service and participation in the war effort went on to function as a catalyst for the further Americanization of thousands of Jewish immigrants.

As the *Forward,* along with the masses of Jewish immigrants that it represented, thus became further caught up in the mainstream of American destiny, its old tie with the Russian revolutionary tradition, no longer enhanced by the glory and the grandeur of a dream, began to disintegrate. From the moment that the Bolshevik regime came into power, many *Forward* writers began openly expressing their hostility to it—Lenin's authoritarian organization had hardly been the vehicle of their social-democratic hopes. But Cahan himself was slow to join in this chorus of condemnation. After all, he maintained, this was the long-awaited Revolution, and one should perhaps suspend judgment upon a regime that had to bring Russia through it and all the ensuing chaos. The very "realism" of this viewpoint suggests that Cahan had already, under the impact of events, abandoned the Russian revolutionary passion of his youth. He had been through the agonies of disappointed revolution a thousand times in his heart; his task was no longer to be led by the nose of naive belief, but to judge carefully and impart his wisdom to a generation in America that awaited understanding of the cataclysm that had taken place back in the old home.

It was not until 1921, when the schism between supporters and opponents of the Communist International then taking place in social-ist parties all over the world split the Jewish Socialist Federation in America, that Cahan finally declared his open hostility to Bolshevism. The Yiddish-speaking Communists of New York promptly created a newspaper of their own, the *Freiheit,* which went on to become—since the *Wahrheit* had suffered a complete demise in 1918—the *Forward*'s chief antagonist in the postwar era. Very well, then; Cahan had dealt with radical opponents before, and now he set to work doing so once again, but this time with an iron will that was the product of sixty years of agonizing self-definition.

CHAPTER 19

# THE LONG TWILIGHT

Some of the gang have become famous. Al Levy was known to us simply as "Stinker"; now he writes wealthy musical comedies.

Abe Sugarman is a proud movie director. He also has become a Spanish nobleman. His Hollywood name is Arturo De Sagaar, no less.

Lew Moses shoots craps with high stakes, with skyscrapers; he is a big real estate speculator.

Others of the boys are humbler comedians. Jake Gottleib is a taxi driver, and feeds his three kids every day. Harry Weintraub is a clothing cutter. Some of the boys are dead.

—MICHAEL GOLD, *Jews Without Money*

WHEN THE FLOW OF JEWISH IMMIGRATION TO AMERICA WAS ALL but cut off completely by the Johnson Act of 1924, the *Forward* was at the height of its power. Its circulation was nearly a quarter of a million—as great as that of any other newspaper in America—and the *Forward* Building was a main center of the burgeoning Jewish labor movement. Cahan was the unchallenged autocrat of this empire. In 1922, Oswald Garrison Villard, editor of *The Nation*, wrote an article on the *Forward* for his magazine entitled "America's Most Interesting Daily," in which he said: "The editor's complete control is never questioned; matters of policy may, however, and do occasionally come before the [Press] Association. Thus there have been two recent meetings of the Association to discuss the paper's attitude toward

Russia and its policy toward the Jewish labor movement. In both cases Mr. Cahan, the editor, and Mr. [Baruch Charney] Vladeck, the business manager, were sustained—they would have resigned had they not been."

By this time, Cahan had firmly defined the main outlines of his policies for the postwar years. His paper was to be ardently anti-Communist, broadly social democratic, and essentially accommodating to the pragmatic unionism of the American Federation of Labor. The candidates it officially endorsed were those of the Socialist Party, but it was ready to support the cause of liberal and progressive politics in America whoever propounded it—except for the Communists. Culturally, the paper was now not merely Yiddish but Yiddishist. In their youth, Cahan and his colleagues in New York had disdained to call themselves anything but "Yiddish-speaking socialists," and they had professed opposition to Jewish nationalism in all its forms. But now, Yiddish was the cultural expression of a worldwide Jewish-proletarian peoplehood for many writers at the *Forward* and elsewhere, and if Cahan had not necessarily become one of the true believers, he was nevertheless a warm supporter of the faith. More so than ever before, the *Forward* was giving a good part of its pages to serious works of fiction and literary criticism, which stood undaunted alongside *A Bintel Brief* and the other more "popular" features.

There were still some final resolutions to be made on specific points within these main outlines. The *Forward* was still, for example, going to have to establish the nature of its Jewish nationalism more clearly. To a certain extent, its Bundist ties were weakening. Since 1917, the Bund had effectively vanished as a force in Russia, and the rump of it that remained in Poland had settled down to the role of a relatively small and sectarian group among several Jewish political parties. Differences were already emerging between Cahan and the Bund as to the correct attitude to take toward Communism and revolution. The Bund was in any case no longer the representative of a broad and generous cultural-political ideal that it once had been, and the *Forward* had grown too large to continue doing homage to it. The Yiddish literary movement was now further removed from the Bund than it had ever been; it had, in fact, shifted its center of gravity from Europe to America. The war had brought both Sholem Aleichem and Sholem Asch to the United States, and though Sholem Aleichem had died before the war was over, so also had the two other major figures and founders of the Yiddish literary movement, Mendele Moicher S'forim and Isaac Loeb Peretz in Europe. Sholem Asch, in New York, was now the most outstanding living Yiddish writer. There was also a thriving school of Yiddish essayists and literary critics who were increasingly becoming centered in New York. Although Warsaw had emerged after the war as a major center for Yiddish letters, it was to continue feeding its writers to New York in the years to come. In any case, the *Forward* was the main literary outlet for Yiddish writers no matter where they lived.

But in the midtwenties, the printed word was not even the most important medium of Yiddish culture in New York. Although the Yiddish theater had fallen into a torpor immediately after Gordin's decline, it had entered upon a renaissance at the war's end and was now better than ever. A number of Yiddish writers of the first rank, including Sholem Aleichem just before his death, and Sholem Asch, had begun applying their talents to drama, and a repertory of good, serious plays had come into being. The foremost school of interpreters of this repertory was in New York. Its preeminent figure was Maurice Schwartz, a native of the Ukraine who, like many Yiddish actors, had been forced to abandon his formal education at an early age but had subsequently discovered the theater to be his university. Schwartz had begun his acting career with a Yiddish troupe in Brooklyn while he was still in his teens. He toured the country a while and then, with the help of Abraham Cahan, who was deeply impressed by his talents, he settled down in New York as a member of David Kessler's company in 1913. His entrepreneurial ambitions grew along with his acting talent, and in 1918 he started a company of his own, at the Irving Place Theater. Three years later he moved his company to Second Avenue and renamed it the Yiddish Art Theater. This became one of the temples of the flourishing Second Avenue Yiddish culture of the twenties.

Although the Second Avenue Yiddish culture continued to bear traces of its socialistic origins, it was nevertheless coming to serve an increasingly middle-class audience, and it relied less and less upon the old explicit ideological commitment as it turned to a broad and sentimental Jewish nationalism. Part of Maurice Schwartz's reputation came to be based upon his interpretations of great figures from Jewish history; this was purely nationalist heroics, free of Gordin's compulsion to make some point of social significance, free of any traces of his anticlericalism—for Schwartz's heroes were figures of religious import often enough. This approach inevitably became touched with elements of Zionism—Schwartz was eventually to include an impersonation of Theodor Herzl in his repertory—despite the fact that Zionism and Yiddishism, especially in its Bundist form, were once entirely antagonistic toward one another. The Balfour Declaration of 1917 had done much to transform the Zionist ideology of a small prewar elite into the aspiration of broad masses of East European Jews wherever they were. Both Yiddish culture and Zionist aims had become more sure of themselves than they once had been, and they no longer had to strive so fiercely to prove themselves against one another. There was now even a Yiddish Zionist press in New York, which claimed its respectability among the other cultural institutions of the Lower East Side.

Zionism became increasingly a matter with which Cahan and the *Forward* had to deal. His generation had tended to remain unrelenting in their anti-Zionism even as their other old ideological antagonisms weakened; even Louis Miller, who had given a good deal of space to Zionist writers in the *Wahrheit,* never personally expressed support for their cause. But with Miller gone as a challenge from the right, and the burden of antagonism now coming from the *Freiheit* on the left, Cahan was more prepared than ever to explore new realms of accommodation to the world's emerging realities. After all, the Jewish national community that was emerging in Palestine was founded upon socialistic agrarian settlements of the sort that had captured his imagination back in the days of the *Am Olam* and his emigration to America. He had to see it all for himself. In 1925, he made a trip to Palestine, visiting the Zionist settlements and speaking to such young leaders of the Jewish labor movement there as David Ben Gurion and Zalman Shazar. In his discussions with them, he remained adamant in his Marxian opposition to the "Utopian" socialist principle that the Zionist communes represented to him. "Mankind," he insisted, "is not developing in the direction of social experiments with small groups." And yet he was deeply impressed with what he saw. "I can't help it," he wrote in his first dispatch to the *Forward* from Palestine, "I must marvel at the heroic fire that burns in them."

After the Arab riots of 1929, Cahan rushed to Palestine again to cover their impact upon the Jewish community there. He still did not consider himself to be a Zionist, but there was no longer any doubt in his mind that he was in some way deeply identified with the fate of the Jewish community in Palestine. As he wrote in one of his dispatches this time:

> There was a time when battles and disputes about this subject used to flare forth between different parties and groups. I am convinced that this is now a thing of the past. Zionist or non-Zionist, party-man or what-have-you—in millions and millions of Jewish hearts a warm feeling has developed, a glorious hope that, in Palestine, a Jewish home is growing.

Cahan was careful to stress that this did not mean he was supporting Zionism. But Zionism was no longer the point, and the *Forward* now began giving more coverage to Palestine. In this it followed the trend of the New York Yiddish press in general, with the notable exception of the Communist and vehemently anti-Zionist *Freiheit*.

This increasing mellowness toward the Zionist form of Jewish nationalism was in part due to the fact that Yiddishism in New York, by the end of the twenties, was already passing its prime. A younger, American-born generation, the sons and daughters of the East European Jewish immigrants, were reaching maturity and already manifesting a pronounced lack of interest, if not hostility, regarding Yiddish culture. The *Forward* and other Yiddish papers had made numerous efforts to capture these young people, using such inducements as English-language supplements, but to no avail. This "second generation" was, for the most part, too American to interest itself in the Yiddish press—ironic testimony to the success of the *Forward* and other Yiddish papers in their aspirations to Americanize the Jewish immigrants and their offspring. In Jewish homes, the *Forward* was suddenly and unexpectedly taking on the role of a central element in the quaint and nostalgic apparatus that surrounded the elderly. Grandmother sat by the kitchen table reading her *Bintel Brief,* grandfather came wearily home from his meeting of retired Workmen's Circle members, his *Forward* tucked under his arm. Responding to a tacit conspiracy of condescension on the part of the young, the *Forward* and its readers retreated steadily into the nostalgia and sentimental Jewish chauvinism that was expected of them. Their culture and their convictions were now above all a defensive wall for a way of life that was threatened with extinction. The Bundist dream of a Yiddish-socialist culture was increasingly part of a nostalgic embracing of the past; it had no more future.

Cahan himself, no longer vexed by the conflicts between past and present that had dominated his youth, now simply settled for looking back upon his entire life, in Russia and in America equally, with a great wave of grandfatherly Yiddish nostalgia. Nostalgia, all-encompassing and all-forgiving, was the element that had been missing when he had attempted to survey his life in *The Chasm,* his unfinished novel of the turn of the century. He now had it in abundance, however, in the midtwenties, when he set to work writing his autobiography in Yiddish, *Bletter fun Mein Leben* ("Leaves From My Life"). This total affirmation of the first fifty-five years of his existence turned out to be a work of immense proportions. The first three volumes, published together in 1926, came to nearly fifteen hundred pages, but they only brought the story down to 1897, with the founding of the *Forward* and Cahan's first resignation from it. The fourth volume, which appeared two years later, was more than six hundred pages long; it bore the essence of Cahan's success story, starting with his career as an American novelist and journalist and ending with the gala fiftieth-birthday celebration that the *Forward* held for him at Carnegie Hall. At that point, the autobiographical novel really ended. Cahan wrote a fifth volume, but it bogged down in miscellaneous chatter about the round of public events with which the editor of a successful newspaper concerns himself, and ended in a 250-page section on the Leo Frank case. Cahan had intended a sixth volume, but there was clearly no more autobiography to write, since it and the *Forward* had become one and the same.

The fifth and, as it turned out, last volume of *Bletter fun Mein Leben* appeared in 1931, at a moment when some rapid and dramatic changes were about to take place in the world. Two years later, Franklin Delano Roosevelt was President of the United States and Adolf Hitler was in power in Germany, and the attitudes of the *Forward* were bound to be affected as a result. The New Deal became an irresistible magnet for the kind of moderate and pragmatic social-democratic trend among Jewish labor leaders that Cahan had long championed. It was not long after Roosevelt took office that Sidney Hillman, President of the Amalgamated Clothing Workers of America, was in Washington working with the National Labor Advisory Board of the National Recovery Administration. Hillman was a prime example of the new generation of labor leaders that had arisen with the coming of age of unionism on the Lower East Side. Born in Lithuania in 1887, he had been a Bundist and had served a six-month prison term during the 1905 revolution. Emigrating the following year, he had lived for a time in Manchester, England, and then crossed the Atlantic to settle in Chicago. There he made his way up through the ranks of the United Garment Workers' local; by the time he went in 1914 to live in New York, where he became president of the newly formed ACWA before the end of the year, he had become thoroughly schooled in the Gompersist conception of pragmatic, nonideological unionism. In the years that followed, Hillman and his union pursued their career untroubled by the kind of tortured and divisive ideological passions that had dominated the garment unions in the nineties. As for the ILGWU, it found an equivalent to Hillman in the young man who succeeded to its presidency after the death of Benjamin Schlesinger in 1932, David Dubinsky. Hillman and Dubinsky, who readily embraced the labor politics of the New Deal—and who seemed to obtain complete vindication for their views with the passage of the Wagner Labor Relations Act in 1935—were two younger men for whom Cahan's teachings had apparently become visceral, disciples of that complete adjustment to the American reality that he had struggled with great difficulty to instill among his contemporaries. Now Cahan needed only to follow these young moderates through to the logical conclusion that their views and actions implied.

And what remained to hold him back, after all? Despite the small pockets of resolutely Socialist and Communist loyalties that remained, the Jewish immigrants were now, under the impact of Roosevelt's personality and policies, becoming overwhelmingly Democrat in their voting preferences. Meanwhile, the Socialist Party, caught up in factional strife between a left wing relatively sympathetic to the Communists and a right wing relatively sympathetic to the New Deal, was steadily growing weaker. Debs was dead, Hillquit was dead, and so also was Meyer London, who had lost his Congressional seat in 1920 and was killed in a street accident seven years later. The old quarrels and the old aspirations now seemed completely buried in the past: Louis Miller, too, had died in 1928, a lonely and forgotten figure on the Lower East Side—he and Cahan had even become friendly again just before the end—and Morris Winchevsky had died in 1932, a member of the Communist Party after having journeyed to the Soviet Union, where he had been received as a cultural hero. What ties remained for Cahan with the Socialist Party of today, a mere shadow of its past? It seemed perfectly reasonable to be a social democrat and yet to support Roosevelt.

By the summer of 1936, when Roosevelt was about to run for a second term, the *Forward* and the garment unions with which it was allied were prepared to make their move. After the Democratic convention in August, a meeting was held in New York under the auspices of Cahan, Hillman, Dubinsky and other labor leaders, at which the American Labor Party was created. This was to be the means of endorsing Roosevelt's candidacy without having to support the Democratic Party, which was tainted with Tammany associations in New York and with racist associations in the South, and was still, after all, a "bourgeois" party. The ALP was to go on functioning as an independent New York party, a conveyer belt of social-democratic support to Democratic Presidential candidates, until the late forties, when it fell apart over the question of Communist infiltration into its ranks, and the Liberal Party was created to succeed it. The *Forward* now had its formula for supporting Roosevelt while continuing to carry the motto "Workers of all countries, unite!" on its masthead. Cahan became more vehement than ever in his denunciation of leftists of all varieties.

As the outlines of the *Forward*'s, socialism thus grew more difficult to discern, its Jewish nationalism, under the impact of Hitlerite persecution in Europe, grew stronger than ever. If Cahan had once perceived socialism as a new form of the traditional religious passion of the Jews, then it could be said that his socialism was now fading back into its Jewish origins. In general, the emergence of fascism seemed to be providing verification for that old Bundist mystique which had perceived, at bottom, some kind of common identity in Jewishness and socialism. To the Nazis in particular, Jews and Marxism were a single enemy. Being Jewish had thus become a pure, objective affirmation of one's identification with the progressive and antifascist cause in the world. For the *Forward,* the growing emergency faced by European Jewry gave rise to a passion to embrace all Jewish values against their detractors, even when the values had not necessarily always been those of the *Forward* and when the detractors were Jews themselves. As war broke out in 1939 and European Jewry entered upon the first stages of what was to be the most enormous disaster in its history, the *Forward*'s anguish at these events became increasingly focused upon a controversy that had broken out over the writings of Sholem Asch.

Asch was by this time not only the preeminent figure in Yiddish literature, but also its major offering to the world at large; for he had come to enjoy, through translations of his works, a general popularity that his greater predecessors had never known in their own lifetimes. The virtue that had made him so much in vogue among non-Yiddish readers was a middlebrowism much more skillful in its execution than Gordin's had been. With a great flair for storytelling, Asch drew upon a vast range of subjects and settings for his works, moving with ease from the *shtetl* to the great East European capitals to New York, and from the nineteenth and the twentieth centuries through the Middle Ages to ancient Palestine. It was in the latter locale, caught up with a mystical vision of Zionist regeneration all his own and with a notion of Judeo-Christian brotherhood partly inspired by the success his novels were enjoying among Gentile readers, that he discovered the figures of Jesus, Paul, and Mary. Even before Asch had done so, Zionist writers, having shaken off the tensions of exile and discovered the roots of Jewish culture in Palestinian soil, were beginning to discern the Jewish personality of the historical Jesus beneath the layers of centuries of Christian interpretation. The whole question was, of course, an extremely sensitive one for Jewish writers of East European origin, since pogroms and persecutions had after all been perpetrated for centuries in Jesus' name, whatever his personal virtues were. Asch, an impetuous spirit in his embrace of all his subjects, was not daunted by the delicacies of the matter, however. The novel that he wrote in 1938, *The Nazarene,* had tendencies in it which many Yiddish readers were bound to interpret as suggesting that Jews should accord Jesus a status not altogether unlike that accorded him by Christians. Indeed, this book and subsequent works and statements by Asch persuaded many that he was advocating mass Jewish conversion to Catholicism. In the course of the controversy that ensued, Asch was never able to come up with a clear statement of precisely what his philosophical view was in the matter.

The trouble began when Asch, then sojourning in Europe, sent in the first chapters of *The Nazarene* to be serialized in the *Forward,* as his novels usually were. Cahan read them and became infuriated. All his old scruples about offending the sensibilities of religious Jews—and perhaps a touch of long-buried orthodoxy of his own— came to the fore, and he refused to publish the novel. Asch protested, and another first-class Yiddish cultural controversy, traditional in its vehemence if not in its content, came into being. Cahan eventually wrote an entire pamphlet to explain his own views in the matter. For him, and for those who supported him in this—and in this instance, he gained support from many who were ordinarily his opponents— there was at stake the question of the integrity of the Jewish people at a moment when masses of Jews were being led to slaughter. One critic in the *Forward* at the end of the Second World War—when the controversy was still raging, and when the details of the Holocaust were first becoming widely known—even described Asch's works as threatening American Jewry with a "spiritual Maidenek." This invocation of the threat of a second Holocaust in the realm of culture seemed excessive even to some of Asch's detractors, but it was reflective of the mood of the time.

Meanwhile, the Jewish civilization of Eastern Europe had been destroyed. Warsaw, the scene of the last great flowering of Yiddish culture on native soil, was a pile of rubble, its name to be indelibly associated in mankind's imagination with the ultimate Ghetto of Europe's thousand-year-old history of anti-Jewish persecutions. In a final act of self-destructive rage, Germany had risen up and annihilated what remained of that ancient Jewish civilization which shared with it a common ancestry in medieval Central Europe; the old interplay between the German and the Ashkenazic Jewish cultures was at an end at last. Most of the survivors of the Jewish civilization were now either in the Soviet Union, where a systematic purge of Yiddish culture was about to take place, or in places of refuge in far-flung parts of the world. Some were eventually to make their way to Israel, others in large numbers to the United States.

The last wave of Yiddish writers reached New York after the war from the now-extinct source, but even this influx did little to stem the steady dwindling of size and energy that the Lower East Side culture was undergoing. Although many of their institutions continued to be located on the Lower East Side, few Yiddish intellectuals even made that neighborhood their home any more; most of them now lived on the Upper West Side of Manhattan. Deriving its creative energies increasingly from pure nostalgia, the Yiddish press shored up its strength for the post-World War II, post-Holocaust era. The old *Tageblatt* had died in the twenties, but the *Morning Journal* survived the war; by the beginning of the fifties, however, it had given up its separate existence and become absorbed by the *Day,* which had begun its own career by buying out the moribund *Wahrheit* at the end of the First World War. The *Freiheit* stayed alive on a shoestring; the first Communist daily newspaper in America, it was also the last. These three survivors of the Yiddish daily press showed considerable staying power. The combined *Day-Morning Journal* lasted two decades, finally closing up shop in 1972. The *Freiheit* still appears weekly. [It ceased publication in 1988—ed.] The *Forward*, which remained a daily until quite recently, now also appears only once a week. Indeed, one member of the *Forward* staff even emerged in the fifties and sixties as a major figure in American literature—albeit in translation from the original Yiddish—Isaac Bashevis Singer. In many ways an anachronism—for he is at least ten years younger than the youngest members of the last great wave of Yiddish writers of Eastern Europe—Singer, a native of Poland and a product of the Warsaw school, is also the least typical of Yiddish writers, for he is the one among them who has utterly repudiated the Haskalah tradition. But it is precisely his demonic vision of a superstition-ridden East European Jewry poised on the brink of disaster that has made his works particularly relevant to the modern sensibility in America and in the Western world at large, and has made them the most qualified in all of Yiddish literature to speak in the wake of the Holocaust. He won the Nobel Prize for Literature in 1978.

With the war's end, Cahan moved on into the rapidly growing silence of extreme old age. In 1946 he suffered a stroke, and control of the *Forward* passed increasingly into the hands of his managing editor, Hillel Rogoff. Cahan still made his iron hand felt whenever he could, however, and sometimes even the old fury poured forth, albeit in odd ways. Shortly after his wife died, he published two articles vigorously denouncing the writings of Turgenev. Some of Cahan's colleagues believed that this was a final answer to his wife, who had always been Turgenev's champion against Cahan's denunciations of him. During her last illness, he had discovered a newly published edition of Chekhov's letters, in which Chekhov had spoken critically of Turgenev. Cahan had eagerly awaited the moment when, upon her recovery, he could press home to her this evidence of his triumph. But she died, and so he published his arguments instead, in these two articles. Thus after sixty years of common experience, nostalgia, some love, more than a little antagonism, and occasional separations, he had made his final farewell to the *barishnya* of his household. Was it in her honor that he had given the name Anna to David Levinsky's last true love, about whom his protagonist had said: "Through all these ephemeral infatuations and interests I am in love with Anna"? One wonders how much of her had been in the ever-present, proud, tormenting women of his stories and novels. In any case, he did not survive the loss of her for very long. In August, 1951, having lived through and presided over the entire life cycle of the Jewish culture of the Lower East Side, from its birth to its decline, he closed his eyes at last upon a world that was no longer his. The Jewish immigrants had been his only children, and they needed his help no longer.

Cahan had lived long enough even to see his grandchildren—the "second generation," offspring of the Yiddish-speaking immigrants—grow up, and to witness in them a cycle of hard struggle, dazzling success, and spiritual anticlimax similar to the one he had himself undergone at an earlier time. They lived the successes and the disappointments of David Levinsky all over again, beginning this time in the American slum ghetto instead of in the Russian *shtetl*, struggling through the Depression of the thirties as Levinsky had done through that of 1893, and coming to rest as often in the new suburbia as in the affluent reaches of uptown Manhattan or the equivalent. Once they had finished that climb and their material struggles came to an end, they found themselves dwelling with growing frequency upon the question, raised by David Levinsky, of what had happened to their inner selves in the process.

For the great majority of middle-class American Jews, particularly those who, like Levinsky, had achieved their successes in business, this question was asked within the framework of the modern, Americanized synagogue, and was addressed primarily to a tradition of Jewish religious and personal moral values which had grown lax. In other words, the question here was the one that David Levinsky addressed to his childhood when he said: "David, the poor lad swinging over a Talmud volume at the Preacher's Synagogue, seems to have more in common with my inner identity than David Levinsky, the well-known cloak-manufacturer." What becomes of those simple pieties of old when one grows rich? This is the wry inquiry that underlies most of the sermons intoned through the microphones of suburban congregations.

But it is the intellectuals of the "second generation," the direct successors, not of Cahan's fictitious businessman but of the author himself, who have had to deal with the even more perturbing question that echoes in the background of the novel. For Levinsky, as we have seen, was really a Jewish intellectual in disguise, who nearly had within his grasp a creed for his maturity that could have fulfilled the religious passions which were the legacy of his boyhood. Levinsky, of course, had let the opportunity evade him altogether; but hadn't Cahan, after all, ultimately lost his grasp on such a creed as well? A firm commitment to moderate social democracy and to the promise of the New Deal hardly entailed the kind of religious passion that accompanied his youthful adherence to *Narodnaya Volya*. The equivalent to this transformation is that of Tzinchadzi trading in his horse for some real estate.

By the time of Cahan's death, the "second generation" intellectuals had gone through a similar transformation. The nineteen-thirties and forties had been for them what the eighteen-eighties and nineties had been for Cahan, a time of youthful radical exuberance and passionate embracing and rejecting of creeds. In a way that had been foreshadowed by Cahan's English-language journalism and fiction in the nineties, the Jewish intellectuals of the thirties helped create a proletarian literary culture that included Jewish traits among its essential characteristics: not only was Michael Gold's description of his boyhood on the Lower East Side, *Jews Without Money,* one of the definitive works of that culture, but there were also included in it many pieces of imaginative writing in which Jews were portrayed in the guise of some other minority or oppressed group, such as the Italians of Clifford Odets' *Golden Boy*. This decisive role played by the offspring of East European Jewish immigrants in establishing the tone of the plebeian culture of the thirties was not exclusively reserved for serious literature, either; indeed, it was in the entertainment arts—above all, movies and radio—that they achieved their greatest fulfillment, as producers, directors, writers, and performers. Surely the most complete embodiment in the popular arts of the day of the average immigrant's liberal-democratic dream was the succession of performances by Paul Muni—formerly Muni Weisenfreund of the Yiddish Art Theater of Second Avenue—in the roles of various great nineteenth-century crusaders for justice and truth.

Like Cahan, the artists and intellectuals of the "second generation" passed from that period of youthful exuberance through a time of social upheaval, war, and revolution, into what was, for the most part, an attitude of moderate, establishmentarian liberalism, and to a certain spiritual disappointment that went with it. And, as it had done for Cahan, this journey brought them ultimately to their best imaginative writing, for the renaissance of American-Jewish fiction that took place in the fifties and sixties was their equivalent to *The Rise of David Levinsky*. Like Cahan, they explored the paradox of being an exiled European intellectual—for even the American-born intellectuals of this generation were ultimately European in the cast of their ideas—adrift in America, filled with dismay by it, and yet in the end strangely capable of mastering its requirements for worldly success. The one great difference between themselves and Cahan is that they no longer found it necessary to tell their own story in the guise of a businessman. Saul Bellow's Moses Herzog, for example—perhaps the definitive fictitious creation of this renaissance—is unabashedly an affluent intellectual, the type who has "made it" just as decisively in the new world of huge faculties, research foundations and communications empires as David Levinsky did in the garment industry (the difference in income between the one and the other is beside the point here). The tragedy of the Herzogs, of course, is that the America which now so amply rewards their creative energies no longer even cares that those energies were first kindled by the light of great European struggles, over which they had suffered all the more by the fact of being separated from them by vast oceans. Their creations, like Cahan's, had been but the dream of the Russian revolution, their successes the legacy of their disappointment in its outcome and in themselves for not having experienced it. What was left for them to do, then, but write the chronicle of that disappointment? Somewhere in that story is the secret of their identity, both utterly American and utterly Jewish at the same time.

# Appendix

# Some Notes on Transliteration, and a Glossary

To those readers who are concerned with the establishment of a system for transliterating Yiddish words, I apologize for the violations they will consider this book to have committed. For my own part, I have found that Yiddish will not readily yield to a single and uniform system, for as any reader of the language knows, there are numerous inconsistencies of spelling to be found, not only between one writer and another but, often enough, within the works of a single writer. In the period covered in this book, Yiddish was a language still in search of its identity, and this search was reflected in, among other things, its uneven orthography and grammar. I found it essential for the story I wanted to tell to reflect this unevenness as an aspect of the language's literary growth.

There is much in this book, for example, about the relationship between the Yiddish and German languages, especially in the early years on the Lower East Side. Now, this is a delicate matter among Yiddishists, who naturally seek to demonstrate as fully as possible their language's cultural independence, above all from the tongue that was spoken by the worst persecutors the Jews have ever known. But the fact remains that the relationship between German and Yiddish is incontestably close at numerous points, and that many of the earlier Yiddish writers had a strong element of pure German in their diction. A proper understanding of the history of the Yiddish language and culture requires that this element be recognized. For example, as this book demonstrates, Lower East Side Yiddish newspapers were often given names that were in fact pure German, such as *Wahrheit* ("Truth") instead of the Yiddish *Emmes,* or even *Vorwärts* ("Forward") instead of, say, *Foroys.* In many cases, such as that of the *Vorwärts* or the *Arbeiter Zeitung,* the name was taken directly from that of a German model or predecessor. It seems to me that it would be misleading to render these names in any spelling but the German.

But, on the other hand, it would be doing violence to both Yiddish and German to try, as some writers have done, to render all of Yiddish in accordance with the principles of German spelling. The results usually are as incomprehensible as they are aesthetically revolting; besides, I too am Yiddishist enough to be unwilling to depict *mamme loshn* in the role of an abortive German dialect. It was therefore necessary for me to strike a compromise and settle for a humane inconsistency in the transliteration. In contexts that seem to me to be pure German—such as the names of many of the Yiddish periodicals, and certain names of organizations—I have used the German spelling; in the purely Yiddish contexts, however, I have transliterated by using the letters whose sounds *in English* correspond most nearly to those of the Hebrew letters as used in the Yiddish original. Hence, the initial sound of the essentially German or Judeo-German newspaper title *Wahrheit* is in most other contexts (i.e., the Yiddish contexts) rendered with a *v,* as in *vos* ("what"). But certain other principles of German spelling which seem to me indispensable are retained in purely Yiddish contexts. This is done partly out of a desire to make comprehension as available as possible to those readers who know German but not Yiddish, and partly out of personal taste. Despite the prescriptions of the YIVO Institute for Jewish Research—to whom all students of Yiddish are at least partly in debt—I cannot bring myself to spell the Yiddish word for "my" as *mayn* instead of *mein.*

English words were frequently incorporated into the Yiddish of the authors quoted in this book, and in these cases I have tried to strike a balance between a spelling that would show up the original English word clearly to the reader and would also render, as closely as possible, the Yiddish pronunciation intended by the author. In the case of a word like *shvindel,* it is easy to do both at once without violating the general principles of transliterating that I have tried to follow. On the other hand, I saw fit to commit a violation in the case of a pair of words like *greener* (a green one, a greenhorn) and *oys-gegreent* ("de-greened," i.e., a seasoned veteran), which would have been spelled *griner* or *griener,* etc., if I were consistent, but which then would not have been so easily recognizable to the English reader.

Still other inconsistencies are due to an effort on my part to be faithful to the spelling of each author, for this sometimes has the effect of being a factor in literary style. Finally, I have settled for some minor inconsistencies on aesthetic grounds, since certain variant renderings are more appropriate to certain contexts than the original rendering. In the body of the book, for example, I have given the *Forward* its original German name (it was even transliterated *Vorwärts* on the masthead in the newspaper's early days); but in the Yiddish titles in the bibliography I have rendered it *Forverts,* since anything else would have been an injustice both to the spirit of these titles and the intentions of their authors.

Let me provide a few general hints about the pronunciation of the Yiddish words as transliterated in this book. Like Yiddish spelling, Yiddish pronunciation is full of inconsistencies, varying greatly according to the region of origin. At best, the reader for whom Yiddish is not a mother tongue can only achieve a very rough approximation of the sounds. Nevertheless, even such an approximation is desirable for enjoyment of some of the poetic passages quoted in this book. Here are some general principles for pronouncing the transliterated words:

*Vowels:* With a few exceptions—such as in *greener*—which will, I hope, be plain to the eye, vowels should be pronounced in the

European rather than the Anglo-Saxon fashion—short *a, e, i,* and *u* (which is an *oo* rather than an *uh*). The *o* sound is subject to great dialectal variation in Yiddish, but it will serve one's purposes here to pronounce it roughly as an *aw.* In Yiddish words of Germanic origin, the German *ei* (pronounced long *i*) and *ie* (pronounced long *e*) are regularly used in this book, as in *mein* and *tziel.* But in Yiddish words of Hebrew origin, the long *i* sound is rendered *ay,* as in *bobba-mayse.* The letters *ey,* as pronounced in the English "hey," are regularly used in this book for that characteristically Yiddish sound. Final *e* is always to be sounded.

*Consonants:* The reader who knows no German at all will have problems here, and I apologize for choosing a course that partially excludes him. As I have said, in words that are obviously pure German, I have used the German spelling, and for Yiddish words I have used an English spelling. This is why, for example, the same sound is spelled with a *z* in some contexts (German) and with a *tz* in others (Yiddish); or, to put it another way, this is why the letter *z* is sometimes used as Germans pronounce it (as in *Zeitung*) and sometimes—the great majority of cases—used as Anglo-Saxons pronounce it (as in *zein,* "to be"). Even the reader who knows no German should, if he is careful, be able to perceive which case is which.

The most crucial consonant sound to deal with in Yiddish is the guttural that corresponds to the hard *ch* in German (*ach*), or to the *ch* sound in the Scottish *loch.* Except in German words, this sound is regularly rendered in this book as *kh.* Some writers render this Yiddish sound with a *ch,* as it is in the German or the Scottish, but I find this undesirable. For one thing, the Yiddish sound is considerably stronger than either the German or the Scottish one, and for another, Yiddish also contains a *ch* sound which corresponds exactly to ours in "Charles," and these letters should be reserved for it.

Below I have assembled a small glossary, not of every Yiddish word that appears in the book (long Yiddish passages in the book are followed in each case by an English translation), but of those that recur without being explained every time. It also includes some frequently used Hebrew, Russian, and German words; in each case, the language or languages that the word properly belongs to in the context of this book is indicated in parentheses. Proper names which appear in the index are not included here.

# *Glossary*

*arbeiter* (Yiddish and German): worker, workers

*badkhen* (Yiddish): a wedding-bard

*barishnya* (Russian): a young lady, a girl of refinement, a girl gymnasium student

*bobba-mayse* (Yiddish): old wives' tale, a tall story. *Bobba* means "grandmother," but in this case it also comes from "Bova," the hero of a fantastic Judeo-German narrative of the sixteenth century.

*Deitshmerish* (Yiddish): a Yiddish diction heavily loaded with Germanisms

*emmes* (Yiddish and Hebrew): truth

*goles* (Yiddish and Hebrew): exile, the diaspora, a state of utter alienation. In modern Hebrew, it is pronounced *galut*.

*greener* (American Yiddish): a greenhorn, a new immigrant. When one has learned the ropes in America, he is considered to have become *oysgegreent* ("de-greened").

*Hasid*, pl. *Hasidim* (Yiddish and Hebrew): literally a "pious one," a member of a pietist Jewish sect—called Hasidism in this book—founded in Eastern Europe in the eighteenth century by Israel ben Eliezer, the "Baal Shem Tov" ("Master of the Good Name").

*Haskalah* (Hebrew): literally, "Enlightenment." An intellectual movement which, under the influence of the Mendelssohnian Jewish "Enlightenment" in Germany, sought to propagate Western knowledge and ideas among East European Jews, but which, unlike its German counterpart, used Hebrew as its medium of discourse. A follower of the Haskalah is a *maskil* (pl. *maskilim*), an "enlightened one."

*Kaddish* (Hebrew): the Jewish prayer for the dead

*Khazzer-Mark* (Yiddish): literally, "Pig Market." This name was given by the Yiddish-speaking immigrants to the area centering upon the intersection of Hester and Ludlow Streets in which, for many years, the day's transactions in the garment industry—including the hiring of labor—took place every morning, amidst great hubbub.

*kosher* (Hebrew): ritually clean according to Jewish law; by extension, anything that is perfectly Jewish or otherwise perfectly all right.

*kruzhok* (Russian): literally, "circle" or "society." In this book, the word refers to the revolutionary circle to which Abraham Cahan belonged as a student in Vilna.

*landsman* (Yiddish): a compatriot, an immigrant from the same town or area as oneself. A society of immigrants from the same home town is a *landsmanshaft*.

*Litvak* (Yiddish): literally, a Lithuanian Jew; but the word has a pejorative or ironic ring, and it usually refers to personality traits popularly associated with the Lithuanian Jew: skepticism, coldness, rationalism. Sometimes the word is used for a person bearing these traits even when he is not from Lithuania. When the word was applied to Abraham Cahan, both meanings were intended as a rule.

*mamme loshn* (Yiddish): literally, "mother tongue," referring, of course, to the Yiddish language. If more than one connotation of the use of *mamme* here meets the eye, this is the point.

*maskil* (Hebrew): see Haskalah

*mazzel* (Yiddish and Hebrew): luck. *Mazzel-tov*, which is shouted at weddings, can be literally translated "good luck," but it means a great deal more, carrying connotations of infinite joy. Its opposite, *shlimmazzel*, refers not only to a condition but to a person, aptly described by Irving Howe and Eliezer Greenberg in *A Treasury of Yiddish Stories* (New York, 1954) as "a luckless creature of infinite misfortune."

*melammed* (Yiddish): a teacher, usually on the elementary levels of the traditional East European Jewish educational system.

*misnagid*, pl. *misnagdim* (Yiddish): literally, "opponent"; specifically, an opponent of the Hasidic movement.

*Narodnik*, pl. *Narodnikii* (Russian): often literally translated "populist," but this has a misleading connotation in America. The word comes from *narod*, meaning "the people"; a *Narodnik* was one of those who literally went "to the people" during the early stages of the nineteenth-century Russian revolutionary movement. Later, the word took on a broader meaning, and referred to any participant in the early, pre-Marxist stage of the Russian revolutionary movement.

*oysgegreent* (American Yiddish): see *greener*

*parveh lokshn* (Yiddish): *parveh* describes any food that is free of either meat or dairy components and can therefore, according to Jewish dietary laws, be eaten with anything. *Lokshn*—"noodles"—is one such *parveh* dish. This term, used by the Yiddish-speaking social democrats to describe the compromise ideal of "nonpartisanship" held up by their anarchist opponents, speaks for itself in the context.

*shtetl*, pl. *shtetlakh* (Yiddish): the typical small town or village of the Russian Jewish Pale of Settlement

*treyf, treyfa* (Yiddish and Hebrew): not *kosher*, ritually unclean; by extension, anything that represents a violation or a compromise of some principle, especially of Jewishness

*Verein* (German and Yiddish): literally, "union," "association," "society," etc. On the Lower East Side it was the term regularly attached to a succession of discussion groups and political clubs.

*yeshiva-bokher* (Yiddish): literally, a "yeshiva boy," a yeshiva student. The yeshiva is the institute of higher learning in the traditional Jewish educational system; graduation from it gives one rabbinical ordination. But *yeshiva-bokher* has many connotations; in this book, it also means an old-fashioned type of pious Jewish boy, who is unworldly and inordinately shy.

# BIBLIOGRAPHY AND NOTES

⁓

ALTHOUGH THESE BIBLIOGRAPHICAL NOTES SHOULD BE OF USE
to those who wish to pursue further the subject matter of this book, it
is not my intention to give an exhaustive list of relevant titles. Rather,
what I want to do here above all is honor those books which have
been of particular use to me in the course of this work. In order to
adhere to this purpose, I have confined my choice of citations here
in two ways. First, I am listing only *books* (with a few exceptions):
a large part of the material in my work comes from newspapers and
periodicals, particularly the Yiddish press, but those sources are indicated in the text and need not be repeated here. And second, I am
listing only those books which have served as *documentary* sources;
numerous *literary* works—mainly poems and fiction—are also discussed in this book, but they, once again, speak for themselves in the
text and need not be listed here.

I am going to cite my principal sources chapter by chapter, but
let me begin by naming a few books that were used throughout this
entire work. Chief among these is, of course, Abraham Cahan's
immense autobiography, *Bletter fun Mein Leben* (5 volumes, New
York, 1926–1931); this work is a treasure-house of information on
Cahan's life and on the history of the Lower East Side, and I have
used it abundantly. There are numerous passages in my work which
narrate scenes from Cahan's life in detail, using even spoken dia-

logue; these, except where otherwise indicated, are from *Bletter fun Mein Leben*. Cahan provided a vast amount of other material, too, some of it between covers and most of it scattered through more than sixty years of journalism; I used much of this, but another *book* of his I used frequently throughout was his novel, *The Rise of David Levinsky* (New York, 1917).

There were a few other books that were helpful to me throughout the preparation of this work. Melech Epstein, *Profiles of Eleven* (Detroit, 1965), is a portrait gallery of eleven prominent figures in the Jewish socialist milieu of the old Lower East Side, written by a man who worked with almost all of them personally. The factual material in it is sometimes fuzzy, but the evocation is always true. Another invaluable source was Hutchins Hapgood, *The Spirit of the Ghetto* (New York, 1902); this is a classic, and I have discussed it in some detail in Chapter 9. Finally, Moses Rischin, *The Promised City* (Boston, 1962), a scholarly study of the Lower East Side Jewish community prior to the First World War, was an ever-useful compendium of information.

Here now are the principal sources used in each chapter:

Prologue. Although I am confining my citations to *books* for the most part, I nevertheless here want to thank Maurice Samuel for his article, "My Friend, the Late Moses Herzog" (*Midstream*, April, 1966, pp. 3–25), which suggested the juxtaposition of Heine and Bialik that forms the epigraph to this prologue. The information on the Heine statue comes from Curt Pabst, *Lore's Leiden* (New York, 1899), a German-language pamphlet issued to accompany its dedication.

CHAPTER 1. My principal sources on the assassination of Alexander II and the revolutionary movement were: Avrahm Yarmolinsky, *Road to Revolution* (New York, 1962); and "Stepniak" (Sergey Kravchinsky), *Underground Russia* (London, 1883). On the history of the Jews in Russia and Poland, the definitive work is still S. M. Dubnow, *History of the Jews in Russia and Poland,* translated by I. Friedlaender (3 vols.,

Philadelphia, 1916); Louis Greenberg, *The Jews in Russia* (2 vols., New Haven, 1944, 1951), is also quite useful. For Yiddish literature, Leo Wiener, *The History of Yiddish Literature in the 19th Century* (New York, 1899), is still the best study in English for the limited period it covers; it is excellently supplemented by Yudel Mark's essay on Yiddish literature in Louis Finkelstein, ed., *The Jews: Their History, Culture and Religion* (4 vols., Philadelphia, 1949). The last part of this chapter is mainly from Cahan, *Bletter,* vol. 1.

CHAPTER 2. Among the various books I consulted on New York history, the two most useful to me were: Edward Robb Ellis, *The Epic of New York City* (New York, 1966), and Nathan Silver, *Lost New York* (New York, 1967). On the Jewish immigration to New York, the most important works used were: Samuel Joseph, *Jewish Immigration to the United States* (New York, 1914); Rischin, *op. cit.,* and Cahan, *Bletter* and *David Levinsky.* On Jewish tenement life and on the garment industry: Jacob Riis, *How the Other Half Lives* (New York, 1890), and Louis Lorwin (Louis Levine), *The Women's Garment Workers* (New York, 1924).

CHAPTER 3. Bernard Weinstein's long career in the Lower East Side labor movement gave him material for two highly useful books that he wrote: *Die Yiddishe Unions in America* (New York, 1929), and *Fertzig Yohr in Die Yiddishe Arbeter Bavegung in America* (New York, 1932): These books provided the anecdote which opens this chapter, as well as other material here and in Chapter 4. Also used, in addition to them and to Cahan, *Bletter,* vol. 2, were Hertz Burgin, *Geshikhte fun der Yiddisher Arbeter Bavegung in America, Russland, un England* (New York, 1915), and Morris Hillquit, *History of Socialism in the United States* (New York, 1903). Emma Goldman provided the material on Johann Most, both in her autobiography, *Living My Life* (2 vols., New York, 1931) and in an article on Most in the *American Mercury,* June, 1926, pp. 158–166.

CHAPTER 4. The account of the Haymarket Affair comes mainly from Henry David, *The History of the Haymarket Affair* (New

York, 1936); this book also was useful for background material on the American labor movement in this period, along with Samuel Gompers, *Seventy Years of Life and Labor* (New York, 1925), and Norman J. Ware, *The Labor Movement in the United States 1860–1890* (New York, 1929). Material on the Jewish labor movement was provided by Melech Epstein, *op. cit.* and *Jewish Labor in U.S.A.* (2 vols., New York, 1950, 1953); Morris Hillquit's autobiography, *Loose Leaves from a Busy Life* (New York, 1934); Abraham Rogoff, *Formative Years of the Jewish Labor Movement in the United States* (New York, 1945); and Elias Tcherikower, ed., *Geshikhte fun der Yiddisher Arbeter Bavegung in die Fereinigte Shtatn* (2 vols., New York, 1943, 1945); as well as the works cited for the previous chapter by Cahan, Weinstein, and Emma Goldman.

CHAPTER 5. The chief source throughout this chapter, in addition to the newspapers themselves, is vol. 3 of Cahan's *Bletter;* also useful on the newspaper background were Mordecai Soltes, *The Yiddish Press* (New York, 1925); Joseph Cohen, *Die Yiddishe Anarkhistishe Bavegung* (Philadelphia, 1945); and Tcherikower, *op. cit.* On Barondess and the 1890 cloakmakers' strike, the main sources were Cahan, *Bletter;* Lorwin, *op. cit.;* Emma Goldman, *op. cit.;* Melech Epstein, *Profiles;* and Jacob Magidoff, *Der Shpiegel fun der East Side* (New York, 1923).

CHAPTER 6. My main source material for this chapter was, of course, the works of the poets themselves, which are available in various collected editions. General background is provided in the works by Leo Weiner and by Yudel Mark cited above. Biographies of the various poets are in Zalmen Reisin, *Lexicon fun der Yiddisher Literatur* (2 vols., Vilna, 1928, 1929). I also drew upon Solomon Liptzin, *Eliakum Zunser, Poet of His People* (New York, 1950), and Kalmon Marmor's biography of Morris Winchevsky in vol. 1 of Winchevsky's collected works (New York, 1927).

CHAPTER 7. Cahan, *Bletter,* vol. 3, is once again the chief source, supplemented by the works cited above by Burgin and Weinstein.

Further material on the events leading to the founding of the *Forward* is in Jacob C. Rich, *Sixty Years of the "Jewish Daily Forward"* (a special supplement to the *New Leader* of June 3, 1957), and Mendel Osherowitch, *Die Geshikhte fun Forverts 1897–1947* (typescript, 1947, New York Public Library, Jewish Collection). Background on the labor and socialist history in this chapter is in Hillquit, *History of Socialism in the United States;* Gompers, *op. cit.;* Ware, *op. cit.;* and David A. Shannon, *The Socialist Party of America* (New York, 1955).

CHAPTER 8. The sources are the works by Cahan that are cited in the text, as well as *Bletter,* vol. 4.

CHAPTER 9. *Bletter,* vol. 4; of course, *The Autobiography of Lincoln Steffens* (New York, 1931); Hutchins Hapgood, *The Spirit of the Ghetto* (New York, 1902) and *A Victorian in the Modern World* (New York, 1939; Norman Hapgood, *The Changing Years* (New York, 1930); and Jacob Riis, *How the Other Half Lives* (New York, 1890).

CHAPTER 10. As in Chapter 8.

CHAPTER 11. Chiefly, *Bletter,* vol. 4; and *The Jewish Daily Forward* in that period; also, Rich, *op. cit.;* and Osherowitch, *op. cit.*

CHAPTER 12. The main treasure-house for the information here is B. Gorin (I. Goido), *Die Geshikhte fun Yiddishen Theater* (2 vols., New York, 1918). Hutchins Hapgood, *The Spirit of the Ghetto,* is another indispensable source. Also useful are Steffens, *op. cit.;* and Zalmen Zylbercwaig, ed., *Lexicon fun Yiddishen Theater* (New York, 1931).

CHAPTER 13. In addition to Gordin's plays, the sources are those listed above, as well as Melech Epstein, *Profiles,* and Kalmon Marmor, *Jacob Gordin* (in Yiddish; New York, 1953).

CHAPTER 14. Two sources in English on the Bund are Bernard K. Johnpoll, *The Politics of Futility* (Ithaca, 1967); and Isaac Deutscher's description of Trotsky's role in expelling the Bund from the 1903 congress of the Russian Social Democratic Party, in vol. 1 of *The Prophet Armed* (Oxford, 1954). For the rest, Cahan provides the material, in *Bletter*, vol. 4, and in the other writings dealt with in this chapter.

CHAPTER 15. Entirely from the *Forward*, the *Wahrheit*, and *Bletter*, vol. 4.

CHAPTER 16. Same as above, as well as: W. A. Swanberg, *Citizen Hearst* (New York, 1961); Hillel Rogoff, *Der Geist fun Forverts* (New York, 1954); Kalmon Marmor, *Jacob Gordin*; and Melech Epstein, *Profiles*.

CHAPTER 17. Chiefly *Bletter*, vol. 5; Lorwin, *op. cit.*; and Epstein, *Profiles*.

CHAPTER 18. The chief sources are Cahan's writings, especially vol. 5 of *Bletter*, and the two versions—as magazine serial and as finished book—of *The Rise of David Levinsky*. Also: Rich, *op. cit.*; and Osherowitch, *op. cit.*

CHAPTER 19. This chapter is the product of wide reading and conversation, but I can make mention of the following: Rich, *op. cit.*; Osherowitch, *op. cit.*; and Epstein, *Profiles*. Cahan's articles on Palestine and his polemic against Sholem Asch were both collected and published in book form by the *Forward*. Also useful on the Asch controversy was Hayim Greenberg's essay, "Sholem Asch's Christological Writings," in *The Inner Eye*, vol. 2, ed. by Shlomo Katz (New York, 1964). For the Yiddish theater in this period, David S. Lifson, *The Yiddish Theater in America* (New York, 1965), was most helpful.

## NOTES

1 That is, the watch is pawned.

2 As a follow-up to successes like these, a separate column eventually was established solely for the purpose of putting out the call for missing husbands, not all of whom were eager to be found.

3 It should be remembered that we are here still discussing the magazine series and not the novel that was later rewritten from it.

# Index

## A

*Abend Blatt*, 169, 170, 176, 268
Abramovich, Sholom. *See* Mendele
    Moicher S'forim
Abramowitz, Bina, 306
Academy of Music, 44
Adler, Charley, 381
Adler, Felix, 67
Adler, Jacob P., 290, 293, 295, 297,
    301, 302, 303, 306, 307, 309
Adler, Sarah, 302
Adler, Viktor, 150
Advice columns
    *Bintel Briefs*, 358–365
    Cahan and Miller's rivalry in
        writing, 356–365, 365
    in *Forward*, 261–262
    as "true novel," 355, 357, 358, 363
    in *Wahrheit*, 354–356
*Age of Innocence, The* (Wharton),
    43–44, 210
*Agunah*, 139
Ahearn, Edward J., 316, 317
*Alef-Beys fun Trade-Unionism, Der*
    (Winchevsky), 145
Aleichem, Sholem. *See* Sholem
    Aleichem
Aleinikoff, Nikolay, 68, 71–72, 73,
    86
Alexander III (Russia), 152–153
Alexander II (Russia)

    assassination of, 12
    attempts on life of, 8–12
    in Jewish assimilation, 26
    reactions to assassination of,
        35–36
    Zunser's poetry on, 131
*Allgemeine Arbeiterbund*, 76
*Alliance Israélite Universelle*, 15
Amalgamated Clothing Workers of
    America, 410, 441
American Federation of Labor, 159,
    164
American Labor Party, 443
American liberalism, 250
American Tobacco Company strike,
    268–269
"America's Most Interesting Daily"
    (Villard), 435
*Am Olam* movement, 38–39, 68, 133
Anarchists and anarchism
    Cahan's rejection of, 85–86
    decline in power of, 158
    formation of rival union by,
        161–162
    Haymarket Affair and, 82–84
    infiltration of *Yiddisher Arbeiter*
        *Verein* by, 88–89
    labor unions and, 87, 95–96
    publication of newspaper by,
        99–100, 111–112
    in union leadership, 114–115

Anglo-Jewish Association, 139
Anti-Semitism. *See also* Pogroms
　the Jewish Question and, 148–150
　Leo Frank trial and, 425–426
Anti-Socialist Law of 1878, 77
"Apostate of Chego-Chegg" (Cahan),
　231–233
*Appleton's English Grammar*, 201
*Arbeiter Freind* (newspaper), 100,
　102, 105, 143–144
*Arbeiter Zeitung* (Chicago
　newspaper), 81
*Arbeiter Zeitung* (New York
　newspaper)
　on Barondess, 123
　Cahan and, 105–111, 156–157,
　　169, 175, 195
　dual unionism impact on,
　　162–163
　founding of, 103, 105–111
　Gordin as contributor to, 299–300
　management conflicts on,
　　155–156
　rivalry with *Die Freie Arbeiter
　　Stimme*, 112
　*Sidra* feature in, 109–110, 185–186
*Arbeiter Zeitung* Publishing
　Association, 106, 156, 177, 371
*Arbel*, 187
Asch, Sholem, 352, 437, 444–445
Ashkenazi, Jacob ben Isaac, 22
Ashkenazic Jews
　Cossack revolt and, 17–18
　in Germany, 18
　immigration to America, 47–48
　in Poland, 17–18
*Ashkenazim*, term, 17
Associated Waist and Dress
　Manufacturers, 399
*Atlantic Monthly*, 225, 236
*Aunt Sosia* (Goldfaden), 282
*Autobiography of an American Jew*
　(Cahan), 417
*Autobiography of Lincoln Steffens*,
　203, 211
Aveling, Edward, 154
Axelrod, Paul, 328

**B**

*Ba'al Eytzah, Der*, advice column,
　365
Baal Shem Tov, 18
Bachmann, M., 85–86
"Back to Dear Old Russia—the
　Disillusionment of Sonia
　Rogova" (Cahan), 324–325
*Badkhen*, 129
Bakers' union, 92
Bakunin, Michael, 76
*Balagula*, 186
Balfour Declaration of 1917, 438
Bandes, Leo, 90, 157
*Barishnyas*, 30–31
*Bar Kochba* (Goldfaden), 293
Barondess, Joseph, 101, 112, 159, 273
　anarchist sentiment of, 114–115
　charges of extortion made against,
　　123–124
　in cloakmakers' strike, 94–95, 173
　in formation of rival union, 161,
　　162
　in sewing-machine operators'
　　strike, 118, 119
　socialist and anarchist disagreement
　　concerning, 121–122
　on typesetters' strike, 371
　vilification of, by press, 120
Beiliss, Mendel, 425–426
Bellamy, Edward, 164
Bellamyite Nationalists Club, 164
Bellow, Saul, 450
Ben-Gurion, David, 439
Bialik, Chaim Nachman, 1
*Bintel, Brief, A* (Cahan), 358–365
Bird watching, 270–271
Black Plague of 1348, 16
*Bletter fun Mein Leben* (Cahan), 441
Board of Arbitration, 175
*Bobba-mayse*, 24
*Bobba mit dem Eynikel, Die*
　(Goldfaden), 283–284
Bochur, Elijah, 24
Bogaraz, Natan, 326–327, 332
"Bontshe the Silent" (Peretz), 192,
　300

*Bova-Book* (Bochur), 24
Bowery, The, 294
Branch 8, of Socialist Labor Party,
    89–90
Branch 17, of Socialist Labor Party,
    90
Brandeis, Louis D., 400
Braslavsky, Abel, 99
Brilliant, Sam, 357
Broder, Ephraim, 277
Brody singers, 277
"Broken Heart, A" (Miller), 354–355
Bronstein, Anna, 74–75
Brooklyn, New York, 213
Brotherhood of Tailors, 404, 406
Bucharest, Rumania, 284
*Bukoviner Israelitishe Folksblatt*
    (newspaper), 280
Bund, The, 327–331, 372, 436
Bundism, 132
Bury, J., 224
Butler, Benjamin F., 84

**C**
Cahan, Abraham, 6, 28–39
    as advocate for tolerance, 256
    on America, 413–414
    on anarchism, 85–86
    *Arbeiter Zeitung* and, 105–111,
        156–157, 169, 175
    on arrival in New York, 40–41
    autobiography of, 441
    on Castle Garden, 42
    as cavalier to female students,
        30–34
    *Commercial Advertiser* and,
        208–209, 212, 215, 223
    on communal movement, 38–39
    countryside sojourn of, 270–272
    in creation of David Levinsky,
        417–425
    on Daniel De Leon, 165–168
    death of, 448
    debate with Roman Lewis, 121
    as drama critic, 276
    on dual unionism, 162–163, 166
    early life of, 28–30

    as English instructor, 66
    on essence of American possibility,
        53–54
    on execution of Haymarket Square
        anarchists, 84
    Gordin and, feud with, 312–314,
        322, 385–387
    on Gordin's *Siberia*, 304–305
    on Gordin's *Tageblatt* denunciation,
        319–320
    *Jewish Daily Forward* and, 204,
        205–206, 207–208, 244, 248,
        251–255, 261–262, 266, 269,
        274, 353
    on Jewish Question, 148–150
    on Jewish success in America,
        416–417
    at Jewish Teachers' Institute, 30
    as journalist, 213–215
    as literary critic, 184
    marriage of, 74
    at meeting on coalition newspaper,
        101–103
    on Miller, 373–374, 379–380
    on musical metaphor, 368–369
    as philosopher, 181
    on pogroms, 331–332
    as *Propaganda Verein* speaker,
        62–64
    on purpose of literature, 180
    on religion, 263–265
    reunion with parents, 154
    in revolutionary movement, 34–38,
        325, 330
    rivalry with Krantz, 155–156
    at Second Congress of the Second
        International, 147–151
    series on socialist movement of,
        245–248
    on sewing-machine operators'
        strike, 119–120
    on shirtwaist makers' strike,
        399–400
    on socialist parochialism, 250
    as socialist speaker, 64–66
    50th birthday celebration of, 389
    "Two Worlds" article of, 107–108

on United Garment Workers'
strike, 408–409
on William Dean Howells,
183–184
on William Randolph Hearst,
378–379
on yearning, 266–268
on Zionism, 439
Cahan, Anna, 219, 225, 252, 269,
326, 447–448
Cahan, Isadore, 154, 388
Cahan, Shakhne, 29
Calendar of Narodnaya Volya, 69
Canal Street, 47, 48
Career of the Nihilist (Stepniak), 333
Castle Garden, 41, 42
Catskill Mountains, 237
Central Labor Union of New York, 82
Chase, John C., 378
Chasm, The (Cahan), 242–243, 270,
332–333
Chekhov, Anton, 188
Chernyshevsky, N.G., 7, 35, 333
Chicago anarchist trial, 82–84
Chmelnitzky, Hetman Bogdan, 17
Chornyi Peredel party, 9, 15
"Circumstances" (Cahan), 225
"Clarinetist" (Cahan), 368–369
Clemenceau, Georges, 70
Cloakmakers' Union, 94–95, 118,
159, 162, 173, 395
Cloakmaking industry
cloakmakers' strike, 94
cutters' strike, 114–124
sewing-machine operators' walkout,
113–114
Clothing contractors, 49–52
Clothing industry. See Garment
industry
Collier's Weekly, 222
Columbusses medina (Zunser), 131
Columbus un Vashington (Zunser),
131
Commercial Advertiser, 208–210,
212, 215, 223
Communal movement, 38–39, 68,
133

Communist International, 434
Comtean positivism, 67
Conley, Jim, 426
Cosmopolitan, 225, 233, 235
Cossack revolt, in the Ukraine, 17–18
Crane, Stephen, 201
"Critique of a Critique" (Miller),
321
"Cross, Skull-Cap and Art" (Miller),
316
Crusades, 16
Customer-peddling, 48
Cutters' strike, 114–124

D
Darwinism, 180, 181
Daughter of Reb Avrom Leib, The
(Cahan), 233–234, 416
Debs, Eugene V., 246
De Leon, Daniel
control of Abend Blatt by, 176–177
dual unionism and, 173–174
Forward's campaign against, 207
impact on Socialist Labor Party,
246
in labor movement rivalry,
163–168
Diamond Shirtwaist Company, 397
Dick, Isaac Meir, 22, 24
Domestic Happiness (Peretz), 347
Dramatishe Velt (journal), 321
Dual unionism, 162, 166, 173
Dubinsky, David, 442
Du Bois, W.E.B., 221
Duffield, Pitts, 223
"Dumitru and Sigrid" (Cahan), 235
Dutchtown, 46

E
Edelstadt, David
background of, 126–127
death of, 124
as editor of Die Freie Arbeiter
Stimme, 112
facility in Yiddish, 125–126
in negotiations for coalition
newspaper, 100

Educational Alliance, 222
Eight-hour working day, 80–81
Elijah the *Gaon*, 28
Elisabeth, Empress of Austria, 2
*Embourgeoisement*, 415
*Emmes, Der* (journal), 171
Engels, Friedrich, 85, 154
Enlightenment, 19
Epstein, Jacob, 218
Epstein, Melech, 411–412
Essex Street, 5, 48
Ethnic archaeology of New York City,
    1–2
Ettinger, Shlomo, 278
*Everybody's Magazine*, 234

**F**
Family virtues
    Cahan on, 257–259
    post-1905 revival of, 348–349
Fascism, 443–444
Feigenbaum, Benjamin, 168, 177, 269,
    352, 385, 389, 397
Feller, Albert, 248, 249, 273
First International, 76
Five Points district, 45
*Folks-Advokat* (newspaper), 132
*Fortbildungs Verein*, 114
*Forward. See Jewish Daily Forward*
*Foyl oder Tzugefoylt* (Winchevsky),
    172, 370
Frank, Leo, 425–426, 441
*Freie Arbeiter Stimme, Die*
    (newspaper), 111–112, 124, 127,
    132, 161
*Freie Velt, Die* (newspaper), 144,
    146
*Freiheit, Die* (newspaper), 3, 78
Frey, William, 67
Friedman, Rosa, 287
*Fun a Vort a Kvort* series (Cahan),
    367

**G**
*Galician Exile* (Gordin), 386
Gallup, Constantine, 145–146
Garland, Hamlin, 202

Garment industry
    clothing contractors, 49–50
    customer-peddling, 48
    German Jews in, 47
    knee-pants trade, 92–93
    shirtwaist factory unionization,
        396–397
    strikes in. *See* Strike(s)
    sweating-system, 50–52
Garside, Thomas, 115–121
General Workingmen's League, 76
George, Henry, 82–83, 88, 164, 165
*George's Mother* (Crane), 201
Germania Theater, 295, 297
German immigration, 46
Germans in United States
    in early socialist movement, 75–76
    relationship with Jews in New
        York City, 2–3
German Social Democrats, 60
Germany
    Jewish culture in, 18
    Jewish reform movement in, 26
    wars of religion in, 17
"Ghetto Wedding, A" (Cahan), 226
Gillis, Meyer, 167
Glossary of Yiddish terms, 457–458
Gnatowski, Anton, 35, 152, 153, 415
*God, Man and Devil* (Gordin), 308
Gold, Michael, 435, 449
*Golden Boy* (Odets), 449
Goldfaden, Abraham, 275, 279–295,
    295, 296, 323
Goldfogle, Henry M., 316, 376, 378,
    381, 411
Goldman, Emma, 84, 95, 96, 117,
    121
Goldstein, Ike, 404
Goldstein, Sacher, 283, 288, 294
Goldstein, Sophie. *See* Karp, Sophie
Gompers, Samuel, 72, 80, 123,
    159–160, 174
Gonikman, Isaac, 427
Gordin, Jacob, 297
    adaptation of other plays by,
        307–308
    background of, 298–299

Cahan and, feud with, 312–314, 322, 385–387
death of, 388
plagiarism charges against, 387–388
realism in plays of, 305–306, 309
relationship with actors, 309–310
*Siberia* of, 302–305
success and reputation of, 311
*Tageblatt* feud with, 315–318
Gordin Circle, 406
"Gordin's Place as a Yiddish Playwright" (Cahan), 386–387
Gordon, David, 151–152
Gordon, Yeva, 152
Gorky, Maxim, 380–381
Gottlieb, Leon, 356
Gottlober, Abraham Baer, 279
Grand Street, 47
Gretch, Mitya, 87
Gretch, Nyuma, 87, 88
Grinevitsky, Ignaty, 12
Grodner, Israel, 278, 280, 281, 282, 283, 285, 287, 289
Grossman, Herman, 395–396
Gutzkow, Karl, 293

**H**
*Ha'Emmes* (journal), 137–138
Haimovich-Heine, Moshe, 290, 294
Haimovich-Heine, Sarah, 294
*Ha'Kol* (journal), 138
*Halacha* and *haggadah*, 262
*Ha'Melitz* (journal), 137
Hapgood, Hutchins, 203, 210, 216–222, 223, 295, 311
Hapgood, Norman, 216, 222
Harkavy, Alexander, 98, 384
Hartmann, Leo, 9, 10, 69–71, 367, 368
Hasidism
founding of, 18–19
opposition to, 28
Yiddish theater and, 277
Haskalah, 19–21, 26, 276
Haymarket Affair, 81–82, 83
Haymarket Square, 81

"He: A Character Sketch" (Winchevsky), 147
Hearst, William Randolph, 214, 260, 370, 375–379, 381
Hebrew, in Jewish nationalism, 137
Hebrew language revival, 20–21
Hebrew Typological Union, 161
Heine, Heinrich, 1, 2
Heine monument, 2, 3
Heins, Vladimir. *See* Frey, William
Held, Adolph, 383, 384, 406
Helfmann, Hessia, 12, 13
Hendrick, Burton J., 416
Henry Street Settlement, 222
Herrick's Cafe, 244
Herzen, Alexander, 26
Herzl, Theodor, 438
"Hester Street Reporter, The" (Cahan), 204
Hewitt, Abram S., 83
Hillkowitz, Morris, 90–91, 92, 101, 112, 155–156, 376, 378, 381, 389, 400
Hillman, Sidney, 410, 441–442
Hillquit, Morris. *See* Hillkowitz, Morris
*History of Greece, A* (Bury), 224
Hitchcock, Ripley, 201
Hitler, Adolph, 441
Hollander, Louis, 404, 406
Holocaust, 445–446
Holt, Hamilton, 400
Holtzman, B., 245
*Homeless* (Gordin), 386
Horowitz, Moshe, 288–289, 296, 304, 323
Horowitzism, 297
Hourwich, Isaac A., 410
Hourwich Affair, 411
Howells, William Dean, 172–173, 182, 183–184, 188, 189, 195, 198, 200
*How Raphael Na'aritzokh Became a Socialist* (Cahan), 169, 191
*How the Other Half Lives* (Riis), 50
Hughes, Charles Evan, 378
Hugo, Victor, 70

Human interest stories, 255, 358. *See also* Advice columns
Hungarian music, 368

## I

Immigration
    development as concept, 41–42
    German, 46
    Irish, 45–46
    Jewish, 46–48
    post-1905 Jewish, 347–348
*Imported Bridegroom and Other Stories of the New York Ghetto* (Cahan), 226–230
Independence League, 375, 381, 382
"In Love With *Yiddishe Kinder*" (Cahan), 255
Intermarriage advice, 357
International Cloak Makers' Union, 162
International Ladies' Garment Workers' Union, 394, 395, 396, 398, 401, 410
International Workingmen's Association, 76
"In the Sweatshop" (Cahan),

193–195
Irish immigrants, 45–46
Irving Place Theater, 3
Isaac Elchanan Yeshiva, 349
*Iskra* (newspaper), 328

## J

Jaffe, Joseph, 99, 143
Jaffe, Marcus, 383
James, Henry, 182
James, William, 181
Jaurès, Jean, 415, 426
Jewish bakers' union, 92
*Jewish Daily Forward* building, 5–6
*Jewish Daily Forward* (newspaper), 203–205, 244, 248
    adaptation to social changes by, 350–351
    in Americanization of immigrants, 384–385

anti-*Tageblatt* articles in, 316–317
the Bund and, 329–330
Cahan as editor of, 254–260, 266, 269, 274
circulation, 265, 389, 435
as clique, accusations of, 371–372
in election campaigns, 376, 381, 383
financial management of, 382–384
founding of, 178
Gordin at, 312–313
Jewish nationalism and, 443–444
lead article in, 254
as "living novel," 353
morning newspaper of, 352
post-WWI policies of, 436–437
relationship with readers of, 261–262
rivalries on, 264–265
United Garment Workers' strike and, 403–409
*Jewish Daily Forward* Press Association, 178, 253, 269, 371, 389
Jewish immigration, 46–48, 347–348
*Jewish King Lear, The* (Gordin), 307–308
Jewish Labor Lyceum, 73–74
"Jewish Massacres and the Revolutionary Movement in Russia" (Cahan), 331–332
*Jewish Queen Lear, The* (Gordin), 310
Jewish Question, 148–150
Jewish Socialist Federation, 434
Jewish Teachers' Institute of Vilna, 30
Jewish Workers' Benefit and Education *Verein*, 138–139
Jewish Workers' Federation, 327
*Jews Without Money* (Gold), 435, 449
Johanssen, Meyer, 95
Johnson Act of 1924, 435
Jonas, Alexander, 74, 82, 86, 121, 175, 389
Joseph, Rabbi Jacob, 349
Judaism, religious

as congruent with socialism,
108–109
revival of, in America, 348–350
Judeo-German dialect, 20, 22, 23
*Juive, La* (Scribe), 293

**K**
Kaminska, Esther Rachel, 310–311
Kaminska, Ida, 311
Kaminska, Ruth, 311
Kangaroos, 246, 249, 272
Kaplan, Paul, 68
Karp, Sophie, 288, 294
Kessler, David, 290, 309
*Khazzer-Mark*, 50
*Khishuf-Makherin, Die* (Goldfaden),
294
Kibalchich, Nikolay, 13, 37
King, Edward, 67, 74, 78, 166, 190,
389
*King Lear* (Shakespeare), 307
Klivansky, S., 373
Knee-Pants Makers' Union, 94
Knee-pants trade, 92–93
Knights of Labor, 59–60, 159
Kobrin, Leon, 311
Kolotkevich, Nikolay, 13
Kossuth, Louis, 41
Krantz, Philip, 102, 105, 106, 107,
110, 113, 143–144, 155–156,
163, 169, 170, 174, 269, 299,
301, 352. *See also* Rombro,
Jacob
Kravchinsky, Sergey, 8, 56, 69, 151,
333
Kremer, Arkady, 328, 330, 331
Kropotkin, Peter, 215

**L**
Labor demonstrations
for eight-hour working day,
80–81
at Union Square, 3
Labor leaders, 384
Labor movement. *See also* Strike(s)
American Federation of Labor in,
159

the Bund and, 330
first Jewish participation in, 59
knee-pants workers' strike and,
93–94
Knights of Labor in, 59–60
longshoreman strike and, 58
reefer makers' strike and, 383–384,
395
United Garment Workers' strike
and, 401–407
Labor unions, 158
anarchists vs. social democrats in,
87, 114–115
dual unions, 161–162, 173
impact of Triangle fire on,
394–395, 401
preferential union shops and, 401
Samuel Gompers' vision for,
159–160
in shirtwaist factories, 396
United German Trades and,
89–90
*Yiddisher Arbeiter Verein* in
organizing, 88
Labor Zionism, 132
La Guardia, Fiorello, 409
*Landsmanshaften*, 350
Lanthorn Club, 201–202
Lassalle, Ferdinand, 61, 149
Lateiner, Joseph, 286, 294, 296, 304,
320, 323
Lavrov, Peter, 151
Lead article, 254, 256–257
*Leaves From My Life* (Cahan), 441
Lebedeff, Aaron, 4
Lefevre, Edwin, 216
Lemlich, Clara, 398
Lenin, Vladimir, 153, 329, 415
Lerner, Joseph, 292–293, 293, 301
Levita, Elia, 24
Lewis, Roman, 100, 111, 120, 121
Lexow Crime Commission, 210
Lieberman, Aaron, 137–138, 139,
171, 327
Lief, William, 248, 249, 250, 273
Liessin, Abraham, 245, 251, 255, 272,
330, 385, 388

Linetzky, Joel, 280
Liptzen, Keni, 290, 309–310, 320
*Litvak*, 28
Local-color writing, 193
London, Ephraim, 400
London, Meyer, 400, 409, 410, 411, 442
Longshoreman strike, 58
*Looking Backward* (Bellamy), 164
Lorelei monument, 2
*Love of Zion* (Mapu), 291
Lovers of Zion movement, 15, 38
Luchow's Restaurant, 3

**M**
*Maggid*, 109–110
Magidoff, Jacob, 90
Manufacturers' Association, 114
Mapu, Abraham, 291
Mark's Cafe, 280, 281, 283
"Marriage by Proxy, A" (Cahan), 234–235
Martov, Lev, 329
Marx, Karl, 149, 262, 327
Marx-Aveling, Eleanor, 151, 154
Marxism
    Cahan lecture on, 64–65
    in early revolutionary movement, 27
    Yiddishism and, 328
Maryinsky Theater, 291, 292, 293
*Maskilim*, 20
Maxim, 373
Mayoral election of 1886, 82–83
*Mazzel*, 260–261
*McClure's Magazine*, 199, 415
*Melammed*, 29
Mendele Moicher S'forim, 24–26, 104, 128, 134, 137, 279, 293, 437
Mendelssohn, Moses, 18, 20
Metropolitan Opera House, 44
Mezentzev, General (St. Petersburg police), 8
Middlebrowism, 308
Mikhailov, Timofey, 12, 13, 37
Miller, Louis, 144, 249, 272, 427
    anti-*Tageblatt* articles of, 315–316
    *Arbeiter Zeitung* and, 112
    Cahan on, 105, 373–374, 379–380
    on Cahan's criticism of Gordin, 320–321
    in creation of Jewish Labor Lyceum, 73–74
    death of, 442–443
    in discussions on coalition newspaper, 101
    in election of Publishing Association members, 176, 177
    *Jewish Daily Forward* and, 323
    political support for Hearst by, 376–377
    rivalry with Cahan, 206, 253, 264–265, 373–375
    support of Samuel Gompers by, 160
    on unions, and need for SLP neutrality, 147
    *Wahrheit* advice column and, 354–356
    "What Is To Be Done?" article by, 157–158
Mintz, Moses, 99
Miravich (labor organizer), 58, 60, 62, 72
*Mirele Efros* (Gordin), 298, 310, 311, 387
*Misnagdim*, 28
Mogilevsky, Zelig, 284
Mogulesco, Sigmund, 284, 285, 289, 291, 293, 295, 297, 301, 303, 304, 320
*Morgenstern, Der* (newspaper), 111, 400
*Morgen Zeitung* (newspaper), 352–353, 365–366
*Morning Journal*, 315, 351, 366
Most, Johann, 121
    death of, 388
    early life and arrival in America, 77–79
    Pioneers of Liberty and, 88–89
"Mottke Arbel and His Romance" (Cahan), 186–188, 192

Muni, Paul, 450
Murphy, Charles, 377, 381
Museum of Natural History, 326

**N**

*Narodnaya Volya* party, 9, 13, 14, 15, 35, 69, 70, 326
*Narodnikii* era, 7
*Nation, The*, 435
National Museum of New York, 326
National Recovery Administration, 441
National Theater, 294
*Nazarene, The* (Asch), 445
*Neie Zeit* (newspaper), 98–99
New Deal, 441, 442
New Milford, Connecticut, 270–271
New Odessa commune, 68, 133
New Year's Eve party, 68–69
New York City
    Cahan on arrival in, 40–41
    ethnic archaeology in, 1–2
    Jewish immigration to post-1905, 347–348
    post-Civil War development, 42–45
New York Clothing Trade Association, 402
New York Social Revolutionary Club, 78
Nicholas I (Russia), 26, 345
Nilsson, Christine, 44
Novakhovich, Lippe Ben-Zion, 136. *See also* Winchevsky, Morris

**O**

October Manifesto, 346
Odets, Clifford, 449
Old Bowery Garden, 294–295
Operators' and Cloak Makers Union No. 1, 162
Orchard Street, 5
Oriental Theater, 295
*Orphan, The* (Gordin), 315
*Our Differences* (Plekhanov), 85
*Oysgegreent*, 266

**P**

Page, Walter H., 226
Pale of Settlement, 16
Palestine, 439
"Pantole Polge" (Gordin), 300–301
Papkin and Marks strike, 122–123
Parsons, Albert, 83–84
*Parveh lokshen*, 102
Patti, Adelina, 71, 367
Paulding, James K., 189–190, 198
*People, The* (newspaper), 167
People's Schools, 279
Peretz, Isaac Loeb, 128, 191, 300, 347, 437
Perkins, Frances, 394
Perovskaya, Sophia, 7–8, 9, 10, 11, 12, 13, 37, 241
Phillips, John S., 199–200
Philo-Semitism, 150
"Phonograph" (Cahan), 367
Pig Market, 50
Pine, Max, 403, 404
Pioneers of Liberty, 88, 99, 100, 111
Plekhanov, Georgy, 85, 328
Poetry
    in *Die Freie Arbeiter Stimme*, 111–112
    in preservation of Yiddish in America, 128–129
*Pogrom, The* (Gordin), 305–306
Pogroms
    of 1905, 345–346
    Cahan on, 331–332
    following assassination of Tsar, 14–15
    in Kishinev, 272, 331
    during medieval period, 16
    in the Ukraine, 17–18
Police Headquarters, 213
Polish Jewry, 16–19
Positivism, 67
*Poylisher Yidl, Dos* (newspaper), 140
Preferential union shop, 401
Prenner, Isadore, 100, 102
*Prinzessin Sabbath* (Heine), 1
Progressives, 209
Proletarian intelligentsia, 327–328

*Propaganda Verein*, 60–64, 71
Protocol of Peace agreement, 400–401
"Protzentniks in Sweatshops"
    (Liessin), 255–256
"Providential Match, A" (Cahan),
    192–193, 195, 226
Pulitzer, Joseph, 260
Purim play, 276
*Purity of Family Life, The* (Gordin),
    318

R
Rabinovich, Helena, 177
Rabinovich (printer), 142–143
Rabinowitz, Sholem. *See* Sholem
    Aleichem
Radkinson, Michael, 138
Rayevsky, Chaim, 74, 98, 272
Realism, in Yiddish theater, 309,
    311
"Realism and Literature" (Cahan),
    353
"Realism" (Cahan), 180–184
*Recruits, The* (Goldfaden), 283
*Red Badge of Courage, The* (Crane),
    201
Reefer makers' strike, 383–384, 395
Reingold, Frank, 122, 123, 124
Reisen, Abraham, 352
Religious tolerance, in socialism,
    263–265
*Revolutionary Catechism* (Bakunin
    and Nechayev), 78
Revolutionary Socialist Labor Party,
    76–77
Rickert, T.A., 402, 403, 410
Riis, Jacob, 46, 50, 222
*Rise of David Levinsky* (Cahan),
    413
    on American success story, 417
    on arrival in New York, 40–41
    on clothing contracting, 51–52
    overview of, 417–425
    second generation intellectuals and,
        448–449
    World War I and, 428–432
Rogoff, Hillel, 384–385

Rombro, Jacob, 140. *See also* Krantz,
    Philip
Roosevelt, Franklin D., 441, 442, 443
Roosevelt, Theodore, 82–83, 209,
    214
Rosenberg, Abraham, 119–120, 410,
    411
Rosenfeld, Morris, 112, 133–136,
    392, 409
Rue Flatters restaurant, 154–155
Rumanian Opera House, 295, 305
*Ruskii Rabochii Soyuz*, 71, 73
Russia
    Enlightenment movement in,
        19–20
    Jewish assimilation in, 26–27
    Jewish exodus from, 15–16, 347
    Jewish migration to, 16
    pogroms in. See Pogroms
    proletarian intelligentsia in,
        327–328
    Yiddish theater in, 289–294, 293
*Russian Jew in America* (Gordin),
    312, 387
Russian-Jewish Workers' Union, 74
Russian Jews
    nostalgic disposition of, compared
        with German Jews, 75
    self-view of, in America, 52–53
Russian Revolution, 432–434
Russian revolutionary movement
    assassination of Tsar Alexander II,
        8–12
    Cahan in, 34–38, 325, 330
    early Jewish participation in, 27
    Jewish émigrés' preoccupation
        with, 60, 68–69
    terrorism as issue in, 9
    women in, 7–8
    Zionism in, 15
Russian Social Democratic Party,
    328–329, 331
*Russisher-Yiddisher Arbeiter Verein*,
    74
Russo-Turkish War, 182, 283, 284,
    289
Rysakov (assassin), 12, 13, 37

**S**

Sachs Brothers Cafe, 113
Sage, Russell, 214
*Salmagundi* (journal), 190
Sarasohn, Hatzkel, 317
Sarasohn, Kasriel, 97, 169
Sarasohn, Rachel, 139
Schach, M., 94
Schewitsch, Sergey, 61, 82, 83
Schlesinger, Benjamin, 383, 384, 395, 411
Schnaubel, Rudolph, 81, 82
Schwartz, Maurice, 3, 437–438
Schweitzer, Benjamin, 403
*Science of Revolutionary Warfare* (Most), 78–79
Scribe, Augustin, 293
Second Congress of the Second International, 147
Segal, Sarah, 287–288
*Serkele* (Ettinger), 278–279
Seward Park, 5
Sewing-machine operators' walk-out, 113–114
Shaikevich, N.M., 293
Shakespeare, William, 307
*Shame of the Cities, The* (Steffens), 223
*Shavuos* theme, 98, 108
Shaw, George Bernard, 398
Shazar, Zalman, 439
Shirtwaist makers' strike, 397–401
*Shmendrick* (Goldfaden), 285
Sholem Aleichem, 25, 128, 191, 437
Shomer (writer), 293
*Shulamis* (Goldfaden), 275, 291–292
*Siberia* (Gordin), 302–305
*Sidra* feature, in *Arbeiter Zeitung*, 109–110, 185–186
Silberman, Moshe, 294, 295
Singer, Isaac Bashevis, 447
Singer, Paul, 149–150
Single Taxers, 82, 83, 165
*Slaughter, The* (Gordin), 313–314
Slonimsky, Haim Selig, 279
Socialism
Cahan on parochialism of, 250

Cahan's series on, 245–248
as congruent with Judaism, 108–109
religion and, 263–265
William Randolph Hearst and, 377, 378
Yiddishism connection to, 128–129
*Socialism: Utopian and Scientific* (Engels), 85
Socialist Labor Party
Americanization trend in, 164
anarchist faction within, 76–77
Cahan membership in, 86
decline in power of, 159
De Leon's impact on, 246
ethnic organization in, 89
Jewish branch of, 89–90
Miller on need for neutrality of, in union affairs, 147
Thomas Garside and, 115
Socialist Party of America, 246, 252, 273, 375
Socialist Trade and Labor Alliance, 174, 394
Social Revolutionary Party of Russia, 372
Sokolov, Vladimir, 35, 36, 153
Solovyov, Alexander, 8
"Song of the Shirt" (Hood), 142
"Soul of *Bintel Brief*" (Cahan), 379
Southern, Charles, 167–168
Spanish-American War, 214
Spencer, Herbert, 180, 181
Spies, August, 83
*Spirit of Labor, The* (Hapgood), 221
*Spirit of the Ghetto, The* (Hapgood), 203, 218–221, 245
Spiritual Biblical Brotherhood, 299
St. Mark's Place, 4
Stachelberg's cigar factory, 72
Steffens, Lincoln, 203, 389
*Commercial Advertiser* and, 210–213
radicalization of, 221–222
on urban corruption, 222–222
on Yiddish theater, 309
Stepniak. *See* Kravchinsky, Sergey

Stokes, J.G. Phelps, 375
Stover, Charles B., 190
Strike-breaking, 56–59
Strike(s)
    at American Tobacco Company,
        268–269
    by cloakmakers, 94
    by cutters, 114–124
    by knee-pants workers, 93–94
    by longshoremen, 58
    at Papkin and Marks, 122–123
    by reefer makers, 383–384, 395
    by sewing-machine operators,
        119–120
    by shirtwaist makers, 397–401
    by typesetters, 370
    by United Garment Workers,
        401–407
Sundelevich, Aaron, 137
Sussman and Goldstein's Cafe, 113
Sweatshop system, 50–52
    Cahan fictional work on, 193–195
    Rosenfeld's poetry on, 133–135

T
*Tageblatt* (newspaper), 97, 169,
    315–318, 319
Tammany Hall, 44, 84, 214, 316, 377
*Teitsh-Khumesh* (Jacob ben Isaac), 23
Terrorism, as issue in revolutionary
    movement, 9
Thomashevsky, Boris, 294, 305
Thomashevsky, Pinchas, 294
Tolstoy, Leo, 183, 189
Tracy, Benjamin F., 208
"Tragedies, Comedies and Ordinary
    Troubles From Real Life"
    (Miller), 355, 358, 365
*Traveler From Altruria, A* (Howells),
    190
Trepov, General (St. Petersburg chief
    of police), 8
Triangle Shirtwaist factory fire,
    391–395, 397
Trotsky, Leon, 329
*Trusty Witnesses* (Webel), 291
Tsederbaum, Lev, 328

Turgenev, Ivan, 7, 324, 447
Tweed, William Marcy, 44–45
"Two Worlds in the World" (Cahan),
    107–108
Typesetters' strike, 370
Typesetters' union, 161–162
Tzederbaum, Alexander, 137
*Tzeyna u'Reyna* (Jacob ben Isaac),
    22–23
"Tzinchadzi of the Catskills" (Cahan),
    236–242, 325

U
Ukraine
    anti-Jewish pogroms in, 14
    Cossack revolt in, 17–18
Ulyanov, Alexander, 153
*Underground Russia* (Stepniak), 69
Union Square labor demonstrations, 3
Union Theater, 306
*Union Zeitung* (newspaper), 162, 169
United Brotherhood of Cloak Makers,
    394
United Garment Workers, 159, 162,
    410
United Garment Workers' strike,
    401–410
United German Trades, 89–91
United Hebrew Trades
    *Arbeiter Zeitung* and, 156
    Barondess and, 95
    founding of, 91–92
    knee-pants trade strike and, 93–94
    in negotiation for coalition
        newspaper, 102
    organization techniques of, 92–93
    in shirtwaist makers' strike, 397,
        398
*Uriel Acosta* (Gutzkow), 293, 297

V
Vanderbilt, William Henry, 44
*Vereinigte Deutsche Gewerkschaften*,
    89–90
*Vereinigte Yiddishe Gewerkschaften.*
    *See* United Hebrew Trades
Vereshchagin, Vassily, 182–183

Villard, Oswald Garrison, 435
Vilna, Lithuania, 28, 153
*Virgin Soil* (Turgenev), 324
Vladeck, Baruch Charney, 436
*Volks Zeitung* (newspaper), 61, 74, 82, 89

**W**
Wagner Labor Relations Act of 1935, 442
*Wahrheit, Die* (newspaper), 99–100, 143, 145, 351, 370, 383, 405
Wald, Lillian, 222
Wedding bard, 129
Weinstein, Bernard, 71, 72, 86, 90, 91, 94, 101, 106, 397
Weitling, Wilhelm, 76
*Well and Weasel* (Webel), 291
Werbel, Elijah Mordecai, 291
Wharton, Edith, 43, 210
"What Is Luck?" writing competition, 260–261
*What Is To Be Done?* (Chernyshevsky), 35, 180, 333
"What Is To Be Done?" (Miller), 158
*White Terror and the Red, The* (Cahan), 333–345
Williamsburg Bridge, 5
Winchevsky, Morris, 105–106, 112, 351. *See also* Novakhovich, Lippe Ben-Zion
  as agitator, 139–140
  on American socialist movement, 172
  background of, 136–137
  as contributor to *Arbeiter Freind*, 143
  death of, 443
  on Gordin's use of Shakespeare, 307
  *Jewish Daily Forward* and, 204–205, 207, 323
  name as pseudonym, 141
  as poet, 141–142
  prologue to *Mirele Efros*, 298
  as publisher, 138–141, 143
  reputation of, 145

on social democrats, 147
on socialist-anarchist ideological struggle, 144, 170–171, 175
William Randolph Hearst and, 377
Wise, Rabbi Stephen S., 394
Wittenberg, Solomon, 8
Women's Trade Union League, 398
Woodbine, New Jersey, 270
"Worker in Moses Our Teacher's Time, The" (Harkavy), 147
World War I, 426–427
World War II, 444–446
Wright, Henry J., 208, 209–210, 270

**Y**
Yakovka (Brody singer), 277
*Yankel the Yankee* (Cahan), 196–199
Yanovsky, Saul, 114–115, 151
*Yehi* (Novakhovich), 141
*Yehi Or* (Winchevsky), 145
*Yekl, A Tale of the New York Ghetto* (Cahan), 178, 199, 201, 224
*Yeshiva-bokher*, 31
Yiddish
  Cahan's socialist lectures in, 64–65
  development of, 22–26
  German language and, 453–457
  in poetry of David Edelstadt, 127
  socialism connection to, 128–129
  as term, 21–22
Yiddish Art Theater, The, 3, 438, 450
*Yiddishe Gazetten, Die* (newspaper), 87, 97, 104
*Yiddishe Kenigin Lear, Die* (Gordin), 310
Yiddish-English dictionaries, 384
*Yiddisher Arbeiter Verein*, 88, 89
*Yiddisher Kenig Lear, Der* (Gordin), 307
*Yiddisher Volks-Zeitung* (newspaper), 99
Yiddish glossary, 457–458
Yiddish literary movement, 127–128
Yiddish prose, 24
Yiddish theater
  ad-libbing in, 303, 306

in America, introduction of,
294–297
audience for, 282
dispute over realism in, 309
historical and Biblical operetta in,
292–293
influence of, 275–276
origins of, 276–277
postwar revival of, 437
relationship between actor and
audience, 303–304
rivalries in, 291
in Rumania, 284–289
in Russia, 289–294
Russo-Turkish War and, 289
women in, 287–288
*Yisrolik* (journal), 280
Yokhelson, Vladimir, 326
Yom Kippur Ball, 99–100, 256
Young Men's Hebrew Association,
66, 68

**Z**
Zametkin, Michael, 74, 103, 121,
168, 207, 322–323, 352
Zasulich, Vera, 8, 9, 328
*Zeitgeist, Der* (weekly supplement),
351–352
Zevi, Sabbatai, 18
*Zhargon*, 22, 24
Zhelyabov, Andrey, 9, 10, 11, 13, 37
Zhitlowsky, Chaim, 372–373
Zhitomir Rabbinical Seminary, 279
Zionism, 15, 329, 438–440
*Znamya* (newspaper), 101
Zuckerman, Lazar, 284, 286, 293
*Zukunft, Die* (journal), 155, 157–158,
162, 176
*Zukunft, Die* (newspaper), 140, 142,
351
Zunser, Eliakum, 129–133, 219